Conflict Resolution in Africa

Conflict Resolution in Africa

FRANCIS M. DENG

I. WILLIAM ZARTMAN

Editors

THE BROOKINGS INSTITUTION / Washington, D.C.

Copyright © 1991 by

THE BROOKINGS INSTITUTION

1775 Massachusetts Avenue, N.W.

Washington, D.C. 20036

Library of Congress Cataloging-in-Publication data:
Deng, Francis Mading, *1938–*
    Conflict resolution in Africa / Francis M. Deng and I. William Zartman.
      p.   cm.
    Includes bibliographical references and index.
    ISBN 0-8157-1798-9.   ISBN 0-8157-1797-0 (pbk.)
      1. Africa—Politics and government—1960–   2. Conflict management—
    Africa. 3. Africa—Economic conditions—1960–   I. Zartman, I. William.
    II. Title.
    DT30.5.D46   1991
    320.96—dc20   91-23604
                                          CIP

9 8 7 6 5 4 3 2 1

Set in Linotron Palatino
Composition by Harper Graphics
  Waldorf, Maryland
Printed by R.R. Donnelley and Sons Co.
  Harrisonburg, Virginia

₿ THE BROOKINGS INSTITUTION

The Brookings Institution is an independent organization devoted to nonpartisan research, education, and publication in economics, government, foreign policy, and the social sciences generally. Its principal purposes are to aid in the development of sound public policies and to promote public understanding of issues of national importance.

The Institution was founded on December 8, 1927, to merge the activities of the Institute for Government Research, founded in 1916, the Institute of Economics, founded in 1922, and the Robert Brookings Graduate School of Economics and Government, founded in 1924.

The Board of Trustees is responsible for the general administration of the Institution, while the immediate direction of the policies, program, and staff is vested in the President, assisted by an advisory committee of the officers and staff. The by-laws of the Institution state: "It is the function of the Trustees to make possible the conduct of scientific research, and publication, under the most favorable conditions, and to safeguard the independence of the research staff in the pursuit of their studies and in the publication of the results of such studies. It is not a part of their function to determine, control, or influence the conduct of particular investigations or the conclusions reached."

The President bears final responsibility for the decision to publish a manuscript as a Brookings book. In reaching his judgment on the competence, accuracy, and objectivity of each study, the President is advised by the director of the appropriate research program and weighs the views of a panel of expert outside readers who report to him in confidence on the quality of the work. Publication of a work signifies that it is deemed a competent treatment worthy of public consideration but does not imply endorsement of conclusions or recommendations.

The Institution maintains its position of neutrality on issues of public policy in order to safeguard the intellectual freedom of the staff. Hence interpretations or conclusions in Brookings publications should be understood to be solely those of the authors and should not be attributed to the Institution, to its trustees, officers, or other staff members, or to the organizations that support its research.

Foreword

The domestic and regional conflicts in Africa pose challenging issues for scholars and policymakers. While they are more limited in scale than the issues that directly engage the major powers, they entail great physical and emotional suffering for the people involved. The toll is monumental in terms of war damage to productivity, scarce resources diverted to armaments and military organizations, and the resulting insecurity, displacement, and destruction to the environment. In this book, African, European, and U.S. experts examine these conflicts and the prospects for their resolution. They review the scholarship on conflict resolution in Africa in light of current changes on the international scene, assess the potential implications of these changes for regional conflict, analyze the specific issues involved in African conflicts, evaluate the prospects for conflict management and resolution, and recommend case studies and themes for further, long-term research.

The book comprises the papers presented at a research conference on conflict resolution in Africa held at Brookings in October 1989. The papers have been revised and updated, but the book has not been subjected to the formal review and verification procedures established for research publications of the institution.

The two editors of this volume have diverse backgrounds in conflict resolution. Francis M. Deng, formerly Sudan's minister of state for foreign affairs and ambassador to the United States, is a senior fellow in the Foreign Policy Studies program at Brookings. For many years he has been involved in efforts to mediate conflict in the Sudan. I. William Zartman, director of the African Studies and Conflict Management programs at the Paul H. Nitze School of Advanced International Studies of the Johns Hopkins University, has published many works that analyze conflict resolution with a special reference to Africa.

The editors wish to thank the many people who participated in the Brookings conference. They are particularly grateful to John D. Steinbruner, director of the Brookings Foreign Policy Studies program, who supported and contributed to the conflict resolution project from the beginning; to Ibrahim A. Gambari, formerly a Brookings visiting scholar, who provided wise and generous advice; and to Patricia Rosenfield, of the Carnegie Corporation of New York, who has assisted them in many ways. The editors would also like to thank Terrence P. Lyons for his work in coordinating the publication process; Gretchen M. Griener for preparing the manuscript for publication; Steve Schwartz, Susan A. Stewart, Wendy J. Glassmire, and Beth Elzinga-Marshall for their assistance in organizing the conference; and Khalid Medani and Ann M. Ziegler for their help in processing the manuscript. Jack Kirshbaum and Caroline Lalire edited the manuscript, and Amit K. Maitra and Mary Kidd prepared the indexes.

The conflict resolution project was made possible by a grant from the Carnegie Corporation of New York. Brookings gratefully acknowledges this support. Other activities supporting this project were funded by the Rockefeller Foundation and the Rockefeller Brothers Fund.

The views expressed in this book are those of the individual authors and should not be ascribed to the people whose assistance is acknowledged above, to the organizations that supported the project, or to the trustees, officers, or other staff members of the Brookings Institution.

BRUCE K. MAC LAURY
President

July 1991
Washington, D.C.

Contents

Part 3 The Contextual Analysis of Conflict

Part 4 The Economics of Conflict

Part 5 Conflict Management and Resolution

Preface

In responding to the challenge of setting the stage for the essays to follow, I intend to highlight some of the critical elements of the conflicts in Africa and suggest ways to manage and resolve them. In attempting this task, I feel encouraged that this conference volume is, in a real sense, the first "outing" of the Africa program at Brookings. And it is appropriate that the book be devoted to an intensive and serious examination of the root causes of conflicts in Africa by an international group of experts on the subject.

A major contradiction of the contemporary international system is that we live in an interdependent world while the world is increasingly dominated by economic and political giants. Nonetheless, no nation, big or small, rich or poor, can expect to exist or prosper in isolation from other states. That is perhaps why African security problems should be examined in their international contexts even though the primary responsibility for solving them must lie with the Africans themselves.

It is therefore gratifying that the Brookings Institution has taken the initiative to establish an Africa program as part of its wider Foreign Policy Studies program. It is even more gratifying to me that there is a growing cooperation between Brookings and similar institutions on Africa studies, as demonstrated by the September 1989 seminar organized by the African Leadership Forum that was cosponsored and hosted by Brookings. This kind of close cooperation and mutual support brings forth the fruitful exchange of ideas capable of enhancing the search for solutions to regional problems in a global context.

Besides the great contradiction between the fact of interdependence of all states and the economic and political dominance of the international system by a few states, there is another contradiction with grave consequences for the discussions in this book. Africa contains the largest number of the least-developed and poorest countries in the world; at the same time it is the arena for some of the world's worst conflicts. In its World Development Report of 1989, the World Bank estimated the average annual growth of real GNP in sub-Saharan Africa between 1982 and 1988 at about 1 percent. This figure is the lowest for any region in the world. Behind these cold statistics is the reality that hundreds of millions of African people have witnessed and continue to experience socioeconomic decline and regression rather than growth and development. The so-called revolution of rising expectations in the decade of independence has been replaced by a new "revolution of rising frustrations."At the same time, the continent is the theater for more endemic deadly conflicts than any other region of the world. There is no subregion in Africa that is immune from conflicts and large-scale violence.

Clearly, then, there is a link between the level of poverty in Africa and the level and incidences of violence and conflict in the continent. These twin afflictions cannot be ignored by African states or the international community. Hence it is to the credit of the Organization of African Unity (OAU) and the United Nations that both organizations devoted special sessions to consider Africa's economic crisis. The 1985 OAU summit adopted an African Priority Program for Economic Recovery, which was essentially endorsed by the United Nations General Assembly and renamed United Nations Action Program for African Economic Recovery and Development (UNAPAERD) in 1986.

At the end of its 1987 special session devoted to the continent's economic crisis, the U.N. General Assembly declared:

> The African development crisis is not an exclusively African problem but one that concerns mankind as a living reality. A stagnant or perpetually backward Africa is not in the interest of the world community. Without durable and sustained economic development in the world's poor regions, of which Africa is a notable example, there is a real danger to international peace and security and an impediment to world economic growth and development. The international community recognizes the importance of genuine peace and security, as well as the strengthening of international cooperation to African development.

Unfortunately, these laudable words were not matched by concrete pledges by the international community to transfer resources to the continent in order to implement UNAPAERD. Nonetheless, the economic and developmental dimensions of the deteriorating African condition have, in recent years, been given some attention.

It is now necessary to accord high priority to the security problems of Africa. Although the absence of conflicts or wars does not guarantee economic development, no real development can occur in an atmosphere of personal, national, and continental insecurity. Moreover, recent changes in international relations do have important implications and consequences for conflicts in Africa. With the relaxation of tensions in Soviet-U.S. relations and the ebbing of the Cold War antagonisms, the superpowers may desire to cooperate in finding solutions to regional conflicts in Africa and elsewhere.

The prestige of the United Nations, especially of its peacekeeping capability and potential, is also on the rise. The relative success in promoting peaceful settlement of the conflicts in Afghanistan, Central America, and Namibia is part of the new lease on diplomatic and political life being enjoyed by the organization. Whatever the difference of opinion over the 1991 Gulf War, it demonstrated the effectiveness of the global system and the emergence of a new international order under the rubric of the United Nations. Africa stands to especially benefit from this trend, which provides new opportunity for close collaboration between the OAU and the United Nations. Would the conflicts in the Horn be susceptible to similar international political pressures and institutional involvement in the direction of peaceful settlement? How about South Africa itself?

Although those disputes in Africa in which superpowers' involvement is pronounced may become more susceptible to peaceful settlement as a result of improved East-West relations, other seemingly intractable conflicts in Africa have deep domestic roots. In any case, we cannot begin to identify trends and opportunities for the peaceful settlement of African conflicts without a clearer understanding of their root causes. Perhaps a good starting point for analyzing the nature and sources of African conflict is I. William Zartman's pioneering 1985 study *Ripe for Resolution: Conflict and Intervention in Africa*. In that book Zartman identified six types of such conflicts: decolonization power struggles that precede and accompany independence (such as Angola, Zimbabwe, Namibia, and Western Sahara); new independence consolidation (Shaba, Ogaden, Chad, and Angola); leftover liberation movements (UNITA in Angola, Frolinat in Chad, and the Western Somali Liberation Front); ill-defined territory (Libya-Chad and Togo-Ghana); structural rivalries (Algeria and Morocco, Ethiopia and its neighbors, and Nigeria in West Africa); and runaway means (Soviet aid to Somalia after 1963, Soviet aid to Ethiopia in 1977).

Some other scholars—for example Olatunde J. C. B. Ojo, D. K. Orwa, and C. M. B. Utete, in *African International Relations* (1985)—analyze the internal and external sources of conflict. On the former, they point to the role of ideology or the adoption of a radical ideology by one country, which may then become threatening to conservative neighbors (for example, the takeover of Flight Lieutenant Jerry John Rawlings in Ghana and the exacerbation of tension in the relationship between that leader and President Gnassingbé Eyadema of Togo). The existence of the apartheid system in South Africa constitutes real threats to the security of neighboring countries in that subregion. A military coup d'état in one state may also lead to conflict with some neighboring countries (for example, Liberia after the coming into power of Master Sergeant Samuel Doe and Guinea's relationship with Ghana after the military overthrow of Premier Kwame Nkrumah). Finally, civil wars are potent sources of insecurity within countries and can also cause problems for neighboring states.

The external sources of conflicts identified are largely territorial disputes. Support for liberation movements often brought retaliatory raids from the colonial or white minority regimes and what Ojo and others call a "militarization and regional arms race"—the latter scenario being amply demonstrated by the Tanzania-Uganda conflict, the Ethiopia and Somalia War of 1977, and Egypt-Libya conflicts and the subsequent military stalemate.

In reality, there can be no separation of the domestic and external sources of conflicts in Africa, because of the dynamic interaction between the two. Intrastate conflicts could easily become interstate (for example, the conflicts among the factions in Chad and the linkages with the Libyan-Chadian War). Conversely, interstate conflicts could have decisive effects on a domestic power struggle (for example, the Tanzanian-Ugandian War). In both intrastate and interstate conflicts in Africa, the result of extra-African interventions has largely been to worsen and prolong the levels of violence.

By posing the question differently, we may also get a clearer picture of the conflicts in Africa. What are the adversaries in the various conflicts in the continent really fighting over? In general, African peoples and states are in conflict over three broad issues. First, there are the conflicts over resources, which may take two forms: the internal struggle over the distribution of national resources and collective wealth, or interstate conflicts over territories that are believed to contain valuable physical or mineral resources. In the first instance, when the individuals and groups competing for power over the allocation of such resources or those seeking greater distributive justice within the state resort to violence, the security of the state is undermined. Examples of the latter include the Libyan-Chadian conflict over the Aozou strip, the role of phosphates in Western Sahara conflicts, the Nigerian-Cameroonian dispute over border area believed to contain crude oil, and the Nigerian-Chadian clashes over fishing rights in Lake Chad.

Second, there are conflicts over the definition of "self" in the struggle for self-determination. The Polisario's pursuit of self-determination in Western Sahara comes into conflict with Morocco's concept of a Greater Morocco. Similarly, the pursuit of Somalia's national mandate to bring all ethnic Somalis under the umbrella of one republic pitches it against Ethiopia's need to preserve its territorial integrity. The termination of the secessionist movements in Katanga and Biafra by force of arms and the Organization of African Unity's pragmatic decision to legitimize colonially inherited "national" boundaries, however artificial they may be, have not resolved the issue of self-determination in Africa. The demand for autonomy made on their respective central governments by the Eritreans and by the peoples of southern Sudan (during the first war) has kept this issue very much alive and constitutes the core of the conflicts in the two countries.

Third, there are conflicts in Africa that concern ideology and competing sociopolitical systems. The clearest illustration of this is, of course, the racist ideology of the dominant Afrikaner regime in South Africa. Apartheid, by its nature, is based on violence and can be sustained only by increasing violence. Hence the racist regime is in perpetual conflict with the legitimate aspirations not only of the country's black majority but of all citizens who seek a nonracial society in South Africa. Moreover, the guardians of the apartheid regime rely on the use of overwhelming force against those neighboring countries that continue to support Africans and others fighting for freedom and justice in South Africa. Witness the incessant and highly destructive raids conducted by the South African Defence Force against the Frontline States in order to destabilize and subdue the neighboring states in the subregion.

The socialist-leaning regimes in Angola, Mozambique, and Zimbabwe also have their internal oppositions, but the causes of the resulting domestic conflicts in these countries transcend differences in ideological persuasions. The efforts being made by the central governments in all these states toward nation-building, social mobilization, and defense of territorial integrity are stoutly opposed by forces largely representing ethnic chauvinism, secessionist tendencies, and sometimes plain banditry, encouraged by outside interests. Moreover, the extension of Cold War considerations and East-West conflict into local conflicts in the socialist-inclined states complicates their security problems.

Scholars may disagree on the nature, sources, and appropriate categorization of the conflicts in Africa. Such disagreements may in fact lead to an eventual clarification of the critical issues by applying new thinking and a fresh approach to analyzing old problems. There is, however, unanimous agreement among scholars and other observers that Africa is paying too high a price for the various wars and conflicts going on all over the continent. These wars undermine and destabilize whole societies. To take as an example the refugee situation in Africa, it is estimated that one-half of the world refugee population is African. And out of the total African refugee population, which was about five to six million in the early 1980s, almost one-half are to be found in the Horn of Africa (the figures are from the United Nations High Commission for Refugees). Somalia alone probably contends with about a million refugees, and the civil war in Sudan has reduced whole populations to living in a permanent state of flux. Unable to cope with the refugee problem, Africa has had to appeal to the international community for repeated assistance (the response has been the mounting of massive relief programs and the work of the International Conferences on Assistance for Refugees in Africa: ICARA I and II).

Conflicts and wars further destroy the fragile foundations for national cohesion, national unity, and domestic political stability in Africa. The damage to Africa's long-term political health is considerable. Worse still, the endemic conflicts in the continent consume a disproportionate share of scarce and declining economic resources. The devastations caused by the incessant and prolonged conflicts in Chad,

Western Sahara, the Horn of Africa, and southern Africa cast serious doubts on postwar economic recovery in these areas. In the Horn of Africa, for example, Ethiopia and Somalia, despite their relative poverty in the continent, spent more on arms imports in 1977–79 (during the Ogaden War) than did the entire Nordic countries plus the Netherlands—that is, 14 percent of their national income as against 0.1 percent for the six European states. The opportunity costs of the conflicts in the Horn and elsewhere in Africa for socioeconomic development are huge and growing. Under these conditions of misplaced priorities and terrible wastage of human and material resources, it is unrealistic to expect the massive—or indeed any significant—foreign investments desperately needed for African development.

Therefore the greatest challenge facing policymakers in Africa is to identify the prerequisites for durable peace, stability, and justice in their own countries. The scholars whose work is gathered here are assisting in this critical endeavor. We need to bring intellectual and other forces together to change the dismal security situation in Africa so that the abundant natural and human resources and the creative energies of the peoples of the continent can be rechanneled toward constructive ends. It is clear to me that the search for the solutions to Africa's conflicts has to be pursued on at least four fronts: the socioeconomic, political, ideological, and institutional.

African leaders must continue to give the highest priority to issues of sustained economic development and the enhancement of prosperity for the peoples of their respective countries. The right balance must be struck in allocating resources between town and country, public and private sectors, agriculture and industry. The cooperative exploitation of physical and mineral resources across national boundaries, the pooling of resources, and the expansion of intra-African trade in the context of subregional economic communities are absolute and urgent necessities. The problems of external debt in Africa and general bargaining with international financial institutions need to be tackled collectively rather than on an ad hoc country-by-country basis.

At the political level, the gap between the elite and the masses and between the state and society in general must be bridged. No domestic peace can exist without social justice and commitment to the defense of human rights of individuals and groups in each African state. Arrangements and structures of governance have to be devised to give full and free expression to the political will of the people. Africa cannot be a secure and lonely island in the global sea of uprising against totalitarian and authoritarian systems.

The ideology of racist domination and oppression has no place in the modern world. Namibia and South Africa must be free, and the people of these countries must be allowed to live in a nonracial political system. Only in that way can the root cause of the conflicts in southern Africa be removed.

At the institutional level, the machinery for peaceful settlement of disputes and conflict resolution in Africa needs to be strengthened. Creative ways must be found to deal with situations of conflict in Africa beyond the present charter provisions and the ad hoc arrangements within the OAU. After a quarter century, the OAU Charter needs to be reexamined with a view to strengthening its capacity for peacekeeping and peacemaking in the continent, perhaps with the assistance of the United Nations. Whether at the OAU, subregional, or bilateral level, confidence-building arrangements need to be established to lower tensions and reduce conflicts. It is through the promotion of African solutions for African security problems that extra-African interventions in the continent's conflicts can be minimized or eliminated.

Within these broad analytical and prescriptive frameworks, several research agendas emerge from the discussions in this volume. A need exists for detailed case studies of conflicts in Africa. Comparative analyses of conflicts within Africa and in other world regions should also be pursued for intellectual profit as well as for practical application by policymakers. This kind of research endeavor would provide a useful basis for collaboration between institutions in Africa and centers of policy and academic research, especially in the areas of conflict resolution and peace studies all over the world.

I can say with confidence and in all seriousness that the African Leadership Forum, which I have the honor and privilege to chair, is ready and willing to engage in such outreach and collaborative research activities. It is also my strong belief that other similar institutions in Africa could engage in this collective search for durable solutions to African security problems in the interest of peace and prosperity for the continent and for the international system as a whole.

Acronyms of African Groups and Organizations

ABAKO	Alliance des Bakongo
ALC	African Liberation Committee (OAU)
ANC	African National Congress
APPER	African Priority Program for Economic Recovery
CONSAS	Constellation of Southern African States
COSATU	Congress of South African Trade Unions
CP	Conservative party (South Africa)
DMI	Department of Military Intelligence (South Africa)
DUP	Democratic Unionist party (Sudan)
ECOWAS	Economic Community of West African States
ECPO	Ethiopian Central Planning Office
EPLF	Eritrean People's Liberation Front
FAPLA	Popular Armed Forces for the Liberation of Angola
FLS	Frontline States
FRELIMO	Front for the Liberation of Mozambique
Frolinat	National Liberation Front (Chad)
IDASA	Institute for Democratic Alternatives in South Africa
KANU	Kenya African National Union party
LLA	Lesotho Liberation Army
MNR	Mozambique National Resistance (Renamo)
MPLA	Popular Movement for the Liberation of Angola
NP	Nationalist party (South Africa)
NRA	National Resistance Army (Uganda)
NSMS	National Security Management System (South Africa)
OAU	Organization of African Unity
PDRE	People's Democratic Republic of Ethiopia
PF	Patriotic Front (Zimbabwe)
Polisario	Popular Front for the Liberation of Western Sahara

Renamo	See MNR
SAAF	South African Air Force
SACP	South African Communist party
SACTU	South African Congress of Trade Unions
SADCC	South African Development Coordination Conference
SADF	South African Defence Force
SPLA	Sudan People's Liberation Army
SSC	State Security Council (South Africa)
SWAPO	South-West Africa People's Organization
TPLF	Tigre People's Liberation Front
UDF	United Democratic Front (South Africa)
UNITA	National Union for the Total Independence of Angola
UNLA	Uganda National Liberation Army
UPC	Uganda People's Congress
UPM	Uganda Patriotic Movement
WPE	Worker's Party of Ethiopia
WSLF	Western Somali Liberation Front
ZANU	Zimbabwe African National Union
ZAPU	Zimbabwe African People's Union

FRANCIS M. DENG & I. WILLIAM ZARTMAN

Introduction

The Brookings Institution chose to initiate its Africa program by focusing on regional conflicts and their resolution because of the challenging humanitarian issues they raise for policymakers and scholars.
Although domestic and regional conflicts are more limited than the
conflicts that directly concern the major powers, they usually invoke
more intense emotions among those immediately involved. They are
the more frequent cause of violence, suffering, and massive denial of
the basic needs of life, resulting in the large-scale influx of refugees
across state borders. They emerge from the interactions of peoples
who maintain separate, antagonistic political identities, and they occur within the boundaries of states as well as across borders. Undem-
ocratic and unresponsive regimes often pursue policies that exacerbate
rather than ameliorate these divisions. The conflicts also seem to be
driven by economic scarcity and the sharp competition for resources
that it engenders. The toll is tremendous: war damage to productivity
and scarce resources diverted to armaments and military organizations, as well as insecurity, displacement, and destruction to the environment. As General Obasanjo says in the preface to this volume,
"Clearly . . . there is a link between the level of poverty in Africa and
the level and incidences of violence and conflict in the continent."

This volume comprises revised versions of the papers presented at
a research conference organized by the African studies branch of the
Brookings Foreign Policy Studies program on October 15–18, 1989,
in which scholars from Africa, Asia, Europe, and North America
participated. The objective of the conference was to review the scholarship on conflict resolution in the light of the changes currently
taking place on the international scene, assess the potential implications of those changes for regional conflict, direct attention to a
contextual analysis of the issues leading to African conflicts, evaluate

the prospects for conflict management and resolution, and recommend a selection of case studies and themes for a longer-term research agenda.

Understanding the critical dimensions of domestic and regional conflicts and devising policies for diminishing them are clearly a central conceptual problem for Africa. The demands of those conflicts impede urgent and complex questions of respect for human dignity, principles of democracy, sustainable economic development, and nation-building.

PERTINENT CHANGES IN THE INTERNATIONAL CONTEXT

The conviction that general thinking on regional conflict needs to be updated derives from several recent Brookings studies that have described major shifts in international politics and in the policies of many countries. As financial and industrial markets have become more international, economic performance has become a prime objective of foreign policy. As China and the Soviet Union have begun to redirect their policies to emphasize economic performance and to overcome their historical isolation from the industrial world, the impulse for superpower confrontation has diminished. As Japan and several other Asian countries have surged in economic importance, new kinds of international relationships have begun to emerge, transcending the standard alliance and adversarial patterns that dominated after the Second World War. In combination, these changes have dramatically affected the context of regional conflict, a strong reason for reconsidering both the dangers posed and the opportunities for constructive resolution.

Some obvious questions arise from this premise: most generally, what are the implications of a "post–Cold War" world for African conflicts and their resolution? If major powers are less eager to acquire clients and fight proxy battles, will that fact dampen regional conflicts or will it stimulate them by removing the restraining danger of superpower confrontation? Is the availability of arms an independent factor in regional conflict? What is the impact of external actors (including the superpowers with global interests, European powers such as France with a traditional involvement on the continent, Middle Eastern states such as Saudi Arabia and Israel, and international organizations of which the United Nations is paramount) on the sources of conflict and the potential for resolution? Does regional conflict normally work to isolate countries from international markets and thereby retard economic development, or can market access operate despite conflict or as a means of resolution? Are the basic changes in the international context producing consistent effects on the attitudes of new generations entering political life, or are discontinuities in those attitudes a root cause of regional conflict? Developed thoughts on some of these questions can be found in the existing literature, but none of them has been settled and all of them need much more systematic reflection and marshaling of evidence than has yet been done.

The first three chapters in this volume consider the impact of international change on African conflicts. Raymond Copson presents a balance sheet, concluding that while some trends suggest a more peaceful future for the continent, others threaten to unleash more conflict. He argues that international change will promote peace in Africa only insofar as it has an effect on the underlying, internal causes of conflicts. Winrich Kühne focuses on the ramifications of Mikhail Gorbachev's reforms in Moscow as they may affect Africa. He concludes that the United States and the Soviet Union will no longer perceive regional conflicts as an opportunity to shift the international balance of power ideologically and militarily but as a burden that distracts them from matters of greater importance to their national interests. Kühne also raises the concern that, as economic aid and international business interest in Eastern Europe rises, Africa risks losing the meager but essential flows of international capital it currently receives.

Next, Ibrahim Msabaha reviews the main themes and changes in the international system from the First World War to the emerging post–Cold War period and its implications for Africa. He concludes that Africans must act on their declarations in favor of economic cooperation across the continent or else face increased marginalization in a world economy of large trading blocs. Msabaha also sees the Non-Aligned Movement as offering an organization that can strengthen African diplomatic positions in the international system.

The impact of international change on regional conflict forms a subtheme in many of the later chapters. Thomas Ohlson and Tom

Lodge, for example, argue that Western attitudes toward political change in southern Africa and the resulting policies regarding economic sanctions will be critical to the transitions in that region.

ISSUES IN THE CONTEXTUAL ANALYSIS OF CONFLICT

Until the end of the Cold War became manifest, the prevailing tendency was to see regional conflicts as actual or potential extensions of the Cold War strategic rivalries of the superpowers, their proxy confrontation in developing countries, and their transfer of weaponry and war technologies to those countries. With the current trend toward economic interaction and cooperation between the superpowers, their confrontation in regional conflicts is rapidly giving way to collaboration, and the internal dimensions, the underlying causes, and the consequences or implications of those conflicts are likely to receive more attention. Such a shift should call for a contextual approach that will address an array of issues: the identities of the conflicting parties, their objectives and perceptions, their methods and strategies, and the structural levels of involvement in the conflicts. It also requires a more broadly conceived concept of security. Along with the traditional threats from external forces, African security, as Ibrahim Gambari has recently argued, must include tensions, conflicts, and violence that arise from socioeconomic and political imbalance and underdevelopment within states. Hence threats to domestic political stability, social cohesion, and economic development should be regarded as constituting security threats to African states at the national and sometimes subregional levels.[1]

Studies of conflict in Africa have identified many underlying causes: incomplete nation-building and differences in identities derived from complex internal factors such as ethnicity, religion, culture, and language; economics and the competition for limited resources; state-society relationships; and political demands that exceed state capabilities—all inspire and perpetuate conflict. The relationships among these factors, and which are independent rather than intervening

---

1. Ibrahim A. Gambari, "An Overview of Threats to African Security," in *Defining African Security* (unpublished manuscript).

variables, are far less clear. Furthermore, external causes, whether regional rivalries or global political and economic trends, also shape conflicts and complicate analysis. Conceptual understanding of the reasons behind conflicts is important to conflict management and resolution because it helps policymakers identify root causes and suggest formulas for mediators to use to reduce disputes.[2] In his detailed and rigorous overview of social science theories and concepts as they may be applied to African conflicts, Ted Robert Gurr argues that general theories of political violence and revolution should be relevant to African cases once distinctly African conditions are incorporated. Gurr suggests a typology to help us analyze conflicts by organizing them according to the issues at stake and to the basis of group mobilization. Understanding the origins, patterns, and possible outcomes of conflicts is indispensable for developing the concepts and means to reduce or resolve them. Along the same proposed line of using theory for the practical end of conflict resolution, Donald Rothchild focuses on the linkages among demands, regime strategies, and the management of conflict. According to this analysis, different forms of collective demands and different regime types have different results for conflict. Distributive issues are more readily negotiable and amenable to political solutions. Subjective and emotionally laden issues such as group status, identity, and survival are often nonnegotiable. And when the claims of rival groups are incompatible, the outcome can be intractable conflicts.

Seeing the problem in context also raises issues of historical perspective, collective memory, and generational differences in response to the form that conflict takes at the different phases of social change. As generations in Africa move away from a long-remembered history of competing or conflicting identities, and adopt a short-term view of the past and the pressing problems of the future, is there likely to be a change in the level of tolerance and in the response to deep-rooted grievances? A correlative question is, are there differences between the responses of the rural masses and those of the educated,

2. Donald L. Horowitz, *Ethnic Groups in Conflict* (University of California Press, 1985), p. 564, states that "a cardinal assumption of this study has been that efforts to ameliorate ethnic conflict must be preceded by an understanding of the sources and patterns of that conflict." The same argument may be made about any type of conflict.

mostly urban, elites to the diversities and disparities or inequities that underlie these internal and regional conflicts? Who, in other words, are the true actors in a conflict situation, or are represented by parties engaged in armed conflict? Answers to such questions might help to identify the core parties in conflict, the interests at stake, and the overall demography of causes and effects.

Despite their impact on the lives of the masses, conflicts usually tend to be approached from the perspectives of the key players from the conflicting factions, especially the leaders whose concerns relate primarily to power struggles and less to the life of the ordinary citizens and the welfare of the community as a whole. Popular aspirations or reactions (backlash) of the masses may be exploited to give legitimacy to the ambitious policies and actions of the leaders of the warring factions. From this standpoint, several basic questions arise for conflict resolution. To what extent do the factors that trigger violence relate to the objectives of the elites, the fighting men, or the populace? Once a conflict has erupted, to what extent is it sustained by the grievances that had triggered it in the first place? Do the value positions of the leaders, the followers, and the people on both sides of the conflict reflect shared concerns and objectives, or do they differ at different levels of the power structure? Answers to these and other questions could help illuminate the causes and consequences of conflict and scrutinize the role, the credibility, and the legitimacy of the leadership from the standpoint of the wider interests of the community.

Atieno Odhiambo's contribution reminds us of the chasm between the perspective of the social scientist and policymaker viewing these conflicts from afar and in the abstract and the perspectives of the marginalized people directly affected. The viewpoints of peoples on the margin in the Horn of Africa "hardly penetrate to the capitals of the hegemonic states that have continually coerced their allegiances: Nairobi, Kampala, Addis Ababa, and Mogadishu are faraway places in 'foreign' lands, centers from which emanate discourses about control and subjection." Superpower discussions are even more distant and faint. To Africans caught in the middle of these conflicts, survival is the imperative, and the family, community, and the state are the arenas.

A contextual analysis of conflict and conflict resolution should also address the problem from a cross-cultural perspective. To what extent do different cultural contexts reflect different techniques of conflict resolution? Assuming a diversity of cultural techniques, can a comparative approach be cross-culturally enriching in developing more effective methods of conflict resolution in the context of cultural pluralism or the emerging universalism?

An important characteristic of conflicts in Africa is that they are often linked to other conflicts. Internally based insurgencies frequently build ties with neighboring states to gain access to safe havens and military resources, thereby adding an interstate dimension to a conflict that originated in local grievances. The complex interweaving of conflicts in a region may have important policy consequences. Peter Anyang' Nyong'o and Thomas Ohlson suggest that the regional character and context may have an important bearing on the prospects for internal conflict resolution. The possibility of regionalized conflict resolution efforts opens up tactical and strategic choices. Given that the conflicts in the Horn are linked, must all conflicts be resolved simultaneously, whether autonomously or in a region-wide restructuring of relations, or should conflict management and resolution efforts in, for example, Sudan proceed without waiting for parallel initiatives in Eritrea? Ohlson's analysis of the regional context of conflict resolution, focusing on the consequences of South Africa's regional strategy for its neighbors in the Southern Africa Development Coordination Conference, argues that heightened economic costs will reduce Pretoria's room to maneuver and force the government to negotiate.

This conclusion supports the increasing tendency in Africa to see conflict in economic terms, more specifically in poverty, competition for meager resources, and general ignorance about the broader challenges of nation-building, such as the need to overcome racial, ethnic, cultural, and religious chauvinism and parochialism. Conflict in turn compels nations to invest heavily in weaponry and the military establishment, thereby aggravating the economic and political life hardships that are created by conflicts.

A tension arises between focusing on the immediate crisis and addressing the deeper economic and social conditions that underlie the crisis. In the chapter on the impact of conflict on the economies of Third World countries, Nicole Ball analyzes in depth the interplay between conflict and military expenditures and their implications for economic and political development. One of her major recommendations is the removal of the military from politics. In that connection she also recommends a serious examination of the relationships among the role of the security forces, economic development, and political development.

Careful study is needed to understand how countries can constructively balance short-term solutions that address the symptoms and the longer-term adjustments that go deeper into the root causes. The debate over the impact of structural adjustment programs formulated and advocated by the International Monetary Fund and the World Bank is the most obvious example of this dilemma. Outside humanitarian intervention and assistance aimed at short-term relief from the consequences or effect of an ongoing conflict also raise significant questions. Any dialogue on the problems of making humanitarian relief available to a population affected by ongoing conflict must inevitably lead to the discussion of the principal cause—the war—and the ultimate objective—peace. Furthermore, making relief available to areas under the control of the adversary and, in particular, the rebel forces always entails negotiating with both sides in a manner that modifies the norms of sovereignty. This circumstance has a way of creating some form of parity between the parties that should facilitate negotiations for peace. Yet, at the same time, such humanitarian intervention is often mistrusted by both sides; they perceive it as favoring the one or the other and as tending to prolong the conflict. What in reality is the effect of humanitarian intervention in conflict situations? Is the benefit from such intervention strictly humanitarian, as is often alleged, or are there aspects that might affect the conduct and perhaps the outcome of the conflict? And if the answer is in the affirmative, in what way does such aid affect the conflict?

Given the multiplicity of actors in African conflicts and the complexities of the issues at all levels, from local to global, speculations on the prospects for conflict resolution cannot be optimistic in the short run. Indeed, a cursory look at the field suggests that conflicts are seldom resolved finally and that, although a temporary settlement may be arrived at, old wounds tend to open up with new conflicts, and the need to negotiate or resolve the whole situation anew may then arise. I. William Zartman argues that "conflict is an inevitable aspect of human interaction" and conflict resolution therefore involves pursuing incompatible goals by nonviolent, political means. Often conflicts are prevented by timely unilateral actions to address grievances; this is the process of "normal politics." At other times those who perceive an injustice must mobilize and organize until they form a group that can negotiate a formula for conflict resolution. Certain conflicts require the introduction of third parties to assist the competing actors in finding the way to pursue their goals without violence.

To prevent inevitable competition from turning into violent conflict, Africa needs to improve and expand mechanisms for conflict management. The past record and future potential of two of the most important existing mechanisms, the Organization of African Unity and certain legal norms, are discussed by William Foltz and Crawford Young, respectively. Foltz's discussion of the OAU as an international "regime" highlights the importance of such norms as territorial integrity and African solutions to African problems. Young analyzes the ambiguity and contradictions between the legal norms of self-determination and territorial integrity in the African state system and suggests that the level of success with the principle of preserving the borders inherited from colonialism should now permit a more flexible application of self-determination without threatening the continent with disintegration.

Tom Lodge's discussion of one of the most salient conflicts in Africa—that between the majority African population and the minority white government in South Africa—demonstrates the laborious process by which conflict may be channeled into nonviolent political competition. The complex and uncertain political process under way in that state, the breakdown and rebuilding of coalitions and interest groups, and the slow process of altering political perceptions suggest that conflict resolution is a political process shaped by many forces. The recent development in Liberia and the eruption of new forms of conflict in South Africa, between rival African groups, indicate that progress on the removal of one form of domination and resolving one conflict may incite other, previously repressed conflicts.

Conflicts at higher levels of political or social organization may in fact consolidate the internal unity and cohesiveness of the conflict groups at lower levels. Conflicts between the center and regional groups, based on race or ethnicity, may force the groups to unite to deal with the center, but once the cementing factor is removed by the actual or impending resolution of that conflict, internal differences are likely to emerge and cause internal conflict. To give an example, although the southern Sudanese united in the seventeen-year war with the central government, once they were granted regional autonomy through the 1972 Addis Ababa agreement, ethnic differences and rivalries among them led to factional alignments with the center. This eventually resulted in the unilateral abrogation of the agreement by President Jaafar Nimeiri, triggering the resumption of hostilities in the south.

One of the main conclusions of this initial phase of the Brookings project on conflict resolution in Africa is that one cannot generalize about conditions in different countries and regions of Africa and that a series of case studies must be conducted before broad conclusions can be drawn about conditions on the continent. Consequently, the chapter by Stephen Stedman is intended to provide a tentative and flexible framework to guide the anticipated case studies now planned to be undertaken in southern, eastern, and western African countries.

CONFLICT RESOLUTION ISSUES IN PERSPECTIVE

Although many of the questions raised in the our original conceptual framework are treated in this volume and will undoubtedly continue to engage researchers in this field, some speculative themes can be formulated from observing the African scene, especially in the light of recent international developments. The issues driving the African conflicts and the prospects for their resolution ultimately crystallize in the complex linkages between the internal context and the dynamics of global interaction and interdependence. Before the recent changes on the international scene, foreign policy analysts concerned with the role of outside powers in African conflicts continually debated whether those conflicts were essentially domestic or regional and should therefore be left for the Africans to manage or resolve, or were essentially generated or sustained by foreign powers, so that resolving them would depend on the relations with and among those powers. Posing the question in terms of "either–or" clearly misconstructed the situation, since those conflicts usually entail elements of both.

The two dimensions, the internal and external, can perhaps be classified into interactive causes and effects. It is safe to argue that the causes are nearly always domestic or regional but that the effects or the operational aspects involving the means, whether in weapons or the financial ability to procure them, are usually external. Whatever the legitimacy of the grievances, without these external resources armed confrontation would be constrained, and conflicts, even if they exploded into violence, would be less destructive. But of course the objective cannot be peace at the cost of justice and human dignity, nor should the external supply of means of destruction be purely a matter of the economics of supply and demand. Both the domestic causes of conflict and the external sources of means of destruction must be considered concurrently or correlatively if an enduring management or resolution of these conflicts is to be achieved.

Regarding the internal context and dynamics, as the contributions to this volume reveal, African conflicts have many domestic or regional causes, in particular the problems of racial, ethnic, cultural, and religious cleavages and stratifications, combined with gross inequities in the distribution of power, wealth, and other resources that render conformity or acquiescence to the status quo untenable. The overriding goal of the liberation struggle against colonial domination usually tended to overshadow these internal differences, and independence was achieved as a gross asset to the nation as a whole, but the issues of who gets what, when, and how soon generated tensions and violent confrontations between the factions concerned. Furthermore, the right of self-determination does not offer a basis for relief against factional domination, since the exercise of that right has so far been permissible only against European colonialism. Because of these rigid limitations on the exercise of self-determination, the increasingly popular alternative now appears to be varying degrees of autonomy, guaranteed through federalism, and perhaps even the looser arrangement of confederacy, with a restructuring of central power so as to be more equitably representative.

As for the external elements of African conflicts, they range from regional interconnections and support to more distant sources of military assistance and sometimes outright intervention. Liberation movements against the center usually cross into neighboring countries and use their territories as bases for waging their attacks. The host countries offer them support either out of conviction for the justice of their cause or for other strategic reasons, including perhaps retaliation against their neighbors' support for their own dissidents or rebel groups. More distant foreign powers also get involved for ideological or strategic reasons that have often been linked to superpower rivalry and proxy confrontation.

The linkage between the domestic causes of African conflicts and the exacerbations of external involvement has generated ambivalences and contradictions in the African management of conflicts. For example, the rhetoric is universally against foreign intervention in African affairs, and the Organization of African Unity has advocated collective opposition to such intervention. Individual governments, however, have often resorted to external sources of military support, ranging from financing to the provision of weapons to, in some cases, the sending of troops. This experience has paradoxically made some people see the intensification of regional conflicts through internationalization and superpower involvement as a means of improving the chances for settlement. Such was the approach adopted by Egypt in 1973, and current developments in southern Africa follow a similar pattern. This strategy has been discreetly advocated by some as a possible way of dealing with conflicts in the Horn of Africa—the civil wars in Ethiopia and Sudan. They have argued that unless the stakes in these conflicts are raised to the global level, the world will choose to ignore them. The assumption is that even though the origins of these conflicts are internal to the countries or the region, dependency on the support of external powers has so altered conditions that ending or sustaining the conflicts is not possible without foreign intervention.

With the seeming end of the Cold War, the external arm of the superpowers, driven by ideological rivalry and proxy confrontation, appears to be withdrawing. But a question can be raised whether external dependency will cease with the withdrawal of the superpowers or will merely be redirected to other sources of external support. Furthermore, it is worth asking whether the change in the attitude of the superpowers is likely to be limited to the withdrawal of support or restraint from involvement or might extend into positive cooperation in resolving regional conflicts.

The international response to Iraq's invasion of Kuwait would seem to signal a new era of global cooperation in the management of regional interstate conflicts. But it may also stimulate a new pattern of global alignment that could overshadow internal contexts of conflict. One source of such alignment rests in the division that the crisis generated in the Arab world. Although international consensus in condemnation of Saddam Hussein's action was overwhelming, the support that a number of Arab countries showed him or their reluctance to join the global action against him, combined with the controversy surrounding the domestic conditions in the now protected countries in the region, is bound to result in ideological cleavages and alliances. Would the governments that supported one or the other position be rewarded by their allies in a way that could consolidate their domestic or regional power without regard to their internal conditions or to the questions of domestic governance or legitimacy? Or would the new momentum of global cooperation be used to address the legitimate grievances of the people or factions within those countries to attack the causes of actual or potential conflicts from within? Furthermore, would the international momentum generated by the war and its aftermath be seized on and used for resolving the Palestinian problem and the Arab-Israeli conflict? Recent developments in the U.S. efforts to do so provide ground for some optimism.

The developments that have recently taken place in other areas of the world—in particular, the trend toward liberalization and democratization in Eastern Europe, South America, and even in South Africa, and the increasing self-assertiveness of minority nationalities in the Soviet Union and in other ethnically pluralistic countries—are likely to affect African countries in several ways. For one thing, they provide examples of political and economic reforms that cannot be ignored where they are badly needed, as in Africa. For another, the superpowers and their major allies may indeed choose to cooperate in promoting those principles in areas of the Third World where they exercise pivotal influence. But perhaps even more important, these developments imply the removal of ideological models that have offered uniting symbols of nation-building in countries that would otherwise be torn apart by ethnic, cultural, religious, or linguistic differences.

Within the African context, these ideological symbols or models have been embodied in the concepts of socialism and the one-party system. "Scientific Socialism" in Africa has generally been modified by the concept of "African Socialism" and justified on the basis of traditional African cultural values and patterns of behavior, even though the content of the policies and the practices associated with those policies were essentially foreign and largely Marxist in origin, with heavy state intervention, central planning, and monopoly in marketing. The one-party system, too, has often been explained in terms of the traditional African cultural orientation toward open discussion, ultimately leading to a consensus. But again, the institutional and organizational model has been the communist one-party system in local variants. Even such ideological slogans as Senghor's Négritude, Nkrumah's Consciencism, Kaunda's Humanism, and Mobutu's Authenticité have been efforts to find domestic roots for concepts and postulates that are essentially external or novel to the African realities.

The removal of these external or new models that provided umbrellas of uniting myths of nation-building is bound to unleash the ethnic, "tribal," cultural, linguistic, or religious diversities that have been overshadowed by these purported symbols of nation-building from the top. The implications of these developments can be both negative and positive. The immediate response is bound to be a greater self-assertiveness by previously oppressed subnational groups, whose survival depended on their submission to the dominant group. And that response will generate greater levels of confrontation and conflict between the center and local nationalities at the periphery of the formal framework of the nation-state. But in the long run, and by the same token, this resurgence of minorities could mobilize and use ethnic, cultural, and even material resources within the subnational groups that might have been incapacitated by repression and lack of recognition. These minorities might not only play a more active role in determining and shaping their own destiny but also contribute their resources and resourcefulness toward building their own society and the country as a whole, whether materially, culturally, or spiritually.

These possible trends need to be carefully monitored and supported in the interest of self-discovery, self-assertiveness, and self-development, while the negative aspects of hostile competition and violent confrontation need to be checked through balanced control and prudent management. It will, however, require more than what the Africans alone can do to build on the positives while counteracting the negatives. The guiding principle in this situation should be to assist the Africans in assuming control of their own development. That can be accomplished only through political and economic growth that will release the energies of the people within the context of the cultural values and institutionalized practices that have traditionally served their communities. Although these values and practices have passed the test of time, they have recently become undermined by externally based ideological concepts of development and nation-building.

Would such a principle be tantamount to recommending isolationism for Africa? It might be, but it need not be, especially since isolationism is no longer an easy or even a feasible option. What we suggest is to modify the exaggerated externalization of the system that has been the natural outcome of colonial domination and dependency. Such a modification, if well conceived and carefully conducted, could be in the interest of everyone, since the African political and economic failures are proving to be not only a burden but an embarrassment to the international community. For Africa, a more creative and constructive approach that uses the cross-cultural framework of nation-building in an interdependent world would delicately balance individualism with social consciousness, liberalism with communal responsibility, self-assertiveness with respect for dialogue, and confrontation with consensus building.

PART 1
Pertinent Changes in the International Climate

Chapter 1

RAYMOND W. COPSON

Peace in Africa? The Influence of Regional and International Change

The final years of the 1980s saw many favorable developments that seemed to portend a reduction in conflict in Africa. The most surprising developments were taking place in the southwestern part of the continent, where Namibia was moving rapidly toward independence and the Cuban army was withdrawing from Angola. The Namibia problem had vexed diplomats for nearly a quarter century, and the Cuban troops had been a disturbing factor in international relations ever since 1979, when their arrival helped catapult Angola onto the Cold War stage. In 1989 both problems seemed to be disappearing. Meanwhile, peace initiatives were under way in some of Africa's major internal conflicts, including the wars in Mozambique and Ethiopia, and hopes were high for a reconciliation within Angola between the Popular Movement for the Liberation of Angola (MPLA) government and the National Union for the Total Independence of Angola (UNITA) resistance, as a result of an African-sponsored mediation effort. The situation in Sudan was uncertain after the June 1989 coup, but a renewal of the peace effort in that costly war seemed possible. Across the continent, Morocco's King Hassan had held discussions with representatives of the Polisario resistance movement from the Western Sahara, and speculation continued on a possible referendum in the disputed territory.

All this apparent progress toward peace in Africa was occurring under the influence of potentially favorable changes in the regional and international state systems. In Africa itself, a new spirit of pragmatism and cooperation seemed to be abroad. Libya and South Africa were conducting themselves with unaccustomed good manners in their relations with their neighbors. The world would evidently have to adjust to cordial South African exchanges with Mozambique and to Muammar Qadhafi's enthusiastic embrace of his North African neighbors in the Greater

Maghreb Union. Morocco and Algeria, once great rivals, now appeared determined to be friends; Ethiopia and Somalia—once bitter enemies—had launched their own rapprochement.

Even more striking were the encouraging changes taking place in the wider international environment. The shift in Soviet policy under President Mikhail Gorbachev was of course the most notable of these. The era when the USSR would freely expend its resources on the wars in Angola, Ethiopia, and Mozambique was at an end. Instead, a commitment to peace, dialogue, and development was to mark the Third World policies of the Soviet Union. Gorbachev had declared that "the bell of every regional conflict tolls for all of us,"[1] and in a remarkable turnabout for Soviet policy, he enthusiastically promoted the United Nations as a force for peace. Indeed, there was renewed worldwide interest in U.N. peacekeeping forces as a solution to regional conflicts, including those in Africa. One such force had already been deployed in Namibia, and another was anticipated in Western Sahara.

Long-time Africa specialists watched these many changes and developments with hope, but also with the caution that comes of experience. They recalled what was in many ways a disaster for the United Nations in the 1960–64 Congo operation, and they remembered the calamitous 1983 breakdown of a much-praised accord that had brought eleven years of peace to Sudan. Libya's destabilizing policy swings over Chad, evidence of continuing South African interference in Mozambique long after the 1984 Nkomati Accord that was supposed to bring it to an end, and Uganda's sad years of suffering after the initially exhilarating ouster of Idi Amin were all too recent memories for experienced observers of Africa.

As the new decade got under way, the doubts and reservations arising from these memories were being borne out in a number of instances. In the final months of 1989 and into 1990, the wars in Sudan, Ethiopia, and Angola intensified and peace initiatives faltered. A final settlement in Western Sahara continued to recede, while Chad was waging a twilight struggle against dissidents taking shelter in a remote region of Sudan. Senegal and Mauritania were locked in a confron-

1. Mikhail S. Gorbachev, "Statement at Plenary Meeting of the United Nations General Assembly," December 7, 1988, p. 15; reprinted in Congressional Research Service, *The Gorbachev Speech to the United Nations, New York, December 7, 1988*, CRS Report 88–776 F (Washington, December 1988).

tation, still short of war, that had arisen unexpectedly in 1989. At the end of that year, Liberia faced an invasion by dissidents in a remote border region that threatened to develop into a prolonged struggle. In short, conflict remained a serious problem for Africa as the 1990s began, despite the favorable developments in the regional and international systems in the final years of the 1980s.

A full assessment of the likely course of conflict in Africa in the years ahead would require an in-depth examination of the many factors that lead to warfare and violence, and an evaluation of all of the changes that might somehow be affecting those factors. Such an examination is beyond the scope of this chapter, which focuses on the influence of changes in the regional and international systems. Nonetheless, a brief review of the dimensions of Africa's conflicts and of some of their more apparent causes suggests that the problem is very grave and deeply rooted in African states and African societies. The regional and international systems represent two sets of factors in the causal pattern, and they are changing in significant ways. But there are other, possibly more important, factors and sets of factors that give rise to conflict. Changes affecting only a part of the total pattern can be expected to offer only a partial improvement, at best, in the problem of conflict in Africa.

Fundamental social cleavages within African states along ethnic and regional lines, sometimes reinforced by religious and income differences, are a major underlying cause of conflict that will not soon disappear. Africa's poverty, which deprives African societies of the means of easing social tensions, is another. The tendency of many African governments to rule through arbitrary and repressive means has provoked violent conflict and armed resistance in many instances. It may be that this tendency is weakening as it has elsewhere in the world, and the developments in South Africa at the beginning of 1990 were a particular source of hope. In some of Africa's major conflicts, however, the beginning of the new decade witnessed a renewal of intolerance and refusal to compromise, affecting both governments and resistance forces and thwarting important peace initiatives. Even the changes in the regional and international systems were somewhat tentative in their effects on African conflict. In Africa itself, the new restraint shown by South Africa was favorable, as were African-sponsored peace initiatives in Angola, Mozambique, and elsewhere. There was, however, little progress toward institutionalizing procedures for conflict resolution in Africa and no clear indication that regional organizations were developing a genuine capability for mediation and peacekeeping.

The contribution of the wider international system to the reduction of conflict in Africa also seemed to falter as the 1990s began. Both superpowers were offering encouragement for peace efforts and negotiated solutions in all of the major conflicts. Yet there was no bold initiative on the part of the superpowers, the Europeans, or the United Nations to resolve Africa's conflicts. Gorbachev's advocacy of regional conflict resolution had once seemed to hold out the prospect of such an effort, but by 1990 the overall direction of Soviet policy was clouded. According to some reports, Soviet arms shipments to Angola and Ethiopia had increased despite Soviet verbal support for a peaceful resolution of these conflicts. U.S. aid to the UNITA guerrillas in Angola was also continuing. No doubt both sides saw their role in Angola as a matter of maintaining commitments and as a necessary prelude to genuine negotiations—but an end to the fighting remained elusive. Many observers, meanwhile, were concerned that Western aid for economic development in Africa would be diverted to Eastern Europe, further weakening Africa's ability to deal with the pressing social needs and divisions that helped cause war.

In summary, despite hopeful trends and developments, major changes that would transform the African situation have not yet taken place. Consequently, the near-term future will probably see continued conflict rather than peace, although larger weapons supplied from outside Africa will perhaps be used less often. Some of Africa's ongoing wars may be punctuated by periods of relative calm as exhausted conflict participants struggle to recover. Some actors in the regional and international systems will encourage and try to prolong these interludes. In most cases, however, there will be a grave danger of a resumption of violent conflict as long as fundamental problems remain unresolved. There will also be a continuing prospect of violent outbreaks in other countries affected by social cleavage, poverty, and repressive government policies.

DIMENSIONS OF AFRICAN WARFARE AND VIOLENCE

During the 1980s, Africa was torn by nine wars, numerous other instances of large-scale violent conflict, and a kaleidoscope of coups, riots, and demonstrations. These hostilities exacted a great toll on Africa in terms of the destruction of human life, cultural damage, economic disruption, and lost investment opportunities. Indeed, it is difficult to foresee significant economic or social development over wide stretches of Africa until the burden of violent conflict is eased.

Of the nine wars, five—in Sudan, Ethiopia, Angola, Mozambique, and Uganda—were major, with death totals, including civilian deaths, ranging from the 60,000 to 100,000 commonly reported in Angola[2] to the million or more thought possible in Sudan.[3] In these large wars, the overwhelming majority of victims were civilians, including countless children, who were deprived of food, shelter, and access to health care because of the fighting. Three other wars, in Namibia, Western Sahara, and Chad, probably resulted in deaths numbering in the 10,000 to 20,000 range. Since these wars took place in lightly populated territories, it seems likely that the civilian toll was less. Little is known about the situation in northern Somalia, although the flight of 350,000 refugees to Ethiopia suggests that substantial fighting has taken place.[4] A human rights organization estimates that 50,000 to 60,000 civilians have been killed in the north.[5] In all, it does not seem unreasonable to estimate that 2 million to 3 million Africans died as a result of Africa's wars in the 1980s. At the end of the decade, there were still

2. Gerald Bender, "Peacemaking in Southern Africa: The Luanda-Pretoria Tug of War," *Third World Quarterly*, January 1989, p. 24. The *Washington Times* has given a figure of 90,000. See "A Freedom Fight Deep in Africa," *Insight*, December 18, 1988, p. 10. The UNICEF figures for Angola and Mozambique include an estimate of child mortality resulting from wartime conditions and are much higher than those published elsewhere. According to UNICEF, 850,000 children who would otherwise have lived died as a result of war in these two countries between 1980 and 1988. United Nations Children's Fund (UNICEF), *Children on the Front Line*, 3d ed. (New York, 1989), p 11

3. This was the estimate used by the Hon. Howard Wolpe, chairman of the House Subcommittee on Africa, on March 2, 1989. See *Politics of Hunger in Sudan*, Joint Hearing before the Select Committee on Hunger and the Subcommittee on Africa of the House Committee on Foreign Affairs, 101 Cong. 1 sess. (Government Printing Office, 1989), p. 1.

4. The number of refugees comes from U.S. Committee for Refugees, *World Refugee Survey: 1988 in Review* (Washington, September 1988), p. 33.

5. Africa Watch Committee, *Somalia: A Government at War with Its Own People* (Washington and New York, 1990), p. 10.

between 9 million and 13 million people seeking shelter from the fighting as refugees or internally displaced persons.[6]

Africa's wars were characterized by hostilities between organized military units over long periods of time. This type of violence was surely the main killer in Africa, but there were many other costly violent conflicts. In some instances, these were brief, spontaneous uprisings that resulted in a high death toll as disorganized groups attacked one another or fought government forces. This type of conflict was perhaps not as common as the popular press would lead one to believe. But important examples include the Hutu uprising in northern Burundi in 1988, resulting in perhaps 7,000 to 13,000 deaths;[7] the recurrent religious violence in northern Nigeria that may have killed 5,000 to 8,000 people over the decade;[8] and the 1989 attacks that may have caused the deaths of hundreds of Senegalese in Mauritania. The violence in South Africa took many forms, including attacks by armed guerrillas infiltrating across the border, probably resulting in a death toll in the hundreds during the 1980s. Internal political violence, such as spontaneous demonstrations, organized police sweeps, and fighting among blacks in Natal, probably killed thousands. Zimbabwe waged a struggle against "dissidents" in the southwestern part of the country that never quite became a war but led to a death toll estimated at between 2,000 and 2,500.[9]

The lesser violent outbreaks in Africa during the 1980s are too numerous to mention here. Suffice it to say that coups and attempted coups, riots and demonstrations, attacks by poachers and rustlers, and simple banditry affected countries throughout the continent. Certainly they exacted an important cost in terms of the human and economic potential of African societies.

6. Committee for Refugees, *World Refugee Survey*, pp. 32–34.

7. Testimony of Kenneth L. Brown, deputy assistant secretary of state for Africa, in *Recent Violence in Burundi: What Should Be the U.S. Response*, Hearings before the House Committee on Foreign Affairs and Its Subcommittees on Human Rights and International Organizations, and on Africa, 100 Cong. 2 sess. (GPO, 1988), p. 9.

8. *Africa Research Bulletin* (London), October 1982, p. 6625; November 1982, p. 6658; and March 1984, p. 7186.

9. Andrew Meldrum, in "An Amnesty for Unity," *Africa Report*, July–August 1988, gives a figure of 2,000 civilians killed in 1983–84.

CAUSES OF WARFARE AND VIOLENCE

A comprehensive discussion of the complex pattern of causation that lies behind Africa's conflict and violence cannot be undertaken here. Nonetheless, some of the major, contributing internal factors need to be discussed in order to assess the effect of changes in the regional and international systems.

Domestic Causal Factors

Most of the wars and other large, violent outbreaks in Africa have reflected ethnic cleavages or other deep social divisions in one form or another. In Sudan, a religious cleavage has deepened the ethnic divide. In Somalia, the rift is between clans within a common ethnic group, whereas in Ethiopia, Eritrean solidarity has emerged more from recent historical experience than from some shared ancient heritage. As elsewhere, contending parties in the Angolan internal war deny that their movements are ethnically motivated and point to representatives of diverse groups within their hierarchies. But in this and many other cases, it is impossible to deny that highly emotive, ascriptive group bonds are a principal factor in conflict. These powerful bonds do not seem to be fading from the African scene. The 1988 Burundi outbreak, the continuing if lower-level violence in Uganda, and the palpable tensions in Kenya testify to their strength.

Poverty contributes to violent conflict in a variety of ways. In Sudan, the poverty of the south compared with the north, as well as the feeling in the south that the region's resources were being exploited by the northern-based government, contributed to the outbreak of war in 1983. Southern Sudan was no doubt more developed in literacy, communication, transportation, and other aspects of modernization than it had been in the past; but increased mobility and greater access to information helped make many southerners more acutely aware of their region's relative impoverishment. In Angola and Mozambique, the resentment felt in rural areas toward an urban, partly mixed-race elite that controlled the instruments of power contributed to the emergence of an armed resistance. Governments in these countries and elsewhere, however, had limited resources for satisfying economic demands even if they had chosen to do so. Nor could they afford to recruit, train, and pay the security forces that would have been needed to curb unrest once it had broken out. This was a particular problem in view of the vast geographic size of most of the countries undergoing internal war. Guerrillas in these countries have had ample space in which to get themselves organized, set up camps and bases, and even build airstrips. Most countries afflicted by war have long borders that cannot be adequately policed with available resources, allowing opposition forces to cross into sympathetic neighboring states and return with ease.

Poverty, manifested in the degradation of unemployment and underemployment, works as an inducement in persuading people to engage in violence. This is fairly obvious for those who have taken up poaching and banditry. The participants in many of Africa's violent demonstrations in recent years, as in Sudan, Zambia, and Nigeria, have been primarily motivated by their deteriorating economic circumstances. Poverty also motivates the participants in Africa's wars. Guerrillas, in joining a resistance army, may obtain food and clothing as well as opportunities for recognition and advancement that would have been unavailable to them in an urban slum or a farming village. Guerrilla leaders too may obtain psychic rewards—and sometimes material rewards—from engaging in war. In recent years, some African guerrilla leaders have become significant figures on the world stage.

The origins of many of Africa's wars and other conflicts are in repressive policies and other political excesses on the part of African governments. President Jaafar Nimeiri's decision to "redivide" southern Sudan, destroying the autonomy the region had gained in the Addis Ababa agreement of 1972, is one such example. His determination to impose a nationwide Islamic system of corporal criminal punishment, even in the non-Islamic south, exemplified the arbitrary measures that have helped spark Africa's wars. Ethiopians endured decades of political excess, including Emperor Haile Selassie's suppression of Eritrea's autonomy and massive human rights abuses on the part of the revolutionary regime that succeeded him, which resulted in decades of war. Mozambique's war was launched by Rhodesian intelligence services, but it drew sustenance in its early years from domestic opposition to the revolutionary policies of the Front for the Liberation of Mozambique (FRELIMO) government.

Political excesses of this sort can be avoided, since they come about through the decisions of individuals and governments. Yet the persistence of some governments, or even a succession of governments, as in Ethiopia and Sudan, in pursuing policies that contribute to conflict is remarkable. Uncompromising stances, however, are by no means an exclusive preserve of governments. Guerrilla movements, once established, can become wedded to demands that complicate peace efforts. Consequently, in a range of African conflicts from Western Sahara to Ethiopia and Angola, would-be mediators have been unable to devise solutions that accommodate the core demands of governments and their armed opponents.

Regional Causal Factors

Conflict in many African states has been promoted by the willingness of neighbors and nearby states to lend their assistance to dissident forces. South African aid to the Mozambique National Resistance (Renamo) in Mozambique and UNITA in Angola, assistance from African states to the African National Congress of South Africa, Ethiopian aid to the SPLA (Sudan People's Liberation Army) guerrillas in Sudan, Sudanese aid to the Eritrean resistance, and Libyan aid to the Chadian opposition are well-known, but by no means the only, examples of this sort of aid. Neighboring states can provide dissidents with arms and training and serve as a conduit for weapons coming from farther abroad. They can also offer headquarters that allow resistance movements to conduct their own foreign relations. South Africa sent troops into Angola partly to back up internal resistance forces, just as Libyan armed forces intervened in Chad in part to support local guerrillas.

Interference is a contributing factor that in theory could be reduced, since it results from the decisions of policymakers. It is nonetheless worth noting that countries become involved in interference against their neighbors for significant reasons. Political belief may play an important part, as when African countries lend their support to the African National Congress, and governments sometimes feel compelled to interfere across their borders in self-defense. Countries like Ethiopia and Sudan, or Chad and Sudan, have been locked into reciprocal patterns of interference on defensive grounds for years.

International Causal Factors

Actors from outside Africa have contributed to the continent's conflicts. That is of course a controversial point, since external powers have often explained their African role as aimed at promoting peace rather than war—and in some cases their claims have seemed justified. The French role in Chad, for example, has probably been a stabilizing influence, on balance, helping to contain Libyan expansion.

Nonetheless, the international role can also be destabilizing. This is perhaps most clearly seen in the mountain of arms that has been used in Africa's violent conflicts. Nearly all these weapons, apart from those made in South Africa, originated outside the continent—primarily in the Soviet Union, which provided nearly $18 billion in military assistance to the continent from 1980 through 1988,[10] and in other Eastern bloc nations. Poachers, bandits, and guerrillas around the continent are armed with the AK–47 assault rifle—as are huge numbers of African soldiers. Banks in Kenya, a country that was once thought of as an island of civil order, are today held up by bandit gangs armed with these automatic rifles, and attacks on tourists by similarly armed outlaws could jeopardize the nation's economy. Meanwhile, tanks and armored personnel carriers rumble around Angola and Ethiopia as vintage MiG aircraft fly overhead.

Even if the flow of new arms could be reduced, past wars, extending back to the Congo crisis of the early 1960s, have left a vast stockpile of small arms that will not quickly be depleted. Larger weapons can also have a very long life. In Somalia, for example, the old Hawker-Hunter fighter-bomber, reportedly piloted by white mercenaries from southern Africa, has evidently been used with devastating effect.[11] In any event, small arms and a variety of larger weapons continue to be available from several suppliers.

External actors have had varied motives for becoming involved in Africa's conflicts, and these usually have had more to do with competitions in the wider international environment than with Africa itself. The superpower rivalry, Cuba's desire to demonstrate its importance as a "nonaligned" leader at a time when it was frustrated in Central America, France's determination to remain a significant middle power in world politics, and the Israeli-Arab dispute have all served as motives for countries' taking some part in African conflicts. As a result, the fighting

10. Richard F. Grimmett, *Trends in Conventional Arms Transfers to the Third World by Major Supplier, 1980–1988*, CRS Report 89–434 F (Washington: Congressional Research Service, August 1989), p. 46.

11. Richard Greenfield, "Somalia: Barre's Unholy Alliances," *Africa Report*, March–April 1989, pp. 66–67.

has often been intensified. The strife in Angola, for example, could not have become so highly militarized or so highly mechanized without Soviet and Cuban involvement, as well as South African intervention, over many years. In 1990, there was some concern that Arab involvement in the Ethiopian conflict would intensify following reports of Israeli arms shipments to the government of Mengistu Haile Mariam.

Beginning in 1986, the United States became involved in Angola through a publicly acknowledged but covert assistance program for UNITA. Analysts may one day judge that this program contributed to regional stabilization by increasing the pressure on the other participants for a compromise. Indeed, some supporters of the program have already reached this conclusion.[12] But for other observers, it is too soon to draw up the balance sheet on the Angolan war.

U.S. military assistance to two of the governments engaged in internal wars—Sudan and Somalia—had virtually stopped by the end of the 1980s, in part because of the human rights violations in each country and the uncompromising stances their governments had taken on their internal wars. Some would maintain, however, that past U.S. aid may have encouraged the governments of those countries to persist in pursuing violent internal solutions because they thought a superpower was on their side. This was true, it is argued, even though the United States, in aiding these governments, was motivated by global strategic concerns and correctly regarded the internal wars as complicating factors. In any event, the sharp recent reductions in U.S. assistance demonstrate one effect of the changes in the international system on U.S. policy. With Cold War tensions reduced, humanitarian rather than strategic considerations have come to be the dominant influence in U.S. policy toward this part of Africa.

CHANGES AFFECTING THE CAUSAL FACTORS

The foregoing review of some of the causes of conflict and war in Africa establishes a framework for assessing the influence of changes in the regional and international environments. Changes in the regional and world systems will promote peace in Africa only insofar

12. Chas. W. Freeman, Jr., "The Angola/Namibia Accords," *Foreign Affairs*, Summer 1989, pp. 131–32.

as they have an effect on the underlying causes and contributing factors that lead to conflict and war. This is a simple point, but one worth making if it helps analysts and observers overcome any unjustified optimism about the course of events in Africa. There were dramatic developments in the international environment at the end of the 1980s—such as progress toward European economic unity, the tearing down of the Berlin Wall, and the movement toward democracy among several countries in Latin America and Asia—that contributed to a general sense of optimism in world affairs but had no direct bearing on Africa's conflicts and wars.

Domestic Factors

Clearly there was little happening in the regional and international systems that would affect the ethnic and other deep social cleavages that lie at the heart of so many African conflicts. Mending these divisions is partly a task of nation-building that must first and foremost be the responsibility of African leaders, African educators and intellectuals, African governments, and African nongovernmental institutions. It is also a broader task of easing the effect of the stereotypes and hatreds that divide people everywhere; and in this sense it is a task for churches and religious authorities, teachers, and Africa's moral leaders, whether in government or out.

Certainly progress has been made in these areas. One thinks of the strong sense of Nigerian nationalism encountered by any visitor to that country or the role of churches in South Africa in attempting to bridge the cultural chasms there. The 1988 reconciliation in Zimbabwe between President Robert Mugabe and Joshua Nkomo represented a serious effort to overcome an ethnic cleavage, and it directly contributed to an end to the dissident violence in the southwest. Still, few observers of the continent would contend that the divisions in African societies, on balance, have been significantly narrowed in recent years, and many would argue that they have deepened. Somalia, for example, once regarded as Africa's one true nation-state, had fallen into "clan anarchy" by the end of the 1980s, according to its leading historian.[13]

13. I. M. Lewis, "The Ogaden and the Fragility of Somali Segmentary Nationalism," *African Affairs*, vol. 88 (October 1989), p. 579.

Poverty, like Africa's social rifts, is deeply entrenched. The growth of production in sub-Saharan Africa was less than 1 percent annually from 1980 through 1987, and per capita income fell, as did saving and investment.[14] There are trends in the regional and international systems that are aimed at alleviating Africa's poverty but no major change that would suggest a substantial improvement in the future. The Economic Community of West African States (ECOWAS) seemed a hopeful regional development when it was created in 1975, but in fact the organization has done little to promote economic growth or integration. The Preferential Trade Area for Eastern and Southern Africa (PTA) has recently grown to sixteen members with the admission of Mozambique, and it has undertaken some notable innovations, including the introduction of a regional traveler's check. But again many barriers to trade remain, and the region has not taken off economically—in part because of its wars and conflicts.

The wider international system is contributing substantial funds to relieving poverty in Africa, but not on a scale sufficient to spark a turnaround. Net capital flows from lending to sub-Saharan Africa have remained positive, in contrast to Latin America's situation, and some industrial countries, led by Japan, have been increasing their official development aid.[15] The United States and other donors are working toward some debt forgiveness for African borrowers. There is no "Marshall Plan" for Africa, however, and few observers anticipate that one will soon be created. Instead, there is deepening concern over the possibility that changes in the wider world will absorb aid and capital resources that might otherwise have gone to Africa. The need for economic assistance in Eastern Europe and Central America, together with the capital needs likely to be created by German unification, could mean that new capital flows for Africa will level off or even decline somewhat in the years ahead. There is a constituency in the United States and other Western countries for economic assistance to Africa, and strong support for humanitarian relief whenever and wherever required, so Western aid will not plummet. But with the United States facing a severe budget deficit and the Cold War incentive for aid to strategically located countries de-

14. World Bank, *World Development Report, 1989* (Oxford University Press, 1989), pp. 7, 12–13, 167.

15. World Bank, *World Development Report, 1989*, pp. 18, 23–24.

clining, a large increase in Western aid is unlikely, despite the recommendations of various commissions and study groups in recent years. Nor is it likely that the Soviet Union will replace its military assistance programs in Africa with economic assistance programs on a comparable multibillion-dollar scale.

Over the longer term, it may be that economic growth resulting from the current changes in international relations will generate new capital resources for Africa. Western European economic unity, a potential economic boom in a united Germany, and a much-anticipated "peace dividend" in both East and West all hold out the prospect of a new era of global prosperity that could benefit Africa. But economists would warn that Africa's comparative underdevelopment will prevent it from fully benefiting in any new era of prosperity—which is far from certain in any case.

The Western donors, instead of providing large new aid amounts, are concentrating on the promotion of economic policy reform in Africa. Under the leadership of the World Bank and the International Monetary Fund, donors are pushing for economic reforms intended to strengthen Africa's private sector, rationalize the public sector, and enhance the continent's financial systems. These are decidedly long-term efforts, and their effect is especially limited in countries afflicted by major conflict. The governments of Angola and Mozambique have been responsive, but real economic progress in these countries must await an end to the fighting. Ethiopia, the world's poorest country, and Sudan, which is hardly richer,[16] have made only limited responses to donor pressures for reform—although Ethiopia was promising substantial changes in 1990. In any event, a debate is raging over whether these programs may in fact increase social tensions and intensify conflict, at least in the short run.

The external pressures for economic rationalization have been paralleled by an advocacy of political moderation and compromise that appeared to be having some effect in the later 1980s. U.S. diplomats, many African leaders, and Soviet officials—at least in their public statements—made it clear that military solutions could not be achieved in Angola, Mozambique, Ethiopia, and Sudan, and that compromise and reconciliation were essential. The incentives for African govern-

16. Based on data from World Bank, *World Development Report, 1989*, p. 164.

ments to respond to this pressure arose from the demands of public image, and from economic as well as military realities. The Angolan government, for example, had to accede in some measure to African peace initiatives in 1989 if it was to avoid a reputation for intransigence that might jeopardize international aid flows and Soviet military assistance. In addition, as foreign observers pointed out, it was clear that Angola faced a stalemate, at least for the time being, in its war with UNITA, adding to the incentives for exploring a negotiated solution. Similar concerns and incentives brought the Ethiopian regime to talks with the Eritrean People's Liberation Front (EPLF), mediated by former U.S. President Jimmy Carter, and with the Tigre People's Liberation Front (TPLF) under Italian auspices. Mozambique also responded to the external advocates of reconciliation—and to pressure from churches within Mozambique—by agreeing to talk with Renamo in Nairobi, with Kenya's President Daniel Moi acting as mediator. Similarly, the Sudanese government respected a de facto cease-fire in its war with the SPLA for several months during 1989 while exploring various peace initiatives, including brief talks sponsored by Carter. Across the continent, the United Nations continued to push for a referendum in Western Sahara, evoking a favorable verbal response from the Moroccan government and leading to meetings between King Hassan and representatives of the Polisario resistance.

Some of Africa's resistance movements also seemed to be responding to international pressures and military realities by adopting more pragmatic stances. The EPLF, for example, was portraying itself as a moderate coalition seeking only a referendum, breaking with its past as a Marxist movement fighting for independence. EPLF leader Issayas Afewerki visited Washington in 1989 to put his views before American officials and opinion leaders. SPLA leader John Garang made a similar visit. Renamo meanwhile reported that it had held its first party conference, evidently in an effort to legitimize itself before negotiations as a genuine political movement.

The most impressive feature of Africa's wars as the decade turned, however, was the refusal of governments and resistance movements to make genuine compromises and bring the fighting to an end. In Angola and Sudan, imperfect cease-fires broke down and large-scale fighting broke out in the final months of 1989. International peace initiatives in Ethiopia were thwarted as the TPLF opened new offensives outside Tigre. In February 1990, the EPLF launched powerful new attacks against the remaining government-held territory in Eritrea, and the new fighting endangered international relief efforts for millions of potential famine victims in northern Ethiopia. There were new incidents of fighting along Western Sahara's border at the end of 1989 as a final settlement continued to be delayed, and ongoing violence in Mozambique seemed to push a negotiated settlement further into the future.

That none of Africa's major wars came to a conclusion reflects the depth of the divisions that had led to war and the strength of the antipathies that had arisen in the course of the fighting. Whether governments or resistance movements would be able to compromise on the core issues remained in question. Would the MPLA government in Angola ever agree to multiparty elections, as UNITA demanded; or would Jonas Savimbi accept anything less? For a time in 1989 it appeared that some solution satisfactory to both sides might be found, but the MPLA and Savimbi pulled back, perhaps under pressure from more radical elements within their movements, and the fighting intensified. Could the Ethiopian government ever agree to independence for Eritrea or to a referendum that would very likely lead to independence—or could the EPLF ever agree to anything less? The new fighting in 1990 made it clear that much more blood would be shed before the answers to these questions would be known. Nor were there answers to the central questions in Sudan, where it had become clear that the new regime would refuse the SPLA's demand for a secular state and regional autonomy. Could the Mozambican government ever grant Renamo, which it had despised as a gang of "bandits" for years, a role as an independent political party? That seemed unlikely, but in the absence of some such compromise it was doubtful that Renamo would lay down its arms.

Regional Factors

A number of African leaders, recognizing the negative consequences wars were having for entire subregions and for Africa as a whole, were showing new interest in promoting the resolution of Africa's wars as the 1980s drew to a close. A case in point was the pressure that African states, led by Zaire, were putting on the MPLA and UNITA for a reconciliation in Angola. Skeptics doubted that Zaire's

President Mobutu Sese Seko was sincere in his search for peace in Angola and argued that he had launched the initiative largely to improve his public image in the West. Nonetheless, Zaire would benefit immensely if the Benguela railway, the traditional export route for Zaire's minerals, was reopened, and this gave Mobutu a practical reason for seeking a settlement. (Zambia, which was also active in the peace effort, had a similar motive for promoting an accord.) Mobutu may also have concluded that UNITA was unlikely to succeed in the long run, after the December 1988 regional peace accord and South Africa's pledge to cut off aid to the movement. Thus he may have may have felt that the time had come to end the war and improve relations with the Angolan government.

Mobutu, however, clearly did not enjoy the full trust of the Angolan government, because of his record in backing UNITA. Zaire's importance as a conduit for assistance to UNITA, it could be argued, gave Mobutu both carrots and sticks that he should have been able to use to bring an end to the fighting. But even though he held some influence over the contending parties, he was unable to budge them from their long-held positions. Kenya's President Moi offered his good offices to help resolve the Mozambique conflict, but this mediation effort also failed to bear fruit—in part because of Mozambican doubts about Kenya's neutrality. A willingness on the part of some African leaders to mediate, in short, has proved difficult to convert into genuine conflict resolution.

A more striking development in the African region at the end of the 1980s was the pullback of Libya and South Africa, two important regional actors, from their entanglements in nearby states. Both were motivated in part by evidence that they had overreached themselves. The 1987 defeat of Qadhafi's army at the hands of the more lightly armed Chadian forces was a particular embarrassment. South Africa, meanwhile, had begun to suffer unacceptable casualties among white soldiers in southern Angola, where it had lost command of the air.

South Africa had other reasons for leaving Angola, including its own domestic problems, a strained defense budget, and the need to fend off international criticism that was adding to the pressure for tougher economic sanctions. These incentives helped persuade South Africa to compromise not only on Angola but also on the Namibia question and to cut back or even terminate its aid to Renamo in

Mozambique, although the final evidence is not yet in. These changes in South African policy contributed to a clear reduction in tensions throughout southern Africa.

Just how lasting the withdrawal of these two regional actors will prove to be is uncertain. Instability in Namibia, particularly actions against white Afrikaner settlers there, could propel a South African reentry, although the international condemnation would probably be severe. Higher levels of unrest within South Africa, moreover, could lead a white government there to blame neighboring states and resume its punishing interventions. Still, President F. W. de Klerk's decision to launch a domestic peace initiative in February 1990 was a hopeful sign. Though much could go wrong, the initiative could be the first step in a long bargaining process that will end apartheid in South Africa and remove the fundamental cause of international tension in the region. The moderation in Libya's policies may turn out to be a more transitory phenomenon intended only to give Qadhafi's regime a breathing spell. Indeed, in the latter part of 1989, there were new reports of Libyan involvement in Chad, Sudan, and Somalia.

It is unfortunate that the Organization of African Unity (OAU) has never acquired a capability for intervening decisively on behalf of peace in Africa's conflicts. The organization did help arrange a ceasefire in the Chad-Libya conflict in 1987, but an earlier peacekeeping effort in Chad was not successful. OAU officials have engaged in quiet diplomacy to ease and defuse other conflicts, but their charter's stricture against interfering in the internal affairs of member states has been a limiting factor. Many observers are hoping that the 1989 choice of Tanzania's Salim Salim, an experienced diplomat, as secretary-general, heralds a more dynamic era for the organization—but these hopes have yet to be realized.

International Factors

The reduction in tensions between the superpowers seems certain to reduce weapon flows to Africa and to create an environment more conducive to negotiated settlement. On the issue of weapon flows, progress is most likely on the larger weapons used in a few major wars rather than the small arms that have become endemic. Presumably, Gorbachev's interest in reducing Soviet expenditures overseas, and his related interest in encouraging regional conflict resolution, will lead to a reduction in military assistance in the form of tanks, artillery, and other heavy weapons for Angola, Ethiopia, and Mozambique. Emphasis must be given to the word *presumably*, since hard evidence of any such cuts is not yet in. Indeed, some have speculated that the Soviets intend to "dump" unneeded weapons in Africa and elsewhere to shore up their faltering economy. Over the long term, however, few of the African governments waging war against armed opposition forces could afford to pay hard currency for such arms, even at bargain prices.

For the United States, the incentive to provide arms to African governments on geostrategic grounds is much reduced. For this reason, humanitarian concerns—always a component of U.S. policy— have assumed greater importance. Pressure from human rights organizations and Congress helped to precipitate the cutoff in U.S. military assistance to Sudan and Somalia, but that pressure would probably have been less effective if the Cold War had still been at its height. U.S. aid for UNITA in Angola will probably also dwindle, either because of possible progress toward a reconciliation there or because of U.S. pressure on Savimbi to agree to such a reconciliation. The Cold War rationale for aiding UNITA in order to hobble the expanding Soviet empire on its fringes is weakened as that empire collapses at the center. Nonetheless, many see Savimbi as a "freedom fighter" and continue to favor increased aid to UNITA. It is not yet clear how the debate on this issue will turn out.

The easing of the Cold War may tend to make the more highly mechanized forms of war, as seen in Angola and Ethiopia, less common. Angola probably has, and Ethiopia may have, adequate heavy arms for carrying out large-scale operations for some time to come. A new Angolan government offensive against the UNITA capital at Jamba, perhaps combining air operations with an advance by armored vehicles, took place in late 1989 and into 1990. At the same time, the Ethiopian regime mounted a counterattack in the north. But we may be entering a period when the modern military capabilities of some governments will wither as tanks, planes, and guns break down for lack of maintenance and spare parts. Such governments will need to become more flexible in negotiations with their armed internal opposition—or face military defeat. The effect of a reduction in superpower arms transfers to Africa will be mitigated, however, to the degree that other countries step in to make up the deficit. Mengistu cast widely in search of new suppliers as his support from Eastern Europe dwindled at the end of the decade, and he succeeded in reestablishing formal diplomatic ties with Israel. Numerous reports of an intensified military relationship followed, and in January 1990 U.S. officials expressed their concern over the possible shipment of Israeli cluster bombs to Ethiopia. Israel denied that any such shipment had taken place. Meanwhile, observers were concerned that President Saddam Hussein of Iraq might use the surplus of weapons accumulated in his war with Iran to try to win influence in Africa.

In any event, the smaller weapons used in so much of Africa's conflict and violence will be there for years to come. The 1983 war in Sudan was begun with captured small arms and weapons stockpiled and hidden at the end of the previous war. Militia programs in Sudan, Mozambique, and Ethiopia have sent vast quantities of arms into the countryside, where their final use cannot be controlled or foreseen. These weapons, and whatever additional arms may come in from willing foreign suppliers, will make lasting peace a difficult objective in many countries even if heavy weapons become less common.

The willingness of external actors to press African states toward conflict resolution is itself an important feature of the current international environment. The United States had a heavy diplomatic investment in the Namibia negotiations, and a flurry of intense U.S.-led negotiations finally crystallized a settlement in southwestern Africa in December 1988. Heightened U.S. attention is now being given to the conflicts in Sudan, Ethiopia, and Mozambique, and there are hopes for some sort of U.S. mediating role in these disputes. As a superpower, the United States enjoys special influence in Africa, and governments as well as guerrillas must pay attention to U.S. concerns. In the Ethiopian case, former President Carter combined his prestige as onetime leader of a superpower with his unique moral influence in a highly unusual peace initiative during 1989. Although the initiative has not borne fruit, Carter surprised many observers with his ability to bring the EPLF and the Ethiopian regime together in two meetings where substantial progress was made on procedural arrangements for substantive talks.

The Soviet Union, after years of discouraging a Cuban withdrawal from Angola linked to a Namibia settlement, lent its support to the Angola-Namibia negotiations in their final stages. It was also encouraging political settlements in Ethiopia and Mozambique as well as an internal reconciliation in Angola. The pattern of Soviet influence in these conflicts, however, is something of a two-way street. Gorbachev may believe that Brezhnev overcommitted the Soviet Union in Africa, but those commitments cannot be coldly terminated without reducing Soviet prestige and influence, at least in Africa and perhaps in a wider environment. It was Soviet involvement in Angola, after all, that gave the Soviets a prominent role in the Angola-Namibia settlement, elevating the views of their Africa policymakers and academic Africanists to a new level of interest in the Western media, think tanks, and universities. The importance of the Soviet Union's Africa role, at a time when its influence in the Middle East is modest and its reputation as a global power generally somewhat tarnished, may give Mengistu, dos Santos, and Chissano some freedom to soldier on for a time with significant Soviet support.

For the Soviet Union's African allies, however, the handwriting is on the wall. In the future, the Soviets will try to maintain their influence in Africa, but they will do so, at least in part, by promoting diplomatic solutions to regional conflicts.[17] Consequently, Soviet allies must enter into reconciliations with their internal enemies or find alternative sources of supply and alternative, less highly mechanized means of carrying on the struggle.

To those who hope for a more peaceful future in Africa, superpower support for negotiated solutions is a positive development. Some wish, however, that Soviet and American leaders would intensify their efforts in this cause. Quiet diplomacy, statements in support of peace, and other efforts are all well and good from this point of view, but many feel that a joint Soviet-American initiative at the highest levels would put far more pressure on the participants in Africa's wars to lay down their arms. With so many changes elsewhere in the world, it is perhaps too much to expect that the top officials of either superpower will assign a high priority to resolving Africa's conflicts. The risk of failure in such an effort would be great. Nonetheless, the mounting toll exacted by Africa's wars ensures continuing support for increased superpower attention to the problem of regional conflict resolution.

An effective international peacekeeping system could help to un-

17. S. Neil MacFarlane, "The Soviet Union and Southern African Security," *Problems of Communism*, March–June 1989, p. 87.

derwrite conflict resolution initiatives in Africa. Peacekeeping forces help to turn cease-fires and peace accords into lasting settlements, since they assure the conflict participants that their interests will be protected during the transition to a new regime. This is the underlying rationale of the United Nations Transition Assistance Group (UNTAG) that has been deployed in Namibia.

The prospects for peacekeeping seemed rather good just a short time ago. The Soviet turnaround on the United Nations under Gorbachev was one of the most surprising recent changes in Soviet foreign policy and appeared to raise the prospect of a new era of international peacekeeping. The creation of UNTAG bore out the hopes raised by the Soviet leader. Today, however, prospects are dimmer. A force may yet be deployed in Western Sahara, but it appears that Morocco's King Hassan has had second thoughts about permitting an international presence that would reduce his control over the course of events in the territory. Governments in Sudan and Ethiopia might feel the same reservations if peacekeeping operations became a prospect in those conflicts. Moreover, peacekeeping forces are expensive, and the developed nations, which would bear most of the financial burden, will not lightly encourage their creation. Many had reservations about the costs of UNTAG and forced a reduction in the projected size of the operation. Even Soviet interest in peacekeeping seems to be cooling. Gorbachev's December 1988 speech to the General Assembly, while reiterating his praise for the United Nations, did not renew his earlier proposals for a comprehensive new international security system within the U.N. framework.[18]

CONCLUSION

Changes in the regional and international systems suggest that the outlook for African conflict during the 1990s is only somewhat more favorable than in the 1980s. There are some tendencies in the regional and international systems working to reduce arms transfers to the combatants in Africa's wars, to reduce external intervention, and to

18. Congressional Research Service, *The Gorbachev Speech to the United Nations, New York, December 7, 1988*, CRS Report 88–776 F (Washington, December 1988), p. 10.

promote negotiated solutions. It is possible that these tendencies will help to persuade the participants in some of Africa's ongoing major conflicts to come to terms. They certainly contributed to the Angola-Namibia agreement in 1988.

Yet underlying internal causes of conflict are not deeply affected by the changes now under way. Consequently, many wars may be expected to continue even if heavy weapons flows are reduced and the more mechanized forms of violence become less frequent. The reintensification of the fighting in Angola and Ethiopia in 1989 and 1990—after hopes for negotiated settlements had been raised—demonstrates the power of these underlying causes of conflict. Elsewhere in Africa, there are other countries that suffer from the deep social cleavages and poverty that cause war, and it is possible that they too will be afflicted by serious violence in the years ahead. Africa's rapid population growth and the depletion of its land and resources may make such violence inevitable.

The changes now being seen in the regional and international systems are hopeful, but they do not yet offer lasting solutions to Africa's conflicts. By the end of the 1990s, the changes in Soviet policy, the stabilization of southwestern Africa, the restraint being shown by Libya and South Africa, and the other promising developments of today may be seen as transitory phenomena or not highly relevant to the more permanent reality of African conflict and violence. Africa and the world will have to undergo much more fundamental change if this future is to be avoided.

Chapter 2

WINRICH KÜHNE

Africa and Gorbachev's "New Realism"

History vigorously poses the question if the socialist idea can survive.
Mikhail Gorbachev[1]

With surprise, the world followed the dramatic developments in Central and Eastern Europe in 1989, as popular pressure led centralistic, Marxist-Leninist, one-party systems to dissolve with great speed. In Hungary and Poland, and later in Czechoslovakia and the German Democratic Republic (GDR), these parties renounced their claim to exclusive popular representation in favor of multiparty systems. The conversion to a market economy was initiated as well. Orthodox Marxism-Leninism, which had dominated the sociopolitical landscape of Central and Eastern Europe since the Second World War, lost any legitimacy for the majority of these peoples. The Iron Curtain slowly disappeared and the East German regime started to tear down the wall in Berlin, once the incarnation of the Cold War in Europe. On January 7, 1990, a decision of immense significance was made in Moscow. The Central Committee of the Communist Party of the Soviet Union renounced its claim to the party's monopoly of power. The Cold War in Europe, or, in technical terms, the "intersystematic, antagonistic confrontation" of East and West, has come to an end.

The East-West rivalry of past decades dissolved in Africa as well. Namibia's independence is the first outcome of this change. For more than a decade, the implementation of Resolution 435 of the U.N. Security Council of December 1978 had been stalled in large part by the global confrontation between Washington and Moscow. On December 22, 1988, however, the treaties for the implementation of the above resolution and for the withdrawal of Cuban forces from Angola

---

1. "Die sozialistische Idee und die revolutionäre Umgestaltung," *Der Spiegel*, January 1990, p. 2.

were signed in New York; U.S. Secretary of State George Schultz and Soviet Deputy Foreign Minister Anatoli Adamishin congratulated each other for the constructive cooperation of the two "superpowers" on the solution of the Namibia conflict.

Those who have been interested in African affairs for some time will recall how different this issue had been treated in the 1970s. In 1976, when the so-called Namibia Contact Group—composed of representatives from the United States, Great Britain, France, Canada, and the Federal Republic of Germany—began to work on a solution to the Namibia problem, Eastern journalists and politicians sharply attacked this "imperialistic plot." When the Contact Group's plan for Namibia's independence was finally adopted by the Security Council in September 1978, the USSR chose not to veto the plan, because it did not want to oppose the "front line states" and other friends in Africa. Instead, Moscow abstained. Western polemics in that period were also confrontational and sharp. The Soviet Union and its allies were accused of supporting international terrorism through the South-West Africa People's Organization (SWAPO) and of pursuing an expansive, hegemonistic policy in southern Africa. "Moscow's fist in Africa" was a standing term for a broad political spectrum in the West.

The rapprochement of Washington and Moscow and the end of the Cold War are essentially the outcome of the "New Realism" in Soviet policy under Gorbachev. It has far-reaching effects on the Third World. (It should be noted that the change in Soviet policy was discernible earlier in the Third World than in Europe. Some Soviet authors used the difficult situation in Africa and other developing countries with socialist orientation to indicate their growing disillusionment with Marxism-Leninism. As a consequence of *glasnost*, they now feel safe enough to express their misgivings directly.) Soviet politicians, diplomats, and journalists emphasize their resolve to stop pursuing global revolutionary goals under socialist banners and the expansion of Soviet military presence. Consequently, the role of Third World conflicts in the international system has dramatically changed. In the past they were a lever to shift the international balance of power ideologically and militarily from one side to the other. Now they have become a burden to the superpowers and their allies, if not a disturbing factor in East-West relations and the problems therein.

Africa must therefore expect a dramatic change in the international environment of its politics, which raises many questions. What is the background to the "New Realism" in Soviet politics? Can it be attributed only to the "subjective" factor Gorbachev, or is it the outcome of long-term, objective tendencies, which will determine Soviet politics even in the case of Gorbachev's downfall? What are the lessons of the collapse of Marxism-Leninism in Central and Eastern Europe for Africa? Will the end of East-West rivalry work for peace on the continent, or will it instead result, as some observers fear, in an increase of local conflicts? Many Africans also worry about the possibility that their continent will be pushed into the background of international attention to humanitarian and economic assistance because of the events in Central and Eastern Europe.

FROM KHRUSHCHEV'S ''ERA OF OPTIMISM'' TO GORBACHEV'S ''NEW REALISM''

The rapprochement of Moscow and Washington regarding the solution of the Namibia question is only one aspect of the change in Soviet policy toward Africa. In 1989, Soviet and Mozambican officials announced the departure of about eight hundred Soviet military advisers from Mozambique by 1990–91. In addition, meetings between Soviet and white South African experts, journalists, and diplomats are no longer unusual.[2] In October 1989, a first conference in the Federal Republic of Germany (Leverkusen) was attended by a group of more than twenty predominantly Afrikaans-speaking white South Africans, by a delegation from Moscow, and by some leading members of the African National Congress (ANC) and the South African Communist party (SACP). The Soviet government has increasingly stressed its preference for negotiated solutions instead of a continuation or even intensification of armed conflicts. Emphasis is now on "dialogue." There are today no significant differences among the

2. On the changes in South African politics, see Winrich Kühne, "A 1988 Update on Soviet Relations with Pretoria, the ANC, and the SACP," *CSIS Africa Notes*, vol. 89 (September 1, 1988), pp. 1–8. An extensive description of Soviet policy on South Africa can be found in Kurt M. Campbell, *Soviet Policy Towards South Africa* (St. Martin's Press, 1986).

United States, Western Europe, and Moscow on the solution of the South African conflict.

Ethiopia, the most important Soviet ally in Africa since the 1970s, is obviously under great pressure from Moscow to end the war in Eritrea, Tigre, and other parts of the country, as well as the mistaken "barrack-communism" of Mengistu Haile Mariam. Arms supplies to the Ethiopian army have slowed down, and Gorbachev is supposed to have threatened to stop deliveries completely when the current treaty runs out in 1990–91. Czechoslovakia suspended its deliveries of military materials and is about to stop all other deliveries. The GDR handed all its diplomatic installations over to the Federal Republic of Germany before unification. Cuba withdrew its remaining troops from the Ogaden War in Ethiopia in the course of a few weeks in 1989. With the successful outcome of Namibia's independence, Cuba is concluding its "internationalist" phase. The retreat of Soviet troops from Ethiopia, as from Angola, turns out to be more difficult. Moscow has to realize that it is easier for a global power to enter a conflict than to leave it without losing face.[3]

The "New Realism" is the result of painful lessons learned not only from multiple setbacks in Africa but also from the economic failure of the socialist system in the Soviet Union itself. Soviet policy in Africa has taken a turn of almost 180 degrees during the last three decades.

In the era of Nikita Khrushchev, the Soviet Union vehemently and optimistically became involved in African politics. The wave of decolonialization, which started to roll in the mid-1950s, seemed strongly to favor the strictly anti-imperialistic goals of Soviet foreign policy. Khrushchev assumed that one country after the other would move away from the capitalist economic global order of the Western states and could gradually be integrated into an alternative socialist model of division of labor. "We will bury the West in the Third World," he once said to a journalist. Of course, this statement added to the anticommunist hysteria in the West. Khrushchev's optimism was based on two assumptions: the revolutionary, anti-imperialistic tendencies

3. The engagement in Ethiopia has been very expensive for Moscow. The value of arms supplies is estimated to amount to more than $7 billion. Moscow cannot seriously hope for repayment. Ethiopia is one of the poorest countries in the world. These debts have apparently been written off in Soviet books to the extent of 1.5 billion rubles.

in the former colonies, and the anticipated economic superiority of the socialist countries. He promised that by 1980 the USSR would catch up with the United States in economic terms.[4] With the exception of Egypt, military means had a subordinated role in Khrushchev's policy toward Africa.

Disenchantment soon followed. In 1964, Khrushchev was overthrown, and in 1966, Kwame Nkrumah, the first president of Ghana and Khrushchev's closest ally in Africa, was toppled by pro-Western officers. In Mali, and later in Guinea, the Soviets encountered further difficulties.

SKEPTICISM AND THE POLICY OF SOCIALIST ORIENTATION OF THE BREZHNEV ERA

Khrushchev's successors were more skeptical about the prospects for socialist development in Africa. Rostislav Uljanovskij, the leading expert on developing countries and deputy director of the influential International Department of the Central Committee of the CPSU, persistently warned of overoptimistic assessments. Although urban petit bourgeois elites with strongly revolutionary tendencies existed in Africa, the objective conditions for socialist development—that is, a strong working class—did not exist.[5] Uljanovskij, Gleb Starushenko,

4. Khrushchev was not the first to make these promises. In 1929, Stalin claimed that the Soviet Union would be the leading producer of grain and that Soviet farmers would soon be the richest in the world. Yuri Rogachev, "What's New in Soviet Agriculture?" *Asia and Africa Today*, no. 5 (1989), pp. 11–12.

5. Two leading Soviet authors and advisers to the government in international relations, W. W. Sagladin, director of the International Department of the Central Committee of the CPSU, and E. M. Primakov, director of the Institute for Eastern Studies of the Soviet Academy of Sciences, wrote: "If the victorious revolutionary proletariat [of the socialist camp] engages in a planned propaganda and if the Soviet government assists with all possible means, it is wrong to assume that a capitalist level of development is impossible to reach for backward countries." See W. W. Sagladin, *Sowjetwissenschaft, Gesellschaftswissenschaftliche Beiträge*, vol. 29, no. 4 (1976), p. 384; and E. M. Primakow, "Länder mit sozialistischer Orientierung: ein schwieriger aber realer Übergang zum Sozialismus," *Afrika, Asien, Lateinamerika*, vol. 9, no. 6 (1981), p. 974.

enko, and others became the founders of the concept of "noncapitalist development with socialist orientation," which stemmed from Leninist theory. Their model tied skepticism to hope. The term *orientation* suggested that revolutionary developments were in no way irreversible in Africa and other parts of the Third World, in contrast to those in the Soviet Union and Eastern Europe as well as Mongolia, Vietnam, and Cuba. These latter states, though developing countries, were qualified as having reached the stage of "socialist development."

Thus Soviet foreign policy would have to reckon with setbacks. Moscow could not guarantee the duration of these socialist-oriented regimes, neither in economic nor in military terms. This had great consequences for "realpolitik." In comparison with merely socialist-oriented countries, Cuba, Vietnam, and Mongolia, which are members of the Council for Mutual Economic Assistance (COMECON) and enjoy key positions in the conflict with China and the United States, received more than 70 percent of Soviet developmental aid, not including price and trade subsidies.

At the same time, Soviet writers continued to believe, or pretended to believe, that the balance of power between socialism and capitalism in the Third World continuously shifted in favor of socialism. The victory of world revolution under Soviet banners was still seen as inevitable. The growing might of the socialist camp would guarantee this by assisting socialist-oriented countries to balance the lack of objective conditions.

But Uljanovskij and others were too realistic to identify this assistance with economic aid, as was true in Khrushchev's era. In the late 1960s, such friendly and progressive regimes as Algeria, Egypt, Tanzania, and Guinea had already been told that comprehensive financial and technical assistance from the Eastern bloc was not feasible. Assistance now meant arms supplies and military aid, in the first place, and backing by the global Soviet military power as demonstrated in Angola in 1975–76 and Ethiopia in 1977 78. In the 1970s, the Soviet Union became the greatest arms supplier in Africa.

The concept of the "noncapitalist development" option was not unopposed by Soviet experts of developing countries. Nevertheless, it clearly dominated Soviet foreign policy in Africa during the Brezhnev era. The developments in Angola, Mozambique, and Ethiopia in the mid-1970s seemed to confirm its validity. Most Soviet writers reacted with euphoria when Marxist-Leninist avant-garde parties of the Eastern kind were established in Angola, Mozambique, and, in 1984, Ethiopia. Others cautioned that the establishment of these parties should not be overestimated. They were right. Because of the developments in these countries, Soviet foreign policy in Africa was forced to adopt a new thinking in the beginning of the 1980s.

THE BACKGROUND OF THE "NEW REALISM"

The attentive observer noticed that signs of a fundamentally new thinking increased in Soviet literature during the late 1970s.[6] Soviet economists began to modify the old anti-imperialist dogma that the existing economic order had to be destroyed in order to establish an alternative socialist model of the international division of labor. The global economy was now considered to be an "organic whole," a "dialectic unit of opposites, in which several international economies of different social systems come together."[7] A Hungarian economist, Lázlo Láng, was even more outspoken: "In the seventies, countries were increasingly aware of the significance of international [nonsocialist] labor division and its eventual merits."[8] The demolition of the global economic order might hit the economically weaker Eastern states and developing countries even harder than the flexible Western industrial states. This sober acceptance of the economic realities became the foundation for the "New Realism."

In the early 1980s, the trend to question the policy of the Brezhnev era continued. Mozambique and later Ethiopia were denied full membership in COMECON. Moscow and Maputo were unable to agree on an extension of Soviet military assistance to counter the military destabilization by South Africa and Renamo. Opportunities to expand

6. See Elisabeth Kridl-Valkenier, *The Soviet Union and the Third World*: *An Economic Bind* (Praeger, 1983); Jerry E. Hough, *The Struggle for the Third World*: *Soviet Debates and American Options* (Brookings, 1986); and Winrich Kühne, *Sowjetische Afrikapolitik in der "Ära Gorbatschow"* (Ebenhausen: Stiftung Wissenschaft und Politik, May 1986).

7. On the details of the debate on the global economic order, see Kridl-Valkenier, *Soviet Union and the Third World*, p. 37.

8. Lázlo Láng, "East-South Economic Interplay in the Eighties: Challenges and Chances" (manuscript).

Eastern influence in countries such as Libya and Burkina Faso or to support revolutionary tendencies in Kenya were not taken up in the Kremlin.[9] Soviet experts on developing countries, such as A. P. Butenko and A. Kiva, increasingly voiced doubts about the feasibility of "noncapitalist development with socialist orientation."[10] Especially in the agrarian sector, which is most important for African countries (as well as for the Soviet Union), the results were also disappointing. A 1985 paper by Soviet counselors in Ethiopia drew much attention from the West. It suggested a greater concentration on elements of private initiative to the regime in Addis Ababa.[11]

Nevertheless, the Soviet political leadership and most Soviet academicians were not yet ready to call things by their name.[12] This phase began only with Gorbachev's *perestroika* and *glasnost*. Liberated of all dogmatic ties, several authors initiated an impressive discussion of past mistakes. Georgy Mirsky admits that "a sober assessment of the present-day situation shows that today there is less evidence than a quarter of a century ago that the newly-independent states are abandoning the capitalist road of development and shifting to the non-capitalist course."[13] W. Shejnis goes one step further and concludes that the "profound contradictions which occur in a capitalist development are not merely a hindrance, but also a source of development."[14] In 1984, Kiva had stated: "One of the problems . . . is the

9. See David E. Albright, *Soviet Policy Toward Africa Revisited* (Center for Strategic and International Studies, 1987).

10. A. P. Butenko, "Der Übergang zum Sozialismus in Ländern mit unterentwickelter Wirtschaft," *Sowjetwissenschaft, Gesellschaftswissenschaftliche Beiträge*, vol. 38, no. 2 (1985), pp. 395–407; and A. Kiva, "Socialist-oriented Countries: Some Development Problems," *International Affairs* (Moscow), vol. 10 (1984), pp. 22–29.

11. Report prepared by the team of Soviet consulting advisers attached to the National Central Commission for Planning of Socialist Ethiopia, "Considerations on the Economic Policy of Ethiopia for the Next Few Years" (Addis Ababa, September 1985).

12. An exception is the above-mentioned Butenko.

13. Georgy Mirsky, "Newly-Independent States: Ways of Development," *Asia and Africa Today*, vol. 5 (September–October 1987), p. 53.

14. W. Shejnis, "Besonderheiten und Probleme des Kapitalismus in den Entwicklungsländern," *Sowjetwissenschaft, Gesellschaftswissenschaftliche Beiträge*, vol. 40 (July–August 1987), p. 398.

difficulty to develop a functioning socio-economic model for the developing countries with socialist orientation."[15] Five years later, he is more explicit: "As regards the administrative command-bureaucratic model, I suppose we have every reason to take a most negative view on it. Fettered from the outside by elements of social retrogression, it is historically doomed to reach an impasse."[16] He castigates himself and his colleagues: "But why did we fail to see in time what was obvious?" One can only agree with the answer Kiva himself gives: "For decades, our social science was hopelessly shackled by dogmatism and subjectivism."[17]

With similar self-criticism, Grigori Polyakov writes: "In trying to apportion blame we make much of 'imperialist intrigues.' . . . As far as economics are concerned the blame is primarily ours."[18] Boris Asoyan discards the hope for the possibility of a "non-capitalist development with a socialist orientation," which for decades was so prominent in Soviet and Third World thinking about economic development: "We have realized that a voluntaristic shortcut from one social formation to another or a leap over development phases is utopian."[19] Nikolai Volkov and Vladimir Popov go even further. They oppose the argument that "neocolonialism" and "neoimperialism" still exist. In their opinion, "non-equivalent exchange" as a systematic element in the relations between Western industrial states and the developing countries is not evident: "By the 1980s there were practically no traces of colonialism left in the world capitalist economic relations. Consequently, there also vanished the real foundation to which one could add the prefix 'neo.' "[20]

The dynamization of change in Soviet policy toward Africa under Gorbachev, however, was not primarily triggered by events in Africa. Rather, the desolate state of the Soviet economy forced the USSR to

15. Kiva, "Socialist-oriented Countries," p. 27.

16. A. Kiva, "Developing Countries, Socialism, Capitalism," *International Affairs* (Moscow), vol. 3 (1989), p. 59.

17. Kiva, "Developing Countries, Socialism, Capitalism," p. 57.

18. Grigori Polyakov, "Economic Cooperation from the Viewpoint of Perestroika," *Asia and Africa Today*, no. 5 (1988), p. 10.

19. Boris Asoyan, "From Illusion to Realism," *Asia and Africa Today*, no. 5 (1989), p. 34.

20. Nikolai Volkov and Vladimir Popov, "Has an Era of Neocolonialism Materialized?" *International Affairs*, vol. 11 (1988), p. 109.

tackle its own problems and give priority to its domestic politics over foreign politics. In addition, it was even more important than before for the Soviet Union to improve relations with the United States, Western Europe, and Japan so as to make progress in arms control and economic cooperation. Africa's decline on the Soviet scale of priorities was an inevitable consequence. In 1987, a Soviet academician stated at a conference at Harare that Africa, especially black Africa, had minimal significance for the Soviet Union.[21]

Within a short period, the change in political priorities led to a dramatic reevaluation of the significance of regional conflicts in the relations between Washington and Moscow. Whereas wars of national liberation and armed conflicts had usually been seen as either an opportunity (by the East) or a danger (by the West) in the ideological and military balance of power between East and West, they now became a disturbing factor in the relations between Moscow and Washington. Greater realism in the capitals of both superpowers on the role of military power in the solution of regional conflicts, which stemmed from the experiences in Vietnam, Afghanistan, Ethiopia, and Angola, reinforced the trend for a new approach to conflict resolution.[22]

During the summit meeting with President Ronald Reagan in Reykjavik in 1985, Gorbachev indicated great interest in cooperating with Washington for the solution of these conflicts, starting with Afghanistan. The Reagan administration responded positively. At this time, Reagan had already decided to enter history as the peace president, and not as the Cold Warrior. The superpowers had to realize that they could stall solutions with their giant military apparatus, but not extort solutions in the same way. Local factors proved to be too persistent.

These remarks may suffice to demonstrate the dramatic changes in Soviet research and policy on developing countries. The anti-imperialist struggle and class struggle of past times, outlined by V. I. Lenin in "Imperialism as the Highest State of Capitalism" and materialized in Africa by Khrushchev, have come to an end. At the meeting of COMECON on January 9–10, 1990, it was officially buried, when the

---

21. See the interview with Viktor Goncharov (deputy director of the Moscow Institute for Africa), *Work in Progress*, vol. 48 (July 1987), p. 3.

22. See *Front File, Southern Africa Brief*, vol. 2 (August 1988), p. 1.

reintegration of COMECON into the world economy was decided. Adamishin, who until recently was the Soviet deputy foreign minister responsible for Africa, put the consequences for Soviet policy to the point: "I do not see convincing evidence for the fact that the confrontation between socialism and capitalism is still the decisive factor for the developments in our world."[23]

LESSONS TO BE DRAWN:
THE VICTORY OF CAPITALISM?

In the West the collapse of the regimes in Central and Eastern Europe and the crisis in the Soviet Union are generally celebrated as the "victory of capitalism." Many claim that socialism is finished. Are things really that simple?

First, if one considers the political and economic reality in Western Europe and other parts of the world, there is more than one kind of socialism, as there is more than one kind of capitalism. Other types of socialism, such as democratic socialism and its multiple variations in Western Europe, are successful and still viable, whatever their significance may be in detail. (The argument that these models are not really a type of socialism is binding only for orthodox Marxists; by the same token, dogmatic capitalists know only their own form of capitalism. Both lines of argumentation have their foundation in the fallacy of abstract and rigidly ideological thinking.) The idea of socialism in Europe dates from before Marx and continues after Marx, as the socialist debate did not concern only orthodox Marxists and Marxist-Leninists.

There is no doubt, however, that Marxism-Leninism, or the "real existierender Sozialismus" (socialism as it really exists), failed to produce a model that is superior to capitalism in economic productivity

23. Anatoli Adamishin, "Zum Zerwürfnis verurteilt?" *Neue Zeit*, vol. 12 (1989), pp. 14–16 A view that is even more in accordance with the conventional thinking of the past was taken by A. Gromyko, the director of the African Institute in Moscow: "New political thinking does not imply renunciation of the class approach, but it develops this approach in a new historical situation." Anatoli Gromyko, "Adopt New Political Thinking in the Practice of International Relations," *Asia and Africa Today*, no. 4 (1989), p. 52.

and as an efficient, human organization of labor. The shocking economic and ecological state of Eastern bloc countries is ample proof. (The so-called Afro-Socialist regimes, such as the Ujamaa model in Tanzania, are to be included in this category, difficult external conditions notwithstanding. These systems were also shaped by the centralistic, bureaucratic command model, although that may not have been the original intention.) This failure touches on the foundation of Marxism-Leninism, since the doctrine of historical materialism scientifically legitimizes Marxism-Leninism precisely because of this superiority. It is also the basis for the Communist party's claim of exclusive popular representation and "proletarian dictatorship." The argument that the Eastern bloc countries did not practice the "right" socialism is unconvincing considering the great number of countries that have experimented with socialism.

Nevertheless, if we focus our attention on Africa, there is little reason for bragging on the capitalist side either. The developments under capitalist banners in Kenya, Zaire, Ivory Coast, and other countries are not impressive at all. The contrast with Benin, and with the Congo, for instance, are marginal if per capita figures are not taken as the sole indicator. And the difference between the capitalist states in Africa and Mozambique, Angola, and Ethiopia would certainly not be so conspicuous if these countries had not been in a state of war for decades. The economic disaster in these countries is due to several factors: war, a misguided economic policy, and natural disasters.[24]

Thus the analysis must go deeper. The debate on capitalism and socialism already fills many books. Yet it is less relevant to everyday African politics than one might assume. The overwhelming dominance of the state—more precisely the relatively centralistic, authoritarian, bureaucratic state and party structures, which are a common feature of most African states—is more important than this ideological controversy. The authoritarian bureaucratic and mental structures, which have their origin in colonialism, on the one hand, and the

24. The Soviet economist Gleb V. Smirnov, employee of the Moscow Institute for Africa, has correctly pointed out that the bad economic results in Africa are not confined to countries with socialist orientation, but are a general phenomenon. Gleb V. Smirnov, "Economic Development of Socialist Oriented African Countries," *Front File, IAIS Conference Special*, vol. 3 (December 1989), p. 6.

authoritarian style of government of the new urban elites and leaders, partly based on traditional African understanding, on the other hand, have formed a repressive symbiosis.

An economic factor that encouraged such formations was perhaps even more important: the almost complete lack of indigenous African capital. Inevitably, the state became the main, if not the only, access route by which Africans could accumulate capital, as it did in many other Third World countries. This coincided with the worldwide mainstream thinking in development theory in the 1960s that the state would have to act as the main "agent of development" to compensate for the lack of internal private capital.

This symbiosis took a more or less fortunate, more or less repressive, more or less corrupt, and more or less socialist or capitalist direction in various states. The "state class" evolved and became a widely discussed phenomenon in the development literature of the 1970s and 1980s. The results, however, were almost always the same: mismanagement, patronage, corruption, and finally the paralysis of private initiative and human creativity in the economic area, especially in the rural sector. (Recall the "marketing boards" of colonial times and their fatal consequences for African farmers.) Indeed, the profound socioeconomic distortions that resulted from colonialism and unfavorable global economic conditions played a major role in the failure in economic development. But "colonial or postcolonial dependence" is not an explanation sufficient in itself, as Hartmut Elsenhans, for instance, showed in his thorough study on "Dependent Capitalism or Bureaucratic Development Society."[25]

It is too easy to attribute the failure of economic development, abuses of power, and corruption to the personal faults of elites or individual leaders. The incredible difficulties some of the new governments had to face at the point of independence must be taken into consideration; these include economic and bureaucratic distortion through colonialism, arbitrary borders, and limited or nonexistent education of officials, technicians, doctors, and professors. In some countries, such as the Portuguese-speaking nations, illiteracy was as

25. Hartmut Elsenhans, *Abhängiger Kapitalimus oder bürokratische Entwicklungsgesellschaft, Versuch über den Staat in der Dritten Welt* (Frankfurt and New York: Campus, 1981).

high as 90 percent at the time of independence. Reasonable politicians would have refused to assume office under these circumstances.

THE INDISPENSABLE MARKET

A thorough examination of the reasons for the economic failure of the centralistic, bureaucratic plan-and-command economy all over the world leads to the conclusion that this failure is mainly due to the dogmatic negation of private initiative and the market and the disregard of their vital functions for economic growth and development. In other words, most orthodox Marxists and similar schools of thought made the mistake of perceiving market and private initiative only under the aspect of exploitation, and thus concentrated their capitalist tendencies. Of course, such tendencies (for example, the danger of an extreme division of the world into poor and rich, workers and capital owners) do exist, but this is only one aspect of the market. At the same time, market and private initiative have other vital functions for economic growth, among them information (through prices) on low-cost allocation of resources, creativity, flexibility, and the ability to innovate. These functions were strangled by the centralistic, bureaucratic plan-and-command economies and their ideologies. In fact, the attempt to enact an all-encompassing system of planning often led to less rationality, freedom, and humanity, in addition to the economic failure. Or, to put it differently, Marxist socialism does not have a workable, refined theory and program for the construction of a socialist political and economic order, and it has not been able to develop one since the October revolution. This is not surprising, because Marxist writing is mostly about capitalism and its contradictions. Marx's few remarks on what a socialist society would look like are neither enlightening nor definite. The same is true for Engels. Indeed, a Marxist from the GDR labeled the systems in the Soviet Union and Eastern Europe as "feudal absolutistic socialism."[26]

In Africa, the negation of the market and of private initiative had particularly adverse effects on the rural sector, where the majority of

26. Martin Robbe, "Jahrhundertwende in Sicht: Versuch einer Standortbestimmung" (manuscript).

Africans live and work. Rural communities and peasants lost interest in producing for the private market or were not even allowed to do so. Consequently, they remained in or withdrew to the subsistence economy. The production of food in Africa has shown a minimal increase of only 1.5 percent since the 1960s. Relative to the population growth of 3.0 percent, this is a de facto decrease. Poverty and famines are now endemic in several parts of Africa. Moreover, it was a large mistake to nationalize trade, as was done especially in countries with socialist orientation. The interchange between city and countryside, which in colonial times had been maintained by small tradesmen in spite of great difficulties, broke down. Farmers could not get rid of their products, or they did not see any sense in selling them in national buyouts at a fixed price. In the cities, markets and shops grew empty.

For a long time the urban elites had an easy explanation for this development: because of the social and economic backwardness of African small farmers and peasants, nobody could expect them to achieve a quick and extensive growth of production and to supply the cities sufficiently. Because of their attachment to traditional cultural values, the elites claimed, African farmers were unable to modernize. Therefore the state had to promote development, either through nationalized farms, collectivization, and nationally operated collectives—in countries with socialist orientation—or through "agribusiness" jointly managed by state and multinational companies in countries with so-called capitalist orientation. Neither model helped African economies. Nationalized farms turned into unproductive capital mongers, and agribusiness did not in the least care for the needs of the indigenous population.[27] Yet urban elites in Africa were not the only ones to articulate prejudices about African peasants. Soviet experts on developing countries, as well as many orthodox Marxists and

27. As Michael Lofchie and others have emphasized, state farms ironically increased the dependency on foreign capital that it was supposed to decrease. More financial and material assistance from Western donors became necessary. In Mozambique, for instance, 80 percent of all foreign currency is used for investments in Mozambican farms. In Ethiopia, Mengistu put 90 percent of the investments into state farms that only produced 6 percent of the country's grain revenues. Michael Lofchie and Stephen Commins, "Food Deficits and Agricultural Policies in Tropical Africa," *Journal of Modern African Studies*, vol. 20 (March 1982), pp. 7–25.

Western agro-technocrats, were equally convinced of the peasants' inability to modernize.[28] Soviet literature on developing countries, even up to today, freely speaks of the "underdevelopment" of the African rural sector, including its cultural aspects.[29] This negative attitude toward the peasants is not surprising considering Stalin's liquidation of millions of Soviet farmers in the 1930s and Marxism's primary orientation toward urban, industrial societies.

This static perception of the African peasants' ability to modernize has, meanwhile, proved to be a crude prejudice. Agricultural production rose by several percentage points in countries that did not force peasants into the tutelage of bureaucratic structures and rigid pricing systems, or that have stopped doing so. Zimbabwe, Tanzania, Mali, Ghana, and other countries are telling examples since they have enacted reforms. Thus traditional values do not keep African peasants from increasing their production and from modernization if prices are adequate and the political framework supportive.[30] In Ethiopia, the land reform benefiting the peasants that was enacted immediately after the downfall of Haile Selassie resulted in lasting growth of production until Mengistu stopped this trend with his policies of forced collectivization and nationalization. After a decade of failure, Mengistu is now capitulating. In March 1990 he announced reforms in favor of private peasant farming.

Another sector highlights the creative enterpreneurial potential of

28. There were some independent Marxists who opposed this opinion. Already in the 1960s, Amin proposed the thesis that progressive regimes with socialist orientation had to "break up" the traditional agrarian sector with capitalist development. S. Amin, "The Class Struggle in Africa," *Revolution*, vol. 1, no. 9 (1964), p. 43.

29. I. Andreyev, *The Non-Capitalist Way: Socialism and the Developing Countries* (Moscow: Progress Publishers, 1977).

30. One should be careful not to consider the growth in production through the "structural adjustment" policy of the World Bank and the International Monetary Fund as the final solution. In the first place, it is unclear whether the effects of this policy will be long-lasting; in the second place, it is questionable whether they are large enough for a growth in capital accumulation sufficient to allow investments in the area of small industry and a gradual development. In other words, "structural adjustment" might serve to break up old static structures, but it can guarantee long-term economic growth only to a limited extent.

the African population: the significance of shadow economies and black markets in several countries, especially in countries with socialist orientation. In Luanda, for instance, black markets called "candongas" are more important than official markets. Acknowledging this fact, the government has revalued black markets with the term "parallel market" (however, they are still only hesitantly shown to foreigners). In a study on Zaire, a group of American experts found that "unofficial sectors" were actually maintaining the economy of the country. Official data show only a fraction of the actual economic activities, which are three times as high as stated in official statistics, especially in the wide field of "informal foreign trade" or "smuggling."[31] Similar observations can be made in many other African countries.

The revival of the market and private initiatives, however, is not the remedy for all problems, as Africans are told by dogmatic "free-marketeers." I earlier stated that the market should not be perceived exclusively as exploitation and the resulting social injustices, as is done by orthodox Marxists. It is equally mistaken to ignore or underestimate the existence of exploitation and the social danger resulting from it. The extremely uneven distribution of income and wealth in developing countries, poverty, famines, and exploitation, as well as the horrendous gap between rich and poor on the North-South axis, are without doubt explosive factors. Exploitation and social antagonism disrupt market economies. One may call it class struggle, social stratification, or whatever. In this context, the negative social and political effects of the "structural adjustment" policy of the World Bank and the International Monetary Fund have been discussed extensively and need no further remarks here.

A sociopolitical discussion of the limits and risks of the market economy and private initiative will therefore be as important in the future as it was in the past. The fact that the controversy between socialism and capitalism is antiquated does not mean that the problems which brought about this controversy are solved. The teachings

---

31. Janet MacGaffey, "Perestroika without Glasnost: The Need for a New Approach to the Real Economics of African Countries," Carter Center of Emory University, *Beyond Autocracy in Africa*, in Working Papers for the Inaugural Seminar of the Governance in Africa Program, February 17–18, 1989, Atlanta, p. 132.

of Marxism, however, will influence this discussion only if they are reduced to what they were in the first place: a sharp analysis of the risks of the capitalist market economy, and not a scientific, workable basis for an alternative, better social order.

This chapter is not concerned with the name of this future discussion. Some speak of "structural adjustment with a human face," or of a "social market economy," borrowing the term from the Federal Republic of Germany. Others suggest a "socialist" market economy or a market economy with "socialist orientation," although they do not refer to the dogmatic meaning of the term "socialism." V. I. Basanetz, Gorbachev's economic adviser, indicated that the Soviet Union supported "socialism with a human face and elements of the market economy." It is not clear, however, where this concept differs from the "capitalist economic order with a human face,"[32] as can be seen in the following advice of Leonid Alajew, editor of the journal *Africa and Asia*, which reflects a way of thinking of a rising number of Soviet economists: "From the newly industrialized countries (South Korea, Taiwan, Hong Kong, Singapore) we could learn, without any 'proletarian prejudices,' how to overcome our backwardness."[33]

"MIXED ECONOMY": A HOPEFUL BUT UNCLEAR CONCEPT

The sociopolitical options just discussed have one thing in common: they are all based on the concept of a "mixed economy." This model, which combines elements of state intervention and private economy, has already become a catchword in the economic and political debate in Africa. One reason for its popularity is its vagueness. Politicians and also experts in—and outside—Africa are therefore challenged to define the practical implications of this concept more exactly. There are multiple questions: Which mixture of private and national elements is optimal for the economic sector in Africa, considering the material, social, and cultural conditions of different countries and regions? What mixture is

32. *Süddeutsche Zeitung*, February 1, 1990.

33. Leonid Alajew, "Den Blick nach Osten richten: Wie die Entwicklungsländer Probleme lösen, die unseren ähnlichen sind," *Neue Zeit*, no. 26 (1989), pp. 13–14.

optimal in the respective sectors? Are there experiences in this field, either outside or inside Africa, that could be generalized? Those colleagues who work on the reforms in the Eastern European and the Soviet economies and those who are concerned with developing countries should cooperate here. What is the significance of the existence of independent trade unions and other social groups for the dynamic social formation of a "mixed economy"? Trade unions and other mass organizations that aid the ruling parties and heads of state are not much help. In early January 1990, President Joaquim Chissano of Mozambique expressed his critical attitude on the traditional dominance of the party and its so-called mass organizations. He claimed that trade unions should be independent and guaranteed the right to strike. In other countries, similar suggestions were made. Freed of apartheid, South Africa, with its strong, independent, and experienced trade union movement, could become a model.

I have doubts that a thorough discussion of the economic and social implications of "mixed economy" and "structural adjustment" will take the place of the controversy between socialism and capitalism. The issue of ecology and ecological restructuring of the economy, state, and society will become a new focus, even though many Africans fear that it will draw too much attention away from economic development.

I very much welcome the coming end to the controversy between socialism and capitalism. Our minds will be free to tackle ecological problems, a task of historical dimension. Nevertheless, some of the people who are now gloating over the collapse of Marxism will grow pensive about the ideological vacuum. The problems of revolution, overthrow, and collective outbursts of desperation and frustration are far from being solved, considering the massive misery in many countries of the Third World and the growing gap in living standards between people in Europe and Africa. Despite its shortcomings, Marxism was a relatively rational concept for the handling of these problems. It remains to be seen how useful it will be in the future, when confronted with revolutionary Moslem movements with fundamentalist tendencies (see the repeated bloody revolts in Nigeria's Kano province) or fundamentalist movements based on African magical traditions, such as the "Holy Spirit Movement" in Uganda, which is led by the twenty-seven-year-old "Mama Alice" Lakwena.[34]

34. Lakwena and her followers believe they become invulnerable by cov-

THE ISSUE OF DEMOCRACY

Africans are disappointed not only by the miserable rate of economic development but also by human rights violations and political patronage. Apart from a few exceptions, the hope for democracy did not materialize during the phase of independence. Africa is experiencing a deep "crisis of governance." The authoritarian ruling style of the first generation of leaders, often wrapped in one-party systems, linked up closely with the bureaucratic structures of colonial times. African ruling elites were not alone in considering one-party systems the most authentic expression of the African understanding of unity and consensus. This perception was shared by most Africans in the first postcolonial phase. (The latent consensus of the African population on authoritarian one-party systems was confirmed in a survey in Namibia shortly before the election of a constituent assembly in November 1989. Two-thirds of black Namibians voted for a one-party system given the choice of a one-party system, a multiparty system, or an all-party government.)[35] Western multiparty systems are considered incompatible with African identity. "There is only one bull in the kraal" is a well-known African saying.

Clearly, the concerns of African politicians about the centrifugal, polarizing force of multiparty systems are justified in view of the ethnic diversity and the strength of ethnic loyalties in Africa (see, for instance, Nigeria's difficult experience with a multiparty system). But this rationale is problematic on the issue of democratization.

What could happen if the people of African countries were to revolt as in Central and Eastern Europe, given the economic problems and the denial of the effect of political participation? Considering the great distance between both continents and the difference in the social and cultural conditions, this question might not make much sense at first sight. Nevertheless, some African regimes are obviously afraid of

---

ering their bodies with a certain tincture. Actually, most of them were killed in the fights with the national troops. The Sungu-Sungu troops in Tanzania and the Makwenya in Kenya also show that there are problems to solve in the conflict of modernity and traditional values in Africa, which lie deeper than the level of the socialist versus capitalist controversy.

35. See Heribert Weiland, "Namibia auf dem Weg zur Unabhängigkeit," *Europa-Archiv*, no. 23 (1989), p. 714.

"contamination." The leadership of pro-Western Kenya, which is not only de facto but de jure a one-party system, reacted in an especially hysterical manner. Oloo Aringo, the chairman of the Kenya African National Union party (KANU), thought it "absolutely insane and crazy" to draw parallels between the political system of Kenya and the events in Eastern Europe.[36]

Is it really that crazy to draw such parallels? Other African politicians showed more flexibility. Especially in the smaller West African countries, such as Benin, interesting parallels to Eastern Europe can be found. In 1974, Benin was one of the first African countries to officially adopt a Marxist-Leninist orientation. Now there is an open opposition to this orientation. In 1989, several parts of the country saw strikes and riots, including a December demonstration in the capital, Cotonou, in which people carried banners with antigovernment slogans. They protested against corruption and the fact that public officials had not received their salaries, as well as demanded the abolition of Marxism-Leninism and one-party rule. They tore down a statue of Lenin. The party reacted like the regimes in Eastern Europe and hastily decided to give up Marxism-Leninism as the official ideology and to adopt the separation of state and party. A "new process of democratization" was initiated.[37]

"Pluralization" is the new catchword. In January 1990, the National Trade Union Association of Benin declared itself independent of any political party.[38] Guinea, which used to be closely associated with the Soviet bloc in the 1960s and 1970s, also wants to advance toward a multiparty system. On the thirty-first anniversary of independence, President General Lansana Conté announced the transition to a two-party system. Madagascar has amended its constitution to permit the formation of political parties after fourteen years in which only parties supporting President Didier Ratsiraka were allowed. In São Tomé and Príncipe the political monopoly held by the ruling Movement for the Liberation of São Tomé and Príncipe may end after a national conference recommendation adopting a multiparty system in a new constitution.[39] Reacting to the developments in Eastern Europe, "Mwalimu"

36. *Monitor-Dienst* (Africa), January 4, 1990.
37. *Monitor-Dienst* (Africa), December 12, 1989.
38. *BBC, "Summary of World Broadcasts,"* ME/0669 B/2, January 23, 1990.
39. *Africa Research Bulletin* (Political Series), January 15, 1990, pp. 5919, 5920.

Julius K. Nyerere, a long-time advocate and practitioner of one-party rule in Africa, declared: "Tanzanians should not be dogmatic and think that a single party is God's wish."[40]

The oldest communist party in Africa, the South African Communist Party, has enacted some breathtaking innovations as well. This party was considered extremely orthodox, if not Stalinist, but it drew radical conclusions from the developments in Eastern Europe. The SACP now supports a multiparty system and stated that "overcentralized and commandist economies of the socialist world helped to entrench a form of socialist alienation." It furthermore claims that socialism is going through its greatest crisis since 1917.[41] Endorsing the concept of a multiparty democracy, Joe Slovo, the secretary-general of the SACP, notes: "We have had sufficient experience of one-party rule in various parts of the world to perhaps conclude that the 'mission' to promote real democracy under a one-party system is not just difficult but, in the long run, impossible."[42] (This critical attitude on orthodox Marxism and socialism as a hope for an alternative economic and social order that might terminate the grievances of capitalism quickly does not correspond to the perceptions of most activists in South African townships. It is understandable that they identify capitalism with apartheid, which was long their practical experience.)

The African renunciation of one-party systems has taken some twists that have an ironic touch. Those countries that were most closely allied with Moscow are the first to discuss political "pluralism." In contrast, traditional Western allies, such as Kenya and Zaire, are reacting defensively. The regime in Zimbabwe, which is only a decade old, seems prepared to adopt a deplorable U-turn into the past. On December 22, 1989, the day when Nicolai Ceauşescu's despotic one-party rule over Romania was overthrown, the ZANU–Patriotic Front

---

40. *International Herald Tribune,* February 28, 1990, p. 8.

41. Internal discussion paper of the SACP, partly reprinted in *Weekly Mail,* January 19–25, 1990. This change contrasts remarkably with the article in *African Communist,* the last official organ of the SACP, on my report of December 1986 in *Africa Analysis* about the radical new thinking in Moscow's policy on Africa. It claimed that the article was a "tendentious piece, full of assertions but short of any evidence." See *Africa Analysis,* December 12, 1986, and *African Communist,* no. 109 (2d quarter, 1987).

42. *Front File, Southern Africa Brief,* vol. 4 (February 1990), p. 4.

party concluded its congress with the resolution to turn Zimbabwe into a de jure one-party system on the basis of Marxism-Leninism. Executive President Robert Mugabe praised Marx and Lenin in a way that would astonish, if not offend, devout Christians. He claimed that Marx and Lenin were like Jesus; they only had a different message on the exploitation of the workers. One of the most intelligent leaders in Africa, Mugabe drew important conclusions from the failures of other African regimes when he became the leader of the country in 1980. Yet, will Zimbabwe have to go through a phase of authoritarian, dictatorial abuse of power like many other countries in Africa? Because Zimbabwe decided at the same congress to continue economic liberalization, a final judgment cannot yet be made. And the majority of the twenty-two members of the politburo are viewed as pragmatic technocrats.[43] According to Mugabe, the party will be organized as a "mass party" and not a "vanguard party," that is, by definition it will not be a Marxist-Leninist party.

In sum, the issue of democratization is on the African agenda in the 1990s. African leaders and regimes will have to learn that their contribution to freedom from colonialism and their resulting national and international legitimacy do not guarantee lifelong power and legitimacy. This lesson may be easier for the new generation of leaders than for the old. The postcolonial state has lost the confidence of the populace.[44] Internal and external forces will press for more accountability, economically as well as politically.[45] At the same time, a revival of traditional ethno-hierarchical structures can be noticed, ones that need to be politically integrated and used as a vital force for the socioeconomic restructuring of African societies. There are positive steps in this direction. The general definition of these structures as hostile to "modernization" and as "tribalism" has driven a wedge between the state and most of the population.

Europeans and inhabitants of the northern hemisphere generally

---

43. *Front File, Southern Africa Brief*, vol. 4 (January 1990), p. 4.

44. See Carter Center, *Beyond Autocracy in Africa*, p. 21.

45. See the interesting controversy about the question of democracy in Africa between Peter Anyang' Nyong'o, "Political Instability and the Prospects for Democracy in Africa," *Africa Development*, vol. 13, no. 1 (1988), and Thandika Mkandawire, "Comments on Democracy and Political Instability," *Africa Development*, vol. 13, no. 3 (1988), pp. 77–82.

are well advised not to consider the issue of democratization merely as a matter of a choice between one-party and multiparty systems. The question is more complicated, especially regarding the reconciliation of traditional ethno-hierarchical structures with the modern territorial state and the difficult task of economic and social change under unfavorable external conditions. The process of democratization concerns first of all the African people.

CONCLUSION: AFRICA NEEDS A "NEW REALISM"

Let us turn back to the developments in Europe and the Soviet Union. The euphoric phase after radical political changes and the collapse of unliked systems has come to an end. Disenchantment is on the rise. In economic and ecological respects, the situation in Central and Eastern Europe as well as the Soviet Union is worse than was assumed before the Iron Curtain disappeared.

A short-term improvement of the economic situation should not be expected. It appears, on the contrary, that the economic descent is just beginning and will only be halted years from now. While the old systems no longer function, the new market-oriented systems do not yet work. As a consequence, food supplies (as well as energy supplies during the winter) might be jeopardized. In the case of the Soviet Union, Bulgaria, Romania, and Poland, even the possibility of famines cannot be excluded. Only the GDR, now united with its economically booming neighbor, the Federal Republic of Germany, will probably escape this fate. It is likely that the economic descent will coincide with explosive political and social problems. The effects of the structural adjustment in Poland have a striking resemblance to those in African countries. Furthermore, ethnic and national conflicts might escalate into violent confrontations (for example, in Yugoslavia). Europe will have to stop speaking of "tribal conflicts" only in reference to Africa.

With this perspective, it is evident that not only the attention but also the material resources of Western Europe, the United States, and Japan will concentrate on Eastern Europe and the Soviet Union in the 1990s. Billions of deutsche marks and dollars must be invested to get the economies of these countries going again. Infrastructure is outmoded and needs to be modernized as a precondition to economic growth. The ecological situation appears to be so bad that it is not certain if the investment of billions will be sufficient to manage this problem. In any case, a vigorous attempt needs to be made.

Africa will therefore enter into direct competition with Central and Eastern Europe for economic resources and cooperation. In February 1990, the European Community (EC) declared that it is willing to associate itself with the Middle and Eastern European countries. What will this association status look like in relation to the African, Caribbean, and Pacific countries that, for instance, have been associated with the EC in the Lomé Treaties regarding preferential trade relations? Central and Eastern European states will soon forget their past "internationalist" solidarity with the Third World. As Europeans, they will pressure for preferential status. Who of the Western European politicians can ignore these claims when the extreme right wing grows stronger and stronger?

Moreover, Western private enterprise will continue to reduce its investments in Africa.[46] Traditionally and increasingly in the new political context, Eastern Europe and the Soviet Union are more interesting to investors than most African countries. (South Africa may be an exception to this rule when it has given up apartheid.) The African share of global trade, which amounts to 1 percent, has been declining over the past few years. Not even a condominium of the two superpowers will occur. They are not interested.

The conclusions are clear. Africa cannot hope that foreign assistance will solve its economic problems. Nor will it help to appeal to the conscience of Western societies and nations. These appeals will no longer be heard, since the results of developmental aid of past decades have been poor, apart from the enormous task of economic reconstruction in Europe. Nevertheless, it is incorrect to call developmental aid a complete failure, especially considering the role of nongovernmental organizations. Although Japan announced that its Africa plan will extend developmental aid to $2 billion, this will not end the difficulties. "Big money" is not the solution to the problem. In addition, Japan lacks experienced personnel and adequate institutions

46. Even French investments in Africa decreased by about 20 percent during 1989.

to use its funds efficiently. Portugal hopes to pick up a big chunk of this money. It will mostly work in favor of its own economy.

Africa has two options to respond to its loss of global attention and assistance: despair or an attitude that uses the events in Central and Eastern Europe as a challenge to initiate a "new realism." Some Africans correctly point out that nothing could be worse for Africa than to become the "social case" of the world, a continent dependent on international welfare. Africa should largely solve its problems by itself and evade ideological daydreams. It should not lose time by complaining about its diminishing status in global politics. What is the relevance? Essentially, Africa will suffer less foreign involvement and get a chance to determine its own fate. The result could be what has so far been lacking in African countries in comparison to Asian countries: the profound, realistic determination to advance. This is not an easy demand. Yet an increasing number of Africans are thinking along these lines.

Europe's contribution to such a determination should be a much more decisive cancellation of debts and the removal of trade barriers. Europe would be well advised not to stop its engagement in Africa. Apart from vital ecological and economic interests, constructive relations with Africa are an important part of the enlightened, nonracist identity of Europe. This fact should not be forgotten while Europe is occupied with its own problems.

Chapter 3

IBRAHIM S. R. MSABAHA

The Implications of International Changes for African States

Since the signing of the Intermediate-Range Nuclear Forces (INF) Treaty between the United States and the Soviet Union in December 1987, the international system has become distinctively different. The superpowers have entered a new era of cooperation symbolized by joint efforts to resolve regional conflicts in the Gulf, southern Africa, and Cambodia. Within the United Nations, for the first time since the world body was formed in 1945, an exceptional partnership exists among the five permanent members of the Security Council, rekindling the hope that the defunct collective security system envisaged in the United Nations Charter, but rendered impotent by the Cold War, could now be revived.

Hand in hand with the continuing collapse of the Cold War has been the political revolution in Central and Eastern Europe, in which virtually all communist regimes have lost their monopoly of power and have instead been replaced by democratically elected governments. Thus the world today is dominated by two main issues: East-West relations and changes in the political landscape of Eastern European socialist states. In the wake of these developments, the question for African states is, what implications do these changes have for the continent? This question is important for several reasons.

First is the issue of similarity of political systems. What has collapsed in Eastern Europe is a single-party system with all its paraphernalia of authoritarian and monopolistic tendencies. In Africa, virtually all governments that took power at independence equipped themselves with mechanisms of perpetual self-reproduction, in which the single party (or the military) has become the predominant feature of political life. The second problem is economic development. The changes in Eastern Europe are partly a result of political and economic stagnation in the region, where economic and political regeneration has proved to be incompatible with ideological rigidity and gerontocracy. Likewise, in Africa, the postcolonial state has coincided with economic and social decadence. Yet as demonstrated in Eastern Europe, history is replete with examples of revolutions where the existing political order has been an obstacle to economic regeneration. The third issue is resources. The most recent European Community (EC) assurances at the 1990 U.N. Special Session on Development notwithstanding, assistance to African states could be lost in the euphoria of a restructured Europe as Eastern Europe occupies center stage in NATO's strategic planning. Indeed, at the time of Namibia's independence, the United States simultaneously approved a $9 billion grant to an Eastern European country and a $500,000 grant to Namibia. The issue is not that Eastern Europe should not be helped, but rather that a good deal of foreign aid might be channeled to the East at the expense of Third World nations, and African states in particular. A fourth consideration is the implications for the Non-Aligned Movement (NAM). NAM was born on the premises of East-West conflict, and the organization has traditionally acted as a counterforce to the East-West division of the international system. In addition, NAM has achieved tangible successes on issues of decolonization and development. The final issue is the United Nations. The relaxation of East-West tensions has produced the possibilities for superpower collaboration in the Security Council. Indeed the United States and the Soviet Union, together with Great Britain, China, and France, have already cooperated in producing the 1988 Security Council Resolution 598 on the Iran-Iraq war and in implementing the 1978 Security Council Resolution 435 on Namibia's independence, and they are now working jointly on the resolution of the Cambodian conflict. The question therefore is, how will such a strategic "alliance" affect the international system and African interests in particular?

This chapter is intended to address these questions of scholarly and policymaking significance given certain postulations. My initial assumption is that recent changes in East-West relations and in Eastern Europe can be comprehended on the basis of the concepts of the international system and that an understanding of these notions could reveal the significant effect of the reforms for African states. Kal Holsti's conception of the international system is particularly useful in this regard.[1] Holsti defines an international system as a collection of political units that maintain a regular pattern of interaction with one another. A key feature is that there is both independence and interdependence in which events in one area affect other areas. Although the dynamics of these relationships continually change, the regular interaction of entities is a constant feature in any international system. Accordingly, an international system is identified by five criteria: boundaries, the nature of political units, the structure of power and influence, the pattern of interactions, and the rules underlying the system. Boundaries refer to geography, issues, and roles within the system. Geography relates to the number of actors and the sphere of international politics. Issues allude to the agenda of international diplomacy in each international system, depending on the type of actors and their preoccupations. As actors participate in international politics, they play certain roles, which vary according to their conceptions of international relations, their main interests, and their capabilities.

The nature of political units applies directly to the inherency of the governmental system that predominates in a particular epoch, especially the relationship between the rulers and the governed. Are governments accountable to the electorate? Is there greater citizen input in public policymaking, and if so how does this phenomenon of political participation affect a country's conduct of foreign relations? The assumption is that the greater the degree of governmental accountability and citizen input, the higher the democratization of the domestic political process. This, in turn, creates complexity in the management of foreign relations.

The third criterion of the international system is power and influence. Power is an age-old concept of political science and international politics, from the classic examples in *The Prince* by Niccolò Machiavelli to the present-day realist conceptions of international politics by noted scholars like Hans Morgenthau. In its simplest meaning, power refers to the ability of an actor to prevail in an encounter. Each nation is considered to have its own power base of aggregate material and

1. See Kal Holsti, *International Politics: A Framework for Analysis* (Prentice-Hall, 1977).

nonmaterial resources in a complex combination of at least four dimensions mentioned by Karl Deutsch: weight, domain, range, and
scope.[2] The weight of power is an actor's ability to change the probability of a particular outcome. The domain of power is the set of all
those affected by an actor, including land, capital goods, and resources under one's control. The range of power, most visible with
nuclear weapons, deals with the difference between the highest reward and the worst punishment or deprivation the power holder can
administer. And finally, the scope of power relates to classes of relations and services under an actor's control. The contention is that
the totality of individual nations' power bases constitutes the overall
potency of the international system. Yet this potency is not evenly
distributed among the members of the system, and so each system
has its own power structure or configuration. A couple of actors may
outclass all the rest in a typical bipolar international system, or a
multipolar sphere may exist in which there are several centers of
power.

These first three criteria obviously influence the fourth, the forms
of interaction. For instance, the growth of international organizations
as new actors has brought about the phenomenon of conference diplomacy and multilateralism in general.

Finally, the rules underlying the system apply to the legal regime
that regulates the relations between states and nonstate actors. They
refer to customary rules of international law as well as to treaties and
conventions.

In short, an international system should be considered as a distinct order, with characteristics of its own that mark it off from the
preceding arrangement. These characteristics can be used to distinguish international systems temporally, not so much to fix transitional dates but to have the balance and perspective of the new
and different. Thus modern world politics can be divided into four
stages: 1917–45, 1945 85, 1985–90, and post-1990. The periodiza-
tion is admittedly arbitrary, but for purposes of this chapter, the
provisional arrangement provides the framework for discussing
major events, basic structural changes, and international political
action.

2. Karl W. Deutsch, *The Analysis of International Relations* (Prentice-Hall,
1978), p. 198.

THE INTERNATIONAL SYSTEM FROM
1917 TO 1945

At the conclusion of the First World War, the boundaries of the international system remained more or less the same as in the prewar period. The main actors were European countries, especially Great Britain, Germany, France, Italy, and Belgium; the issues were Eurocentric—for the most part security and colonial questions—and the roles were designed to ensure that Europe remained the arena of international politics. Africa and Asia were essentially colonial continents and therefore could not participate in international politics. Both the Soviet Union and the United States adopted a temporary policy of isolation from European affairs, especially the politics of the League of Nations.

It was the Bolshevik revolution and the Soviet entry into international politics that substantially transformed the international system. The 1917 revolution led to an attempt by the new communist regime to introduce changes in the existing international system by spreading revolution beyond Russian frontiers. Between 1917 and 1921 the Soviet Union faced a civil war and external intervention. The revolution could not be crushed, and it left the conflict between the newly born "Eastern bloc" and the "old West" unresolved. The conflict grew from its essentially ideological roots to become geopolitical, and it is this mixture of ideological and geopolitical concerns that has continued to characterize East-West relations.

In terms of the structure of power and influence, the bipolar division that would come to dominate in the international system had not yet clearly emerged, but the illusion of the Western European nations that Europe would continue to play a pivotal role in international politics was beginning to fade. The war exhausted the European powers. As Geoffrey Barraclough correctly notes, the First World War resulted in "substantial and irreversible changes in the balance of economic power, and in relation to overall growth the countries which had taken the lead in pre-World War—Germany, for example, the United Kingdom, France, and Belgium—were falling back."[3] It was

3. Geoffrey Barraclough, *An Introduction to Contemporary History* (Penguin Books, 1977), p. 27.

the League of Nations, conceived as an instrument of collective security, that became the primary medium of interaction during the interwar years. Ironically, it was the impotence of the league, and especially the temporary absence of the United States and the Soviet Union, that brought about the collapse of the European international system as fascism rose in Germany, Italy, and Japan. Despite its leading role in establishing the league, the United States withdrew into isolation for fear of becoming deeply involved in European affairs. The Soviet Union was eliminated by revolution, subsequent civil war, and foreign intervention.

As for the rules underlying the international system, many of the modern concepts of interstate relations were solidified during this period. The sovereign national state continued to be the primary legitimate actor; territorial integrity, though occasionally violated, became an acceptable norm of international relations, and the rights and duties of states were codified under the Montevideo Convention.

Despite these supportive standards, the international system—which had its origin in the Treaties of Westphalia of 1648—began to crumble. Although it had been temporarily strengthened by colonial acquisition in the nineteenth century, it was shaken by the First World War. By the end of the Second World War, the old order had been fashioned by death, destruction, and social upheaval. The former powers of Europe were relegated to secondary positions, and communist regimes were set up by the Soviet Union throughout Eastern Europe. The international system became bipolar, and NATO and Warsaw Pact alliances entered the postwar order as robust competitors.

THE INTERNATIONAL SYSTEM FROM 1945 TO 1985

The rise of the superpowers and the continued colonial occupation of mostly African and Asian countries not only determined the shift of emphasis from Europe but also became the harbinger for two concurrent salient features of the international system: the East-West conflict and the North-South divide of world politics.

Boundaries of the System

Before 1945, the international system was geographically Eurocentric. It took the decolonization process to bring about a change in the number of actors and the globalization of the international system. Since then, the number of actors recognized within the system has greatly increased, with varying degrees of influence accorded a wide range of states, international organizations, and liberation movements. One example of the postwar expansion is the emergence of the United Nations as the hub of world politics. Another is the rise of the liberation movements as actors in their own right. For instance, both the Palestine Liberation Organization and the South-West Africa People's Organization (SWAPO) have enjoyed observer status in the U.N. General Assembly. The system has expanded geographically toward recognizing that nation-states are not the only legitimate and influential actors.

Following the height of the Cold War in the 1950s and 1960s—symbolized by the Korean War, the Congo crisis, and the Cuban missile crisis—new concepts of conflict have had a major influence on interstate behavior and on what constitute basic issues in international diplomacy. Two trends could be observed: the East-West conflict and the North-South division. Anatol Rapoport classified the East-West relationship into fights, games, and debates.[4] Fights are the most automatic and seemingly mindless; they are characterized by a great power confrontation and include escalation preceding actual conflict. An example of such behavior is when one nation's level of arms expenditures becomes the basis for the other nation's decision on how much to spend to exceed that "safe" margin or to obtain parity in order to ensure security. Games occur when players maintain a more rational control over their moves. Strategies and tactics play a central role in determining risks, probabilities, and consequences of the different moves. Interstate threats and promises are evidence of these games as tension mounts into crisis and troops are mobilized. Debates, the most rational of the encounters, provide forums through which nations can discover mutually acceptable solutions because the actors have a better chance of discovering exactly what each other's

4. See Anatol Rapoport, *Fights, Games and Debates* (University of Michigan Press, 1960).

expectations and opinions are. The Soviet-American arms race and arms control negotiations typify this conception of conflict as fights, games, and debates.

The other critical issue during this period was the North-South confrontation over the nature of the international system and the Third World's subordinate status in it. The Non-Aligned Movement championed the idea that Third World poverty was partly a result of structural international inequality. Expressing a similar conception, the paper tabled by the delegation of Tanzania to the Lusaka Summit of NAM in 1970 stated:

> The poverty of the Third World and the economic dependence of the nations of the Third World are . . . an integral part of the present world economic order. To a degree, the Third World is poor and will remain poor because the rest is rich and getting richer. The functioning of the present international system ensures that this is so. For national wealth, development and effective economic independence on the one hand and national poverty, underdevelopment and extreme economic dependence on the other hand are all complementary parts of the whole economic system as it exists at the present time.[5]

The conception of the unjust international order became the dominant agenda of international diplomacy in North-South relations. It also defined the respective roles of NAM members as one of heralding changes in the international system through decolonization and the establishment of a New International Economic Order.

The Nature of Political Units

Two trends have affected the nature of political units in this period. First, there was a greater degree of governmental accountability to the electorate, especially in the Western industrialized countries. The increasing number of special interest and pressure groups, including trade unions, has had a growing influence on governmental domestic and foreign policies and so has affected relationships within the international system. Second, communist nations in Eastern Europe

5. Tanzanian delegation, "Cooperation against Poverty," paper presented to the Lusaka Summit of the Non-Aligned Nations, 1970.

developed monolithic political systems, and with time these one-party states developed crises of governance. In Africa, most governments emulated the Eastern European political model. At the time of independence and in the years following, there was an understandable and exclusive emphasis on national unity. Building the new state encouraged the elevation of one leader, the adoption of a single ideology, and the domination of an exclusive political party. Indeed, by the end of the 1960s the monolithic political system that was adopted across Africa became a salient feature of the regional system. After the first decade of independence, however, the focus on maximum national consensus brought with it the problems of citizen alienation from genuine political participation, resultant underground political opposition, political instability, and violence. The new state and society remained apart, and sustainable economic development became impossible.[6] The regimes that took power at independence had equipped themselves with mechanisms of perpetual self-reproduction: the authoritarian legacy of the colonial era, a patrimonial power structure, single political parties, and the ossification of authority under de facto or de jure life presidents. But these features of the domestic political units in Africa and Eastern Europe would become the main sources of economic and political decadence, as well as the chief impetus for political transformation in Eastern Europe and transition in East-West relations. The changes in Europe would, in turn, become a prime model for the transformation of African domestic and international politics.

Power Configuration

Hand in hand with the modification of the nature of postwar political units has been the alteration in the structure of power and influence. After the First World War, several powers vied for global dominance: Great Britain, Belgium, France, Germany, Japan, and Italy. Weakened by the Second World War, these nations saw their influence decline in the new power structure that emerged. The bipolar order that arose produced imbalance in economic, industrial,

6. See Carter Center, "Beyond Autocracy in Africa: Working Papers for the Inaugural Seminar of the Governance in Africa Program," Emory University, February 17–18, 1989.

and especially military power, with the advent of nuclear weapons. The intense East-West conflict of the 1950s and 1960s could be seen in the arms race and in the voting pattern at the United Nations.[7] That same period witnessed a decline in North-South issues between the developed and the developing countries except for the decolonization agenda. By the 1970s, however, a multipolar structure had emerged, especially in the nonmilitary sphere. There were several factors in this development. The emergence of NAM and its coalition diplomacy was a significant contribution. Beginning with the Bandung Conference in 1955, when NAM was first conceived, the organization had a ringing appeal to Third World nations as a symbol of the idea of unity. In the context of the bipolar international system, NAM's real objective was to organize a formidable counterforce to the superpowers' interference in the affairs of the small nations and to speed the movement for the granting of independence in the colonial territories. The Algerian war of independence, the Congo crisis, the Bay of Pigs invasion, and general competition for influence in the Third World by the superpowers crystallized the composition of the "resistance movement" of Third World nations.[8] Effective use of natural resources by some Third World countries also contributed to the reordering of the structure of power and influence. Not only did the Arab oil embargo of 1973, as well as successes by the Organization of Petroleum Exporting Countries (OPEC) in establishing new oil prices, become the symbol of the struggle of the weak for equity and justice in the world of the mighty, but it also had demonstrative value. The lesson was that one does not have to be economically developed to have an economically powerful influence. When certain critical resources are used as leverage, Third World nations can play a reformist or revolutionary role in the international system.[9]

By way of summary, as the international system became more diffuse and multipolar, two capability models emerged. On the one hand, the industrialized nations have used industrial and military

7. See Hayward R. Alger and Bruce M. Russett, *World Politics in the General Assembly* (Yale University Press, 1965), pp. 134–37, 276–79, 293.

8. See Robert A. Mortimer, *Third World Coalition in International Politics* (Praeger, 1980).

9. See Robert L. Rothstein, *Global Bargaining: UNCTAD and the Quest for a New International Economic Order* (Princeton University Press, 1979).

power to obtain influence; on the other hand, developing countries have counted on their numerical strength and resources to produce a transformation of their subordinate status in the international system.

Forms of Interaction

As a result of the increasing complexity of the international system from 1945 to 1985—given the multipolarity of actors, variety of issues, and diffusion of power—diplomatic interplay is largely organized through the United Nations and regional organizations and groupings. Group interaction falls into several categories. They are regional, such as the Organization of African Unity (OAU); subregional, including the Association of Southeast Asian Nations, the Western European Community and the Eastern European Council for Mutual Economic Assistance; and functional, such as the Non-Aligned Movement and the Group of 77. On the whole, the emergence of international organizations brought about multilateral and conference diplomacy and provided the context for Third World coalition diplomacy in international politics. In essence, this predominant mode of interaction has played a role for international relations analogous to Kelsen's legal conception of the "ground norm" in the domestic legal system, which sets the trend for lesser laws. Likewise, conference and multilateral diplomacy has set the pattern for bilateral diplomacy.

Rules

As the boundaries, political actors, structure of power, and modes of interaction continuously evolve, so do the relevant rules underlying international relations. For instance, the duties and rights of states have been accepted for generations, but with the emergence of the United Nations and the incorporation of these legal norms into its charter, duties such as good neighborliness, nonuse of force, respect for territorial integrity, and the sovereignty of the nations have gained prominence. And since the 1970s, the question of resource sharing has become particularly important, as demonstrated by the 1982 Convention on the Law of the Sea. *Mutatis mutandis*, the same may be said of the economic regime. In particular, Third World nations have been relentless in their call for a new international economic order in which the position of the developing nations would be improved.

Thus what emerges from the period is a complex international environment both for East-West relations, especially on security issues, and for North-South relations, in particular on the development question. Ali Mazrui has aptly described the international system in relation to African states as one of economic stratification with the rigidity of the caste system of India. And while the global system therefore has the appearance of stability and rigidity, it is also characterized by active, imminent, and latent instability because of the burdens of the Third World nations.[10]

THE INTERNATIONAL SYSTEM FROM 1985 TO 1990

Ali Mazrui's comments might also be applied to the entire international system, given the security anxieties in East-West relations that produced the INF Treaty and the failures of the communist regimes in the Soviet Union and Eastern Europe that produced the reformist movement and political revolution in the period from 1985 to 1990. The events are "regional," but because of the global predominance of the actors involved, their implications profoundly affect African states.

The Main Actors: The Soviet Union and the United States

Although this is essentially a summary of U.S.-Soviet interaction, it is only appropriate to emphasize the Soviet role, since the present changes were inspired by the emergence of a new leadership in the Soviet Union.

The historical quest of the Soviet Union, like that of all states, has been the struggle for survival. Russia was invaded by the Western powers at the time of the Bolshevik revolution, and during the Second World War it lost about 20 million of its citizens. Consequently, the Soviet Union has historically sought refuge in military power, some-

10. See Ali Mazrui, *Africa's International Relations* (London: Heineman, 1977), p. 4.

times at the expense of social and economic development. It has also aimed for strategic parity with the leading Western power. With the achievement of strategic parity in the 1970s, Soviet and American interests converged on the necessity for mutual survival. The continued control of nuclear weapons became the fulcrum of the Soviet-American relationship. The emergence of a new dynamic leadership in the Soviet Union in 1985 produced a new momentum. Mikhail Gorbachev recognized the distinction between the Soviet military as a superpower and the Soviet economy as a Third World system. The Soviet leadership reasoned that unless this contradiction was resolved, Soviet decline was inevitable, even in the military field. As Jonathan Haslam explains the Soviet strategic dilemma:

> The gap between requirements and capabilities has to be set against the background of increasing difficulties faced by Soviet air defense forces which arose from the rapid growth of US technology: a problem compounded by a relatively underdeveloped infrastructure. Time was also a major problem. The rapid growth in the technology of the enemy has meant that their air defense forces have less time to prepare for battle. This requirement placed a premium on efficiency, not only technical but also managerial efficiency. It is at this point that the demands of high technology have met with the backwardness of Soviet society.[11]

The solution was the Soviet-American "discovery" of a mutual interest in survival through arms control. Both countries sought to avoid war or to make it less destructive should one occur, to reduce the uncertainties created by modern weapon systems, and to reduce the economic costs of the arms race. It is the desire to create strategic stability that promoted the Soviet-American convergence through political-military relations of mutual interest in peaceful coexistence; avoidance of direct entry of NATO–Warsaw Pact forces in regional conflicts; relaxation of international tension; and settlement of regional disputes by peaceful means. Several technical factors also contributed to the redefining of the security problem by the Soviet Union under the new policy of *perestroika:* the impressive display of American air power in Vietnam; the continuing American effort to reinforce its

11. Jonathan Haslam, *The Soviet Union and the Politics of Nuclear Weapons in Europe, 1969–87: The Problem of the SS20* (London: Macmillan, 1989), p. 23.

superiority, especially with the emergence of the Strategic Defense Initiative under the Reagan administration; the deployment of Cruise and Pershing II missiles in Europe; and the shift in NATO doctrine toward the option of limited nuclear war.[12] The necessity to restore Soviet confidence and strategic stability brought about the signing of the INF Treaty in December 1987 and the new era of détente.

The triumph of *perestroika* in the arms control debate epitomized the changes in East-West relations, which in turn foreshadowed a political revolution in Eastern Europe. The new era of East-West relations represented a remarkable shift in the determination of Soviet strategic interests. As Haslam aptly points out, the Soviets have redefined their age-long security dilemma by looking to a political rather than a military solution.[13]

This is not the first time the Soviet Union has redefined the security problem and shifted its attention from defense to diplomacy in order to meet more pressing economic problems. At the conclusion of the Russian civil war and the war of intervention in 1920–21, V. I. Lenin undertook a major realignment of domestic and foreign policies. This realignment resulted in the introduction of the New Economic Policy and the demobilization of the Red Army. In the period 1929–32, Joseph Stalin engineered another transformation, in which the first Five-Year Development Plan was a key element. In both periods, the Russians stressed the importance of disarmament, of Western companies working in the Soviet Union, and of détente. However, both changes were temporary. The question therefore is whether the present changes are big enough to maintain a lasting convergence in East-West relations.

Eastern Europe

The transition from communist regimes to liberal democratic governments that has been allowed to take place in Eastern Europe is the most significant indication of how profound *perestroika* has become and of how "permanent" the present thaw is in East-West relations. Never before has the Soviet Union allowed such political transformation. Far from it, in 1956 and 1968 the Soviet Union intervened in

12. Haslam, *Soviet Union*, p. 30.
13. Haslam, *Soviet Union*, p. 177.

Hungary and Czechoslovakia to stamp out reformist regimes that would have threatened the communist monopoly of power. Today, however, the same forces that are at work introducing domestic changes in the Soviet Union itself through *glasnost* are responsible for the changes in Eastern Europe. As in the Soviet Union, changes in Eastern Europe are a result of political and economic stagnation in the region, where regeneration has proven incompatible with ideological rigidity and gerontocracy, a situation paralleled in Africa.

THE POST–1990 INTERNATIONAL SYSTEM AND IMPLICATIONS FOR AFRICAN STATES

Given the similarities in political systems of Eastern Europe and African states, it is necessary to address the implications of the two chief events in the contemporary international system for the African states in the post-1990 period.

Boundaries of the System

Although geographical boundaries may remain relatively stable for African states, the nationalism sweeping across the Soviet Union and Eastern Europe could influence secessionist tendencies in the African continent. For instance, if the present composition of the Soviet Union breaks apart because of independence movements in the Baltic states and Asian republics, the example could rejuvenate such breakaway African regimes as Biafra, Katanga, and Southern Sudan. Assuming that the present structure of boundaries of the African states as inherited from the colonial powers is the most appropriate political arrangement for Africa, then African foreign policy should encourage the preservation of the political units and the integration of these states into larger regional and eventually continental unions.

East-West convergence poses a new complexity. On the one hand, increased Soviet-American cooperation reduces international tension and contributes significantly to the resolution of regional conflicts, as evidenced in the Iran-Iraq war, in Namibia's independence struggle, and in Afghanistan, Mozambique, Angola, and Cambodia. In fact, cooperation of the superpowers and the other permanent members of the Security Council is a prerequisite for the success of the United Nations in its present form. Because of their global geopolitical interests, these powers can play an obstructionist role in the United Nations through the use of veto and economic power. On the other hand, this cooperation also raises the specter of superpower condominium with negative consequences for the democratization of international relations. Constitutionally, the U.N. Charter does not anticipate independent action by the superpowers or, more precisely, by the permanent members ("Big Five") of the Security Council, because this would hold the rest of the international community hostage to the strategic interests of the Big Five. Indeed, the position of the Big Five does not always coincide with the interests of the international community. The implementation of U.N. Security Council Resolution 435 on Namibia's independence is the most recent example. Despite a vigorous campaign by NAM and OAU to preserve the original strength of the U.N. Transition Assistance Group at 7,500, as approved by the Security Council in 1978, the permanent members voted the figure down to a mere 4,500. Initial mishandling of the implementation period accounted for major conflict in Namibia between SWAPO and South African forces in the first week of April 1989.

While the relaxation of tension should help the resolution of some regional conflicts, it may also heighten North-South conflict in the short term over the nature of political systems to be followed by developing countries. In an April 1990 article, the British representative to NATO, Sir Michael Alexander, contended that the revolution which swept across Eastern Europe in 1989 laid to rest the ghost of communism that has haunted Europe since Karl Marx's declaration of the "Specter of Communism" in 1848.[14] What Alexander failed to say is that a new specter is now haunting Africa: Western gospel to Africa, with its uncompromising moralism about the multiparty system. The attempt to impose Western models may lead to Western withdrawal from the "imperfect" African world in the form of marginal economic assistance, or it could produce unrestrained interventionism by the United States and other Western powers under the pretext of supporting prodemocracy movements. Either tendency could

14. Michael Alexander, "NATO's Role in a Changing World," *NATO Review*, no. 2 (April 1990), p. 1.

lead to the balkanization of the continent.[15] The likelihood of the second possibility coming to pass is based on the rear-guard battle that leaders in most of these states are fighting to preserve the one-party system and thus their own survival. As recent events have shown in Mali, Zambia, and Kenya, the obduracy of these leaders can lead to bloodshed when citizens demonstrate their determination to oppose the one-party system. The existence of domestic opposition can in turn lead to direct or indirect foreign intervention.

There is another possible source of fresh South-South conflicts as East-West conflicts wane. One of the ironies of the Cold War is that it had demarcated "spheres of influence" for the superpowers, where a sudden change of government in one area represented a shift in the balance of power. Because of this prospect, superpower intervention was always a possibility for hastening or forestalling change that would affect the status quo. The present atmosphere of collaborative relationships between the Soviet Union and NATO, however, has removed the "zero-sum" nature of their dealings in the Third World. Although this atmosphere removes the urgency of major power intervention in support of protégé regimes, it also creates a vacuum that could be filled by regional powers and hence create new conflicts.

The Iraqi invasion of Kuwait on August 2, 1990, represents the most recent and pertinent example. The invasion has enormous geopolitical consequences for the countries of the region and for the Western world in particular. Iraqi control of Kuwait's huge oil reserves changes the balance of power in the Gulf in favor of Iraq and could significantly affect the politics of OPEC. It also calls into question Western claims over the protection of small Gulf states and Saudi Arabia. No wonder, then, that there was a swift condemnation of the Iraqi invasion by the United States, NATO members, and the other major powers.

The point that should not be lost in all of this is that during the Cold War years, Iraq would have thought twice before contemplating such an invasion, because it could easily have led to immediate physical intervention of American forces in the Gulf. The present détente, however, has not only created a vacuum but has also slowed the tempo of American reaction and refocused attention on the significance of the United Nations. In an unprecedented move, the United

15. Stanley Kober, "Ideal Politik," *Foreign Policy*, no. 79 (Summer 1990), pp. 8–9.

States and the Soviet Union issued a joint statement to condemn the invasion. Within the United Nations, there has been growing consensus on the need for swift, comprehensive, mandatory economic sanctions against Iraq. The lesson to be drawn here is that unless there is truly a determined international response to interventions such as the one in Kuwait, there is the likelihood of intensified regional conflicts in the post–Cold War period, wherein regional powers rather than superpowers contend for hegemony.

Under the circumstances, how should African states respond? First, any relaxation of East-West conflict must be supported for the simple reason that a safer international environment is a better place for international relations. Accordingly, African states should continue to support a revitalized United Nations, which has been a major foreign policy goal of these states since independence. Efforts to broaden the mandate of the U.N. Security Council, however, must be approached cautiously. As long as African states—or NAM, for that matter—do not carry the veto power in the Security Council, broadening the council's mandate might infringe on the mandate of the other U.N. organs that are more democratic than the council. It might also interfere with Article 2(7) of the U.N. Charter on noninterference in domestic affairs of member states. African foreign policy must therefore be directed at a mixed strategy of cautious support.

Nature of Political Units

The changes in Eastern Europe have spearheaded a new revolution in the nature of governments. Whereas from 1945 to 1985, Eastern Europe, the Soviet Union, and much of Asia, Africa, and Latin America were characterized by monolithic political systems, the collapse of communist governments in Eastern Europe has sent shock waves throughout the African continent. If there is a single lesson to be learned from Eastern Europe, it is the necessity for democratic reforms that reorient state-society relationships so that the political accountability of the rulers to the governed is the hub of political life. The process could be gradual, messy, pitiful, and rife with imperfections. Nonetheless, as noted at the 1989 workshop organized at the Carter Center of Emory University, there must be movement away from rigid and repressive authoritarianism, including the excessive use of the security apparatus of the state; movement toward a liberal policy in which human rights violations are terminated or minimized; release of political prisoners; considerable freedom of expression and political organization even in the absence of effective competition for power; political leadership prepared for voluntary relinquishing of power; initiative for democratic regime transformation from civil society in the form of popular organizations that provide the means for the articulation of interests, assertion of rights, and an arena for the development of the norms and practices of democratic citizenship; and new institutional structures to ensure accountability.[16]

By way of prediction, three scenarios may be postulated for Africa's future trend of democratization. First, the success of the present wave of prodemocracy movements in such African states as the Ivory Coast, Benin, Algeria, Kenya, Mozambique, Tanzania, and Zambia would imply the triumph of *glasnost* African-style, in which there is gradual improvement in economic conditions. This would result, in turn, in greater mass support for multiparty systems. In its most dynamic stage, this process would lead to the unification of the African continent and the creation of a single economic market by the year 2000. Achievement of this goal would require the backing of, rather than intimidation by, the international community, especially the Western democracies.

Second, assuming the interim failure of the prodemocracy movements across Africa, as has already happened in Kenya, prodemocracy leaders would be seized and put in detention. But the continuing globalization of *glasnost* has built up sufficient pressure on African leaders to make continued detention of leading opponents of the one-party system impossible in the long run. Zambia, for example, in late July 1990 released four leading opponents who were serving life sentences for plotting to overthrow President Kenneth Kaunda. That this would happen barely a month after the latest coup attempt in Zambia speaks much about the pressure African leaders are experiencing today. In short, the Africanization of *glasnost* has become virtually irreversible.

The third scenario postulates that the prodemocracy movement neither succeeds nor fails and that the African continent, beleaguered by the ensuing confusion, slides into anarchy. This development is possible in states such as Tanzania, where the debate over party

16. Carter Center, "Beyond Autocracy in Africa."

system has been orchestrated by the country's retiring mentor Julius K. Nyerere. Not until it became clear that he didn't believe the ruling party could hope to exist alone indefinitely did the other leaders as well as the media pick up the theme. Yet one still finds an air of cynicism about the intentions of the ruling party. For example, several changes might be made in the constitution to allow independent representation by workers, women, and parent and youth organizations, which are now organs of the supreme party, but these changes will be used as justification for retaining the one-party system. Although this approach might ensure the short-term survival of the single-party state, it is unlikely to still the outcry against it. In the absence of any genuine alternative, the African condition would become unpredictable, engendering a higher incidence of military coups reminiscent of the 1960s and 1970s. The emerging military regimes would offer no solution to the abysmal economic condition of Africa.

In short, the lesson is that democratization of civil society is necessary, because the single-party state predominant throughout the continent coincides with economic stagnation and decay. Democratization is also needed to diminish state violations of civil rights and exploitation of the population, which have contributed to Africa's economic crisis. In the final analysis, Africa's economic malaise is a political malaise.

Structure of Power and Influence

African states need to combine their economic resources to enhance the prospects for international cooperation. Because Eastern Europe occupies the center stage in Western strategic planning, a good deal of foreign aid may be diverted to the East at the expense of the African states and the Third World. What has alarmed the African states are the developments that took place immediately after the major changes in Eastern Europe began to take hold. The Western alliances have been keen to ensure that the reforms under way are soon consolidated. In July 1989, the Paris summit meeting of the seven main Western industrialized countries confirmed this strategic objective by offering support to Poland and Hungary: "We welcome the reforms underway and the prospects of lessening the division of Europe. . . . Each of us is prepared to support this process and to consider, as appropriate and in a coordinated fashion, economic assistance aimed at transforming and opening their economies in a durable manner."[17]

As Frans Andriessen explains, two principal approaches have since been employed: action in a multilateral context and a European community initiative. The multilateral approach involves the initiative of twenty-four countries, including the United States, Austria, Canada, and Iceland. The EC was given the mandate to coordinate aid to Poland and Hungary. One week after the Paris summit, Poland was granted ECU 130 million for a food policy program, whereby the funds gained by the Polish authorities through food sales at market prices would be channeled to fund specific programs designed to improve the structural basis of Polish agriculture.[18]

This kind of assistance is to be extended to the countries of Eastern and Central Europe, as well as the Soviet Union. At its December 1989 ministerial meeting in Brussels, the Group of 24 confirmed its willingness to respond positively to other countries of Eastern and Central Europe.

The point here is not that Eastern Europe should not be assisted. Rather, unless African states take concerted action, their development agenda could be lost in the euphoria of the restructuring of Europe. This is particularly the case since Europe as a whole is preparing for a common market by the year 1992. A balkanized African continent will be too weak to face a united Europe.

As Julius K. Nyerere pointed out recently, when launching the South Commission Report, five elements should be stressed:

—[The fact] that development is about people, about human beings. Their advancement and well-being is its purpose.

—A development policy of national self-reliance. . . . Without national self-reliance, the reality of national independence is compromised. True independence is possible only on the basis of equal self-reliance.

—The collective self-reliance of the South . . . bilateral, subregional, and regional cooperation as a base for inter-regional and global South-South cooperation.

17. Cited in Frans H. J. J. Andriessen, "Change in Central and Eastern Europe: The Role of the European Community," *NATO Review*, no. 1 (February 1990), p. 1.

18. Andriessen, "Change in Central and Eastern Europe," p. 3.

—South-South solidarity in all international negotiations . . . conducted separately or together.

—The importance of promoting and using science and technology for the future development prospects of the South.[19]

There is another challenge posed by the resurgence of Europe. A reformed Eastern Europe faces the problems of reintegration into the world's capitalist economic system. While this prospect poses the likelihood for competition with the African states for Western European and American markets, it also raises the question whether Eastern Europe can be counted on as a partner in the Third World's efforts for the establishment of a new international order. This issue is important for African leaders because the communist parties that were in power in these countries at least had a favorable conception of African problems ranging from apartheid to economic development. These newly elected governments are at best ignorant when it comes to African states. Evidence from Hungary supports this contention. After the collapse of the communist regime in 1989, one of the principal revisionist foreign policy acts of the new regime was to invite the South African foreign minister to Hungary and to encourage the emigration of Hungarian experts for work in South Africa, acts that had the implication of circumventing the international isolation of the apartheid regime. The advice for African states might be to adopt a two-pronged strategy toward the new Eastern European governments. On the one hand, they should seek to educate these regimes on the nature of African issues. On the other hand, African states should mount a concerted diplomatic campaign to isolate those governments that continue to turn a blind eye to African problems.

Forms of Interaction and Rules

The significance of multilateral diplomacy and regional organizations have already been mentioned. The issue that has yet to be fully discussed is the role of the Non-Aligned Movement in the post-1990 period. Because NAM was born at the height of the Cold War, the

19. From an address given by Mwalimu Julius K. Nyerere, chairman of the South Commission, at the launching of the South Commission Report, Caracas, Venezuela, August 3, 1990, printed in *Daily News* (Tanzania), August 4, 1990, p. 4.

question is whether the movement can continue to be effective in the new international system that has eclipsed the Cold War. NAM's role is significant since it might affect the pattern of diplomatic interaction in effect during the 1945–85 period. As described earlier, NAM has become an instrument of Third World coalition diplomacy. There is, however, another dimension. The economic dimension of NAM has been clear since the Lusaka Summit in 1970, at which it was noted that the poverty of developing nations was a structural weakness of the existing international system. Because NAM has since emerged as the "Philosopher King" on the necessity for a New International Economic Order, the organization should continue to play a leading role in international politics.

There is another reason why NAM is important and why African states should therefore offer their fullest support to the organization. From 1945 to 1985, intimidation against the Third World came from both camps, East and West. This became the *raison d'être* of NAM. From 1985 to 1990, intimidation was different in that the pressures emerged from another source: the major Western powers led by the United States. This kind of threat is potentially more dangerous, because the traditional instrument of statecraft—playing off one power against the other (East-West)—no longer exists in the post-1990 period.

Western intimidation of African countries has already begun, and several countries, including Tanzania, Uganda, and Zimbabwe, have already decried this policy. The Western world has created a linkage strategy that makes the extended provision of foreign aid contingent on the implementation of political reforms. The linkage was first applied to the German Democratic Republic, Czechoslovakia, Bulgaria, Romania, and Yugoslavia when they prepared their reform plans and requested the extension of benefits enjoyed by Poland and Hungary from the Group of 24 countries.[20] With most of Central and Eastern Europe now qualified to receive Western assistance, the next obvious candidates for the Western linkage strategy are the African states, which are in any case much more vulnerable to economic coercion. It is possible that one African state after another will succumb to external pressure. In short, African states are now more vulnerable than ever before.

20. Andriessen, "Change in Central and Eastern Europe," p. 4.

CONCLUSION

After examining the implications for African states of the changing international scene as a result of a thaw in East-West relations and a political revolution in Eastern Europe that has toppled communist regimes, I can fairly conclude that the international system is now in a state of transition to a new international system for which African states had better be prepared. My advice for African states is to invest in the collective power of the Organization of African Unity, thereby resisting American and European intimidation, and to take a significant, less subordinate role in the new order.

PART 2
Implications for Conflict Resolution

Chapter 4

PETER ANYANG' NYONG'O

The Implications of Crises and Conflict in the Upper Nile Valley

Winding through the plains, hills, and valleys of what later came to be known as Kenya colony, the railroad from Mombasa to the East African hinterland was originally built without the intention of creating a British colony there; this goal came later, as a "commercial afterthought." The original aim was to reach the source of the Nile in Uganda. When the railroad builders got some four hundred kilometers inland, they were happy to find fresh, clean water at a place in the Maasai countryside called Nairobi, meaning "place of good water." Thus, ironically, in searching for the source of the Nile, British colonialism had inadvertently found its future center in the Upper Nile Valley. Kenya has remained the "place of good water" not only for the British but also for other nations in the Western world that find it provides a "healthy climate for investment" and a welcome holiday site for the pleasure-chasing tourist. In contrast, Uganda, the "jewel on the British Crown" and "the Pearl of Africa," which was so dearly sought after, has known almost nothing but fratricidal conflicts since gaining its independence in 1962. Sudan, whose history of internal conflicts is similar to that of Uganda, must also trace "the original sin" to British colonialism and its preoccupation with the Nile.

When discussing conflicts and conflict resolution in northeast Africa, one should pay attention to the Upper Nile Valley and not just to the region usually referred to as "the Horn." The Nile River is as much the lifeline of Egypt as it is of those countries around its source: Ethiopia, Kenya, Uganda, and Sudan. At the dawn of this century, major European powers scrambled for control of this part of Africa, principally because of the Nile. Today, it is not inconceivable that Egypt would go to war with any of the Upper Nile Valley countries were one of them to decide to divert the waters of the Nile for its own use, thus affecting the volume flowing downstream to the Mediterranean. Yet such an eventuality is not impossible: Ethiopia, Kenya, and Sudan have drought problems that could be alleviated by major irrigation works using some of the water claimed by Egypt from the Nile. Uganda's Owen Falls Dam, situated near one of the Nile's sources on Lake Victoria, can be expanded only with the agreement of Egypt. A conflict over the Nile would hurt not only socioeconomic development in the Upper Nile Valley but also many foreign interests that are present and active in the region.

Over the past twenty-five years, the Upper Nile Valley countries, except for Kenya, have been torn apart by such serious internal conflicts that their development has been severely set back. In a sense, they all have the Nile to blame for this; the origin of their conflicts is closely related to the colonization of these countries because of their proximity to the Nile. Yet when one is talking about the crisis in the Horn of Africa, one rarely thinks of the Nile and its relationship to the Horn. The crisis in the Horn is so much a crisis "in the Nile" that, historically and currently, the two aspects must be taken into account together for there to be a meaningful perception of conflict resolution in this region. Historically, the seeds of regional conflict were sown by colonialism. Currently, the political economy of this area provides the basis for understanding the patterns of conflict in Africa and the possibilities for its resolution. Success can be achieved only by taking a *regional perspective.*

ETHIOPIA

When the Italians lost out in the competition for the Nile, they settled for one thousand kilometers of land along the Red Sea, now called Eritrea, so as to strategically check British control of the Nile. But after its early blunders in the Second World War, Italy lost Eritrea to Great Britain in 1941. In 1962 Ethiopia annexed Eritrea, with the connivance of the West, thus sowing the seeds of the present conflict.

Peoples, Resources, and Potential

With a per capita income of $110 in 1986, Ethiopia is now reckoned to be the poorest country on earth (or perhaps a close second to

Mozambique).[1] Yet this miserable position is ordained neither by God nor by Ethiopia's lack of agricultural production. What is lacking, however, is an enabling environment—appropriate government policy and a growing home market—in which to translate this potentiality into reality. The civil war in the north continues to sap needed resources for development while threatening to plunge Ethiopia into total disintegration as a state. Thus it is the crisis in politics, much more than economic underdevelopment, that must be solved if Ethiopia is to begin the long, arduous march toward development.

Both the World Bank and the Soviet advisers to the Ethiopian Central Planning Office (ECPO) have argued that the heavy-handed state control of the economy must be relaxed if economic growth is to be ensured. In a 1986 report issued by a team of Soviet advisers to the ECPO, "Considerations on the Economic Policy of Ethiopia for the Next Few Years,"[2] the team observed that Ethiopia needed to adopt the World Bank–type reforms if its economy was to perform better. Such reforms would include more economic incentives to peasants; reduced state intervention in, and control of, the commercial sector; the disbanding of some, if not all, of the state farms.

It is also interesting to note Soviet attitudes on the political situation. As early as mid-1988, it was generally believed that the Soviet Union had been advising Ethiopia to seek a political settlement to the wars in Eritrea and Tigre. It was becoming increasingly clear that the influence of *perestroika* was rubbing off on Ethiopia, affecting policies in both the economic and political domains. Such an evolution would presuppose a political environment in Addis Ababa in which an ideological about-face and rational economic decisions could be made. Given the preoccupation with the war and the deficit in political legitimacy, there was perhaps little prospect for such change in the near future; hence the possible impatience by the generals who finally attempted to remove Mengistu Haile Mariam on May 16, 1989.

Roots and Patterns of Conflict

Colonized only during the 1936–41 Italian occupation and regarded as one of Africa's oldest civilizations, Ethiopia has been held in pride

1. See, for example, Salim Lone, "Mozambique: The Economic Rehabilitation Programme One Year On," *Africa Recovery*, vol. 2 (March 1988).
2. This report was available only for limited circulation.

as the seat of Africa's symbol of future greatness—the Organization of African Unity (OAU). Unfortunately, today Ethiopia has become a metaphor for perpetual civil war, recurring famine, and an unimaginative and dogmatic approach to dealing with underdevelopment.

In the early 1960s, when most of Africa was emerging from colonial rule, Ethiopia could pride itself on having twice fought European invaders and emerging triumphant on both occasions. Emperor Haile Selassie, though ruling Ethiopia with an iron fist in the postwar period, tempered his reign with modernization policies that were aimed at spurring his society to catch up with the developed world. Like the typical imperial ruler that he was, Haile Selassie's policies were handed down to his subjects in a patronizing manner, and one of the most important beneficiaries—the educated intelligentsia—soon grew weary of the emperor's domination and demanded a more participatory and modern polity. But perhaps the emperor's most important unfulfilled mission in his modernization program was the iron-fisted attempt to integrate politically the disparate parts of his empire.[3]

Ethiopia, most historians agree, is a loosely knit state in which different nationalities had been brought under the imperial rule of an essentially feudalist Amharic ruling class over the last hundred years. Given the predominance of the Amharans and their language and culture, members of other nationalities—including Eritreans, Somalis, Oromos, and Tigreans—saw themselves as second-class citizens and demanded the right to some form of self-determination during Haile Selassie's rule. Eritrea has had the strongest claim to self-determination. It could be argued that the Oromos, Somalis, and Tigreans are more deeply incorporated into Ethiopia, and that—except for Ogaden—it would be geographically more difficult to establish separate and viable states for these nationalities.

Throughout his rule, Haile Selassie maintained that Ethiopia had to remain one entity, that rebellion must be crushed, and that his foreign friends had to help him to achieve this. The more he sought to put the Eritrean nationalist movement down by force of arms (without much success), the more restive and weary the Ethiopian army became. The bonds of military loyalty to the crown finally snapped

3. J. Markakis and Nega Ayele, *Class and Revolution in Ethiopia* (London: Spokesman, 1978); and F. Halliday and Maxine Molineux, *The Ethiopian Revolution* (London: Verso, 1981).

in 1974, when the imperial regime was disgraced by a massive famine that it clumsily and tragically sought to conceal from the rest of the world. Students and workers joined the fray in open dissent. By May 1975, the revolution was an accomplished fact.[4]

The springtime of freedom brought to the surface demands for political rights by other repressed nationalities seeking to distance themselves from historic Amharic domination and Amharicization, which the emperor considered synonymous with Ethiopianization.

The question today remains whether the new revolutionary regime led by Mengistu Haile Mariam is attempting to solve the nationalities problem in any way differently from Haile Selassie. After the emperor was overthrown, a new regime, under the leadership of an elusive group of military officers called the Derg (Armed Forces Coordinating Committee), assumed the captaincy of the ship of state. By 1976–77, it had become increasingly clear that Mengistu Haile Mariam, supported by a close-knit group of military collaborators, was the man in charge. There are many similarities in the attempt to overthrow Mengistu in 1989 and the overthrow of the emperor in the mid-1970s. The main difference is that the latter succeeded and the former failed. Nevertheless, Mengistu's soldiers are as tired of "elusive victories" as Haile Selassie's were.

Mengistu's political opponents often argue that no change for the better has occurred in Ethiopia. In contrast, his supporters tend to exaggerate and tout his government as the most revolutionary and progressive regime in Africa. Neither represents the true situation. It cannot be denied that, in 1974, a revolutionary process started in Ethiopia. With the land reform program launched in 1975, the revolution became a reality to peasants in the countryside. Subsequently, at the level of the polity, a new ruling class emerged.

At the level of economic relations, feudalism in agriculture was virtually abolished; smallholder peasant agriculture mushroomed, though disrupted by chaotic government policies; and the state established substantial control in the commercial, industrial, and service sectors—not always for the good of the economy. These are clearly revolutionary changes; however, their outcomes, positive or negative, need to be analyzed separately.

On that note, one must add that, while claiming to build a People's

4. See M. Chege, "A Revolution Betrayed," *Journal of Modern African Studies*, vol. 17 (1979).

Democratic Republic of Ethiopia (PDRE), the government of the Worker's Party of Ethiopia (WPE) under Mengistu's leadership rarely used democratic methods to manage or solve the nationalities question in Ethiopia. Indeed, the Constitution of the PDRE (1987) generally regarded nationalist movements in Eritrea and other regions as mere manifestations of "chauvinism and narrow nationalism."[5] In this respect, the approach to the nationalities question bore no substantial difference from that of Haile Selassie.

External Intervention

In both Ethiopia and Sudan, internal conflicts have been fueled by external intervention. The longer these conflicts continue, the greater is the military dependence of the warring parties on their arms suppliers. In the 1960s and early 1970s, the United States was Ethiopia's friend, protecting Haile Selassie's regime against internal rebellion from his subjects and external aggression from Somalia.

According to John Spencer, Ethiopia originally sought U.S. protection in the postwar period after Great Britain attempted to impose a protectorate on it.[6] The United States was interested in Ethiopia for two reasons: it had the location and physical characteristics needed for a major communication center, and it could serve as a convenient link in the air routes to India and the Far East. America's most important interest in Ethiopia became the Kagnew base outside Asmara; in return, Ethiopia received military training and equipment from the United States, becoming by 1963 the biggest recipient of such aid in sub-Saharan Africa.

The dominant factor in Ethiopian-U.S. relations during this period was military, and the interest in this type of relationship was mutual. Total U.S. military aid was estimated at $159 million from 1953 to 1970. Although that was considerably less than the $228 million in economic aid for the same period, the military program was very large for Africa. U.S. military aid to the entire continent, until 1970, was put at $305 million.[7]

5. See article 2(2) of the constitution.
6. John Spencer, *Ethiopia, The Horn of Africa and U.S. Policy* (Cambridge, Mass.: Institute of Foreign Policy Analysis, 1977).
7. Spencer, *Ethiopia.*, p. 24.

Whether perceived or real, Somali aggression drove Ethiopia to request and expect more American military aid and to put more men under arms at considerable strain to its public purse. The period between 1970 and 1974 saw a rapid increase in this dependence. As Somalia became militarily stronger by dint of aid from the Soviet Union, Ethiopia sought more assistance from the United States, subordinating other concerns for social and economic development to the arms race. One might argue that Haile Selassie had had a choice; he could have concentrated on internal programs of socioeconomic reform and development. As far as the emperor was concerned, however, the choice was not to be cast in this framework. He assumed that he was doing sufficiently well for his subjects, and even if he were to sacrifice just a little more for the survival of the empire, that sacrifice was worth it. Again the question arises whether the approach of the Mengistu regime is any different.

After the revolution of 1974, the Derg successfully courted Soviet friendship. Indeed, for a few years the Soviet Union was able to maintain the delicate balancing act of having close relations with both Somalia and Ethiopia. But when Somalia invaded Ogaden in 1977, the Soviet Union was faced with a dilemma; it decided to throw its full military weight, assisted by Cuba, behind Ethiopia, making the latter its most important outpost in Africa after Angola. Somalia, for its part, severed all links with the Soviet Union, embracing instead the United States.

Subsequently, the Ethiopian government's heavy reliance on the military became increasingly conspicuous, and the military dependence on the Soviet Union equally enormous. The resources devoted to putting down the internal conflicts far outstripped those devoted to development. What is different, however, is the rhetoric devoted to an ideology meant to create the new Ethiopian citizen, who should be free of chauvinistic tendencies. If this rhetoric is meant to educate and persuade, then the continued, increased militarization of society and the pursuit of the military option to Ethiopia's internal conflicts are sure signs that the rhetoric has not worked.

Gains and losses in the battlefields will continue to fluctuate. The resistance movements in Eritrea and Tigre have made some important military gains, forcing the Ethiopian government to the negotiation table. The armed might of the Ethiopian state will not put an end to these struggles. Conversely, it is difficult to see how the resistance movements are going to succeed. While the conflicts continue, much human life continues to be lost, resources needed for development are being diverted to armaments, another generation of Ethiopians is growing up with the negative consciousness of the "we" and the "them" divided along nationality lines, and foreign powers continue to play the midwife to these conflicts—all the while defending their so-called strategic interests. Although transformations have taken place in the global political system, the scene in Ethiopia does not seem to have changed. Today, Israel has emerged as the external supporter of the Mengistu regime, whereas the Arab Gulf states seem to align themselves behind Eritrea.

KENYA

Kenya's rather impressive past economic performance now faces challenges. A high rate of population growth, deteriorating terms of trade, drought, and debt combine to threaten the economy. In an effort to restore economic growth, the government has begun to pay close attention to policies that will make both the agricultural and the industrial sectors perform better. In agriculture, the main objective is to attain self-sufficiency in food production as well as diversification in agricultural exports. This must be accompanied by appropriate policies for intensive and cost-effective use of land. Thus far, such policies have not systematically been made, let alone enforced. In industry, the very low capacity utilization of almost all plants points out the inefficiency and low productivity in that sector. It has been argued that low capacity utilization is due to two factors: the collapse of the East African Community, which had provided Kenyan industries with an immediate market; and the high cost of production, which makes it nearly impossible to penetrate foreign markets.[8]

What is usually not seriously discussed is how a home market can be carefully nurtured in Kenya to support these infant industries. To accomplish that end, difficult policy decisions will have to be made, but the government cannot make such policies unless it is sure, be-

8. For more detailed analyses, see the relevant chapters in P. Coughlin and G. Ikiara, *Industrialization in Kenya: In Search of Strategy* (Nairobi: Heinemann, 1988).

forehand, that the people will be prepared to make the necessary sacrifices to ensure successful implementation. There must therefore be a *politically enabling environment* if such difficult objectives are to be pursued.

The crisis in Kenya at the moment is that such an environment is not easy to husband. The state has to take imaginative steps to see that conflicting social forces, which perceive different outcomes from policy options, accept the system of the authoritative allocation of values. For them to do so, they must perceive the state as legitimate, or at least ideologically accept the legitimacy of its policy options. If not, given the potentially explosive economic issues, this miracle of economic growth and political stability could easily burn itself out. It would be a mistake not to consider this problem in a regional context; that is, within the context of a regional economic cooperation already being spearheaded by the Preferential Trade Area.

SUDAN

The crisis is even more severe in Sudan, where dire poverty combines with the historical intransigence of rival factions to forestall significant improvements in the social and economic spheres.

Peoples, Resources, and Potential

Sudan remains one of the least developed countries in the world with a per capita gross domestic product (GDP) of about $393 (1984). Most of the population lacks access to such basic amenities as health and educational facilities, clean water, and electricity. For the mass of human resources needed for development, Sudan still has a long way to go. This situation has been compounded by civil strife that is making it almost impossible even to initiate the process of development.

Since 1978, the Sudanese government has tried a series of structural adjustment programs comprising devaluation and the adoption of a flexible exchange rate policy, the relaxation of price controls, the establishment of strict demand control measures, and the privatization of state enterprises operating in commercial fields and increased autonomy for the remaining ones. The effect of these policies has, on the whole, been disappointing. The real GDP growth averaged only 0.4 percent yearly during 1980–84, while per capita GDP fell at an average annual rate of 2.1 percent.

To implement needed reforms the government in Khartoum must be strong enough to pursue them consistently, and creditors must have confidence in the economic prospects of the country. As the civil war worsens in the south and the west, none of these conditions is likely to be met soon. The coup d'état by Brigadier Omar Hassan Ahmed al-Bashir has not made things any better; if anything, it has checked a political process that was beginning to outline specific options for conflict resolution in Sudan. So far, Bashir has not presented a clear model of what he is offering Sudan. The strong arm of the law is not enough; it cannot be established under the present conditions and it has not worked in the past. Moreover, settling debt obligations assumes that the people of Sudan accept such obligations. This assumption cannot be valid in a context where there is no viable political process to test it. A democratization of society has to take place before the imposition of such an obligation on the Sudanese people.

Roots and Patterns of Conflicts

The origins of the present conflicts in Sudan must be traced to its colonial past, when Great Britain employed "divide and rule" tactics effectively. Apart from using Egypt under the Condominium Agreement as an intermediate power to rule Sudan, the British fostered real division between the north (Arab and Moslem) and the south (African and non-Moslem). In 1919, the southern provinces were formally cut off from the north and were declared closed to all northerners except government officials. Southerners were taught English, not Arabic, and they were isolated from Arab and Islamic traditions.

At the same time, northerners were taught about the south, and an ideology of looking down on the southerners as pagans was fostered. The southern region was thrown open to Christian missions in order to establish spheres of influence for crusades among the nonbelievers who, if they were not saved for Christ, would at least be lost to Allah.[9] Therefore, when Sudan became independent in 1956, it was a country with south and north deeply different from one another. Great Britain's southern policy had bequeathed a perpetual source of division within the new multinational republic.

Within the Arab Moslem communities of the north, the British further entrenched clan and religious division. The Ansar Muslims, led by the Mahdi, had put up stiff resistance against British colonialism in the nineteenth century. For years after "the conquest of the Sudan," Great Britain feared that the Mahdist movement, though defeated on the battlefield, would sweep the country once again. But a safeguard was at hand, in the form of another religious sect or *tariga*, the Khatmiyya, led by the Mirghani family. There was implacable rivalry between the Khatmiyya and the Ansars, which was deeply rooted in history and shrewdly manipulated by the administration.

The greater part of contemporary Sudanese political history turns on the axis of these two opposing sects and their opposite orientations. Political party moves and allegiances, otherwise seemingly inexplicable, were a mirror of their conflicts. Even the unity of the army command was rent by opposing sectarian allegiances. Every government of the traditional parties has had to come to terms with, or break under, the all-pervasive influence of these two major *tarigas*.

After the fall of President Jaafar Nimeiri and the reestablishment of civilian rule in 1986 under the premiership of Sadiq al-Mahdi and his Umma party's alliance with Mohammed Osman al-Mirghani's Democratic Unionist party (DUP), it might have been assumed that the two opposing sects had finally closed ranks. The alliance, however, was a marriage of convenience, since neither party could form a government on its own. The overthrow of Nimeiri had come about for many reasons, one of them being the opposition to the *shari'a* (Islamic law) and another being the debilitating civil war in the south. Al-Mahdi's government made no progress on either front. If anything, the government bowed to pressures from the Moslem

9. Ruth First, *The Barrel of a Gun: Political Powers and the Coup d'Etat* (London: Allen Lane, 1970), pp. 126–43.

fundamentalists—the National Islamic Front (or Moslem Brothers)—clinging to the *shari'a* and plunging even more deeply into the
civil war in the south. The composition of the coalition government
formed by al-Mahdi in May 1988 signaled the rising influence of
the National Islamic Front when its leader, Hassan al-Turabi, directly presided over the destiny of the *shari'a* as the minister of
justice.

In March 1986, the National Alliance for the Salvation of the Country—a broad democratic front grouping together trade unions, progressive intellectuals, and other popular organizations—met with the
rebellious Sudan People's Liberation Army (SPLA) in Ethiopia so they
could work out a formula for ending the conflict and building a politically stable society. It was agreed that, for Sudan to develop, all
the major social forces must be committed to the development of a
new Sudan based on the principles of justice, equality, peace, and
democracy. However, this peace initiative was not seriously pursued.
The government in Khartoum under both al-Mahdi and Bashir has
continued to find ways by which it can both defend the *shari'a* and
bring to an end the rebellion in the south. In doing so, it has been
able to rely on the support of several Arab states. Egypt has always
felt that its historic influence should be asserted in Khartoum at all
times. Libya, in an effort to check Egypt, has sought to promote its
own factions in Khartoum. Thus, while the Democratic Unionist party
remains Egypt's closest ally, the National Islamic Front, close to fundamentalists in Egypt, is a source of much concern in Cairo. But
toward the south, these rival northern parties essentially have a common approach: a tough military posture and continued retention of
the *shari'a*.

The SPLA's military successes in the south have always provoked
strong response from Khartoum. When the SPLA took over the
town of Kurmuk near the Ethiopian border, most of the Arab world
was mobilized by Prime Minister al-Mahdi for its recapture. Mirghani, the DUP president, toured Arab capitals and secured the
support of Riyadh, Baghdad, and Cairo. While the Saudis provided
fuel and hand weapons, Iraqi military planes supplied the heavy
military artillery that the Sudanese army needed to dislodge the
SPLA from Kurmuk and Geisan.[10] The tales of massacres and po-

---

10. *Africa Analysis*, no. 43 (March 18, 1988).

groms continue to come out of Sudan as military confrontations move from one town to another in the south. As the civil war rages on, the refugee problem also worsens. Refugees have fled both west and east, some walking as much as 1,500 kilometers to camps on the Ethiopian border. The escape routes are described as being littered with the remains of children and old people who have died of hunger and disease on the march. As long as the Khartoum government sticks to its policies toward the south, and the SPLA, for its part, remains equally adamant about "liberating zones" and forcing a political agenda on Khartoum that will favor its goals, Sudan will remain mired in bloodshed and destruction. Clearly, without peace, no meaningful socioeconomic progress can be made in either the north or the south.

There appears, however, to be a distant glimmer of hope. The call by the SPLA leader, John Garang, in May 1988 for the launching of a national dialogue in which all major political forces would participate "without any conditions"[11] represented a great opening. This gesture was welcomed by all the political parties in Khartoum, and serious efforts began to launch a process that could have led to a negotiated settlement to the Sudanese conflict. That the Democratic Unionist party was prepared to endorse a negotiated settlement was a major breakthrough. But sadly, no sooner had this happened than al-Mahdi felt besieged and resorted to inaction, warranting the coming in of yet another military regime offering no viable options.

UGANDA

Like Ethiopia and Sudan, the former "Pearl of Africa" faces acute economic problems that are not being addressed in a serious, concerted, long-term way. Again, the obstacle is interminable conflict, which undercuts any effort at social progress.

11. See Agence France Presse dispatch of May 30, 1988, from Addis Ababa, containing an interview with John Garang.

Peoples, Resources, and Potential

While a remarkable measure of peace and security has been established in the south and the west of Uganda, the north and the east are still torn by internal strife. Moreover, government policies on the political and economic fronts have been episodic, thus betraying lack of both resolve and definite direction. In the meantime, as the civil war drags on inconclusively, more and more resources will continue to be wasted. The attitude of some officials in Kampala that rebellion in both the north and the east is caused by discordant forces with no coherent demands—hence not worth negotiating with—is unconstructively defensive and in the long run counterproductive.

An economic recovery plan for Uganda should include the following: restoration of peace, internal security, and democracy as a precondition for economic recovery and development; emergency provision of relief for, and resettlement of, citizens deprived and displaced as a result of the ongoing combat; and a medium-term rehabilitation program with the long-term objective of developing an "independent, integrated and self-sustaining national economy."[12]

Roots and Patterns of Conflicts

When Great Britain colonized Uganda at the end of the last century, it made a distinction between the Bantu Kingdoms of the south and west and the acephalous Nilotic nationalities of the east and north. The kingdoms of Buganda, Bunyoro, Ankole, and Toro were preserved intact and the British ruled them under a formula called "indirect rule," whereas the rest of Uganda was brought under direct British administration. Buganda agents were, in fact, used in the northern and eastern parts of the country as administrative hirelings of the British crown. Later on, to man the security apparatuses of the colonial state, the British recruited soldiers and policemen from the Nilotic north and east, men regarded as being

12. See United Nations Economic Commission for Africa, "Africa's Submission to the Special General Assembly Meeting on the African Crisis," Addis Ababa, May 1986.

"naturally warlike." Thus the seeds of interethnic conflict were sown by colonialism.

That the Buganda countryside was climatically favorable to coffee production and that tea could be grown further to the west made these regions emerge as the economic heartland of colonial Uganda. The north remained a subsistence farming area, and pastoralism dominated the eastern grasslands. Once more, economic differentiation resulting from the way in which Uganda was incorporated into the market economy would later have a significant effect on its politics.

Religious rivalry brought in by Christian missionaries became deeply rooted in Uganda's history. Catholicism and Protestantism not only became vehicles for economic advancement in colonial Uganda through a missionary-based education system but were also a condition for acquiring political power. Because the Anglican British government favored Protestants, the kings of the southern kingdoms were by and large Protestants. When Uganda became independent, the British were happy to see Milton Obote's Uganda People's Congress (UPC), a predominantly Protestant party, accede to political power, much to the chagrin of Benedicto Kiwanuka's Democratic party, a Catholic-based coalition. The Moslems, always a minority, were marginal in almost all walks of life.

The UPC managed to gain power by establishing a Machiavellian alliance with the Kabaka of Buganda's political party, *Kabaka yekka* (Kabaka only), after skillfully playing on the Protestant connections in both parties. When the alliance broke down in 1966 and the UPC held onto power, the army became Obote's backbone, since here, again, colonial arrangements favored him as a northerner and a Nilotic. In time, Obote's government increasingly became imprisoned in military dependence as a means of political survival. The internal contradictions of the regime led to its downfall in 1976.

Political scientists have written sufficiently about why the Obote regime fell. For our discussion, it is important to ask, what were the problems that arose out of the geopolitics of the Upper Nile region and their impact on the domestic politics of Uganda?

In the 1960s, southern Sudanese Anya Nya rebels, who were fighting the Khartoum government, sought sanctuary in northern Uganda. Being predominantly from the southern Sudanese Nilotic nationalities, they found northern Uganda a congenial environment both culturally and linguistically. The UPC government in Kampala, then being led by Milton Obote, a Nilotic northerner, needed no persuading to give support to kinsmen across the border, who were viewed as persecuted and discriminated against by a Khartoum government dominated by Arabs and Moslems.

Jaafar Nimeiri's coup in Sudan in May 1969, termed "a putsch with a popular front," changed things. Seeking political legitimacy, Nimeiri pronounced as one of his major aims the ending of the civil war in the south. Claiming that the goal of his "revolution" was to build a socialist society, Nimeiri found himself in the same ideological camp as Milton Obote, who had declared a "Move to the Left" strategy of socialism for Uganda. Nimeiri therefore initiated dialogue with Obote to enlist the latter's support in ending the civil war in Sudan. This move could have been purely strategic on the part of Nimeiri, who knew full well that, without Obote's support, the southern Sudan crisis could not be solved. For Obote to change sides, however, would have been against the interests of Israel, the major outside supporter of the Anya Nya rebels. Exploiting the differences between Obote and his army commander, Idi Amin, Israel supported an anti-Obote coup, which in January 1971 pitted Amin—a Moslem—against the UPC government.

The tales of military misadventure, political repression, economic mismanagement, and massacres of political opponents that characterized Amin's eight-year rule have all been told. When the chickens finally came home to roost, with the help of the Tanzanian army and financial backing from some Western powers, Amin's regime was removed from power in 1979.

This paved the way for Obote's "second coming." In the elections of December 1980, the UPC was returned to power amid allegations of ballot rigging. After much protest, the main opposition party, the Democratic party (DP), accepted the outcome of the elections and took their seats in the new parliament. However, militant members of a small opposition party, the Uganda Patriotic Movement (UPM), which had won only one seat in the elections, adopted a different attitude. They rejected the election results and took to the bush to wage a guerrilla war against the new UPC government. As their base, they chose the woodlands of Luwero in the center of Buganda, a DP stronghold where there was no love lost for Obote and the UPC. Five years of guerrilla war, marked by shifting alliances and deals in the forest among the opposition forces, almost doomed the resistance to failure in the face of the might of the government army. Thanks, however, to the excesses of the army and to the manipulation of ethnic sentiments in the region, the guerrillas of what came to be known as the National Resistance Army (NRA), led by Yoweri Museveni, were able to implant themselves firmly in the Buganda countryside.

When the second Obote government fell in 1985, because of an internal split within its own army, a military junta led by the aging General Tito Lutwa could hold the reins of power for only six months. Attempts by some civilian forces in Lutwa's government to make the best out of a bad situation by working for a government of national unity and reconciliation in which the NRA would also participate were stillborn.

After protracted negotiations between the Lutwa government and the NRA under the chairmanship of Kenya's President Daniel Arap Moi, an agreement to end the civil war and form a government of national unity was signed in Nairobi in December 1985. It is clear, however, that even as the Nairobi Peace Talks were taking place the NRA had already decided to take power in Kampala. Given the Lutwa government's broad coalition, it had within it elements, such as the Democratic party, which were prepared to shift to an NRA government provided they were assured substantial political gains. Moreover, the NRA was able to take full advantage of the fact that in Lutwa's army discipline and morale had broken down and graft was rampant. Within weeks of signing the Nairobi Peace Agreement, Museveni's forces stormed Kampala and took over the reins of power on January 25, 1986.

The overthrown soldiers, coming mainly from the east and the north, retreated to their "home areas" with arms and whatever else they could loot from Kampala. Others escaped into exile in neighboring countries, particularly southern Sudan. Attempts by Museveni's NRA to wipe them out in hot pursuit soon created new problems: the NRA's own excesses against the peasants of the north and the east made the Uganda National Liberation Army (UNLA) soldiers welcome as possible defenders. Thus began a new era of warmongering and the mushrooming of "liberation movements" in the northern and eastern regions against the new government in Kampala.

Much has been said about the priestess Alice Lakwena's Holy Spirit Movement and how it tried to mobilize peasants in the north and east against Museveni's NRA government. This movement—whose soldiers were reported to face machine guns with open chests, with shields and sticks as their only weapons, believing that their real defensive power was God and the Holy Spirit—was finally defeated by the NRA at the beginning of 1989. There are, however, armed opposition groups still holding out in the north and the east against the NRA; they have as many names as they have factions. One thing is certain: they represent dissatisfaction with Uganda's politics and cannot simply be wiped away by force of arms. The causes of this dissatisfaction need to be seriously addressed at a deeper political level.

The NRA regime has tried to create a broad-based government. Museveni's latest cabinet, comprising forty-four ministers and twenty-two deputy ministers, is the largest in Uganda's history. Yet the heavy southern dominance is striking even in that list, where northerners and easterners seem to be more numerous at the level of deputy minister, a reminder of their "second fiddle" position under Museveni.

The economy continues to do rather poorly, with inflation getting increasingly out of control, and Museveni's foreign policies within the region have not made matters any better. Relations with Kenya worsened in 1987, and the two neighbors almost went to war. Kenya suspected that, in collusion with Libya, the NRA government was trying to destabilize the Moi government. Uganda reacted by calling Kenya names and even seeking an alternative route for its coffee exports through the port of Dar es Salaam in Tanzania rather than using Mombasa in Kenya. When matters were finally sorted out at the beginning of 1988, the damage had already been done: there was little trust left between Presidents Moi and Museveni.

Uganda's continued ties with Libya worry some of its neighbors. The two countries do have military relations: Libyan pilots and technicians are in Uganda to man the Czech-made LO39 trainer-fighter bombers that were received in 1987. In addition, Western sources maintain that over the past two years, Muammar Qadhafi's confidant, Musa Kusa, has paid several visits to Kampala. The visits of Kusa, reputedly the head of the Mbatha Anti Imperialist Training Center of the former U.S. Wheelus airbase near Tripoli, is said to cause "blood pressures to soar" in both Kenya and Zaire. But Kusa, though he almost certainly is responsible for the training of various "liberation fighters," is also one of Qadhafi's trusted economic negotiators.[13] The Libyan connection notwithstanding, it is clear that the West has much more influence in Uganda now than does any other set of foreign powers. Uganda has tried all the IMF–World Bank formulas to treat its ailing economy. Although it has found little success, Uganda remains pro-IMF, pro–World Bank, and pro-Western in its approaches to economic management and development.

Still, the most important challenge facing the NRA government is the ethnic and political polarization that runs deep in the country. Will the NRA be able to embark on a genuine process of national reconciliation that can draw back into the fold a significant section of the country that now feels marginalized, if not excluded? If it cannot, it will be difficult for Uganda to make much progress, and internal conflict is bound to continue as part of its political life and as a harbinger of more chaos to come. To say this is not to wish Uganda ill luck, but to urge the resolution of these conflicts by finding political formulas that will make the state more legitimate and the people more endeared to a common destiny.

CONCLUSION: TOWARD REGIONAL CONFLICT RESOLUTION

In spite of its potential as a region well endowed with agricultural land (except in Kenya) and natural resources (including the Nile itself), the Upper Nile Valley countries—with the exception of Kenya—are falling apart from internal civil strife and economic collapse. Yet even in Kenya, the ability to address the fast-growing crises in governance may point to a much more deeply rooted crisis: that of social reproduction. Sudan, once projected to become Africa's "breadbasket," could remain Africa's dreaded "death basket" if its civil war continues.

Common patterns of internal strife do emerge in Sudan, Ethiopia, and Uganda. First, in all three cases, the internal conflicts are patterned along nationality and ethnic divisions: in Sudan, it is the Arabs versus the Africans; in Ethiopia, it is the Eritreans, Tigreans, Western Somalis, and Oromos versus the predominantly Amhara regime in Addis Ababa; and in Uganda, it is the Nilotic ethnic groups versus

13. See *Africa Analysis*, no. 46 (April 1988).

the predominantly Bantu government of Yoweri Museveni. Second, there is a rather common regional pattern, the north versus the south: the Arab north versus the Christian south in Sudan; the northern resistance movement versus the southern-based military government in Ethiopia; and northern Nilotics versus the southern Bantus in Uganda. But these forms are the dynamic and subjective reflections of concrete and objective socioeconomic differences that stem from the history and political economy of the region.

It is important that parties interested in conflict resolution in any one of the countries, whether internal or external, adopt a regional approach. The objective of this chapter has been to point out the regional character and context of the internal conflicts, and hence the need to regionalize conflict resolution efforts and competence-building projects. Because of the political histories of these conflicts, none of them is susceptible to a military settlement; they require political solutions. That is the overriding challenge facing Ethiopia, Sudan, and Uganda—not to mention Somalia. Only then will these countries have the political environment necessary to enable them to channel the enormous potential of the Upper Nile Valley into the process of economic and social development.

Chapter 5

TOM LODGE

Perspectives on Conflict Resolution in South Africa

Both the representatives of the South African government and their most radical opponents have for decades viewed their country's conflict as an arena for international conflicts between superpowers and competing socioeconomic systems. At least since 1948, South African officials have portrayed their domestic opponents as the local expression of a global communist conspiracy. Conversely, the refusal of most Western countries until the mid-1980s to implement economic sanctions against the Republic of South Africa as well as the expansion of European and American investment in the Republic during the 1960s lent substance to radical antiapartheid representations of South Africa's ruling order as protecting interests that were important for the prosperity of international capitalism.[1]

Those two perceptions have received some influential external support and have certainly helped to shape foreign policies toward South Africa, but their underlying assumptions do not survive se-

---

1. This opinion is pervasive. It is reflected in a speech made by the leader of the Uitenhage Youth Congress on March 27, 1985, in the aftermath of the Langa massacre: "The Western Imperialists do not see or hear the cries of the black majority. Their eyes are covered by gold dust, and their ears by diamonds. They are only concerned about the wealth they are raping out of our country." "The Bosses' False Horror," *State of the Nation* (Johannesburg), May 1985, p. 12. At a more academic level, the following reasoning is usual: "The main reason why U.S. policy has supported white minority rule in Southern Africa is this: the section of the U.S. population with the most influence over policymaking (corporate leaders and top officials in government agencies) has also been the section with the greatest stake in maintaining the status quo in South Africa." Kevin Danager, "The U.S. Struggle over Sanctions against South Africa," in Mark Orkin, ed., *Sanctions against Apartheid* (Cape Town: David Phillip, 1989), p. 131.

rious scrutiny. Though communists have made a significant historical contribution to the development of organized popular opposition to minority rule, they have been and continue to be only one influence among many, and they are formed by a locally generated radical political tradition.[2] Western strategic preoccupations with the region have historically arisen from its geological and geographic features. In 1899, Great Britain committed nearly 500,000 soldiers to ensure imperial control over South African gold deposits and the Cape of Good Hope shipping lanes. Whereas the list of South African minerals of strategic importance has since then grown considerably longer, today the issue of who governs their territorial location is unlikely to arouse comparable concern among the great powers. Substitutes exist for most South African strategic minerals, and no substantial alternative markets for them exist.[3] In the event of superpower conflict, international shipping could be disrupted much nearer home than in the remote reaches of the South Atlantic.[4] Notwithstanding its relative size as an African economy,

2. On the roots of this local tradition see Jack Simons and Ray Simons, *Class and Colour in South Africa* (Harmondsworth, U.K.: Penguin African Library, 1969), pp. 201–15, 386–415; and Sheridan Johns, "The Birth of the Communist Party of South Africa," *International Journal of African Historical Studies*, vol. 60, no. 3 (1976).

3. For different views on South African strategic minerals and the extent to which importers could find alternate sources or substitutes for them in the event of an embargo on their purchase, see Commonwealth Committee of Foreign Ministers on South Africa, *South Africa: The Sanctions Report* (Harmondsworth: Penguin, 1989), pp. 95–98; "Will Industry Stop without South African Minerals?" in Joseph Hanlon and Roger Osmond, *The Sanctions Handbook* (Harmondsworth: Penguin, 1987), pp. 243–59; and Stephen R. Lewis, *The Economics of Apartheid* (New York: Council on Foreign Relations, 1990), pp. 60–61. During the Reagan administration, the report of the Foreign Policy Advisory Committee on South Africa, "while recognising the importance of specific mineral imports from South Africa, refused to accept that the difficulties resulting from counter-sanctions or a breakdown in the South African economy should influence, let alone determine, U.S. policy." Christopher Coker, "Disinvestment and the South African Siege Economy," in Shaun Johnson, ed., *South Africa: No Turning Back* (Indiana University Press, 1989), p. 284.

4. Jack Spence, "Does Pretoria Have a Cape Card to Play?" *Times* (London), September 1, 1988; and Larry Bowman, "The Strategic Importance of South

investment and trade with South Africa is proportionately insignificant for the leading industrial economies.[5]

As regards the Soviet Union, while its involvement in the southern African region has increased considerably since the early 1970s—most notably in the scale of resources it has committed to defending the MPLA administration in Luanda—Soviet African experts remain unenthusiastic about the prospects for a successful socialist revolution in the Republic.[6] Soviet military assistance to the African National Congress (ANC) has been modest,[7] the Soviet Union maintains a discreet cooperation with South African corporations over the management of the international market for gold and diamonds,[8] and recently its diplomatic representatives have played a vital role in helping to negotiate a nonrevolutionary transfer of power in Namibia. Soviet Africanists argue in favor of the accession of a reformist majoritarian administration, one that would maintain many of South Africa's existing trading and financial relationships and a substantial proportion of its present internal economic structure.[9]

Africa to the United States," in D. Aluko and T. M. Shaw, eds., *Southern Africa in the 1980s* (London: Allen and Unwin, 1985), pp. 139–40.

5. In the case of Great Britain, for example, the main source of foreign investment in the South African economy, its 40 percent share of South African foreign investment represented 2.2 percent of total British direct investment overseas. Martin Holland, "The EEC and Sanctions against South Africa," in John D. Brewer, ed., *Can South Africa Survive?* (London: Macmillan, 1989), pp. 69–70. Since the Second World War, South Africa has accounted for 1 percent of U.S. foreign trade and 1–2 percent of U.S. direct foreign investment. William J. Foltz, "United States Policy toward South Africa," in G. D. Bender, J. S. Coleman, and R. L. Sklar, eds., *African Crisis Areas: U.S. Foreign Policy* (University of California Press, 1985), pp. 32–48.

6. On recent Soviet thinking, see Winrich Kühne, *A "New Realism" in Soviet–South African Relations* (Ebenhausen: Stiftung Wissenschaft und Politik, 1988).

7. On the scale, nature, and purpose of Soviet military assistance to the ANC, see Steven Davis, "Season of War: Insurgency in South Africa, 1977–80," Ph.D. dissertation, Tufts University, International School of Law and Diplomacy, 1982.

8. With the recent conclusion of a loan and diamond marketing agreement with a Swiss-based De Beers subsidiary, this cooperation is today much more open. See Deborah Stead, "Talking Deals," *New York Times*, August 2, 1990, p. D2.

9. Gleb Starushenko, "For Peace, Co-operation and Social Progress," printed in *Southern African Record* (London), no. 46 (April 1987), pp. 77–88. Viktor

That the South African conflict does not involve economic resources or strategic concerns that are central to the relationship between the great powers does not mean, of course, that it is of negligible importance to them. For example, South African–sponsored insurgencies in the region can threaten governments whose fall could damage Soviet prestige more generally in the Third World.[10] Then there is the anxiety shared by both great powers about nuclear proliferation and the implications of the Republic's capacity to construct a nuclear arsenal.[11] Increasingly too, South African politics has acquired a symbolic resonance affecting the domestic popularity of American administrations; in the 1980s African Americans have become a vital constituency helping to influence U.S. policy on southern Africa. That the region is increasingly perceived to be unlikely to become an arena for superpower hostility does not mean that its politics will be a matter of international indifference. Indeed, the 1980s witnessed an unprecedented expansion of externally directed measures intended to coerce political democratization in South Africa, and it is likely that these pressures will continue.[12] Both the Soviet Union and the United States

Goncharov, deputy director of the Institute for African Studies, USSR Academy of Sciences, has stated: "I believe that in the end South Africa will be socialist, maybe not in 25 years but in a century. . . . I am an optimist." Interview in *Work in Progress* (Johannesburg), no. 48 (July 1987), pp. 3–7.

10. On South African support for the Mozambican National Resistance (RENAMO), see William Minter, *The Mozambican National Resistance as Described by Ex-Participants*, research report submitted to the Ford Foundation and the Swedish International Development Agency, Washington, March 1989. See also Phyllis Johnson and David Martin, *Apartheid Terrorism: The Destabilization Report* (Indiana University Press, 1989). For a succinct analysis of Soviet strategic concerns in the region, see G. R. Berridge, "The Role of the Superpowers," in Brewer, *Can South Africa Survive?* pp. 10–13.

11. The first suggestions that South Africa was developing nuclear weapons came from partisan sources. See Afro-Asian Solidarity Committee of the German Democratic Republic, "Danger to Africa," *African Communist*, no. 19 (October 1964), pp. 16–35 (on South African–West German nuclear collaboration). That South Africa has nuclear weapons is now more generally believed; for a review of the evidence, see Michael Cherry, "The Other Indaba," *Leadership* (Cape Town), vol. 7, no. 4 (1988), pp. 42–46.

12. For a list of the more important of these measures, see Charles Becker, "The Impact of Sanctions on South Africa and Its Periphery," *African Studies Review*, vol. 31, no. 2 (1989), pp. 62–63.

favor a negotiated political settlement,[13] which would require that the popular forces opposing the South African government accept the impossibility of a unilateral victory. At the same time, it would need to be obvious to the rulers and their supporters that the costs of holding on to power were becoming intolerable.

The analysis in this chapter makes the following assumptions about the international domain affecting South Africa. First, the various conflicts within the southern African region will not involve issues of sufficient importance to the great powers to provoke large-scale military intervention, either directly or through proxies. Second, sanctions and internal political turbulence will continue to restrict the Republic's external financial and trading linkages.[14] Third, within the scope of the limited pressures they are willing to bring to bear, the United States and the Soviet Union, along with smaller powers with significant interests in the region, will continue to favor a nonrevolutionary transition to a majoritarian democracy. Given this external environment, three features of South Africa's present political culture may prove to be decisive in bringing about a negotiated transfer of power: South Africa's ruling group is deeply divided; within the white population, there is widespread political dissent; and within the black community, leadership is predisposed toward conciliation. Each of these points requires elaboration.

13. In October 1989, Deputy Minister Anatoli Adamishin publicly stated Soviet willingness to help arrange talks between the South African government and African nationalists. Five months earlier, Yuri Yukalov, department head of the Soviet Foreign Ministry for Africa, was quoted by a Moscow journalist on the USSR's preference for "a political settlement and a political solution to the apartheid problem." Alexander Devitt, "Moscow and Pretoria," *Weekly Mail*, May 23, 1989, p. 7.

14. Two assessments by South African private sector agencies of the likely long-term effects of sanctions are helpful: Mike Perry, *The Business Environment under Sanctions* (Johannesburg: Perry and Associates, 1986); and Federated Chamber of Industries, *The Effect of Sanctions on Employment and Production in South Africa* (Johannesburg: FCI Information Services, 1986). Even if sanctions were lifted, their effects on trade and investment might continue; companies that have disinvested may feel no compulsion to resume South African operations, and new suppliers of raw materials may have proved themselves to be cheaper and more efficient than previous South African exporters.

DIVISIONS IN THE WHITE COMMUNITY

The 1980s witnessed a decisive breakdown in the consensus that had characterized white electoral politics in the preceding three decades. An emergence of a strong conservative parliamentary opposition signaled the dissatisfaction of certain white constituencies with the government's advocacy and implementation of limited political and socioeconomic incorporation of sections of the black community.[15] The Conservative party (CP), which embraces the traditional tenets of Verwoerdian apartheid, enjoys the support of white blue-collar workers, smaller farmers (especially those producing for the domestic market), and lower-echelon civil servants. Its constituency is predominantly, though not exclusively, Afrikaans-speaking. It did well in the 1988 municipal elections with the effective capture of about seventy councils. How tenaciously the party's electoral following supports its program is questionable. In two municipalities, Boksburg and Carletonville, Conservative-controlled councils resegregated parks and social facilities, prompting black consumer boycotts and a subsequent wavering of white voter support.[16] The recent general election demonstrated that its support remains constrained by social and geographic limitations. With about 30 percent of the white vote, the CP is strong in the smaller industrial towns of the Witwatersrand and the northern Free State, especially in those electoral districts that include sizable numbers of rural voters as well as city dwellers. It is well entrenched in the Transvaal maize belt, where small farmers have been hit by the removal of subsidies and the escalating price of foreign inputs. In larger cities, junior civil servants and industrial workers feel vulnerable to the inroads made into their hitherto protected status through black job mobility, and they have been the prime

15. On the emergence of the Conservative party, see Craig Charney, "Class Conflict and the National Party Split," *Journal of Southern African Studies*, vol. 10 (October 1984).

16. In Boksburg, running against the trend represented by the Conservatives' victory in municipal elections, the Nationalist party retained its seat with an increased and comfortable majority of 2,390 votes. In Carletonville, local mineworkers' leader Arrie Paulus successfully defended a Conservative seat with a small majority of 955. Here the consumer boycott petered out after a couple of months and had less effect on the local economy.

white victims of economic recession. Their disenchantment with the Nationalist party, though, is more than offset by the sheer size of the professional and managerial middle class. White workers and farmers constitute only about a third of the total of whites employed.

Conservative opposition lacks substantial support from business and from the media—state controlled or otherwise. Partly for this reason, it has emphasized tight local organization on a neighborhood basis, a strategy traditionally neglected by white parties, which for a long time have mainly been instruments of electoral mobilization campaigning at a considerable distance from their supporters. The white right has substantial influence in the police force, but there are few indications of a comparable degree of sympathy for the right in the officer corps of the South African Defence Force (SADF). South African electoral analysts today suggest that Conservative support has peaked; notwithstanding the element of wishful thinking in such assertions, it seems reasonable to conclude that unless the Conservatives can make ideological inroads into the thematic discourse of white "reformist" politics, their following will be unable to vote them into power.[17] Here the Conservatives' weak intellectual base is significant; comparisons with the Nationalist party during the historical phase of its accession to power are illuminating. Afrikaner nationalism's triumph was preceded by its domination of literature, scholarship, philosophy, theology, and the arts.[18] Racial rancor, homespun

17. A useful summary of the reasoning underlying this argument is Rupert Taylor, "CP's Electoral Strength Is Limited and No Threat," *Star* (Johannesburg), May 31, 1989. In the September 1989 election, the CP won 39 out of a total 166 parliamentary seats. Thirty-four additional seats were won by the Nationalist party with fewer than 1,000 votes more than their right and left opponents; it is reasonable to presume that Conservatives might gain support in a large proportion of these constituencies. Even so, this would leave them well short of a majority in the house of assembly. *Monitor: The Journal of the Human Rights Trust* (Port Elizabeth), December 1989, p. 53. On political attitudes of South African policemen, see John Brewer, "The Police in South African Politics," in Johnson, *South Africa: No Turning Back*, pp. 277–78.

18. An illuminating analysis of the construction of Afrikaner nationalist identity in popular literature is Isabel Hofmeyr, "Building a Nation from Words: Afrikaans Language, Literature, and Ethnic Identity, 1902–1924," in Shula Marks and Stanley Trapido, eds., *The Politics of Race, Class and Nationalism in Twentieth Century South Africa* (London: Longman, 1987), pp. 95–124.

morality, folksy nostalgia, and *dirigiste* economics are unlikely to win Conservatives many converts in the leafier suburbs.

The right does not have a monopoly of white dissent. To the left of the Nationalist party, there is the tradition of liberal parliamentary opposition represented by the Democratic party, formed in 1989 from an alliance between the Progressive Federal party and the Independent movement. The Progressives had been steadily losing support as Nationalist party policies (as demonstrated in the 1983 constitutional referendum) became more appealing to traditional Progressive voters, who tended to be English speaking, affluent, and urban. In 1987, party leaders considered support among university students to be sufficiently important for them to blame the party's electoral decline on students' staying away from the voting booths. The Democratic party draws on traditional Progressive constituencies, but the main determinant governing its ability to mobilize nearly a fifth of the white vote in the September 1989 poll was its capacity to attract Afrikaners. Its candidates included former Nationalist MPs, senior government functionaries, television luminaries, Stellenbosch university teachers, and even a recently retired SADF major-general. The Democrats drew advantage from leadership disarray within the government, but their real strength was ideological; compared with the previous contest, "security" issues were less conspicuous and voters were being asked to deliver a mandate on the government's vaguely conceived strategy toward racial power sharing. They were of course helped by 20 percent inflation, deteriorating public services, revelations of bureaucratic venality, and ministerial squabbling, but this should not obscure the fact that in its public projection the Democratic party emphasized its commitment to a nonracial restructuring of the political order based on universal suffrage. Voters are probably equally drawn by the *realpolitik* emphasis in Democratic discourse; that so many of its principals are defectors from the government rather than members of the traditional liberal opposition makes them all the more credible to whites as potential intermediaries between the state and its more radical opponents.[19]

See also T. Dunbar Moodie, *The Rise of Afrikanerdom* (University of Calfornia Press, 1975), pp. 146–74.

19. On the Democratic party and its supporters, see Heribert Adam, "The Polish Path?" *Southern African Review of Books* (London), October–November

There is also a small but vocal, extraparliamentary, white left opposition, clustered around student organizations, the End Conscription Campaign, the arts, and an "alternative" press. This group has an influence out of all proportion to the actual number of activists and committed participants, helping to shape the discourse of more mainstream white and black opposition politicians. Charitable agencies also help to subvert suburban culture with a powerful vein of social criticism: "Operation Hunger," such frivolities as its televised lottery proceedings notwithstanding, is important in this respect.

White "left" dissent should not be sought only in the institutional matrix of political organizations and pressure groups. The worsening decline of South African currency and international creditworthiness and the increasingly obvious limitations of industrial development that cannot be directed effectively at export markets because of political constraints have prompted a sharp reduction of business confidence in the South African state.[20] Increasingly, business executives are beginning to find common topics of discussion and even common platforms with radical opposition.[21] The widening social differentiation of the Afrikaans community—a function of educational expansion, bourgeoisification, and growing secularization—supplies the background for understanding the opening up of moral debate and political disagreement even within the Nationalist establishment. Leading churchmen join newspaper editorialists, financiers, artists, and sports officials in sanctioning negotiations with African nationalist leaders. Government itself is increasingly susceptible to factionalism, which not only divides coalitions of cabinet ministers and party administrators but is also manifested in a shifting balance of strength

---

1989, pp. 3–4. See also *Monitor: The Journal of the Human Rights Trust* (Port Elizabeth), special issue on the white Democrats (July 1989).

20. This is described in detail in Michael Mann, "The Giant Stirs: Business in the Age of Reform," in Philip Frankel, Noam Pines, and Mark Swilling, eds., *State, Resistance and Change in South Africa* (Johannesburg: Southern Book Publishers, 1989), pp. 79–82.

21. Christo Nel, "Group Therapy," *Leadership*, vol. 7, no. 4 (1988), pp. 35–41 (on the formation of the Consultative Business Movement after the meeting in August 1988 between eighty prominent business leaders and UDF representatives). See also Bob Tucker (chairman of the South African Permanent Building Society), "Economic Justice," in Five Freedoms Forum, *Conference Proceedings*, Johannesburg, September 25, 1987, pp. 10–12.

between conservatives, pragmatists, and reformers-through-negotiation within each state department or ministry.[22] In the context of a split white political constituency and deep divisions within the ruling bureaucracy, the formation of any long-term ruling strategy with a coherent ideology and a rational allocation of resources to underpin it becomes extremely difficult, if not impossible.

THE BLACK COMMUNITY

Meanwhile, within black politics, despite the multitude of political and functional organizations, the popular legitimacy of the oldest standard bearer of African nationalist identity, the African National Congress, is not seriously contested. There is no national body that commands a comparable extent of popular sentiment (though the conservative Inkatha remains a significant regional rival in Natal).[23] The ANC's leadership is more or less openly acknowledged by the larger of two trade union organizations, COSATU (Congress of South African Trade Unions), and the organizations loyal to the United Democratic Front (UDF). In certain respects the ANC represents a broad popular movement, since it is not ideologically or socially monolithic. Despite its strength in the industrial working class (political organization in the countryside has been historically sporadic and superficial), its leadership is a social alliance. One should therefore be wary of attributing to this movement a fixed ideological character or strategic orientation. Nevertheless, in the last several years, ANC statements and activities together testify to an effort to discover common ground with people customarily regarded as hostile. The ANC

22. Ivan Sarakinsky, "The State of the State and the State of Resistance," *Work in Progress,* no. 52 (March 1988), pp. 47–51; Mark Swilling, "The Politics of Negotiation," *Work in Progress,* no. 50 (October 1987), pp. 17–22; Mark Swilling, "Is FW the Man to Lead Us to Peace?" *Sunday Star,* June 17, 1989; and Anton Harbor, "The Two Nat Camps: One Which Will Talk to the ANC, One Which Opposes Talks," *Weekly Mail,* January 27, 1989, p. 6.

23. John D. Brewer, "Inkatha Membership in Kwa Mashu," *African Affairs,* no. 84 (1985); Roger Southall, "A Note on Inkatha Membership," *African Affairs,* no. 85 (1986); and Nkosinathi Gwala, "Political Violence and the Struggle for Control in Pietermaritzberg," *Journal of Southern African Studies,* vol. 15 (April 1989), pp. 506–24.

has entertained at its Lusaka headquarters a succession of deputations from South Africa, including some from conventional arenas of white political and social life: business leaders, parliamentarians, priests, newspaper editors, and rugby players. From dialogue with these groups as well as from discussions with representatives of Western governments, the ANC has experienced increasing pressure to define in detail a postapartheid program.[24] It has responded to this pressure with the elaboration of a series of constitutional "guidelines." Although they advocate considerable economic redistribution, these guidelines fall well short of a total restructuring of the political and economic systems. In October 1987 the ANC announced its willingness to negotiate with the South African government—not the first of such statements, but phrased with softer preconditions and qualifications than before.[25]

The ANC and Negotiations

The recent ANC predisposition toward a negotiated transition to social democracy may derive from five factors. First, there are its own ideological traditions, including a consistent advocacy of racial reconciliation. Since 1969, the ANC has included whites in its membership, and today there are two white members on the ANC national executive committee. In the 1950s, the ANC functioned within the Congress Alliance, which brought together Indian, colored, and white congresses as well as a multiracial trade union movement. ANC lead-

24. An informative discussion of the different external agencies prompting the ANC's economic planning is Witney W. Schneidman, "Who's Where in the Debate on "Nationalization" in South Africa," *CSIS Africa Notes*, July 1, 1990. See also John Kifner, "Planning Is Begun on South Africa Aid Bank," *New York Times*, July 5, 1990.

25. Its present position was defined in African National Congress, *Statement of the National Executive Committee of the ANC on the Question of Negotiations*, Lusaka, October 9, 1987. In this document the conditions needed to create a "climate conducive to negotiations" include the release of political prisoners, the lifting of the state of emergency, the unbanning of banned organizations, the withdrawal of the security forces from the townships, the repeal of politically restrictive legislation, and the return of exiles. The ANC succeeded in obtaining OAU support for these terms in the August 1989 Harare Declaration.

ers at that time also maintained friendly contacts with a broad spectrum of white liberals. The ANC's program, the Freedom Charter, adopted in 1956, projected a South Africa that would "belong to all who live in it, black and white" as "equals, countrymen, and brothers." ANC officials defended this program against acrimonious internal criticism culminating in the secession of the self-styled Africanists who founded an "exclusivist" nationalist Pan-Africanist Congress in 1959. The "multiracial" culture of the 1950s' political campaigning was a formative influence on today's older generation of congress notables. There is also the older heritage of Protestant mission-school liberalism that was an important feature of the congress's early history, a history that still inspires respect and affection among modern ANC intellectuals.[26] Though the whites who can be directly associated with the ANC's postwar history remain a small group of several hundred or so, their role has been conspicuous and of great symbolic importance. The concept of negotiation again finds resonance within the ANC's history: as late as 1961 the initiation of guerrilla warfare through a sabotage campaign was still linked to a demand for a national constitutional convention.[27] The ANC maintains a strong degree of legalism in its own procedures and actions, perhaps a reflection of the influence of the lawyers who have made such a telling contribution from the congress's formation to the staffing of the organization's upper echelons. This legalism finds expression in the carefully hedged and qualified language of ANC policy statements, in its painstakingly drafted internal constitutions, in facets of its behavior—it remains the only insurgent organization to be a signatory to the Geneva Convention—and in its consciousness for precedents set by its own history.

Second, the ANC's military strategists may have less faith in the likelihood of an insurrectionary accession than they had at the height

26. See, for example, Pallo Jordan, "The Life and Times of W. B. Rubusana," *Sechaba*, January 1984, pp. 5–13.

27. For the history of the ANC's commitment to negotiations and a constitutional convention, see Ian Philips, "Negotiations and Armed Struggle in Contemporary South Africa," *Transformation* (Durban), no. 6, pp. 38–51. For the ANC's position in 1961, see "Resolution of the All in African Conference," Pietermaritzberg, March 25–26, 1961, printed in Thomas Karis, Gwendoline Carter, and Gail Gerhart, *From Protest to Challenge* (Stanford: Hoover Institution Press, 1977), pp. 632–33.

of the 1984–86 unrest. At that time, it is true, both within the ranks of the guerrilla army, Umkhonto we Sizwe, and among the post-1976 exiles who today supply an important current of intellectual radicalism within both the ANC and the South African Communist party (SACP), there was evidence of increasing impatience with the notion that the armed struggle should merely serve as a source of leverage rather than as the prime mechanism for a revolutionary "seizure of power." Such feelings were expressed in an arcane debate conducted within the columns of *Sechaba* and *African Communist* and, possibly, in insurgent attacks on "soft targets" such as shopping centers and bus terminals.[28] Because of the proliferation of organized mass assertion, the South African state was then widely perceived to be immediately vulnerable. In fact, senior Umkhonto commanders and ANC officials, while falling in with the rhetorical language of a "people's war," continued to argue that in the end victory would have to be bargained for and that the ANC was a long way from matching the firepower of the SADF.[29] Significantly, the SACP has recently redrafted its policy program, in doing so conceding the absence of "immediate prospects of inflicting an all round military defeat on the enemy."[30] Umkhonto's armory is modest, and the number of operational guerrillas is not a serious obstacle to the routine functioning of either the state or the economy.[31] The guerrillas' actions are vital, though, in supplying an effective

---

28. Comrade Mzala, "Has the Time Come for the Arming of the Masses?" *African Communist*, no. 89 (1982); Thanduxalo Nokwanda, "The Dangers of Militarism," *African Communist*, no. 91 (1982); Cassius Mandla, "Let Us Move to All-Out War," *Sechaba*, November 1986; and Ronnie Kasrils, "People's War, Revolution, and Insurrection," *Sechaba*, May 1986. For reports of disagreement within the ANC over Umkhonto attacks, see "South Africa: Hani's Rise," *Africa Confidential*, vol. 29 (August 12, 1988), pp. 1–3. See also John Battersby, "The Man Behind the Men Behind the Bombs," *Weekly Mail* (Johannesburg), June 10, 1988, p. 5.

29. "I don't envisage in any near future the liberation forces meeting and defeating, on any frontal basis, the military force on the other side." Joe Slovo, "The Struggle Goes On," *AfricaAsia*, no. 33 (September 1986), p. 16.

30. Quoted in Gavin Evans and Thandeka Gqubule, "Goodbye Joe Stalin," *Weekly Mail*, August 25, 1989, p. 13.

31. In 1989 the police recorded 289 guerrilla "incidents," mainly grenade and limpet mine explosions as well as exchanges of fire with policemen. *SA Barometer*, vol. 4 (March 2, 1990), p. 43.

and heroic reminder of the ANC's presence to black South Africans and their white compatriots.

Third, international action against South Africa in recent years may have served to rekindle confidence within the ANC in the utility of external leverage and diplomacy. Since 1957, the ANC has urged economic sanctions, which it believes can play a critical part in "changing the balance of power," hence shortening the conflict and limiting its destructive consequences. ANC spokespersons buttress the case for sanctions by pointing to South Africa's heavy dependence on imported capital goods, foreign electronic technology, and loans from "transnational financial institutions."[32] Notwithstanding the shortcomings of the sanctions packages reluctantly endorsed by British and American administrations in 1986, the ANC contended that their effect was politically decisive. Moreover, it said, the bankers' refusal that year "to roll over loans . . . [was] an important victory in our struggle."[33] Of course, foreign government sanctions, corporate disinvestment or divestment, and hardening attitudes among bankers were responses to much more powerful impulses than those that could be orchestrated by ANC diplomats, but nevertheless all three occurred in a context of intensifying contacts between ANC officials and senior business leaders and Western officials.[34] The sanctions campaign also helped to generate within the United States and Great Britain important new public audiences for the ANC.

Fourth, ANC principals have long argued that the white minority was not a monolith.[35] Events in the 1980s have vindicated this view.

32. Neva Makgetla, "Why We Call for Sanctions," *Sechaba*, September 1985, pp. 9–15.

33. African National Congress, *Attack, Advance, Give the Enemy No Quarter*, national executive statement, Lusaka, January 8, 1986, p. 12.

34. Anthony Sampson, *Black and Gold: World Capitalism and the Apartheid Crisis* (London: Hodder and Stoughton, 1987), chap. 13.

35. African National Congress, "Strategy and Tactics of the South African Revolution," in Alex La Guma, ed., *Apartheid* (London: Lawrence and Wishart, 1972), p. 197. In its 1969 strategic program the ANC emphasized the possibility of working-class defections from the white minority. Since then, ANC theorists see a much more diverse constellation of class interests within the white community emerging in opposition to apartheid. See, for example, Harold Wolpe, *Race, Class and the Apartheid State* (London: James Currey, 1988).

Tensions and divisions within white politics present opportunities for the ANC to, if not enlist fresh adherents, at least detach certain groups from active complicity with minority rule. ANC thinkers share a perception with many economic analysts that South Africa is in the grip of an endemic economic crisis in which a necessary condition for recovery is radical political reform. Political measures by themselves, though, will be insufficient to eradicate the poverty that is one important source of this crisis. Advocates of radical postapartheid restructuring concede that the surplus that could be appropriated for redistribution through nationalization of industry owned by "monopoly capital" is "quite small" and would not significantly augment the resources that could be directed toward the poor.[36] Extension of public ownership might also disrupt the economy's external linkages; ANC overtures to business leaders suggest a recognition among its leaders that a postapartheid South Africa would have to maintain existing connections with the international capitalist economy. Although prescriptions may differ, these economic preoccupations may supply at least elements of common discourse when the ANC hosts delegations of South African business leaders. At the very least, they share an interest in preserving intact a relatively advanced industrial order.[37]

Finally, perhaps Soviet reluctance and even inability to extend its commitments in the region would help to reinforce the imperative for a strategy of liberation in which the ANC's political standing rather than its military capacity becomes the crucial variable. Here, though, a note of caution is sensible. It is tempting to interpret in recent SACP statements a responsiveness to Soviet *perestroika* thinking that may have a wider audience in the ANC itself, but the Soviet reevaluation of southern

36. Terence Moll, "Macro-economic Policy and Income Distribution in Latin America and South Africa," in John Suckling and Landeg White, eds., *After Apartheid: Renewal of the South African Economy* (London: James Currey, 1988), p. 31.

37. See, for example, Oliver Tambo, "South Africa: Strategic Options for International Companies," address by the president of the African National Congress of South Africa at the Business International Conference, London, May 27, 1987. See also Tambo's remarks on capitalism in House of Commons, Foreign Affairs Committee, "The Situation in South Africa," October 29, 1985, p. 4; and on nationalization in "Notes of a Meeting at Mfuwe Game Lodge, Zambia," September 13, 1985 (summary of exchanges between ANC and South Africa business delegation, in author's possession).

African politics has been conducted at some distance from South African exiles. Soviet and Eastern European support for the ANC is hardly on a scale to be indispensable or even irreplaceable from other sources. In any case, the Soviet Union would gain nothing from reducing the present flow of resources it channels to the ANC. The ANC's difficulties in expanding the scope of military operations do not reflect a shortage of essential supplies but rather the logistical barriers confronting the infiltration of combatants into the Republic and maintaining communications with them thereafter. These are not new problems. But whatever the likely nature of future Soviet military assistance, what is increasingly evident is that a postapartheid administration cannot hope that a decisive injection of Eastern economic aid will underwrite radical structural change.

The ANC Guidelines

Although ANC leaders may currently favor negotiations, there are tight limits to what they may consider to be negotiable. The constitutional "guidelines" drawn up in 1988 after a series of internal seminars in Lusaka are a helpful indication of what these limits might be. The document begins with a preamble that stresses the requirement for "corrective action" to guarantee an irreversible redistribution of wealth and the "opening of facilities" to all. The preamble calls for the protection of individual human rights but argues that the protection of group rights would preserve the existing inequality of property ownership. The twenty-five clauses that follow are divided into sections concerned with the state, franchise, national identity, a bill of rights and affirmative action, the economy, land, workers, women, the family, and international relations. The clauses specify a nonracial form of popular sovereignty based on universal suffrage represented in a central legislature, executive branch, judiciary, and administration. To enhance efficient government and popular participation in decisionmaking, powers should be delegated from the central government to more localized administrative bodies. Judicial, police, and military organs should be popularly representative and democratically structured. The constitution would guarantee "free linguistic and cultural development," the eradication of racial discrimination, the prohibition of racism, fascism, nazism, and ethnic or regional sectionalism; subject to these constraints, it would guarantee freedom of association, thought, worship, and the press. Within the economic sphere, the guidelines prescribe a mixed economy in which "the State shall have the right to determine the general context in which economic life takes place" and in which the private sector "shall be obliged to cooperate with the State in realizing the objectives of the Freedom Charter." Apart from the public and private sectors, the economy should include cooperative and small-scale family enterprises. The state would direct a program of land reform. Workers' trade union rights (including the right to strike) as well as the equality of women would receive constitutional protection.[38]

The papers presented at the seminars out of which the guidelines developed help to illuminate the thinking that informed their drafting. The guidelines and the discussion that produced them envisage a state and society radically different from today's. Popular participation as the defining characteristic of democracy, an electorally accountable judiciary, and the transfer of ownership of productive assets to those with "productive skills" would, taken together, represent a major reallocation of power and resources. But such a reconstruction would also permit a considerable degree of conservation and piecemeal adaptation of existing institutions and social relationships. For example, a paper by Tony O'Dowd, a lawyer in the 1956–61 treason trial, suggested that a large proportion of the existing body of legal doctrine could remain in force, and, indeed, in criminal courts "many present judges could probably remain in office." Albie Sachs, the ANC's most intellectually creative legal theorist, contended that an ANC in power would show some sympathy for those "white farmers with a deep attachment to and love for the land." The guidelines do not include mention of the Freedom Charter's specific commitment to nationalizing the mines, banks, and monopoly industry. The inclusion of a bill of rights represents a fresh interest within the ANC to define appropriate civil liberties, though Albie Sachs did argue that "second generation rights" (health, shelter, nutrition, etc.) should at times take precedence over individual freedoms. The constitutional discussion was based on an extensive review of international models and historical experiences and drew strongly on Anglo-Saxon and more generally Western bourgeois liberal heritages.[39]

38. The guidelines are reprinted in *SA Barometer*, vol. 4 (March 16, 1990).

39. Papers presented at a seminar in Lusaka on March 1–4, 1988, included Albie Sachs, "Towards a Bill of Rights in a Democratic South Africa"; Zola

It is likely that within the ANC the guidelines are viewed as conforming to the most minimal popular expectations of change. Certainly they place the ANC philosophically well to the right of the Black Consciousness movement and its insurgent rival, the Pan-Africanist Congress.[40] With the measure of caution, the degree of qualification, and the eschewal of utopianism in these guidelines, the ANC is taking considerable risks: the congress's moral and political hegemony at the moment extends well beyond the disciplined ranks of its properly organized adherents. Outside its own bureaucratic structures, though, it cannot take for granted that its political ascendancy will endure through the complicated passage of a negotiated transition to power, as the following examination of the ANC as a social movement will make clear.

The ANC as a Social Movement

The ANC today is a tightly constructed bureaucracy, which makes it markedly different from the loose assembly that it was in the 1950s, when it functioned as a legal mass movement. It is a body that has been shaped by the requirements of surviving under conditions of exile outside South Africa and clandestinity within the Republic. I have argued elsewhere that in certain respects it resembles a state more than a political party.[41] For those who join it, the ANC affects a much wider range of their daily experience than is normally true of a political organization. The external ANC maintains an army,

Skweyiya, "Parliamentary and Presidential Systems of Government"; Dan Cindi, "International Relations in Post Apartheid South Africa"; Tony O'Dowd, "The Legal System and Judiciary in South Africa"; and Kader Asmal, "Electoral Reforms: A Critical Survey." See also David Niddrie, "Building on the Freedom Charter," *Work in Progress*, no. 53 (April 1988), pp. 3–6.

40. On the Pan-Africanist Congress, see Harold R. Isaacs, *Struggles within the Struggle: An Inside View of the Pan Africanist Congress of South Africa* (London: Zed Press, 1985); Phil Molefe, "As the PAC Sees It, The New News Is Just the Same as the Old News," *Weekly Mail*, February 9, 1989, p. 6; Cassandra Moodley, "Who's Who of the New Africanist Leaders," *Weekly Mail*, December 8, 1989; and Howard Barrell, "The Outlawed Liberation Movements," in Johnson, ed., *South Africa*, pp. 72–78.

41. Tom Lodge, "State of Exile: the African National Congress of South Africa, 1976–1986," *Third World Quarterly*, vol. 9 (January 1987), pp. 1–27.

administers schools and vocational training, exercises judicial authority over its members, receives quasi-diplomatic recognition from many governments and international agencies, and even has a modest productive base in the farms and workshops it runs in Zambia and Tanzania. Outside South Africa, the ANC probably represents a total of 10,000 to 15,000 people, scattered through as many as twenty-five countries but mainly concentrated in Tanzania, Zambia, and, until 1989, Angola. The largest group of these people form the ranks of the ANC's army, Umkhonto we Sizwe, now in the process of being transported from their former training facilities in Angola to camps in Tanzania. Recruits to the ANC are usually offered a choice, though, of enlisting in the army or furthering their studies at the ANC college in Morogoro, Tanzania. The ANC also claims the adherence of about 1,500 students at universities in Europe and America, some of them recipients of scholarships from the ANC.

The congress has a compartmentalized and complicated hierarchical structure that administers all these activities. Its various departments and divisions are ultimately subject to the authority of a National Executive Committee (NEC), which is elected every five years or so at a general conference (according to the rules instituted at the last of such meetings in 1985). The NEC appoints three leading officials: a president, secretary, and treasurer, whose identities have remained unchanged over the last two or three decades; they, together with about a third of the other NEC members, supply the present ANC with its most manifest historical links with the days when it openly functioned inside South Africa. Only a minority of leading ANC officials have recent experience of political activity inside South Africa.

The ANC, though, does have a strong internal presence within South Africa. It maintains this presence in two ways: through the direct insertion of externally trained cadres to construct an underground political network or to wage insurgent warfare, and by virtue of its role as a central element in popular political culture—partly by the activities of its underground cadres but also through the generation of a powerful historical mythology.

The internal activists are separated into military and political functionaries, each of which are locked into separate chains of command. The soldiers' duties are more publicly obvious; in 1988, they were responsible for about three hundred insurgent attacks, more than half of them limpet mine explosions, principally in the Witwatersrand,

Vaal, and Pretoria areas. The nonmilitary side of the ANC's internal presence is understandably less easy to record or measure. Both ANC people and the police concur that it is much less well developed than the guerrilla agency. ANC literature has stressed the importance of the organization developing a cluster of disciplined adherents in legal mass organizations—trade unions and political bodies such as the UDF. There have also been a few indications of efforts to infiltrate people into the police and the homeland civil services.[42] The guerrillas have regional command structures inside the country that coordinate the activities of three- to five-person cells, but sometimes the lines of communication extend directly from each cell to the command centers located in territories adjacent to South Africa. For example, what the ANC termed "the machinery" for directing guerrilla operations in the North East Transvaal was, at least until 1988, based in Swaziland. In practice, guerrilla units exercise considerable tactical autonomy in the field, and they also distribute weapons (and instructions on how to use them) to groups of sympathizers in the townships.

The second sense in which the ANC constitutes an internal force is in the way in which its moral leadership is accepted by a very large number of people who are not active within or even knowledgeable about its clandestine structures. The brave deeds of Umkhonto guerrillas have excited widespread admiration, especially among young people. The resurfacing in trade unions and legal mass organizations of effective and impressive leaders whose careers date from the ANC-led mobilization of the 1950s has also enhanced the organization's support. But probably as important as either of these factors has been the popular celebration and consumption of resistance history. This process began in the late 1970s and can be linked with both the political awakening of the 1976 uprising and the academic revival of South African historiography that began in Great Britain in the early 1970s and was effectively entrenched in South African universities by the end of the decade.[43]

The ANC is one of a group of related organizations that function

42. Louise Flanagan, "Cadres in the Civil Service," *Work in Progress*, no. 55 (August 1988), pp. 34–37. For earlier examples, see Tom Lodge, "The African National Congress in South Africa, 1976–1983: Guerrilla War and Armed Propaganda," *Journal of Contemporary African Studies*, vol. 3 (April 1984), p. 175.

43. Belinda Bozzoli and Peter Delius, "Radical History and South African Society," *Radical History Review*, nos. 46–47 (Winter 1990), pp. 13–45.

in exile. Its allies include the remnants of the old trade union feder-ation, the South African Congress of Trade Unions (SACTU), which, with the reassertion of political trade unionism inside South Africa, has a function that is increasingly difficult to define. More important is the South African Communist party. All SACP members belong to the ANC, though within the ANC they constitute a minority. How influential a minority they are is subject to academic debate. They certainly have had a profound influence on the ANC's intellectual development in the last twenty years, but they do not monopolize the ANC's ideological discourse. Still, as the only organized political tendency within the ANC, they are in a position to play a more dominant role than independent socialists, noncommunist Marxists, liberals, or conservatives. Their influence is apparent in the forms of internal organization used by the ANC, in much of its printed liter-ature, and in the incorporation into the ANC's strategic program of the SACP's "internal colonialism" analysis of South African society. The SACP sees itself as a vanguard within a vanguard (both orga-nizations use the term) and as the effective guarantor of ultimate working-class hegemony in postrevolutionary South Africa. Not all working-class leaders inside South Africa are comfortable with this assumption; the SACP's generally uncritical depiction of socialist sys-tems in Eastern Europe did call into question for some the validity of what it conceives working-class interests to be.

Like the SACP, the ANC attributes to the working class a "leading role" in the process of national liberation, and its own documents depict the South African struggle as being part of an international historical progression toward the attainment of socialism. The ANC, though, disavows any socialist identity, for its theorists argue that a broad alliance of classes can most effectively oppose apartheid and that not all the constituents of this alliance would find their interests accommodated in a socialist order. The ambiguities in this formulation are astutely exploited by ANC spokespersons, but it is also true that within the ANC, or at least within its leading echelons, there are people with quite different long-term political principles.

In one sense the ANC is a largely external organization, whose disciplined adherents inside the country possibly total about 1,500, but probably number rather less.[44] In another sense, it is a much

44. If each of the nearly three hundred guerrilla attacks during 1989 was carried out by a different five-person unit, then military insurgents would

broader cultural movement, for people who endorse its leadership and sympathize with its activities often see themselves as ANC followers. If they are predisposed toward political activity, they will probably most often express their loyalty to the ANC by participating in the life of those organizations that are affiliated to the series of committees constituted as the United Democratic Front.

The United Democratic Front

The UDF is not merely a legal surrogate for the ANC (which is the way it is portrayed by the South African government). This is not to make the simple legalistic point that it has no discernible organizational connection with the ANC; it is really rather different in character. To be sure there are many connections. When the UDF was set up in 1983 to oppose the tricameral constitution, it borrowed a form that was a favorite ploy of SACP strategists in the 1940s—creating a federal alliance of functional organizations to serve as a political mobilizing agency for constituents who often did not originally have clearly defined political goals. In theory, the UDF claimed to be ideologically heterodox, but in practice, support for the Freedom Charter (or at least acquiescence to it) was a distinguishing characteristic of many of those groups and individuals who participated in its campaigning. Right from the beginning, old congress notables were accorded a conspicuous position at its helm. Its gestation came after antipathy between Black Consciousness supporters and "Charterists" was already strongly institutionalized. At UDF meetings, ANC slogans, symbols, myths, iconography, songs, and flags predominated. ANC leaders would have liked it if the UDF had represented a dependable internal wing of their organization—that is, a legal front in the sense in which the Sinn Fein substitutes for the IRA in Northern Ireland—and this is certainly the role that many UDF activists understood themselves to be playing. Yet such a perception of the UDF's role is misleading.

---

total fifteen hundred. This is unlikely—the attacks tended to be locally concentrated and can probably attributed to relatively few units in each area. Through the 1980s, the development of ANC nonmilitary structures lagged well behind the progress of its internal guerrilla organization and embraced a much smaller group of people.

First of all, because of the UDF's looseness of structure, there is much more room for open expressions of ideological disagreement within its ranks than within the ANC. To be sure, there are certain core components of UDF ideology—and allegiance to the ANC is one of them—but what the ANC represents and how its program can be interpreted vary considerably according to constituency. Within UDF leadership echelons—not just formal elected officeholders but also the intelligentsia who predominate in much of its public discourse— there are discernible tendencies toward the right, the center, and the left. In the right-wing camp can be placed many of the older generation of spokespersons—the churchmen, social notables, and professionals whose voices substituted for organized opposition in the immediate aftermath of the 1976 Soweto uprising. In the center are people whose predisposition is toward the ANC-SACP view of the revolution as being "popular democratic" with a tactically submerged socialist kernel. To the left are those whose prime concern is that the working class be able to exercise its own leadership within any political alliance; within the UDF their voice is muted but still significant.

Aside from the greater variety of ideological discourse in the UDF, there is a difference in the social and intellectual experience that informs the more effective sections of UDF leadership. Many UDF leaders—especially the younger ones—had their political formation in the Black Consciousness movement and brought with them into the UDF a different intellectual heritage from that of the old ANC stalwarts. In certain respects, it was a richer heritage, informed by the existence of a larger indigenous intelligentsia and a political tradition that paid more attention to cultural and philosophical considerations than did the ANC. The UDF was formed in the shadow of a massive and sophisticated trade union movement and borrowed from it much of its organizational code, especially the emphasis on accountable leadership, internal democracy, and constituency-derived mandates. Trade unionists played an important role in constructing the more durable neighborhood affiliates of the UDF.[45] The UDF also drew much of its strength from classroom revolt and dropout unemployment. The schoolchild and youth affiliates probably supplied most of its esti-

45. Jeremy Seekings and Matthew Chaskalson, "Politics in Tumahole, 1984–85," Association of Sociologists of South Africa Conference, Durban, June 30, 1986, paper 59, p. 22.

mated 50,000 activists, and they brought a generational consciousness, a utopian socialism, an antiauthoritarian iconoclasm, and a susceptibility for brutal violence that were quite unprecedented in the culture of black South African political organizations. Throughout the 1984–86 township uprising, the UDF was increasingly pulled along courses determined by this most energetic and volatile of its constituencies.[46]

The occupation of the townships by the South African Defence Force during 1986 did succeed in halting this movement and, for a while, demobilizing some of its following. Fragments of its organizational substructure survive, though, and continue in certain centers to inspire popular loyalty, reactivating themselves as soon as the army presence is withdrawn. Legal restrictions make it difficult for the UDF hierarchy and bureaucracy to function openly. Since 1986, many of the most compelling demonstrations of popular political emotions have been orchestrated and led by trade unionists. COSATU officials are currently playing a conspicuous role in the Defiance Campaign, though the huge numbers participating in stay-aways and marches in even the smaller towns testify to the continuing vitality of community organizations as well as an undiminished culture of self-sacrificial political assertion.

PROSPECTS FOR A NEGOTIATED SETTLEMENT

The ANC's bargaining power in any future negotiations will largely depend on the extent to which its leadership is still unchallenged among politically mobilized workers and youth. These are not constituencies whom the ANC can "deliver" unconditionally. It is true that COSATU trade unionists, after protracted internal debate, now support the Freedom Charter, but according to COSATU leaders, their implicit loyalty to the congress is in the interests of the working class, because only "by . . . locating ourselves in the hub of the struggle

46. Colin Bundy, "Street Sociology and Pavement Politics: Aspects of Youth and Student Resistance in Cape Town, 1985," *Journal of Southern African Studies*, vol. 13, no. 3 (1987); and Shaun Johnson, "The Soldiers of Luthuli: Youth in the Politics of Resistance in South Africa," in Johnson, ed., *South Africa*, pp. 94–152.

for democraticization of society" can workers hope to exert more effective pressure for socialist transformation.[47] Many trade unionists expect wide-ranging nationalization "on the basis of workers' control."[48] Promises of highly visible acts of redistribution, both of economic resources and political power, will be even more necessary in maintaining the ANC's ascendancy among the huge numbers of unemployed young men and women. As with workers, their loyalties are by no means unqualified.[49]

To be sure, South Africa's rulers and the community they represent are a long way from being sufficiently demoralized to countenance the concessions that black leadership needs to secure if it is to negotiate a compromise that will not jeopardize the ANC's popular moral authority. Yet the present political dynamics within the white minority do not suggest a social setting conducive to the patient and enduring acceptance of endless sacrifice as the price of continued political supremacy. As economic problems and political insecurity have persisted, the numbers on whom the government can depend for unquestioning support have greatly diminished. Increasingly the government's own constituency is rooted among people whose support is not governed by any emotional or ideological identification with its policies; a narrow minority of its supporters are English-speaking South Africans among whom the traditional cadences of Afrikaner nationalism have little appeal.[50] Such a constituency is likely

47. Jay Naidoo, "COSATU—The Struggle for Socialism," quoted in Rob Lambert, "Trade Unions, Nationalism and the Socialist Project in South Africa," in Glenn Moss and Ingrid Obery, eds., *South African Review 4* (Johannesburg: Raven Press, 1987), p. 247.

48. Lambert, "Trade Unions, Nationalism and the Socialist Project," p. 247.

49. UDF and ANC anxieties about the difficulties of carrying their youthful constituents into the phase of negotiation politics are testified to in Ivor Powell and Thandeka Gqubele, "Slow Down FW. We Still Have to Educate People," *Weekly Mail,* January 26, 1990.

50. After the 1987 election, Heribert Adam concluded that about half the NP's support came from English speakers. "Observations on the South African Elections," *CSIS Africa Notes*, no. 73 (June 4, 1987). This may have been an overestimation. Rupert Taylor suggests that over half the English-speaking population voted for the Nationalist party in 1989, about 40 percent of its total support. "The South African Election of 1989," in Glenn Moss and Ingrid Obery, eds., *South African Review 5* (Johannesburg: Raven Press, 1989), p. 63.

to be shifting and volatile in its political choices and preferences. The young middle-class recruits to political and administrative office in the next decade are likely to have been deeply affected by the uncertainty and disagreement that have characterized Afrikaner intellectual and cultural life in the last decade.[51] As opinion polls repeatedly demonstrate, there is among middle-class urban whites a steady diminution of support for residential, economic, and educational segregation, and increasing acceptance of the inevitable necessity for negotiations with such leaders as Nelson Mandela.[52]

Of course there remains a considerable gulf separating the meaning of the discourse of reform and negotiation as it is understood within mainstream white politics and what black South Africans would recognize as processes leading toward the creation of a liberated society. This gulf exists even though the conflict is between people who share more elements of a common culture than is often recognized.[53] The

See also H. Pakendorf, "The NP: Challenged by a Changed Support Base," *Africa Insight*, vol. 17, no. 3 (1987), pp. 188–91.

51. This has been evident in a wide range of fields of intellectual activity. The defection from the Nationalist party to the Democrats of the influential Stellenbosch economist, Sampie Terreblanche, is a case in point. For his criticisms of the "structural" inadequacies of the South African economy, the effect of thirty years of growth in "an inappropriate and skewed way," see S. J. Terreblanche, "Anticipating the Future: A Future Economy," paper read at an IDASA (Institute for Democratic Alternatives in South Africa) conference, Port Elizabeth, September 1988. For other examples, see Gerrit Olivier, *Praat met die ANC* (Johannesburg: Taurus, 1985).

52. See "HSRC Poll Says Most People Back Sharing of Power," *Star*, May 17, 1986; "Poll Finds Urban Whites Split on Release of Mandela," *Star*, May 9, 1986; "600,000 Votes for True Democracy. . . . The Problem Is How to Harness Them," *Weekly Mail*, March 25, 1988; Jill Nattrass, "Management on the Political Economy of Change," *Indicator SA* (Durban), vol. 4 (Winter 1986); and Carmel Ricard, "Segregate? Not Even Whites Seem to Care," *Weekly Mail*, May 26, 1990.

53. See Leo Kuper, *An African Bourgeoisie: Race, Class and Politics in South Africa* (Yale University Press, 1975); and Heribert Adam and Kogila Moddley, *South Africa without Apartheid* (University of California Press, 1986), pp. 196–214. Andre Brink has stated: "White Afrikaners and Black Africans . . . have much in common: in both there lingers the memory of a nomadic, agrarian, even peasant past; both of them have been largely shaped by a tribal experience; both know what it means to live with the rhythms and patterns of

Nationalist party's insistence that "group" or racial identity should continue to be the basis for any reformed system of parliamentary representation reflects a defensive ideology of communal survival that is probably the most unifying bond within its social following. Nor are defensive reflexes confined to Nationalists. Even among Democrat politicians there is pronounced hostility to any curtailment of "free enterprise" and a predisposition toward "keeping the role of government as small as possible." In this view, the most minimal extensions of the welfare state should await the establishment of vigorous free market–generated growth.[54] Free market ideologues excitedly project to wistful audiences a vision of democratization that will impose on whites no material sacrifices at all; indeed, they imply, if anything, even in the short term democracy will make whites wealthier.[55] There are exceptions to this prevalent escapism in liberal thinking. Some Afrikaner Democrats and reformist economists at Afrikaans-language universities believe that massive social investment in black education, transport, housing, and public health should come first and will itself help to generate the necessary conditions for a growth rate outpacing the tide of demographic expansion. In this thinking, a strong and centralized administration is an indispensable corollary.[56] New Afrikaner social democracy springs from a community whose prosperity is largely derived from a benevolent and potent state. Mainstream liberal emphasis is instead on reducing the state's economic and social domain. This view is carried over into the constitutional field with prescriptions of federalism that reflect reluctance to accept the implications of black enfranchisement. More generally, though opinion

---

Africa; both have been conscientisized by a struggle for freedom and independence." "Afrikaners and Change," paper read at the Smithsonian Institution, February 8, 1988. For a view that emphasizes cultural differences and oppositions, see Rian Malan, *My Traitor's Heart* (New York: Atlantic Monthly Press, 1990).

54. Interview, Zan de Beer, *Monitor*, July 1989, p. 29.

55. Clem Sunter, *The World and South Africa in the 1990s* (Pretoria and Cape Town: Human and Rousseau, Tafelberg, 1987), pp. 88–111; and Leon Louw and Frances Kendall, *After Apartheid: The Solution for South Africa* (Bisho, The Ciskei: Amagi Publishers, 1987).

56. See Pieter Le Roux, "The Economics of Conflict and Negotiation," in Peter Berger and Bobby Godsell, eds., *A Future South Africa* (Pretoria and Cape Town: Human and Rousseau, Tafelberg, 1988), pp. 200–39.

polls may express diminished white commitment to social segregation and even recognition of Nelson Mandela's personal stature, they do not yet show substantial resignation to the ultimate accession of a predominantly black government.

South African political culture demonstrates the features of a social and economic order under extreme pressure. Certainly the economic growth of the 1960s played a role in bringing about some of the sociological developments that have contributed to these trends— social differentiation within the Afrikaans community, for example, or the empowerment of black trade unions that has been so important in making black opposition effective and visible. But the fluidity and divisiveness of white politics reflect an ideological crisis that at least in part stems from economic recession. A restoration of economic prosperity would probably help to reconstruct political consensus within the white community. It would enable the government to maintain white (and some black) living standards and at the same time fulfill the level of security provision (at the moment it is being forced into choices between the two).

Conversely, a continued deterioration in South Africa's international economic relationships will reinforce and even quicken the cycle of black communal unrest and impose increasingly heavy economic burdens on whites. It can be predicted to magnify opposition to the government within the white community. The government will probably try to expand its support base among its traditional liberal opponents as well as among more or less conservative black politicians; under economic recession, it cannot restore the well-being of its forsaken white working-class constituency. This redefinition of its constituency is likely to enhance the position of those within the (increasingly divided) bureaucracy who argue in favor of a negotiated political settlement as the only instrument through which to secure economic resilience. It is difficult to perceive comparable sources of compulsion toward a negotiated resolution in a situation in which the state presides over a stable economy. Inasmuch as economic sanctions contribute to this political fluidity within the state and its immediate beneficiaries, they should be seen as an indispensable component of any strategy for South Africa's liberation from minority rule.

Progression toward a negotiated settlement is not inevitable, nor is it likely to be rapid. The degeneration of the economy will probably be a halting decline rather than an accelerating collapse, and most whites can reasonably expect to be sheltered from its more serious consequences for several years to come.[57] Among the uncertainties that could affect the duration of the conflict and its outcome are the idiosyncrasies of key decisionmakers, the loyalty to the government of sections of the bureaucracy, the volatility of the white electorate, and the ability of the ANC and its allies to maintain their popular support within their black constituency while offering the concessions required to win legitimacy or at least acquiescence among whites. External actors may help to make the road easier with a carefully calculated mixture of threats, inducements, and penalties. Threats and penalties in particular can be more effectively directed at the South African government than at its opponents; small as the scope here is for effective leverage, it is greater than any that foreign powers can exercise over the ANC or comparable forces in the arena of black politics. Effective deployment of external pressure, though, will require consistency and commitment that may be difficult to maintain.

GENERAL IMPLICATIONS

What are the implications arising from this South African case study for a more general discussion of conflict resolution in Africa? It has to be conceded that in certain respects the South African conflict is exceptional. At least within South Africa's borders, it is one in which warfare plays a subsidiary role to other forms of insurgency and revolt. The main arenas of conflict are urban rather than rural. The South African state as well as the national economy is unusually resilient and possibly less susceptible to external pressure than other African political economies. Perhaps more than any other confrontation in Africa, the South African struggle concerns political and

---

57. Whites have the political means to defend themselves from the worst effects of economic decline. The white share of unemployment is disproportionately small. Whites are affected by rising interest rates, foreign exchange shortages, restrictions on luxury consumption, and the deterioration of public services, but these represent a different order of deprivation from that of blacks.

economic issues that are still widely perceived by both sides to be essential to their own well-being. Nevertheless, the South African experience should not be excluded from any general consideration of African conflict, chiefly because the efforts by South Africa's rulers to defend racial privilege extend well beyond South Africa's borders, stunting the economic development of the southern African region and vastly enlarging the destructive scope of civil wars in Angola and Mozambique.

Looking beyond the region, though, one can draw lessons from this South African study that may be useful in analyzing conflicts throughout the continent. First, even in a country as relatively rich and strategically important as South Africa, the prime concerns of the great powers are largely political, relating to the safeguarding of their foreign relations with other countries, their prestige or status in the Third World, and, in the case of the United States, the government's command of domestic electoral support or the achievement of a bipartisan foreign policy over a range of different areas. Of the medium-level powers, Great Britain remains important in the region. Because of the relative importance of its economic links with South Africa, its membership in the Commonwealth, and the existence of about 800,000 potential British citizens in the Republic, Great Britain has a stronger interest than the United States or the Soviet Union in facilitating a peaceful settlement in South Africa. But the same generalization that is valid for the southern African policies of the superpowers applies to Great Britain. There are important concerns involved, but they are not always considered by policymakers to be of fundamental or vital significance. They do not suggest an array of motivations that could inspire policies backed by a heavy commitment of resources. If that is true in regard to southern Africa, can one expect a more profound engagement of great powers in other African conflicts?

Moreover, even if great powers are successful in their efforts to induce or coerce the contending parties to agree on the conditions for a transfer of political authority, the prospects for an enduring peace will be fragile. In South Africa, at the very least whites will expect security of livelihoods—jobs and pensions, as well as the maintenance of fairly high standards of health care and education. The state currently employs, directly or indirectly through publicly owned corporations, nearly a third of the white work force. While the state may have to continue to underwrite white prosperity, it will also be under massive popular pressure to finance schemes for land reform and rural development, expand the ranks of the bureaucracy to absorb unemployed black dropouts, and make rapid and visible improvements to township schools and housing. Under the most optimistic scenario, a proportion of the resources for these initiatives could come from cutbacks in defense expenditure, and the private sector could be prompted to devote more funds to black housing. All the same, however, it is difficult to see a politically viable program of socioeconomic reconstruction being funded from internal resources alone. That would be especially difficult if the successor administration inherits the foreign indebtedness of the present one. Great powers (and especially Western ones) may have a more important role to play in sustaining peace than in bringing it about. But their willingness and ability to commit resources on a sufficient scale seem at present very questionable.

A final problem concerns great power policies on African conflict resolution. This chapter has suggested a historical process in which the principal determinants of a negotiated political transition are internal. Both sides have to reach the point of recognizing that unilateral victory is impossible but that substantial gains or concessions can be extracted from a negotiated compromise. A rough parity of power will facilitate this recognition. The leadership of the black opposition forces will have the tremendously difficult task of reconciling the expectations that will be generated by high levels of mass mobilization (the principal source of black leverage) with popular acceptance of the need for a postapartheid state to sanction a continuing degree of de facto racial inequality.[58] As for today's ruling group, economic degeneration and white political divisions will help to reduce the resources available to the state. Exchanging political monopolies

---

58. South African economic inequalities remain the highest of any in the fifty-seven countries in the world for which data are available. Francis Wilson and Mamphela Ramphele, *Uprooting Poverty: The South African Challenge* (Norton, 1989), pp. 16–26. A majoritarian administration that accedes to power through negotiations may alleviate black poverty to a modest degree through more progressive taxation and the redistribution of land, but major political barriers will confront the redeployment of public expenditure in favor of the poor.

for social and economic safeguards may in time become a more compelling option for white politicians. But both economic decline and political fragmentation are slow processes that may take several years to work themselves through. White demoralization and ideological disaffection are especially crucial given the state's virtual monopoly of coercive resources, which are likely to remain institutionally intact even at the point of administrative transition. What is subject to change is the will to use them to their fullest extent. Foreign policymakers tend to make short-term judgments about the efficacy of measures directed at promoting change; sanctions are a case in point. Great power policies, to be politically effective, need to appear to be consistent in the long term. Sharp shifts in such policies, even shifts that are largely rhetorical, undermine their credibility and effect.

The South African experience suggests that the resolution of conflict requires profound alterations in the social, economic, and ideological conditions that affect political perceptions on both sides. Many of the analyses that address ways of democratizing South Africa concern themselves with the design of constitutional formulas rather than the investigation of what needs to happen before one group can be persuaded to renounce power and another to lay claim to something less than total victory. Indeed, both sets of protagonists will be hampered rather than aided by too precisely delimited a blueprint; more than ever before, in coming to a settlement, leaders must use the language of ambiguity to address each other and simultaneously reassure their respective constituencies. Leaders may influence their supporters, but in the final analysis they have to represent them; one of the surprising features of South African politics is the extent to which political authority still rests on popular sanction, with whites as much as blacks. Here, surely, are lessons that are widely applicable. Generally, prescriptions for African conflict resolution must be sensitive to changes in the political cultures and political economies within which leaders function. Policymakers who dispense with historical and sociological analysis are unlikely to make lasting contributions to the construction of a peaceful political order.

The general conclusions that can be derived from this case study may seem extremely pessimistic for those concerned with the design of more constructive and effective African policies for the great powers. In South Africa at least, conflict arises from historically determined competition over the allocation of resources and power; it is difficult to conceive of a resolution in which no one loses. Conflict does not arise from delusion or misunderstanding; the problem is not one that can be resolved merely through better communication. To contribute decisively and constructively, third parties must be more than diplomatic brokers; they must make significant material commitments. The prospects of this happening are unlikely in a context in which African affairs are increasingly perceived to be of marginal significance to the strategic and economic preoccupations of the dominant world powers.

POSTSCRIPT

Since this essay was written, the prospects for a negotiated democratization of South African politics look much brighter. The release of Nelson Mandela, the unbanning of the ANC and other prohibited organizations, the ANC's suspension of guerrilla hostilities, and the onset of constitutional discussions between its leaders and members of the de Klerk administration—all are developments that seem to reflect swifter and more powerful compulsions toward reconciliation than are suggested by this chapter's emphasis on gradual economic decline and internal political fragmentation.

In 1989, Namibian independence and the upsurge of township revolt represented important setbacks for opponents of negotiation within the government. The general election results, Conservative party gains notwithstanding, may have helped to convince President de Klerk and his colleagues that a majority of whites favored political reforms that would lead to African participation in central government. Shifts in American regional policy in the final year of the Reagan presidency may have encouraged this recognition,[59] though sharp deteriorations

59. Pauline Baker argues that in the final year of the Reagan administration, Assistant Secretary of State Chester Crocker was partly responsible for a "major failure in South African (regional) strategy," turning a blind eye to the escalation of the Cubans' military role in Angola after realizing that "South Africa's military attacks on its neighbours went well beyond the needs of

during 1989 in the levels of foreign exchange reserves and the state's fiscal resources probably made more important contributions to the decision to talk with the ANC.

If willingness to parley is more evident today than it was a year ago, the task for leaders on both sides in maintaining their followers' support for the politics of compromise remains formidable. For the government, the retention of existing patterns of ownership in the industrial economy as well as collective safeguards for whites are likely to be the essential issues in the bargaining to come. To date, President de Klerk professes in public to view negotiation as a path toward sharing power, not yielding it. The ANC, meanwhile, understands negotiations as the means through which political authority will be transferred to an administration representing the majority. For the ANC, making concessions that allow the preservation of white "group" rights or private control of mining industry would alienate a significant number of its supporters as well as open up divisions in its leadership. Naturally, in adopting such a course, it may win fresh adherents in the "middle ground" of South African politics that is quickly opening up; that may compensate for any losses of popular support to the ANC's competitors on the left. In any case, neither the ANC nor its more radical rivals today command the strength and resources needed to dictate terms of surrender to President de Klerk.

The prospect of a relatively rapid and fairly peaceful accession to political office might make constitutional concessions of a symbolic or transitional character seem acceptable to black politicians. Government proposals are likely to feature a two-chamber parliament, in which an upper house would be composed of communal or racial representatives with limited veto powers and a lower house would be elected through a common-roll universal suffrage. A postapartheid administration whose program was subjected to constitutionally entrenched vetoes of this nature might find it difficult to expand the state's role in the economy. Most black leaders to the left of Chief Mongosuthu Buthelezi believe that a degree of state intervention would be a necessary precondition for reducing poverty. Such a resolution

legitimate defense." Pauline H. Baker, *The United States and South Africa: The Reagan Years*, South Africa Update Series, Ford Foundation (New York: Foreign Policy Association, 1989), p. 71.

of South Africa's conflict would at best be incomplete: political de-mocratization without economic redistribution will merely redefine the lines of social fission in South Africa, not eliminate them. Perhaps, though, that is the best one can hope for. Socioeconomic inequalities as profound as those that exist in South Africa are unlikely to be significantly alleviated through constitutional bargaining, diplomatic maneuvering, and political finesse.

PART 3
The Contextual Analysis of Conflict

Chapter 6

TED ROBERT GURR

Theories of Political Violence and Revolution in the Third World

Since the 1960s, the countries of Africa south of the Maghreb have been wracked by more deadly conflict than any other world region except Southeast Asia. Consider some of the evidence:

—Since 1960, 18 full-fledged civil wars have been fought in Africa, in addition to the protracted proto-revolutionary conflict in South Africa.[1]

—Nearly one-third of all overt military interventions between 1960 and 1985 (53 out of 171) were targeted at African countries. Contrary to common wisdom, 55 of the 81 interveners were other African states, compared with 16 interventions by former colonial powers.[2]

—Eleven genocides and politicides occurred in Africa between 1960 and the late 1980s, compared with 24 elsewhere in the world. The mass murders perpetrated in Uganda during Idi Amin's reign and the killing of civilians in southern Sudan during the first phase of the civil war were the most deadly of the African episodes that, in the aggregate, claimed between 500,000 and 1,700,000 civilian lives.[3]

1. Eight African civil wars are recorded for 1960–80 in Melvin Small and J. David Singer, *Resort to Arms: International and Civil Wars, 1816–1980* (Beverly Hills, Calif.: Sage Publications, 1982), pp. 231–32. By my count ten others occurred in the next decade (through 1990). This and the following comparisons include all of continental Africa and its offshore islands with the exception of Morocco, Algeria, Tunisia, Libya, and Egypt.

2. My tabulations are from Herbert K. Tillema, "Foreign Overt Military Intervention in the Nuclear Age," *Journal of Peace Research*, vol. 26, no. 2 (1989), pp. 192–95. Some of the interventions had multiple interveners, so their number exceeds the number of interventions. South Africa, which participated in five of the interventions, is counted as an African state.

3. From Barbara Harff and Ted Robert Gurr, "Toward an Empirical Theory of Genocides and Politicides: Identification and Measurement of Cases since 1945," *International Studies Quarterly*, vol. 32, no. 3 (1988), pp. 359–71.

—At the beginning of 1990 more than 2.5 percent of all Africans were refugees, most of them fleeing from political violence. These included 4.7 million Africans in need of assistance outside their home countries and another 8.6 million internally displaced people—altogether 43 percent of the global population of refugees.[4]

—The worst may be yet to come. In a recent global survey of minorities at risk of involvement in future conflict, and at risk of victimization, James R. Scarritt and I identified 72 such communal groups in Africa. In the aggregate they make up about 45 percent of the total regional population, a proportion far higher than in any other world region.[5]

In his introductory remarks to the Conference on Conflict Resolution in Africa, General Olusegun Obasanjo observed that, although managing and solving African problems is an African responsibility, understanding the root causes of civil conflict in Africa is a task to which outside observers can contribute. The difficulty, in my view, is that Western scholars' theoretical explanations of violent conflict in the Third World and their models for management of regional conflict make little use of African evidence. As a consequence, their relevance for African analysts and practitioners remains to be demonstrated. Prevailing explanations and prescriptions tend to reflect Western assumptions about human nature, the nature of society and polity, and the inherent possibility and desirability of constructing and testing valid general theories of social phenomena. Such theories may be useful in providing a sense of understanding to Western-trained scholars, journalists, policymakers, and others confronted with chaotic and deadly political happenings, but whether they are meaningful and similarly useful in an African cultural context is more problematic.

There are two basic positions on how one should go about understanding violent conflict within African societies. One is to apply directly

4. My tabulations from *World Refugee Survey: 1989 in Review* (Washington: U.S. Committee for Refugees, 1990), pp. 30–32

5. Ted Robert Gurr and James R. Scarritt, "Minorities Rights at Risk: A Global Survey," *Human Rights Quarterly*, vol. 11 (August 1989), pp. 375–405. The same criteria were used to identify minorities at risk throughout the world. Twenty-eight of the thirty-six African societies in the survey have at least one such group.

the theories and techniques of Western social science. Otwin Marenin, commenting on an earlier version of this chapter, makes the point succinctly: "A theory by definition starts out universalistic, true for all cases. There can be a distinct 'African theory' of conflict only if particular variations in the general variables of the theory occur systematically in Africa. But then you still have a general and not an African theory because the same distinctive pattern of variation could be found elsewhere." This position is reflected in a number of studies. René Lemarchand's comparative analysis of Rwanda and Zanzibar made sophisticated use of the analytic concepts available some twenty years ago for the study of revolution, arguing that events in these societies could be interpreted using Western theories of revolution.[6] Pamela Ann Arthur has interpreted the process and political outcomes of the Ethiopian Revolution as an example of "revolution from above."[7] And when Marxist scholars analyze conflict in African societies, they tend to look for the economic class relationships that, it is assumed, underlie the "false consciousness" of ethnic and racial identifications.[8]

The opposing argument is that African societies have distinctive features that are not taken into account by supposedly universalistic theories. The most extreme version of this argument, sometimes voiced by historians and area specialists, is that there can be no valid general

6. René Lemarchand, "Revolutionary Phenomena in Stratified Societies: Rwanda and Zanzibar," *Civilisations*, vol. 18, no. 1 (1968), pp. 1–34.

7. Pamela Ann Arthur, "The Ethiopian Revolution: A Revolution from Above and Its Outcomes," Ph.D. dissertation, Northwestern University, 1982. The theory of "revolution from above" was developed by Ellen Kay Trimberger, *Revolution from Above: Military Bureaucrats and Development in Japan, Turkey, Egypt and Peru* (New Brunswick, N.J.: Transaction Books, 1978). Similarly, many empiricists who study the causes of coups d'état assume that military interventions in Africa can be explained by the same kinds of theories that account for coups elsewhere in the Third World.

8. A comparative study that uses Marxist concepts but breaks away from narrow economic determinism is Stanley Greenberg, *Race and State in Capitalist Development* (Yale University Press, 1980), an examination of the changing class alignments underlying the racial orders of South Africa and three capitalist societies in the Northern hemisphere. Unlike some Marxists, Greenberg does not try to explain away race and racism as an expression of underlying economic relations; rather, he looks at the ways in which economic classes and the state use race in the service of class interests.

theories of conflict: riots and rebellions, whether in Africa or else-where, can be understood only in their own immediate context. The more moderate position recognizes that general concepts and theories are necessary to help interpret particular cases, but also questions whether prevailing theories do in fact include variables and concepts that fit African realities. The Marxian concept of class, for example, is an inadequate tool for the description of social relations in most of rural Africa. More directly relevant to conflict analysis is the question of the cultural evaluation of political conflict and violence. E. V. Wal-ter's study of the political uses of violence in precolonial African societies suggests that some rulers practiced, and their subjects tol-erated, much higher levels of personal violence than those prevalent in most contemporary societies.[9] Ada Bozeman makes the contro-versial argument that modern Western concepts of conflict do not apply in Africa, because peace is not a preferred fundamental value and neither war nor rebellion is feared as the worst of conditions.[10] Whether or not Walter and Bozeman are correct—Walter's interpre-tations seem to have been accepted, whereas Bozeman's views have been sharply criticized—their observations have one clear implication: the applicability of conflict theories to African cases depends on whether they allow for, or specify the consequences of, differences in cultural orientations toward conflict and violence.

It may seem safer, in the face of concerns about the cultural deter-minants of meaning and action, to limit the analysis of episodes of political violence in Africa to description and interpretation that make only cautious use of a few concepts and categories from Western social science. In fact much of the literature on violent conflict in Africa is precisely of this sort: case and comparative studies that neither test nor use general theories and limit their generalizations to African cases. An example is Robert Rotberg's edited volume, which consists of comparative studies of local rebellions against colonial rule.[11] An-other example is Crawford Young's comparative analysis of the ori-

9. E. V. Walter, *Terror and Resistance: A Study of Political Violence* (New York: Oxford University Press, 1969).

10. Ada B. Bozeman, *Conflict in Africa: Concepts and Realities* (Princeton University Press, 1971).

11. Robert I. Rotberg, ed., *Rebellion in Black Africa* (London: Oxford Uni-versity Press, 1971).

gins and consequences of contemporary secessionist movements in Katanga, Biafra, and Eritrea.[12]

EXPLAINING CONFLICT IN AN AFRICAN CONTEXT

In the spirit of Francis Deng and I. William Zartman's introduction to this volume, I assume that the truth lies in between: that general theories of violence and revolution are in principle relevant to African cases, but only insofar as they incorporate whatever concepts and variables are needed to make sense of distinctly African conditions. What may be assumed constant in other world cultural settings is not necessarily constant in Africa, and vice versa. One example concerns the relative significance of class and ethnicity as sources of group mobilization and conflict. It cannot be assumed a priori that African conflict occurs mainly along lines of communal or ethnic cleavage, even when opposing groups invoke communal symbols, any more than it can be assumed that communally based conflict is concealed class conflict. It should be an open question, which is to say an empirical question, whether conflict derives from communal identifications, economic interests, political associations, or some combination thereof. The task for theory that is relevant in an African context is to specify the circumstances in which different sources of group formation and intergroup hostility are most important, and how they affect the processes and outcomes of conflict.

A second example concerns the context in which conflict occurs. Modern Africa, more than any other world region, is afflicted by material scarcity and economic stagnation, whereas most theories of civil conflict and conflict management assume that societies have slack resources that efficient governments can mobilize to deal with social problems, demands, and threats, both internal and external. Political violence can be forestalled or suppressed only if governments make effective use of their authority to reallocate and deploy resources. In

12. Crawford Young, "Comparative Claims to Political Sovereignty: Biafra, Katanga, Eritrea." In Donald Rothchild and Victor A. Olorunsola, eds., *State Versus Ethnic Claims: African Policy Dilemmas* (Boulder, Colo.: Westview Press, 1983), pp. 199–232.

Theda Skocpol's influential theory of social revolution, for example, the first structural requisite of revolution is the resistance of the traditional land-owning class to reforms through which the state might tap those slack resources and use them to deal with crises. In most of contemporary Africa there are no such classes and few slack resources.[13] Rather, conflict takes on the characteristics of a negative-sum game in which each party must fight to defend its share of a shrinking pie against increasingly forceful challenges from other groups. In such societies there are strong tendencies toward increasing and entrenched inequalities, intensified conflict, and reliance on authoritarian forms of political organization as a means of protecting existing patterns of distribution and controlling conflict.[14]

Another set of considerations distinctive to Africa concerns the nature of its national political institutions. It has become a commonplace to say that most of Africa's new states are institutionally weak and dominated by the personalistic rule of autocrats. They are "soft states," limited in their control over society, constrained by the unavailability of human and fiscal resources, and pressured by domestic and international demands.[15] In a number of theories of internal con-

---

13. Theda Skocpol, *States and Social Revolution: A Comparative Analysis of France, Russia, and China* (New York: Cambridge University Press, 1979). She does not claim that her theory is universally applicable, only that it accounts for the French, Russian, and Chinese revolutions and possibly a few others. Nonetheless, Skocpol and others have commented on its applicability to other cases: see for example Theda Skocpol, "Rentier State and Shi'a Islam in the Iranian Revolution," *Theory and Society*, vol. 11 (1982), pp. 256–83; and Michael Burawoy, "State and Social Revolution in South Africa: Reflections on the Comparative Perspectives of Greenberg and Skocpol," *Kapitalstaat*, vol. 9 (1981), pp. 93–122.

14. I develop this argument at length in "On the Political Consequences of Scarcity and Economic Decline," *International Studies Quarterly*, vol. 29 (March 1985), pp. 51–75.

15. Early statements of this interpretation were Aristide R. Zolberg, *Creating Political Order: The Party-States of West Africa* (Rand-McNally, 1966), and "The Structure of Political Conflict in the New States of Tropical Africa," *American Political Science Review*, vol. 62 (March 1968), pp. 70–87. It has since been amplified and modified in many writings, for example by Robert H. Jackson and Carl G. Rosberg, "Why Africa's Weak States Persist: The Empirical and Juridical in Statehood," *World State and Nation in the Third World:*

flict, such weakness on the part of regimes is said to be strongly linked to widespread, often revolutionary political conflict.[16] These theories might lead us to expect higher levels of political violence than have in fact occurred in most African countries. What theorists should take into account is that "weakness" is a relative concept, relative both to the strength of competing groups and relative to the cultural context. Samuel Huntington has argued that a key indicator of a government's institutionalization (hence its strength) is its adaptability.[17] In fact, for thirty years the governments of postindependence Africa have proved remarkably resilient in maintaining national independence, forestalling successful movements, and avoiding challenges by mass revolutionary movements. Robert Jackson and Carl Rosberg attribute the persistence of African states in the face of this "instability" to the existence of regional organizations that "have served as 'post-imperial ordering devices' for the new African states, in effect freezing them in their inherited colonial jurisdictions and blocking any post-independence movements toward self-determination."[18] Part of their effectiveness might also be credited to the success of autocrats in building mass parties that serve simultaneously as channels of participation, means of upward mobility, and instruments of political control. Coups have been numerous, but most of them have been the outcome of conflicts within the new elite and have seldom led to widespread violence or to fundamental institutional changes.

Other Western conceptions of regime strength emphasize the state's capacity to extract resources from society and reallocate those resources. David Abernethy's study of government growth shows that the rate of increase in government consumption in African states in

---

The Western State and African Nationalism (St. Martin's Press, 1983). The concept of the "soft state" is applied to Africa in the introduction to Rothchild and Olorunsola, *State versus Ethnic Claims*, pp. 7–9.

16. For variations on this theme see Samuel Huntington, *Political Order in Changing Societies* (Yale University Press, 1968), chaps. 4 and 5; Ted Robert Gurr, *Why Men Rebel* (Princeton University Press, 1970), chap. 9; Charles Tilly, *From Mobilization to Revolution* (Reading, Mass.: Addison-Wesley, 1978), chap. 4; and Skocpol, *States and Social Revolutions*, passim.

17. Huntington, *Political Order in Changing Societies*, chap. 4.

18. Jackson and Rosberg, "Why Africa's Weak States Persist," p. 21. Young, "Comparative Claims to Political Sovereignty," offers a similar interpretation for the failure of secessionist rebellions.

comparison to private consumption from 1970 to 1977 was the highest among the world regions, and that the absolute growth of government consumption from 1960 to 1977 was second only to that of the oil-wealthy Middle Eastern countries. Moreover, the average wage of African civil servants about 1980 was six times that of gross domestic product (GDP) per capita, more than twice the ratio in Asian and Latin American countries.[19] Thus the general picture is one of African governments that are markedly effective in extracting surplus from poor economies and in using it to maintain themselves and the state apparatus. These are not the hallmarks of "weak regimes." Yet they could be argued to be the source of illegitimacy. Given Western political values, the extraordinary privileges of most African rulers and bureaucrats and their use of state power for private gain would be regarded as prima facie evidence of illegitimacy and a potent incentive for political challenges. In practice, resentment seems largely confined to less-advantaged members of the elite—especially younger, university-trained people who have assimilated Western political values that condemn corruption and who themselves have higher personal ambitions.[20]

One could make a counterargument that the concentration of wealth, privilege, and "corruption" in government in the African context can help build support for the state rather than undermine it. In societies in which the private economy provides relatively little wealth or status, government positions are much sought after by ambitious people. If the paths to opportunity are not blocked by class or communal barriers, these people are likely to devote their energies to obtaining the educational and political credentials needed for governmental posts. This means working within and for the system, not against it. Such arrangements should contribute to political stability, provided that the majority of the population, which has no prospect of benefiting from office, acquiesces to them. This in turn depends partly on acceptance of personalistic, autocratic rule that may often seem harsh

19. David B. Abernethy, "Bureaucratic Growth and Economic Stagnation in Sub Saharan Africa," paper read at the Annual Meeting of the American Political Science Association, Washington, D.C., 1984, pp. 8–9.

20. A case study of the making of the "Ghanaian culture of political corruption" is Victor T. LeVine, *Political Corruption: The Ghana Case* (Stanford, Calif.: Hoover Institution Press, 1975).

and capricious, and tolerance for inequalities based on the possession of authority rather than competence in its exercise. This does not imply that Africans have a greater tolerance than people elsewhere for regimes and rulers that they regard as illegitimate. Rather, many Africans have different criteria by which they judge legitimacy than those which prevail in Western polities and theories of political conflict.

Thus far the principal threat to autocratic and self-serving rulers in new African states has come when ambitious potential members of the elite find, or perceive, that their opportunities are threatened by discrimination based on their communal or class origins. By this interpretation, the Ethiopian Revolution of 1974 took place because a traditional leader was not responsive enough to the demands of an increasingly well-educated and vocal segment of the elite who demanded different policies and greater political access. The origins and persistence of the rebellion in Eritrea also are due in significant part to the castelike character of rule by Amhara (and assimilated Oromo) elites under the old imperial regime and the revolutionary Derg. The rebellion at first was led by Eritrean Muslims, who were almost completely excluded from regional politics after Eritrea's reluctant union in 1952 with the empire. The same kind of exclusionary policies eventually alienated most of the Christian Eritrean elite as well, pushing them into coalition with Muslims. The rebellion that began in the Tigre province in the mid-1970s had the same genesis: resentment by Tigrean students, and more traditional leaders, about their lack of access to power in the regional or central governments.[21]

Access to power for ethnic or regional elites provides no guarantees against instability. Many African governments are controlled by an unstable multiethnic coalition—a pattern that exists in quasi-democratic countries like Kenya and Nigeria, in countries governed by a single party like Guinea and Zambia, and in military-ruled countries like Benin. Leaders of specific ethnic groups move in and out of such coalitions. Any present coalition member who was in opposition in

21. On Eritrea, see Haggai Erlich, *The Struggle Over Eritrea, 1962–1978: War and Revolution in the Horn of Africa* (Stanford, Calif.: Hoover Institution Press, 1983). For a general assessment of the Ethiopian revolution and of regional rebellions, see Christopher Clapman, *Transformation and Continuity in Revolutionary Ethiopia* (Cambridge: Cambridge University Press, 1988).

the past will probably be suspected by others of having oppositional tendencies and, along with his followers, may as a consequence be subject to discriminatory treatment. Similarly, any coalition member who leaves or is forced out risks political repression and restricted political opportunities for others in his group. These are the kinds of circumstances that intensify communal hostilities and increase the risk of riots, plots, and rebellions.[22]

WHAT IS TO BE EXPLAINED: MAGNITUDES OR EVENTS?

More general theories of conflict and the findings of empirical research provide one possible basis for understanding collective political action and violence in African societies. The quantitative comparative approach to conflict uses aggregate national data to test explanations of why properties of conflict, such as "magnitude of political violence" or "deaths from domestic group conflict," vary among countries and across time. These properties of conflict are measured using information drawn from journalistic and other sources for each country during a specified time span. The independent or causal variables are those identified in a set of hypotheses, sometimes formalized in a "model," a set of linked equations. In cross-sectional analysis, which is more common, the test of the argument is whether the measured properties—conflict and its causes—are significantly correlated across the countries studied. One can compare the results for different subgroups of countries. An example is my study of the correlates of political violence in the early 1960s. For all 119 countries in the study I found that the level of economic development (per capita GDP) did not correlate significantly with total magnitude of violence. The size of the public sector (government revenues as a percent of GDP), however, was negatively correlated with violence (partial $r = -0.39$). In other words, governments that commanded a substantial portion of national resources experienced fewer violent political challenges. In a separate analysis of 29 African countries, I found essentially the same result: the size of the public sector correlated -0.38 with violence.

22. This is James Scarritt's argument, developed in Gurr and Scarritt, "Minorities Rights at Risk," pp. 387–88.

But the effects of economic development were strikingly different than in the global analysis: the more developed an African country, the greater its magnitude of violence (partial $r = 0.57$).[23]

The positive relation between political violence and economic development in Africa in the 1960s demonstrates that there are empirical as well as theoretical reasons for expecting the dynamics of African conflict to be different from those in other world regions. But it does not necessarily require a uniquely African explanation. There is a general argument to the effect that the early stages of Western-style economic development cause rapid social change and instability, whereas at higher levels of development continued growth has a stabilizing effect. Since most African countries were near the beginnings of the "development" process in the 1960s, this would account for the observed relationship. It also implies that the relation over time between development and political violence in each country should be curvilinear, not linear: at some point in development a threshold is reached beyond which violent conflict tends to decline. Such thresholds may occur at different levels, depending on the country. If ethnic and class inequalities are relatively low, as they appear to be in Tanzania and Malawi, for example, then their developmental threshold of political stability may be far lower than in more prosperous countries like Kenya and South Africa, where there are sharp inequalities across class and ethnic divisions.

This kind of relationship should ideally be tested using a "longitudinal" research design, in which time-series data on two or more indicators, usually collected annually, are correlated to determine how closely they vary over time within a given country. What is lost in generality is gained in specificity: the results, if statistically significant, suggest that changes in one variable cause changes in the other in each of the countries studied. If the positive relationship observed between economic development and violence in African countries in the early 1960s reflects a general causal relationship rather than the

---

23. These findings are from Ted Gurr and Charles Ruttenberg, *The Conditions of Civil Violence: First Tests of a Causal Model*, Research Monograph 28 (Princeton, N.J.: Center of International Studies, April 1967), table 6. The partial correlations are from best-fit multiple regression analyses, which were done for all countries in the study and a number of alternative subgroupings of them.

special circumstances of that period, longitudinal studies that correlate annual measures of per capita income and political violence for each country should show positive results. I do not know of any published studies of conflict in Africa using this kind of research design, probably because few African states have been independent long enough to provide sufficient annual "cases" for time-series analysis: thirty to forty data points are a practical minimum for most kinds of longitudinal analysis.

Another way to test for time-dependent effects is to repeat cross-sectional analyses for several different periods. The question is whether relationships observed at one period are the same at a later time. This technique has been used by Stuart Hill and Donald Rothchild in a study of whether political conflict in African countries was affected by diffusion from conflict elsewhere in the world in 1962–66 and in 1971–75. They found distinct contagion effects in the first period, but only in countries with previous protest. The effects were dampened in African countries with a high degree of ethnic diversity. By the 1970s, however, levels of domestic conflict in Africa had dropped markedly and varied only with past levels of domestic conflict, with no significant diffusion effects.[24] The conclusion is that contagion effects in Africa were specific to the early years of independence rather than universal. It may be that the positive connection between development and political violence also was specific to the same period.

A more detailed example of the cross-sectional approach is Mary Welfling's study of the correlates of magnitudes of turmoil and rebellion in twenty-five African countries. Her model incorporates such causal variables as social stress (short-term deprivations), social strain, and conflict traditions. The causal variables most strongly associated with conflict in Africa prove to differ somewhat from those in global analyses. For example, the strains associated with ethnic diversity and group discrimination had greater effects on conflict globally than they did in Africa in the 1960s. In contrast, traditions of past conflict and regimes' lack of institutional support were more important correlates of turmoil and rebellion in the African context than elsewhere.

24. Stuart Hill and Donald Rothchild, "The Contagion of Political Conflict in Africa and the World," *Journal of Conflict Resolution*, vol. 30 (December 1986), pp. 716–35. Their findings are more complex than this brief summary suggests.

Welfling also calls attention to the substantial problems of measurement error in aggregate analyses of African countries: error in measuring both the properties of conflict and the conditions said to cause conflict.[25]

One can be more confident of results if other statistical studies, using different measures or techniques, lead to similar conclusions. Welfling's results gain credibility because they are reinforced by Mark Cooper's study of the correlates of turmoil (riots, demonstrations, clashes) in various world regions. Among African states, he finds that a history of strife is a more important cause of present turmoil than in other world regions, which parallels Welfling's findings about the relative importance of conflict traditions in Africa. Cooper also finds that African countries with more associational means for articulating interests (parties, interest groups) have less turmoil than others, a finding consistent with Welfling's evidence about the conflict-inhibiting effects of African regimes' institutional support. The effects of these variables on African conflict are substantially stronger than in other world regions. Moreover, Cooper's measures of short-term economic and political deprivations are more strongly correlated with conflict in Africa than in other regions.[26]

The same general approach has been used in many cross-national studies of coups in Africa. In such studies the dependent variable is typically the number of coups and attempted coups reported for each country. African coups, unlike some other kinds of conflict, are unambiguously similar to military interventions elsewhere and thus invite such comparative analysis.[27] Although these studies differ greatly

25. Mary B. Welfling, "Models, Measurement and Sources of Error: Civil Conflict in Black Africa," *American Political Science Review*, vol. 69 (December 1975), pp. 871–88. The causal model tested was developed by Ted Robert Gurr and Raymond D. Duvall, "Civil Conflict in the 1960s: A Reciprocal-Theoretical System with Parameter Estimates," *Comparative Political Studies*, vol. 6 (July 1973), pp. 135–70, who report the global findings against which Welfling contrasts her results for Africa.

26. Mark N. Cooper, "A Reinterpretation of the Causes of Turmoil: The Effects of Culture and Modernity," *Comparative Political Studies*, vol. 7, no. 3 (1974), pp. 267–91.

27. Morrison and others, *Black Africa*, p. 122, report there were more than 100 attempted coups, half of them successful, in sub-Saharan states between 1958 and 1981. Representative studies are Raymond D. Duvall and Mary B.

in detail, there are some common conclusions. Coups and other elite conflicts have been particularly common in African countries that lack an institutionalized party system, have high levels of social mobilization, and are dominated by one large ethnic group. Of particular significance is Robert Jackman's finding that coups are substantially more likely in African countries with a dominant ethnic group (one with more than 44 percent of the population) than in more heterogeneous countries.[28] Other studies ask whether the correlates and effects of military intervention have been appreciably different in African countries than in other world regions.[29] The answer, in a nutshell, is "only a little." It appears that coups in Africa are more readily explained by general theories than are turmoil and rebellion, whose correlates are appreciably different in Africa than in other parts of the world.

An essential question about such studies is whether measures of the scope and intensity of protest and rebellion, or the frequency of coups, are as meaningful in an African context as they are from the perspective of global theories. Donald Morrison and Hugh Stevenson

---

Welfling, "Social Mobilization, Political Institutionalization, and Conflict in Black Africa: A Simple Dynamic Model," *Journal of Conflict Resolution*, vol. 17, no. 4 (1973), pp. 673–702; Alan Wells, "The Coup d'Etat in Theory and Practice: Independent Black Africa in the 1960s," *American Journal of Sociology*, vol. 79, no. 4 (1974), pp. 871–87; and Robert W. Jackman, "The Predictability of Coups d'Etat: A Model with African Data," *American Political Science Review*, vol. 72 (December 1979), pp. 1272–75.

28. Jackman, "Predictability of Coups d'Etat."

29. For example, Donald G. Morrison and Hugh M. Stevenson, "Measuring Social and Political Requirements Stability: Empirical Validation of an Index Using Latin American and African Data," *Comparative Political Studies*, vol. 7, no. 2 (1974), pp. 252–64; Morrison and Stevenson, "Social Complexity, Economic Development and Military Coups d'Etat: Convergence and Divergence of Empirical Tests of Theory in Latin America, Asia and Africa," *Journal of Peace Research*, vol. 11, no. 4 (1974), pp. 345–47; William R. Thompson, "Regime Vulnerability and the Military Coup," *Comparative Politics*, vol. 7, no. 4 (1975), pp. 255–76; Robert D. McKinlay and A. S. Cohan, "Performance and Instability in Military and Nonmilitary Regime Systems," *American Political Science Review*, vol. 70, no. 3 (1976), pp. 850–64; and Rosemary H. T. O'Kane, "Towards an Examination of the General Causes of Coups d'Etat," *European Journal of Political Research*, vol. 11, no. 1 (1983), pp. 27–44.

have argued persuasively for an alternative basis for conceptualizing African conflict, one that distinguishes types of conflict based on the groups involved: elites, communal groups, and mass movements.[30] The implication of the distinction is that there should be separate theoretical and statistical explanations for *elite instability, communal instability,* and *mass instability.* For events of each type, the analyst may ask where and with what frequency episodes will occur, and with what scope or intensity.

Several empirical studies of African conflict during the 1960s have employed Morrison and Stevenson's distinctions, using measures of the frequency of episodes of elite and communal instability, and episodes of turmoil (including riots, demonstrations, and strikes, irrespective of the type of initiating group). One study reports consistently strong correlations between African states' coercive potential and the occurrence of elite and communal instability—a finding that provokes a question about which was cause and which was effect.[31] Another study found that inequalities among ethnic groups, measured on a number of dimensions, consistently predicted all three types of conflict—more so than social mobilization or ethnic pluralism alone.[32] This evidence supports the hypothesis proposed in the preceding section that inequalities and discrimination along lines of ethnic and regional cleavage are a potent source of conflict in African societies.

TYPES OF POLITICAL CONFLICT IN AFRICA

There are several grounds for questioning Morrison and Stevenson's classification of African conflicts in terms of elite, communal,

30. Donald G. Morrison and Hugh M. Stevenson, "Political Instability in Independent Black Africa: More Dimensions of Conflict Behavior within Nations," *Journal of Conflict Resolution,* vol. 15, no. 31 (1971), pp. 347–68; also in Donald G. Morrison, Robert Cameron Mitchell, and John Naber Paden, *Black Africa: A Comparative Handbook,* 2d ed. (Paragon House and Irvington Publishers, 1989).

31. Donald G. Morrison and Hugh M. Stevenson, "Integration and Instability: Patterns of African Political Development," *American Political Science Review,* vol. 66, no. 3 (1972), pp. 902–27.

32. Walter L. Barrows, "Ethnic Diversity and Political Instability in Black Africa," *Comparative Political Studies,* vol. 9, no. 2 (1976), pp. 139–70.

and mass instability. Let me suggest first that *the classification does not permit sufficiently precise distinctions among types of collective political action.* In particular, it is not sensitive either to substantial differences among conflict episodes *within* the categories of communal instability and mass instability or to overlaps between them. There is a very substantial difference in the form, intensity, and potential effect of conflict episodes that focus on limited issues—such as particular policies and personalities—in contrast with conflicts in which the structure of authority or the integrity of the state is at issue. These differences underlie the distinction made in quantitative studies between "turmoil" (or protest) and "rebellion." There is an equally significant distinction between "rebellions" that aim to restructure central authority in a revolutionary way and those that aim at greater autonomy or secession.

The distinction between "communal" and "mass" instability is also problematic because it implies a sharp division that is often contradicted by African realities. How should we categorize a violent strike by a political association of Zulu laborers in a multiethnic South African township? Are they acting on the basis of communal identities, class position, or membership in a political movement? Another problematic example is provided by the Maitasine riots which began in Kano in 1980. Muhammad Marwa (known as Maitasine) was a fundamentalist Moslem with a substantial following among the workers and the poor in northern Nigerian cities who was sharply critical of political leaders and policy. Some of his followers clashed with other Moslems on an Islamic holy day, leading to a massive riot in which the police were overwhelmed. Commentators have offered communal, class, and political interpretations of the episode.[33] I suggest that group conflict in Africa usually involves mobilization of people based on several overlapping identities: ethnicity and class, class and political association, ethnicity and political association—sometimes all three. Political association is often the key element: demonstrations by workers, riots by ethnic minorities, and secessionist movements typically follow from mobilization by leaders who make selective political appeals to com-

33. I am indebted to Otwin Marenin for his summary and interpretation of this example and for pointing out the importance of the interaction of communal, occupational, and class cleavages (personal communication).

munal and class groups and use the organizational tactics of modern political movements. Riots and pogroms against immigrant workers are another, increasingly common type of conflict that defies simple categorization. The victims are distinguished by, and targeted because of, their economic, ethnic, and national status.

The actual forms and content of conflict reflect approximately but not precisely the particular combination of interests upon which action is based. Conflicts that are primarily based on communal identifications are usually directed at other communal groups in the form of riotous clashes or, in extreme cases of intercommunal rivalries, in mass slaughters such as those the Tutsis perpetrated against the Hutu in Burundi in 1972 and 1988. To the extent that such communal identities are mobilized by or subordinated to political associations, conflict is likely to take more "modern" forms; for example, demonstrations asking that authorities provide more equitable treatment for a communal group, or revolutionary or secessionist movements.

Figure 6-1 presents a typology of conflicts in Africa that attempts to take into account the above distinctions and interactions. Rather than define and label precise categories, I have identified clusters of conflict types that tend to be associated with particular combinations of (1) conflict issues and (2) bases of group identification. Three general kinds of conflict issues and four bases of group identification are identified. Not all potential categories are sharply distinct: I assume, for example, that revolutionary movements, urban uprisings, and peasant rebellions all challenge the legitimacy of political authority but are likely to be mobilized on the basis of some combination of political and class interests rather than on one or the other. Similarly, the typology combines (at the extreme right of the figure) civil wars and rebellions based on the interests of regional groups on grounds that they involve political as well as communal mobilization. This category thus encompasses such cases as insurgency in southern Sudan, which is usually interpreted as a reflection of southerners' communal aspirations, and the National Union for the Total Independence of Angola's ongoing revolt against the Popular Movement for the Liberation of Angola government in Angola, which is ordinarily regarded as "political" because of its rhetoric and external support, but which also reflects the communal interests of many of the Ovimbundu people.

FIGURE 6-1. *A Complex Typology of African Conflicts*

Primary basis of group mobilization	Central issue of conflict		
	Policies and distributional issues	Positions and structures of authority	Integrity of the state
Occupational and class interests	Strikes Boycotts Economic sabotage	Peasant rebellions Urban uprisings	
Political association	Political riots Demonstrations	Political revolts Revolutionary movements	Regional civil wars
Communal (ethnic) identification	Communal riots, clashes	Communal warfare Genocide	Irredentist/ autonomist rebellions
Institutional position	Mutinies	Coups Purges | Revolutions from above State terror Politicides	

The typology also incorporates the principal kinds of conflict initiated by political elites. Some of these, such as mutinies and coups, are manifestations of rivalries among factions within the elite. Communal identifications usually provide the primary basis for military factions. Ordinarily the contenders are concerned with distributional issues: which faction and its communal supporters will enjoy the perquisites of power. Sometimes there is a reformist or revolutionary element to these conflicts, as when a radical faction seizes power aiming to eliminate corruption or to implement fundamental socioeconomic and political changes. Generally we can only judge in retrospect whether a "revolutionary" seizure of power will lead to the imposition of revolutionary change, as in Ethiopia after 1974, or to predatory factionalism under a new label, as in the Congo Republic after 1963 (and many similar cases).

There is another kind of elite-initiated violence that has been ne-glected in most empirical research on African conflict, one that is potentially more deadly than all others except civil war. This is the reliance of elites on purges, terror, and politicides to establish and maintain their power. Idi Amin's practice of terror in Uganda from 1972 to 1979 is the best-known but not the only or necessarily the worst African case. The death toll in proportion to population prob-ably was greater under Macias Nguema's reign of terror in Equatorial Guinea after 1974. In Zaire, Mobutu Sese Seko used similar tactics, on a smaller scale, to crush a number of localized challenges to his rule in the late 1970s and early 1980s. These kinds of conflicts are also included in the typology.

The complex relations among the various kinds of elite-initiated conflict are represented schematically in figure 6-1. Mutinies, coups, and revolutions from above involve seizures of power, the issues and outcomes of which generally determine how we label and categorize them. Purges, state terror, and politicides are generally policies used by new elites after the seizure of power to consolidate their rule and to eliminate the possibility of future challenges to it.[34]

One question implied by the typology is whether the statistical explanation of cross-country variations in the frequency of general types of conflict is sufficient. Clearly the answer depends on the purposes of the analyst. Most country specialists and policymakers have more particularistic questions. Which regions or ethnic groups in country X are most susceptible to communally based instability? What determines the frequency, timing, and outcomes of military coups in Benin, or Nigeria? What are the prospects for a cohesive revolutionary movement in South Africa? Some general answers to these questions may be suggested by aggregate analyses of conflict, especially those which are specific to Africa, but detailed answers require more extensive theoretical analysis of particular conflict types. In the sections that follow, some general theoretical ap-proaches to elite, revolutionary, and communally based conflicts are discussed.

34. Barbara Harff has coined the term *politicide* for mass political slaughters; see Harff and Gurr, "Toward an Empirical Theory of Genocides and Politi-cides." Seven of the eleven African episodes identified in the same source, pp. 364–65, began immediately after new leaders came to power.

THEORIES OF ELITE INSTABILITY AND
STATE VIOLENCE

A recent global study of coups concludes that they are most likely to occur in countries that have undergone previous coups, that have been independent for some years, that are divided by social cleavages and suffer from poor economic conditions, but that have relatively high levels of literacy.[35] This level of abstractness will leave most Africanists dissatisfied, especially in light of comparative studies of African coups that demonstrate the relevance of many other factors. Claude Welch's pioneering work on African coups in the 1960s highlighted the relevance of institutional weakness in civilian regimes and the organizational capacities of armies to seize power and bring about change.[36] Samuel DeCalo argues that coups in Africa are most satisfactorily explained by examining the internal dynamics of African military hierarchies, including personal factors, and the extent to which wider societal cleavages are reflected in the armed forces.[37]

The common-sense approach to comparative explanation of coups in Africa is to combine the general with the specific. The general tendency of a country toward coups depends on the factors that have demonstrated correlation with past coups: a history of military intervention, relative poverty, and the presence of a dominant ethnic group. The specifics, which determine which of the countries "at risk" is most likely to have a coup and when, depend on immediate economic and political crises and on the internal dynamics of the military.

It is more difficult to explain elites' reliance on state terror and political slaughter as instruments of rule because there is not much general theory or evidence about state coercion and violence. The prevailing model

35. From O'Kane, "General Causes of Coups d'Etat," who bases her conclusions on a number of aggregate-data studies. She tests various contending theories and concludes that the theory advanced by Zolberg, "Structure of Political Conflict," to explain political conflict in new African states is the most strongly supported theory of coups throughout the Third World.

36. Claude E. Welch, Jr., ed., *Soldier and State in Africa: A Comparative Analysis of Military Intervention and Political Change* (Northwestern University Press, 1970), and *Civilian Control of the Military: Theory and Cases from Developing Countries* (State University of New York Press, 1976).

37. Samuel DeCalo, *Coups and Army Rule in Africa: Studies in Military Style* (Yale University Press, 1976).

used in explaining violent conflict is one in which protesters and rebels act and governments react. But rulers responsible for many cases of state terror have initiated policies of extreme coercion with little provocation by their victims. One kind of example is provided by the Afrikaners' introduction of apartheid policies after 1949, and the systematic use of state coercion and terror to maintain the system for the next four decades. These systematic policies contrast sharply with the almost-random uses of state terror sanctioned by Idi Amin in Uganda and Jean-Badel Bokassa in the Central African Empire during the 1970s. In South Africa and Uganda, one can point to long-standing tensions, racial in the first instance, communal and political in the second, which predated but in no sense fully explained the extremity of official violence. One can also cite the ideological rigidity of the Afrikaner elite and question the sanity of individual autocrats, but these are ideographic explanations, not general ones.

The more general issue, which has now begun to be specified and investigated in a systematic way, is why some regimes and rulers rely mainly on coercion and violence as instruments of rule. Until recently most general theoretical discussions have assumed an action-reaction model in which elites respond, or overrespond, to some functional need to maintain control in the face of actual or potential challenges.[38] I have recently proposed a more general model of the determinants of state violence that takes into account not only the character of challenges but a number of other historical, structural, and situational factors. State violence is particularly likely to be used by minority elites in highly stratified societies who have gained and maintained power through violence, and who have organized instruments of violence such as secret police, revolutionary militia, or special military contingents at their personal disposal.[39]

38. See, for example, Tilly, *From Mobilization to Revolution*, chap. 4; Steven Jackson and others, "Conflict and Coercion in Dependent States," *Journal of Conflict Resolution*, vol. 22, no. 4 (1978), pp. 627–57; and Mark Irving Lichbach, "Deterrence or Escalation? The Puzzle of Aggregate Studies of Repression and Dissent," *Journal of Conflict Resolution*, vol. 31 (June 1987), pp. 266–97.

39. T. R. Gurr, "The Role of the State in Political Violence: A Theoretical Analysis," in George A. Lopez and Michael Stohl, eds., *Government Violence and Terrorism: An Agenda for Research* (Westport, Conn.: Greenwood Press, 1986). See also Raymond D. Duvall and Michael Stohl, "Governance by Terror," in Michael Stohl, ed., *The Politics of Terrorism*, 2d ed. (New York: Marcel

Rhoda Howard has developed a simpler, three-variable theory of the conditions that can be expected to lead to the institutionalization of state terrorism in Africa. The first condition is the development of class-based political organization; the second is exclusive ideologies among opposition or regime; the last is foreign support for the regime. Howard's application of the theory to Kenya is less than convincing because, as she acknowledges, Kenya has not yet institutionalized state repression.[40] My own sense is that, among the African states that have developed the most thoroughgoing systems of repressive rule—South Africa, Ethiopia, and (more tentatively) Zaire—South Africa is the only one in which all three of Howard's conditions are satisfied.

Theories designed to explain state repression generally are not enough to account for the extraordinary violence of genocide and mass political killings. Recent studies by Leo Kuper and Barbara Harff have begun the comparative analysis of genocides with this kind of question in mind, using African as well as non-African cases to illustrate general processes. Harff identifies three factors that combine to make genocides and politicides likely: national upheaval, defined as an abrupt change in the political community; the existence of sharp internal cleavages, combined with a history of intergroup conflict; and the lack of foreign powers' interest in or constraints on the ruling elite.[41] The simple version of the theory appears to fit the circumstances of most of the eleven post-colonial African episodes. But it remains to be demonstrated that the crucial conditions were absent in the majority of African countries that did not have genocides and politicides.

Dekker, 1973), chap. 6; and George A. Lopez and Michael Stohl, eds., *The State as Terrorist* (Westport, Conn.: Greenwood Press, 1984).

40. Rhoda E. Howard, "Repression and Terror in Africa: The Case of Kenya," paper presented to the Conference on State Organized Terror, Michigan State University, East Lansing, November 2–5, 1988.

41. Leo Kuper, *Genocide: Its Political Use in the Twentieth Century* (Yale University Press, 1981), offers comparative generalizations but no explicit theory. The initial statement of Barbara Harff's theory appears in "The Etiology of Genocide" in Michael N. Dobkowski and Isidor Walliman, eds., *Essays on Genocide* (Westport, Conn.: Greenwood Press, 1986), pp. 41–59.

THEORIES OF POLITICAL VIOLENCE
AND REVOLUTION

Many global theories about the causes and processes of political violence and revolution should be relevant to the explanation of political
riots, revolts, and revolutionary movements in Africa. Some of these
theories offer general explanations of all forms of violent political
conflict; others are specific to revolution. Both are relevant: revolutions can usually be regarded as one possible outcome of conflict
processes that have small beginnings. To understand the transitions
from peaceful protest to riots and then revolt, it is necessary to trace
the complex interactions between activists' tactics and demands, and
how governments respond to them. And to understand why some
political movements have revolutionary consequences, it is necessary
to understand why some regimes lose or lack the capacity to accommodate rebels or to repress them.

Whereas political riots have become relatively common in Africa,
revolts and revolutionary movements are rare. In a survey of political
instability in independent black African countries through 1971, Donald Morrison and his collaborators identified only four revolts and
revolutionary movements based primarily on *political* associations rather
than communal identifications.[42]

—Niger, 1960s: a revolt by exiled members of the outlawed SA-
WABA party, carried out mainly in raids and attacks from neighboring
countries.

—Zaire, 1963–66: a series of revolts in northeast and southwest
Zaire, loosely coordinated by the Comité National de Liberation.

—Sudan, October 1964: ten days of demonstrations and a political
strike that forced the abdication of a military government.

—Malawi, 1964–67: an unsuccessful armed revolt led by dissident
ministers, first within the country and then from exile, against the
government of Dr. Banda.

There is, however, potentially much more to explain than cases like
those. First are the nationalist revolutionary movements of former Por-

42. Morrison and others, *Black Africa*, p. 124. The only post-1971 examples
they cite are "peasant uprisings and support for secessionist movements in
Ethiopia."

tuguese Africa, Cameroon, Zimbabwe, Namibia, and South Africa. While some of these movements were dominated by a particular communal group, for example, the Shona in Zimbabwe, all were or are associational political movements bringing together people of diverse backgrounds in the common interest of national liberation, not communal autonomy. Second are communal rebellions and regionally based civil wars, many of which are organized along political lines and some of which use the rhetoric and strategies of revolutionary movements. Theories of revolutionary movements may prove to be relevant to understanding the origins and dynamics of such groups as the Eritrean People's Liberation Front and UNITA. Such theories also should be instructive about the conditions under which (communal or regional) rebels are likely to win or lose. Finally there is the question, why not revolution in Africa? Why have so few of the political conflicts in independent Africa led to revolutionary seizures of power and concerted efforts at socioeconomic transformation? If general theories are correct in specifying the conditions that have led to revolutionary movements in Latin America and Eurasia, they should also help us understand why attempted revolutions have been so rare in independent Africa, and under what circumstances this is likely to change. The other side of this argument is that an analysis of revolutionary potentials in Africa may lead to modification of the general theories.

The remainder of this section does not try to answer these questions, but rather summarizes the principal scholarly approaches to explaining mass political violence generally and revolution specifically. Prevailing explanations of political violence can be grouped into four broad categories. First are *volition theories* that emphasize the importance of discontents, cultural and ideological dispositions, and rational choices in the making of political violence and revolutions.[43] In these theories, the states of mind of prospective leaders and par-

---

43. Major statements of such theories are James C. Davies, "Toward a Theory of Revolution," *American Sociological Review*, vol. 27, no. 1 (1962), pp. 5–19; Gurr, *Why Men Rebel*; Gordon Tullock, "The Paradox of Revolution," *Public Choice*, vol. 11 (Fall 1971), pp. 89–99; Edward N. Muller, *Aggressive Political Participation* (Princeton University Press, 1979); and James DeNardo, *Power in Numbers: The Political Strategy of Protest and Rebellion* (Princeton University Press, 1985). A useful overview of these theories is James B. Rule, *Theories of Civil Violence* (University of California Press, 1988), chaps. 1, 7.

ticipants are the critical variables, though there are sharp differences among them in the relative importance they give to deprivation, alienation, political beliefs, and personal and strategic calculations.

In *structural theories*, the causal emphasis is on tensions created by patterns of social relations. Some of these theories emphasize disruption of relations between value systems and environment, referring to such disturbances as "dysfunction" or "disequilibrium."[44] The contradiction between most educated Africans' desires for high-status positions in the public sector and the relatively limited number of such positions is an example of a widespread "dysfunction": the achievement of a set of values is frustrated by material and political constraints. Other structural theories, including those of Marxists, attribute violent conflict and revolution most fundamentally to inequalities and to the worsening of exploitation by the dominant class.[45]

Political process theories explain political violence by reference to the characteristics of political institutions and those who challenge them. Theorists in this vein treat revolution "as the 'ultimate' political conflict, in which the normal struggle between interest groups is escalated—by both the intensity of the conflict and the magnitude of resources that interest groups bring to bear—to the point where normal political processes for conflict mediation and resolution fail, and the political system is violently split apart."[46] Emphases differ: Samuel Huntington is concerned with the characteristics of political institutions that make them resilient in the face of political pressures for change, whereas Charles Tilly places weight almost entirely on the capacity of challengers to mobilize for collective action against governments.[47]

44. For example, Chalmers Johnson, *Revolutionary Change* (Little, Brown, 1966); and Mark Hagopian, *The Phenomenon of Revolution* (Dodd, Mead, 1974). See the discussion in Rule, *Theories of Civil Violence*, chap. 5.

45. The most general such statement is Johan Galtung, "A Structural Theory of Aggression," *Journal of Peace Research*, vol. 1, no. 1 (1964), pp. 95–119. Marxist contributions to the empirical understanding of revolutionary causation are summarized in A. S. Cohan, *Theories of Revolution: An Introduction* (Wiley and Sons, 1975), chaps. 4, 5.

46. Jack Goldstone, "Theories of Revolution: The Third Generation," *World Politics*, vol. 22, no. 3 (1980), p. 429.

47. Huntington, *Political Order in Changing Society*; Tilly, *From Mobilization to Revolution*. For an excellent review and comparison of these theories, see Stan Taylor, *Social Science and Revolutions* (St. Martin's Press, 1984), chap. 4.

Two general observations can be made about these three groups of theories. One is that they are not mutually exclusive, despite claims that they are or should be.[48] Rather they identify a dovetailing set of explanatory factors. Structural and cultural factors both shape general dispositions to action, which in turn lead to strategic decisions about campaigns of political action. The actions and responses of regimes and challengers are both influenced by the same general structural and cultural constraints. The character of their actions and responses determines the nature of the conflict episode as well as its outcomes— reform, repression, revolution, or nothing.

The second observation is that, even if they could be formally synthesized, these theories remain collectively incomplete on several counts. First, they say little about why and how regimes respond to oppositions. Second, they do not take into account the international linkages and constraints that shape internal conflict—an omission that is especially important in the African setting. Finally, they say nothing systematic about the outcomes of conflict—who gains, who loses, and why.

There are a number of recent theories of revolution that attempt to correct some of the lacunae in these general theories of political violence. They do so at the expense of generality by focusing narrowly on particular types of revolutionary movements in the Third World. Jeffrey M. Paige develops a theory of the effects of agrarian social structure on the potential for revolution and includes Angola among his case studies.[49] Ellen Kay Trimberger links the existence of a dis-

48. See Harry Eckstein, "Theoretical Approaches to Explaining Collective Violence," in T. R. Gurr, ed., Handbook of Political Conflict: Theory and Research (Free Press, 1980), chap. 4.

49. Jeffrey M. Paige, Agrarian Revolution: Social Movements and Export Agriculture in the Underdeveloped World (Free Press, 1975). Other influential works on the role of rural people in Third World revolutions are Eric Wolf, Peasant Wars of the Twentieth Century (Harper and Row, 1969); Joel S. Migdal, Peasants, Politics and Revolution: Pressures toward Political and Social Change in the Third World (Princeton University Press, 1974); James C. Scott, The Moral Economy of the Peasant: Rebellion and Subsistence in Southeast Asia (Yale University Press, 1978); Samuel L. Popkin, The Rational Peasant: The Political Economy of Rural Society in Vietnam (University of California Press, 1979); Craig Calhoun, The Question of Struggle (University of Chicago Press, 1982); and John Walton, Reluctant Rebels: Comparative Studies of Revolution and Underdevelopment (Columbia University Press, 1984).

tinctive kind of elite structure, in which bureaucratic and military officials are separated from landlord and merchant classes, to the occurrence of "revolutions from above."[50]

A major contribution of Trimberger's analysis is her attention to the consequences of differences in state structure and in the class support of rulers, factors that she shows have profound influence on processes of revolutionary change. Her view is of course "from the top down," whereas Theda Skocpol takes a more abstract "structural" view of the conditions necessary for the occurrence of what she calls *social revolutions*. Her question is why such revolutions have occurred in some countries but not in others experiencing generally similar conditions. Social revolutions have only occurred in "agrarian-bureaucratic" societies in which a bureaucracy, with the support of landlords, subsists mainly on agricultural surplus. In such societies there is an inherent tendency toward conflict between state and landlords over the division of surplus, and a potential for peasant rebellions whose intensity varies with the autonomy and organizational strength of peasant communities. When the state is threatened by international pressures but lacks enough leverage to increase its share of surplus, there is a revolutionary situation. But Skocpol's analysis is limited to explaining why structural differences between France, Russia, and China, on the one hand, and Prussia, Japan, and England, on the other—together with differences in international pressures—account for the fact that successful social revolutions occurred in the first three countries but not in the latter.[51] She does not attempt to apply it elsewhere.

Are the elements of Skocpol's theory applicable to contemporary African societies? In Africa, bureaucracies have developed unchallenged means of extracting surplus from peasant producers that are effective in the short run but undermine the longer-run incentives to produce. The major internal threat to the state is probably the disaffected peasant producer, but the threat is more likely to be manifested in the peasant's withdrawal from cash-crop production than in overt rebellion.[52]

More appropriate to Africa may be John Walton's ideas about the causes of revolts in contemporary agrarian societies. The first cause

50. See note 7.
51. Skocpol, *States and the Social Revolution*.
52. See references in note 13.

is the " 'crisis of modernization' attendant to the full-scale implementation of dependent capitalism." This crisis of uneven development is manifest in new forms of inequality "implemented in law and
economic policies that become the focus of local grievance and, later,
nationalistic protest."[53] The second cause is the political mobilization
of classes centered on these issues. The crises of these two conditions
push dominant classes into new and potentially more effective coalitions. The final cause has to do with the weakness of these states
and the policy choices made by ruling coalitions. Most Third World
states in such situations have lacked the will and resources to remedy
popular discontents, and as a consequence are vulnerable to revolt
and revolution. Walton's only African case study in support of this
theory is the Mau Mau revolt, and it is an open question whether the
theory is applicable to independent Africa. Uneven development is
clearly present in most African states, but nationalism and ethnoregional separatism are thus far the only issues that have a demonstrated capacity to generate political mobilization on a large scale.
Class-based action by the rural or urban proletariat has not yet occurred with much frequency or political effect, despite the existence
of objective conditions that theory suggests should have such effects.
One plausible reason is the capacity of most African peasants to shift
from cash-cropping to subsistence agriculture. Another is the persistence of communal loyalties that inhibit the development of broader
identifications based on class or economic situation.

These theories of revolution also give more explicit attention to the
international factors that shape internal conflicts, such as Skocpol's
emphasis on international pressures as a source of crisis in prerevo-
lutionary states. A more complete accounting of relevant international
factors includes the following:

—*External capitalist penetration into rural economies* and the consequent effects of agricultural commercialization on class conflict.[54]

—*Dependency on foreign trade, capital, and technology,* which tends to

53. Walton, *Reluctant Rebels*, pp. 157, 162.

54. See Wolf, *Peasant Wars*; Paige, *Agrarian Revolution*; Scott, *Moral Economy
of the Peasant*; Walton, *Reluctant Rebels*; and Edward L. Kick's more general
argument, "World System Properties and Mass Political Conflict within Nations: Theoretical Framework," *Journal of Political and Military Sociology*, vol.
8, no. 2 (1980), pp. 175–90.

restrict the state's policy options, stimulate the growth of a dependent bourgeoisie aligned with international rather than national interests, and require authoritarian patterns of rule and reliance on coercion to protect the interest of international capital and its local clients.[55]

—*International political pressures*, including foreign military threats, intervention, and alliance involvements, all of which tend to increase the state's allocation of resources to military purposes, increase hostile external support for opposition movements, and reduce the state's freedom of political maneuver with respect to opposition.[56]

THEORIES OF COMMUNAL CONFLICT

Conflicts that develop around communal loyalties pose a different set of problems than do revolutionary conflicts: many African cases, few general theories. Most studies of communal conflict are specific to a set of related episodes, such as the explanations offered for racial conflict in the United States during the 1960s, or theories that purport to explain the persistence of factional religious conflict in such countries as Northern Ireland or Lebanon.

The most general approach to the explanation of group violence based on communal cleavages is to interpret it within the context of broader theories of political violence of the kinds reviewed above. A basic principle of volitional and structural theories as applied to communal conflict is the emphasis on inequalities among groups: the greater the inequalities, the more likely the disadvantaged groups are to take collective action. This is particularly likely if the inequalities are reinforced by custom and legal barriers established by dominant groups. Denial of the opportunity to reduce inequalities is a particularly potent source of grievance. A related principle, consistent with political process theories of conflict, is that com-

---

55. See Trimberger, *Revolution from Above*, chap. 4; Jackson and others, "Conflict and Coercion in Dependent States"; and Raymond D. Duvall and John R. Freeman, "The State and Dependent Capitalism," *International Studies Quarterly*, vol. 25, no. 1 (1981), pp. 99–108.

56. See James N. Rosenau, ed., *International Aspects of Civil Strife* (Princeton University Press, 1964), and the review of evidence in Kick, "World System Properties," pp. 178–79.

munal identity provides an easy basis for mobilization. Where communal identity remains strong and is not yet eroded by new, cross-cutting loyalties to class and associational groups, it is relatively easy for leaders evoking symbols of common ethnic interest to propagate ideologies of resistance and to organize group members for political action. In many African societies, these identifications seem to be sufficiently strong that it is difficult to mobilize people on any other basis.

Probably the most useful theoretical frameworks for the analysis of communal conflict are emerging from the growing body of comparative research on ethnopolitics. Only a few of the relevant works can be discussed here.[57] An early example of a formal, general theory is Alvin Rabushka and Kenneth Shepsle's "theory of democratic instability" in plural societies. They define plural societies as ones in which there exist separate cultural groups with generally incompatible sets of values: "The hallmark of the plural society . . . is the practice of politics almost exclusively along ethnic lines. . . . Permanent ethnic communities acting cohesively on nearly all political issues determine a plural society and distinguish it from a culturally homogeneous, nonplural society."[58] Their analysis of politics in such societies makes use of formal rational-choice theory, based on assumptions of intra-communal consensus and intercommunal dissensus. From this they construct a paradigm of the political process in plural societies during and after the transition to independence. Case studies of eighteen such societies, most of them in the Third World, provide evidence for the existence of a series of stages in that process.

The end of the process is likely to be the resort to autocratic rule, either by a dominant ethnic group or by the military. From the

57. A classic study is Arend Lijphart, *Democracy in Plural Societies* (Yale University Press, 1977). A magisterial overview is Donald L. Horowitz, *Ethnic Groups in Conflict* (University of California Press, 1985). An excellent new collection of case studies and comparative analyses of conflict management strategies in plural societies is Joseph E. Montville, ed., *Conflict and Peacemaking in Multiethnic Societies* (Lexington, Mass.: Lexington Books, 1989).

58. Alvin Rabushka and Kenneth A. Shepsle, *Politics in Plural Societies: A Theory of Democratic Instability* (Columbus, Ohio: Merrill, 1972), pp. 20–21. Also useful, though less systematic, is Cynthia H. Enloe, *Ethnic Conflict and Political Development* (Little, Brown, 1973).

viewpoint of those studying African conflict, however, this analysis is incomplete because it does not specify what the sources of communal violence are likely to be *in the absence of free democratic competition*. Whereas virtually all plural African states lack the free political competition assumed by Rabushka and Shepsle, they differ greatly in the level and intensity of communal conflict, and for an outside observer the most significant difference is not in the extent of superordinate political control but in the quality of relationships among ethnic groups. In other words, some African countries seem to fall in Rabushka and Shepsle's category of "pluralistic countries, where coalitions often vary from issue to issue [and] the cultural categories tend neither to be carefully demarcated nor always politically salient."[59]

The further theoretical question is what conditions or policies reduce or increase the salience of ethnic divisions in autocratically ruled countries. The use of federal or confederal relationships is an approach advocated by Rabushka and Shepsle for democratic societies, one that has been used with mixed success in Sudan and Nigeria in response to communally based regional revolts and civil war.[60] Donald L. Horowitz distinguishes these "structural" approaches to conflict management from "distributive" approaches. The structural approaches include separation ("radical surgery"), regional autonomy, and federalism. All are risky solutions because, depending on circumstances, they may channel and intensify rather than resolve conflict. The alternative distributive approaches involve differential allocation of government positions and resources to less-advantaged groups. Redistribution also has its pitfalls, not the least of which is backlash from more advantaged groups.[61]

Horowitz makes a convincing argument that the relative effective-

---

59. Rabushka and Shepsle, *Politics in Plural Societies*, p. 21.

60. Rabushka and Shepsle, *Politics in Plural Societies*, pp. 213–15. For a case study of federalism in Nigeria, see J. Isawa Elaigwu and Victor A. Olorunsola, "Federalism and Politics of Compromise," in Rothchild and Olorunsola, *State vs. Ethnic Claims*, chap. 14. A case study of federal policy in Sudan is Dunstan M. Wai, "Geoethnicity and the Margin of Autonomy in the Sudan," chap. 15 in the same source.

61. Horowitz, *Ethnic Groups in Conflict*, chaps. 14–16.

ness of all such strategies depends on whether they bring into play more specific conflict-reducing mechanisms, and identifies five such mechanisms:[62]

—Disperse interethnic conflict "by proliferating the points of power so as to take the heat off of a single focal point." Regional decentralization is only one of a variety of means to this end.

—Establish political arrangements that increase intraethnic conflict, thereby diverting energies from conflict between ethnic groups.

—Create incentives for interethnic cooperation. Certain kinds of electoral arrangements can provide such incentives, as can some policies of preferential allocation of positions and resources.

—Encourage political alignments based on interests other than ethnicity. This follows from the argument and evidence that "cross-cutting cleavages" reduce the intensity of intergroup conflict. (See my comments, above, on the potential significance of class-based alignments in changing the character of political violence in African states.)

—Design policies that reduce disparities between groups. Note that redistributive policies are not the only way to do so.

A limitation of both Horowitz's and Rabushka and Shepsle's theories is that they focus mainly on the reduction of conflict in the political realm. Some of the cultural and economic conditions that drive communal conflict are not necessarily susceptible to political management (though, of course, one must begin somewhere). The quantitative studies reviewed at the outset of this chapter point to the general importance of *conflict traditions* as sources of contemporary conflict in African countries; traditions of hostility and clashes between ethnic dyads are a persisting source of intergroup hostility and potential violence in contemporary societies. The *relative size of ethnic communities* is another consideration. Rabushka and Shepsle distinguish four "ethnic configurations," suggesting that those characterized by a dominant majority such as Rwanda, Zanzibar, and Ethiopia are likely to have more violent instability than those

---

62. Horowitz, *Ethnic Groups in Conflict*, pp. 597–99. Eric A. Nordlinger identifies six conflict-regulating political practices that are generally consistent with Horowitz's prescriptions in *Conflict Regulation in Divided Societies*, Occasional Papers in International Affairs 29 (Harvard University Center for International Affairs, 1972), pp. 21–33.

characterized by balanced competition (they cite no African examples) or fragmentation among many groups, as in Zaire and Nigeria. In the "dominant minority" pattern, typified by South Africa, systematic repression is typical.[63] Quantitative evidence consistent with the "dominant majority = violence" argument is Robert Jackman's finding, cited previously, that coups have been most likely in African countries where the largest ethnic group has 44 percent or more of the population.

The extent of inequalities between classes and communal groups in the distribution of wealth, status, and political position is a third major variable that is emphasized in a number of the conflict theories cited in this chapter. Many quantitative cross-national studies have shown that material inequalities are substantially correlated with both protest and rebellion, irrespective of communal cleavages.[64] When inequalities coincide with communal cleavages, the consequences are often explosive. Redistributive policies of the kinds Horowitz evaluates are designed to reduce such discrepancies. I suggest that the greater the inequalities, and the larger the disadvantaged group, the more difficult it is for any government to design effective catch-up policies. The economic costs and the potential resistance from more-advantaged communal groups are likely to be prohibitive. The emphasis on redistributive policies also assumes good will on the part of the governments that in fact may be committed to maintaining the powers and privileges of one communal group.

The outlines of a general theory of communal conflict can be derived from this discussion. Intense communal conflict in multiethnic African societies is most likely in these circumstances:

—where there are two or more dyads of communal groups with historically based hostilities;

63. Rabushka and Shepsle, *Politics in Plural Societies*, pp. 88–91. On systematic repression in the "dominant minority" pattern, see Gurr, "Rule of the State."

64. For a comprehensive review, see Mark Irving Lichbach, "An Evaluation of 'Does Economic Inequality Breed Political Conflict?' Studies," *World Politics*, vol. 41 (July 1989), pp. 431–70. A recent empirical study that encompasses more countries than previous studies is Edward N. Muller, "Income Inequality, Regime Repressiveness, and Political Violence," *American Sociological Review*, vol. 50, no. 1 (1985), pp. 47–61.

—where ethnic identities are highly salient and have not yet been significantly diluted by cross-cutting identifications with newer class, corporate, or associational groupings;

—where there are substantial inequalities across ethnic groups in income, status, and access to political power;

—where disadvantaged groups in the aggregate are relatively large compared with advantaged groups;

—when political and economic inequalities are reinforced by discriminatory patterns of social behavior and public policy;

—when government and politics are controlled by members of a dominant minority or majority ethnic group; and

—when few or none of Horowitz's conflict-reducing mechanisms are in place.

This model does not specify the circumstances that trigger outbreaks of communal violence or say whether it will be limited to protest and clashes, or take the form of revolts and civil wars. I suggest that one of the most common precipitants of communal conflict is the introduction of new government policies that reinforce or are seen to symbolize existing patterns of intercommunal inequalities. If the burden of those policies is most evident to members of the aggrieved communal group in the modern sector, those living in towns or cities and engaged in the money economy, then protest and clashes are most likely. If the burden of new discriminatory policies falls most heavily on rural and regional communities, the more likely consequences are rural revolts and support for separatist movements.

THE OUTCOMES OF POLITICAL CONFLICT

Most theory and research on political violence has focused on the causes and processes of conflict rather than its outcomes. The "new theories" of Third World revolution reviewed above have offered some generalizations about the ways in which class coalitions, state power, and international constraints limit revolutionaries in the kinds of changes they can implement once they are in power.[65] But these

65. On the policies pursued by revolutionaries in power, see Jack A. Goldstone, ed., *Revolutions: Theoretical, Comparative, and Historical Studies* (Harcourt Brace Jovanovich, 1986), pp. 207–317.

"generalizations" are in fact specific to historical revolutions in countries rather different from those of contemporary Africa, which has had few if any revolutions to which they might be applied. In William Foltz's view, expressed at the conference on which this book is based, only two "real revolutions" have occurred in modern Africa: in Ethiopia and, perhaps, Liberia.

There is also a substantial literature about the effects of limited forms of political action on public policy in the United States historically and during the ghetto riots and rebellions of the 1960s.[66] Similar questions are being asked about the effects of protest on government policies in some contemporary Asian countries and in the USSR.[67] All these studies suggest that under specifiable circumstances democratic governments tend to make substantial concessions and reforms in response to protest, whereas authoritarian governments do so under more restricted circumstances. The hypotheses of these studies and the methods used to test them could easily be applied to the study of urban protest in Africa. There remain the large numbers of communally based protests and revolts in Africa whose outcomes seem not to have been studied in any systematic way. Nor is there any significant body of theoretical or empirical generalizations about the outcomes of communal conflict elsewhere in the Third World.

CONCLUSION: UNFINISHED BUSINESS

Some readers may be discomfited that this review does not conclude by proposing a synthetic "theory of African conflict." I think that is a misguided objective. It is preferable to test and revise general theories of conflict in light of the African record. With the exception of

66. An empirical study using historical materials is William A. Gamson, *The Strategy of Social Protest* (Homewood, Ill.: Irwin-Dorsey, 1975). A review of findings on the outcomes of protest and violence by American blacks is James Button, "The Outcomes of Contemporary Black Protest and Violence," in T. R. Gurr, ed., *Violence in America: Protest, Rebellion, Reform* (Newbury Park, Calif.: Sage Publications, 1989), chap. 10.

67. See, for example, Michael O'Keefe and Paul D. Schumaker, "Protest Effectiveness in Southeast Asia," *American Behavioral Scientist*, vol. 26 (1983), pp. 375–94; and Myungsoon Shin, "Political Protest and Government Decision-Making: Korea 1945–72," same issue, pp. 395–416.

cross-national quantitative studies of coups, most of whose results are too general to satisfy the area specialists, and a few analyses of the correlates of conflict magnitudes, most comparative research on revolution and political violence in the Third World has proceeded separately from substantive studies of conflict in black Africa. Theories of "Third World" conflict have been much more influenced by and applied to the rebellions and revolutionary conflicts of Asia and Latin America than the political violence of independent Africa. Either the theorists have not been sufficiently interested in African developments to take them into account when formulating their theories, or Africanists have found general theories of limited relevance to their African cases. If Western theories of revolution and mass political violence are at all appropriate to Africa, they should at least have some insights to offer about prospects for violence and political change in South Africa. But except for Diana Russell's comparative analysis of the role of military force in maintaining regimes such as those of South Africa,[68] Western analysts since the 1950s have contented themselves with simplistic predictions of "revolution soon." Few if any have anticipated or offered convincing explanations of the cyclical pattern of repression, resistance, conservative reform, and escalated protest, followed by a return repression, that has characterized South African racial politics for more than a generation. And virtually all have been surprised by President F. W. de Klerk's abrupt but sustained shift, late in 1988, toward the politics of accommodation and incorporation.

It is thus a reflection of Western conflict theorists' relative ignorance of Africa that this chapter has been largely limited to pointing out some points of potential relevance. General theories of elite instability, state violence, and communal conflict appear potentially more applicable to Africa than do most theories of political revolution. The sketch offered here for a general explanation of communal violence in Africa illustrates what I believe to be a valid approach. The theory sketch is specific to one type of conflict. It builds on general theories and evidence about communal conflict and also incorporates variables that seem to be particularly important in African societies, in this example the persisting importance of communal loyalties and tradi-

68. D. E. H. Russell, *Rebellion, Revolution, and Armed Force* (Academic Press, 1974).

tions of intergroup conflict. And it is sensitive to the conditions that distinguish among African societies and regimes: the extent of intergroup inequalities, patterns of ethnic dominance, and the kinds of conflict-minimizing policies followed by states. I recommend a similar strategy for those who would apply general theories to the explanation of other forms of political violence in Africa. When accounting for protest, revolts, revolution, and their outcomes, it will also be essential to follow the precepts of the "new theorists" of revolution and consider the effect of international economic and political factors, as well as the crucial parts played by African states and elites. Equally important will be to examine the ways in which communal, political, and emerging class bases of identification interact to shape and reshape patterns of conflict. It should not be assumed, though, that international forces or the national state or the emergence of class bases for action will necessarily have the same kinds of effects on conflict in Africa as they have had in Latin American or Asia. Western theories of the causes, processes, and resolution of conflict should be tested and revised in light of the African experience, not imposed on the evidence.

Chapter 7

DONALD ROTHCHILD

An Interactive Model for State-Ethnic Relations

To gain an understanding of conflict management, it is necessary to acquire a comprehensive view of the various interconnected processes in evidence. This is best done by relating latent grievances and different types of societal and extrasocietal claims to regime strategies and capacities. It is only as the analyst explores all elements of the interlinked and reinforcing systems of relations that comprehensive insights into the dynamics of a particular policy process will be possible. Hence this chapter attempts to provide an initial look at the logic of events at work, focusing, as figure 7-1 suggests, on the connections that may be present between the social and political environments and the regime types (that is, the pattern of behavior accepted by the dominant political elite as the legitimate formula for exercising political power).[1] At that point, it will be possible to note the ways that these organizing regime principles act to structure policy outcomes on intergroup relations.

THE SYSTEMIC CONDITIONS

Given Africa's objective circumstances in postindependence times, the record of political relations among ethnic and regional interests is, on balance, a relatively favorable one. In terms of economic conditions, the performance of the sub-Saharan African states has cer-

I wish to express my appreciation to Arend Lijphart, Alexander J. Groth, Stuart Hill, S. W. R. de A. Samarasinghe, and Edmond J. Keller for comments on the first draft of this chapter.

1. On this logic of events, see Leo Kuper, *The Pity of It All* (University of Minnesota Press, 1977), p. 9.

FIGURE 7-1. *A Systems Approach to State-Ethnic Relations*

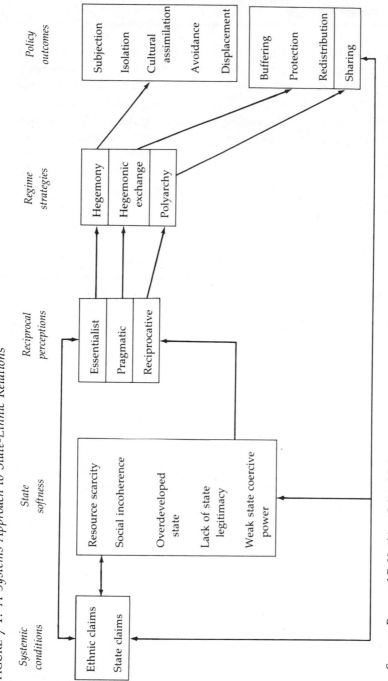

Sources: Raymond F. Hopkins, *Political Roles in a New State: Tanzania's First Decade* (Yale University Press, 1971), pp. 51, 55, 56; and letter from Shaheen Mozaffar, December 19, 1986.

tainly been disappointing, with inflation and unemployment on the rise and per capita income falling in the 1980s to a level three-fourths that reached in the 1970s.[2] External debts remain high, export earnings have fluctuated while imported goods have risen dramatically in cost, and populations are increasing considerably faster than economic growth rates in many countries, placing heavy constraints on social services, infrastructures, and physical environments.

Moreover, the state and its institutions are in decline, unable to implement their regulations effectively throughout the territory ostensibly under their control. Paradoxically, the modern African state seems overcentralized and a major consumer itself of scarce resources, yet "soft" and lacking in the ability to carry out its ambitious programs. It is frequently resented by the majority living in the rural periphery, who look upon it as an alien superstructure that extracts resources while allocating little to the development of the periphery.[3] State efforts to increase economic opportunity through structural adjustment programs run the risk of widening regional disparities, thereby creating new grievances among the relatively disadvantaged in the periphery. The estrangement of these rural dwellers leads at times to a process of disengagement, as an informal economy and local associational life achieve a new vitality of their own. The result, commonly, is to leave the state less capable of exerting a top-down, hegemonic control over society.

In such a context of economic scarcity and state weakness, the intermediaries of ethnic, regional, and religious groups carry on an active competition for the scarce resources controlled by what is in reality a "lame [state] leviathan."[4] The fact that regularized political routines have emerged at all under such circumstances reflects well on the political acumen of Africa's state and societal elites. To be sure, such political routines are less apparent in Africa's various

2. World Bank, *World Development Report, 1988* (New York: Oxford University Press, 1988), p. 28.

3. Goran Hyden, "Problems and Prospects of State Coherence," in Donald Rothchild and Victor A. Olorunsola, eds., *State Versus Ethnic Claims* (Boulder, Colo.: Westview Press, 1983), p. 69.

4. See Thomas M. Callaghy, "The State as Lame Leviathan: The Patrimonial Administrative State in Africa," in Zaki Ergas, ed., *The African State in Transition* (Macmillan, 1987), pp. 87–99.

hegemonic regimes (with their hierarchically organized one- and no-party systems); however, they are frequently practiced by elites in the hegemonic exchange regimes (systems that combine the parameters of one- or no-party governance with norms and practices of balanced group inclusion in decisionmaking, proportionality in appointments and allocations, autonomy, political exchange, and reciprocity) and polyarchical regimes (inclusive, accountable, and openly competitive two- or multiparty systems). In fact, those countries making use of the latter two regime types have at times exhibited a fairly high level of political responsiveness, developing norms of reciprocity and rules for political exchange under adverse economic conditions.

Latent Grievances

At the outset, it seems necessary to relate the regimes of hegemony (bureaucratic centralism), hegemonic exchange, and polyarchy to the latent grievances in the environment (over inequality, status, identity, recognition, and so forth). These grievances can be tapped by political elites intent on making demands for change as well as for maintenance of the status quo (that is, counterdemands). In general, it can be surmised that those situations tending toward the establishment of hegemonic regime patterns will reflect the subjective factors giving rise to intergroup conflicts, and those situations tending toward hegemonic exchange and polyarchical regime types are likely to indicate competing interests over tangible goods. Whereas the former frequently involve destructive, even intractable, conflicts where group security and survival seem to be threatened in one manner or another, the latter, which bring less intense passions to the fore, allow greater scope for creative conflict procedures based on understood norms of political exchange and reciprocity. Whether an ethnically related group acts like any other interest group competing in the marketplace for publicly controlled resources is therefore likely to reflect the systemic conditions and reciprocal perceptions that prevail in each situation.[5]

Contrary to commonly held impressions on the inevitability of zero-sum interethnic relations, Africa in fact exhibits a wide range of con-

5. See Donald L. Horowitz, *Ethnic Groups in Conflict* (University of California Press, 1985), p. 104.

flict-creating grievances and encounters.[6] Certainly, profound differences, not easily negotiable, have surfaced and led to deep chasms between distinct identity groups in the same society. The forces in operation that produce these intense political attitudes and commitments are likely to reveal a heavy emphasis on subjective, mainly psychological, concerns. Included in this broad psychological-symbolic array of conflict-producing factors are the following: a fear of restratification and the loss of political dominance;[7] an assertion of group worth and place;[8] the existence of negative remembrances and images; the determination to resist a controlling group's effort to spread its language, culture, or religion; and evidences of a sense of superiority on the part of a politically or economically dominant minority.[9] Where ruling state elites and their constituents fear the consequences of a fundamental reordering of regime procedures or where political minorities remain deeply anxious over their subordination or their cultural or physical survival, ethnic conflicts are likely to be intense and, in some cases, highly destructive of lives and property. Adopting an "essentialist" perception regarding their ethnic adversaries—that is, one in which leaders and groups, viewing their rivals as fundamentally threatening to their cultural or physical survival, regard any political compromises on their part as weakening their position—allows little scope for negotiated, mutually beneficial outcomes. Conflict, therefore, seems most likely to proceed in a heavy-handed, even violent, direction.

Important as these psychological and symbolic factors are in explaining high stakes, emotionally laden conflicts, and the resort to hegemonic forms of control, they are not by any means the entire story of Africa's interethnic relations. In the period since Africa's

6. For an earlier discussion of these issues, see Donald Rothchild, "Interethnic Conflict and Policy Analysis in Africa," *Ethnic and Racial Studies*, vol. 9 (January 1986), p. 86; and D. Rothchild, "State and Ethnicity in Africa: A Policy Perspective," in Neil Nevitte and Charles H. Kennedy, eds., *Ethnic Preference and Public Policy in Developing States* (Boulder, Colo.: Lynne Rienner, 1986), pp. 15–61.

7. See René Lemarchand, "Revolutionary Phenomena in Stratified Societies: Rwanda and Zanzibar," *Civilisations*, vol. 18, no. 1 (1968), p. 47.

8. Horowitz, *Ethnic Groups in Conflict*, p. 186.

9. Donald Rothchild, *Racial Bargaining in Independent Kenya* (London: Oxford University Press, 1973), chap. 5.

decolonization, the leaders of a number of countries have regularly managed to elude worst-case scenarios, channeling demands along predetermined paths and developing new routines for conflict avoidance. By emphasizing the tangible or distributive side of these state-societal relations (and playing down the subjective sources of conflict), these elites have defused some of the passions of ethnic rivalry and created new political cultures based on mutual adjustment.

The extent to which ethnic and other rivalries take place over such distributive goods as cabinet appointments, civil service recruitment, and regional allocations is far-reaching. In societies that are scarcity prone and have weak state institutions, issues of recruitment and allocation among societal interests and administrative units lend themselves to "neutral" distributive principles such as proportionality (that is, the distribution of state resources and political and administrative positions among ethnic peoples or regional units on the basis of their relative numbers). Where political routines have become widely understood and accepted and a bargaining culture has emerged, leaders can find compromise formulas to bridge the differences between the relatively advantaged and relatively disadvantaged on such basic questions as subregional need versus derivation (the place of extraction) in allocative policies (oil-based wealth in Nigeria), merit versus proportionality in recruitment policies (Kenya), legislative representation based on subregional parity or population size (Nigeria), or centralization versus decentralization of power (Ghana, Zambia, Nigeria, and Sudan in 1972). In Zambia and Uganda (under Milton Obote's first administration), governments have engaged in unofficial political exchange practices with the representatives of ethnoregional interests, including them on a roughly proportional basis in their cabinets. Although hegemonic exchange did not gain legitimacy in these two countries, their political leaders acted in terms of political necessity, appointing ethnic intermediaries to high positions of state in accordance with rough guidelines on balanced representation. Such practices gained more acceptance in Jomo Kenyatta's Kenya and Félix Houphouët-Boigny's Côte d'Ivoire, where something tantamount to an inclusive grand coalition developed, which avoided adversarial politics and allowed the dominant elite to negotiate policy questions quietly among themselves.

Moreover, central government practices in many countries reveal a keen regard for maintaining a balance among groups and subregions when recruiting members of their civil service. In Ghana, for example, a breakdown of the ethnic composition of senior staff members of the central government in 1972 showed, with few exceptions, a remarkably close parallel between ethnic proportions in the civil service and the society at large.[10] Furthermore, an analysis of public expenditure patterns in Nigeria and Kenya indicated recurrent use of the proportionality principle in the mid-1970s to early 1980s in order to achieve a degree of fairness (even corrective equity) in the expenditures on roads, health, and education among the countries' subregions.[11]

In brief, distributive issues between different ethnic interests that share a sense of common destiny normally are policy questions with tangible referents—goods, jobs, taxes, roads, schools—and frequently amenable to political solutions. There are of course exceptions to this generalization. Where differential rates of modernization and political and economic practices have combined to create a profound sense of comparative group deprivation, the objective *and* subjective sources of conflict can reinforce one another and exacerbate latent tensions. When discussing the increasing strains in north-south relations in the Sudan in the period following the 1972 Addis Ababa agreement, Dunstan Wai wrote: "A feeling of *relative economic deprivation* is growing, and the intransigent refusal of the Arab Sudanese to share real political power and revenue from within and aid from without with the Southern Sudanese will gradually erode any desires in the South to identify with the 'Sudanese state.' "[12] In this case, southern Sudanese are inclined to view economic and political relations as part of the structure of relations, and hence less tractable

10. In relationship to the total population, my survey showed the Fanti and Ga-Adang to be significantly overrepresented, whereas the northerners were underrepresented. Others, such as the Ashanti, Boron, Akim-Akwapim, Nzima, and Ewe, showed no statistically significant variance from proportionality. See Donald Rothchild, "State-Ethnic Relations in Middle Africa," in Gwendolen M. Carter and Patrick O'Meara, eds., *African Independence: The First Twenty-Five Years* (Indiana University Press, 1985), p. 85.

11. See Donald Rothchild, "Africa: Hegemonial Exchange and Resource Allocation," in Alexander J. Groth and Larry L. Wade, eds., *Comparative Resource Allocation* (Beverly Hills, Calif.: Sage Publications, 1984), pp. 173–75.

12. Dunstan M. Wai, "Geoethnicity and the Margin of Autonomy in the Sudan," in Rothchild and Olorunsola, *State versus Ethnic Claims*, p. 320 (italics added).

than might be anticipated where unranked equal collectivities compete over distributable goods.[13]

The Nature and Intensity of Collective Demands

In the development of predictable hegemonic or exchange routines, a pivotal factor has been the nature and intensity of ethnic and regional demands. Made by elite representatives on those in power at the political center, these demands represent the injection of a dynamic element into the relations between state and society. Such background factors as the number and distribution of ethnic groups, the inequality of rates of modernization among subregions, unequal exchange, degree of social mobilization, the communications revolution, and the fragility of political institutions no doubt explain much about the collision among social forces; yet an understanding of the interactional process at work in a particular country requires more in the way of specifics—in particular, a probing of latent grievances, the role of intermediaries in the shaping of ethnic demands, the structuring of state-ethnic relations, and the responses of state elites.[14] Clearly, the possibilities for conflict management are increased when group demands are reasonable and moderate (that is, negotiable) and do not challenge the integrity of the political order. Non-negotiable demands for a restructuring of power and territorial separatism are likely to pose a fundamental challenge to a state's organizing principles and informal rules of engagement and therefore to bring on an aggressive response on the part of state officials. Different kinds of

13. Naomi Chazan, "Israel and South Africa," *New Outlook* (Tel Aviv), vol. 32 (February 1989), p. 5.

14. Important examples of these general explanations of ethnic conflict include Harold Issacs, "Basic Group Identity: The Idols of the Tribe," *Ethnicity*, vol. 1 (April 1974), pp. 15–41; Ali A. Mazrui, *Post Imperial Fragmentation: The Legacy of Ethnic and Racial Conflict*, University of Denver Studies in Race and Nations, vol. 1, no. 2 (1969); Karl W. Deutsch, "Research Problems on Race in Intranational and International Relations," in George W. Shepherd, Jr., and Tilden J. LeMelle, eds., *Race among Nations: A Conceptual Approach* (Lexington, Mass.: Lexington Books, 1970), pp. 123–52; Karl W. Deutsch, "Social Mobilization and Political Development," *American Political Science Review*, vol. 55 (September 1961), pp. 493–514; and Samuel P. Huntington, *Political Order in Changing Societies* (Yale University Press, 1968).

state and ethnic claims are influenced by the reciprocal perceptions that rival elites have of one another, and they, in turn, relate and reinforce the kinds of regime strategies put into play by those in power.

Given the centrality of ethnic group demands to the processes of conflict and conflict management, it is hard to explain the relative lack of scholarly attention to the nature of demands and counterdemands. Because of the far-reaching consequences of demands for a revision of state procedures, security guarantees, a restratification of political power, or separation and secession, these demands have actually received greater scrutiny than their less threatening negotiable counterparts. In some cases, the demand for ethnic self-determination is not only non-negotiable but has an "externalist" quality about it —that is, it can only be satisfied through the establishment of separate, independent countries.[15] The negotiable demand for self-determination, which clusters around coalitional and various forms of autonomous integration within the state and allocative issues, is "internalist" in its aim and can be accommodated by state elites prepared to respond effectively to legitimate demands. Certainly, the nature of these demands can change over time. In some situations, ethnic groups begin with negotiable demands involving modest resource costs. If the state does not meet these claims, however, they can lead to extreme, non-negotiable demands.

Each of these types of demands and their implications for the negotiation process will be examined in turn. Less disruptive, and therefore less newsworthy, than the demands for the restructuring or the breakup of the state, negotiable demands are nonetheless common in many middle African states. Where ethnic leaders and their constituents are prepared to compete for public resources according to prevailing societal rules, and where they perceive their rivals in pragmatic terms (that is, they assume a basic conflict of interests in their relationships with other groups, while not precluding the possibilities for conciliatory behavior on specific issues), they may be prepared to make moderate demands that can be satisfied within the state. Ethnic difference does not in and of itself exclude the possibility of collaboration. Provided an overarching sense of shared fate is present among

15. See Donald Rothchild, "The Two Senses of Ethnonational Self-Determination," *Africa Report*, vol. 26 (November–December 1981), pp. 56–58.

diverse ethnic and other interests, state and ethnic leaders may be able to join forces to solve common problems.

To gain an insight into the demand process, it is necessary to distinguish between the felt dissatisfactions of the general public and the ethnic intermediary's critical role in selecting and shaping these points of discontent for presentation to high state officials. The gap that exists between the public's latent grievances and the way their representative filters and communicates them to those in power has enormous implications for systemic stability. Where the ethnic go-between—a member of the dominant political "class"—fails to display sufficient sensitivity to the feelings of that person's constituents, the operating norms of a clientelistic relationship may weaken and lead to the patron's loss of credibility.[16] Consequently, the intermediary's survival depends on a continuing process of negotiations at two levels: with constituents at the local level, and with other intermediaries and members of the state elite at the political center.

An idea about the general public's felt dissatisfactions can be secured from the results of three surveys administered or processed by me in Kenya (1966), Zambia (1969–70), and Ghana (1973).[17] In all three cases, members of the general public focused on distributive issues, expressing the most modest and restrained kinds of grievances. In Zambia, villagers in Northern Province, only minimally aware of the relative neglect of their area, put forward limited demands for clinics, an improved water supply, shops and marketing facilities, a nearby school, road repairs, improved housing, community and homecraft centers, grinding mills, and agricultural schemes. Similarly in Ghana, villagers in the relatively disadvantaged Northern and Upper regions stressed the need for sanitation, market stalls, road improvement, and piped water; their counterparts in the more-

16. See Richard L. Sklar, "The Nature of Class Domination in Africa," *Journal of Modern African Studies,* vol. 17 (December 1979), p. 550; and Larry Diamond, "Class Formation in the Swollen African State," ibid., vol. 25 (December 1987), pp. 585–86.

17. For a more extended summary of these findings, see Donald Rothchild, "Collective Demands for Improved Distributions," in Rothchild and Olorunsola, *State Versus Ethnic Claims,* pp. 172–198. See also Anthony Oberschall, "Communications, Information, and Aspirations in Rural Uganda," *Journal of Asian and African Studies,* vol. 4 (January 1969), p. 48.

advantaged Western and Ashanti regions and Greater Accra voiced the need for a broader array of improvements, including such costly items as modern markets, electricity services, schools, and hospitals. In general, the "revolution of rising expectations" was a phenomenon most evident among the relatively advantaged; by comparison, the less advantaged, in the urban as well as the rural areas, made essentially reasonable demands for public services and amenities.[18] The effect of this was to place reduced pressure on heavily burdened governments to redistribute scarce resources, and hence to allow them to temporize or "satisfice" on key development projects—for the time being at least.

When demands made by the relatively disadvantaged on the state are limited in scope and intensity, state elites are sometimes able to surmount the heavy constraints of the political and economic environment and to engage in exchange relationships with ethnic intermediaries at the top of the political system. To the extent societies are in a position to develop recurrent patterns of interaction, the result is a gain in political system responsiveness and stability. There are, however, limits to such relationships. Where "there is no similarity whatever between the loyalties which the transforming center requires and those to which the local community adheres," then, Manfred Halpern predicts, bargaining will be unable "to overcome the underlying incoherence." In such a situation, he explains, "convertible values" will be lacking, leading to a weakening of connections between government and societal interests.[19]

Non-negotiable demands, characteristically rigid and highly wrought, tend to cluster around such subjective and emotionally laden issues as group status, worth, identity, subordination, and survival. These profound anxieties, which arise from a diffuse sense of danger, have the effect of limiting and modifying perceptions, and therefore becoming the sources of extreme collective reactions. Where such psychological determinants come into play, ethnic leaders are likely to go beyond economic-interest perspectives and stress the need to cope

18. Joan M. Nelson, *Access to Power* (Princeton University Press, 1979), p. 241.

19. Manfred Halpern, "Changing Connections to a Multiple World," in Helen Kitchen, ed., *Africa: From Mystery to Maze* (Lexington, Mass.: Lexington Books, 1976), pp. 15–16.

with a perceived threat to their self-esteem or survival, even at a cost to themselves in terms of comparative economic advantage. To the extent that the resulting claims of rival groups are incompatible, the outcomes can be essentialist perceptions and intense, even intractable, conflicts.[20]

Non-negotiable demands are likely to emerge where state elites and ethnic representatives hold incompatible values. Where state leaders (especially in an ethnically or racially dominated state, such as Burundi or South Africa) and other ethnic representatives disagree over fundamental principles, not tangible interests, conflict tends to become intense and frequently unmanageable. For example, when writing about polarizing ideologies among dominant and subordinate groups in such repressive contexts as Rwanda, Burundi, preindependence Algeria, and postindependence Zanzibar, Leo Kuper describes minority domination as "constitut[ing] a system" that excludes reform along the lines of power sharing. "While dominant polarising groups see reform as a stepping stone in the reversal of power, not as a process in the sharing of power, subordinate groups consider it a delusion to hope that the State, which is the instrument of their oppression, will bring about effective change, and they see reformism as a device in the maintenance of power."[21] The web of relations linking state and ethnic elites is therefore torn asunder, and the different ethnic identity groups retreat to the safety of their separate communal "containers."[22]

Clearly, intractable conflicts, involving intense demands for power, status, territory, and the protection of cultural and physical identities, were built into Africa's vertically stratified societies (South Africa, Burundi, colonial Zanzibar, and colonial Algeria) from the outset. Because the dominant minority denies the principle of equality and enforces inequitable practices through top-down, hierarchical control, a system of vertical stratification often comes to feature non-negotiable claims from both the ruling (but vulnerable) minority and the excluded (but resentful) majority. Adopting essentialist perceptions about each

20. Horowitz, *Ethnic Groups in Conflict*, p. 196.
21. Kuper, *Pity of It All*, pp. 122, 271.
22. Manfred Halpern, "Choosing Between Ways of Life and Death and Between Forms of Democracy: An Archetypal Analysis," *Alternatives*, vol. 12 (January 1987), p. 13.

other's intentions, the antagonists perceive acts of conciliation and compromise as indications of weakness that threaten their status or security. Lacking a sense of common fate, group demands may become unreasonable and inflexible. The reciprocity that does occur between group intermediaries is negative in nature, and it sometimes involves claims that escalate to the point where the security or survival of one group takes place at the expense of the other.

As survey data on white Rhodesian attitudes in the late 1960s showed, a large number of respondents viewed power sharing as threatening and tended to limit their realistic choices to the stark alternatives of minority dominance or emigration.[23] In modern-day South Africa, Botha's Afrikaner-led state's refusal to negotiate with the African National Congress and its determination to hold on to the reins of political power (that is, "grand apartheid") similarly reflected its perception of threat (in particular, its fear of *swartgevaar*, or being overwhelmed by the black majority).[24] And the violence of Burundi in 1972 revealed a minority people, the Tutsi, in control of the state apparatus, responding with extreme ferocity to initial attacks by bands of Hutu and "Mulelist" rebels in Bujumburu and some of the provinces in the south; Tutsi army "counterviolence" followed the Hutu majority's assumption of power in neighboring Rwanda and showed acute Tutsi fears of a possible spreading of the rebellion to engulf their country as well.[25] Violence can be viewed, then, as "inherent" in relations of dominance and superiority.[26] The systemic conditions and reciprocal perceptions of group leaders are sufficiently negative for minority leaders to feel impelled to demand a concentration of power at the political center to ensure their group's opportunities and survival;

23. Barry M. Schutz, "Homeward Bound? A Survey Study of White Rhodesian Nationalism and Permanence," *Ufahamu*, vol. 5, no. 3 (1975), pp. 81–117.

24. See Donald Rothchild, "From Exhortation to Incentive Strategies: Mediation Efforts in South Africa in the Mid-1980s," in Edmond J. Keller and Louis A. Picard, eds., *South Africa in Southern Africa: Domestic Change and International Conflict* (Boulder, Colo.: Lynne Rienner, 1989).

25. On the Tutsi's "orgy of counter-violence," see René Lemarchand, *Selective Genocide in Burundi*, Report 20 (London: Minority Rights Group, 1974), p. 18.

26. Salvador Minuchin, *Family Kaleidoscope* (Harvard University Press, 1984), p. 191.

however, this inevitably occurs at a heavy cost in terms of developing the kinds of legitimate routines necessary for negotiation and joint problem solving.

The non-negotiable demand is by no means limited to "ranked" or hierarchically ordered societies; it also appears in "unranked," ethnically coexisting societies. The unranked ethnic system, writes Donald Horowitz, does not involve superiority and subordination; rather, "parallel ethnic groups coexist, each group internally stratified."[27] Yet despite the parallel nature of these groups, conflicts can still become intense; this can lead to situations where demands are put forward in uncompromising terms for power, status, territory, and autonomy.

To take the example of territorial autonomy, it is important to note that where such demands do not raise questions about the legitimacy of the state and its normative order, they need not be threatening to the political system. State elites, perceiving these ethnoregional claims as reasonable and creating scope for enhanced efficiency, may seek to accommodate these pressures by conceding a limited administrative responsibility on certain specified matters. Hence a variety of subregional councils, planning boards, district assemblies, autonomous administrative authorities, and federal relationships have emerged, all of which have provided a limited capacity for local initiative and action while stopping short of separatism and secession. As former President Jaafar Nimeiri of the Sudan is reported to have said (but not to have allowed to develop in the 1980s), a federal system is necessary "to reconcile the country with itself."[28] In situations where perceptions are mutually pragmatic and claims negotiable, territorial autonomy can contribute creatively to state coherence.

However, it is when the demand for territorial autonomy comes to be presented in a confrontational and abstract or nontangible manner, and when it thus comes to raise questions about the legitimacy of the political order itself, that conflict tends to become destructive. In general, it seems reasonable to hypothesize that the more rigid the demand, the more inflexible the state's response. To be sure, ethnoregional leaders have justified the call for territorial self-determination in Biafra, Katanga, and Western Sahara, or the claim to irredentist reunification in Somalia and among the Ewe and Bakongo, by pointing to the

27. Horowitz, *Ethnic Groups in Conflict*, pp. 22–23.
28. Quoted in *Weekly Review* (Nairobi), February 3, 1980, p. 3.

artificiality of the colonial divisions; nevertheless, Africa's successor states, invoking the international legitimacy conferred on them at independence by other governments, have insisted on the territorial integrity of the new states as against all other claimants, internal or external. The colonial territory's quest for state self-determination had turned, with independence, into a demand on the part of state elites for the maintenance of the status quo.[29]

In certain cases (such as Biafra, Katanga, and Eritrea, which did not recognize its union with Ethiopia as legitimate), ethnoregional leaders have refused to negotiate their differences with state authorities on the basis of this status quo, persisting in a demand for separation. The demand by a sectional elite for a further grant of self-determination in postindependence times amounted to a radical assertion of group rights, potentially destructive of the organizing principles of the state. Such a claim precluded reform and implied that no compromises would be sufficient guarantees of group survival within the existing political order. The inevitable consequence was high conflict, often violent.

Under what circumstances might such a non-negotiating stance be justified? This question, posed most poignantly during the Nigerian civil war, brought inconclusive answers. Some contended that a valid claim to national self-determination rested on the need to preserve the survival of the affected group. For Tanzania's president, Julius Nyerere, this was indeed the case. When his government recognized the state of Biafra, he argued that secession "was declared because the Ibo people felt it to be their only defence against extermination."[30] But other observers at the time were equally emphatic in denying that federal troops had engaged in acts of genocide against the Ibo people or that Colonel Odumegwu Ojukwa had exhausted all the possible remedies under the system before breaking connections.[31] The pro-

29. John H. Spencer, "Africa at the U.N.: Some Observations," *International Organization*, vol. 16 (Spring 1962), p. 381. See also Robert H. Jackson and Carl G. Rosberg, "Why Africa's Weak States Persist: The Empirical and the Juridical in Statehood," *World Politics*, vol. 35 (October 1982), pp. 12–16.

30. The United Republic of Tanzania, *Tanzania Government's Statement on the Recognition of Biafra* (Dar es Salaam: Government Printer, 1970), p. 1.

31. See, for example, Organization of African Unity, *No Genocide* (Lagos: Federal Ministry of Information, 1968), pp. 6–11.

ponents of the federal government's position also emphasized the overriding imperative of maintaining Nigeria's territorial integrity. Thus in Ali Mazrui's novel *The Trial of Christopher Okigbo*, one of his characters, Kwame Apolo-Gyamfi, put the case for the state's counterdemand most forcefully: "But just because we permitted an empire to break up is not an adequate reason for permitting our respective countries to follow suit. Imperial disintegration is a good thing. Let us not permit it to become less good by allowing it to lead on to national disintegration."[32] In brief, the non-negotiable demand for separation had given rise to an equally unyielding counterdemand, with violent struggle as the logical outcome.

STATE RESPONSES TO ETHNIC DEMANDS AND COUNTERDEMANDS

Drawing on latent grievances in their communities, ethnic and regional intermediaries make various and contradictory claims on state authorities. These leaders, who are members of the same dominant political "class," play a key role in the way they shape demands and channel them to those in authority. In particular, their demands can be creative or destructive, tangible-practical or symbolic-psychological, leading alternatively to accommodations within the political system or to possible disruptions of the state and its procedures. How the state will react to these collective demands is situational and depends largely on the intensity of demands, the structure of power relations, the political culture, the perceptions of elites, and the skill and effectiveness of leaders. Much as the nature of demands sometimes changes over time, the responses of state leaders can also be expected to shift as governing coalitions realign and elite preferences alter.

Certainly, regimes (that is, the legitimate formulas for exercising power) are critical in structuring the way that state elites will respond to ethnic and other group demands. Regimes make a significant difference in the management of conflicts, for their frameworks set parameters on choice. Thus hegemonic regimes that consolidate power at the political center and emphasize hierarchical control by govern-

32. Ali A. Mazrui, *The Trial of Christopher Okigbo* (London: Heinemann, 1971), p. 118.

ment and party often tend to impose serious restraints on the aggregation and channeling of group demands to decision elites; when communal intermediaries do manage to articulate their claims, state leaders in such regimes may respond slowly and reluctantly, leading to a greater likelihood of antagonistic relations. Hegemonic exchange and polyarchical regimes, by contrast, are more prepared to accept routines that organize predictable state-society interactions, providing avenues for the voicing of communal demands at the political center. Where the hegemonic regime seeks to control and resist demands, its hegemonic exchange and polyarchical counterparts allow access to ethnic intermediaries and are more prepared to enter into direct or tacit negotiations with these interest group intermediaries. The greater openness and flexibility of the latter regime types has a positive feedback effect: ethnic-related demands can be more moderate because group leaders have reason to anticipate a greater responsiveness on the part of state officials.

In the hegemonic exchange and polyarchical regimes, leaders, fully aware of the fragility of their institutions, are more inclined to enter into ongoing negotiations with a wide array of interest groups in order to promote their state-building objectives. Such negotiations may involve high decisionmaking costs: the various group representatives are likely to take longer to reach agreements in these contexts than might be the case if the power of decision were limited to a few actors; moreover, negotiations entail an implicit recognition of the legitimacy of sectional interests, something that the leaders of a hegemonic regime find distasteful.[33] Yet the tendency on the part of hegemonic regimes is to exert central control and to repress social conflicts. The hegemonic regime, a resister of collective demands, thus tends to repress oppositions, inhibit free expression, limit the arena of decisionmaking, restrict public accountability, and, with the exception of the highly ideological states, allow only narrow and restricted opportunities for mass participation.

To be sure, the regimes discussed here overlap one another in specific situations; some reciprocity inevitably occurs in hegemonic regimes between rulers and ruled, and a tendency in polyarchies to concentrate power at the political center is common. Yet the substance of their

---

33. James M. Buchanan and Gordon Tullock, *The Calculus of Consent* (University of Michigan Press, 1962), p. 111.

organizing processes is distinguishable, with distinct consequences in terms of state-society relations. These regime types differ in openness to interest group demands, central discipline, roles of political parties, regularity of elections, ideological commitments and preferences, and so forth. They also diverge quite noticeably in their willingness to bargain with domestic class and ethnic interests as well as in the relative costs they are prepared to pay in terms of decisionmaking efficiency.

How do the leaders of the different state regimes organize their societies to cope with ethnic-related conflict? The hegemonic regime, which comes into being as a result of a voluntary decision by party leaders to abandon opposition politics or by assumptions of power on the part of civilian or military elites, results in a process of governance by hierarchical control, or what Robert Dahl and Charles Lindblom describe as a substantial degree of "control by leaders" over nonleaders.[34] By consolidating power at the political center, the hegemonic-type regime, in theory at least, is in a position to impose a number of policies, potentially both creative and destructive, on a reluctant society. By resisting ethnic and regional demands, the hegemonic regime sometimes manages to put off raising such claims to a level requiring a political response, thereby temporarily increasing state capacity during times of economic scarcity. Moreover, the containment of participation can circumscribe certain domestic conflicts, denying them a legitimate arena in which to fight out their differences. This capacity to act as a deterrent to internal conflict leads Daniel Geller to conclude that "centrist systems suppress moderate or high levels of turmoil more rapidly than polyarchies" and that "centrist systems manifest less violence and for briefer durations than either polyarchic or personalistic states."[35] Within limits, then, the "unidirectional nature" of the hegemonic regime's route of general deterrence can contain social conflict, at least over a limited period of time.[36]

34. Robert A. Dahl and Charles E. Lindblom, *Politics, Economics and Welfare* (Harper and Row, Harper Torchbooks, 1963), p. 227.

35. Daniel S. Geller, "The Impact of Political System Structure on Probability Patterns of Internal Disorder," *American Journal of Political Science*, vol. 31 (May 1987), p. 230. See also Alan Rabushka and Kenneth A. Shepsle, *Politics in Plural Societies: A Theory of Democratic Instability* (Columbus, Ohio: Merrill, 1972), pp. 207, 217.

36. Donna Bahry and Brian D. Silver, "Intimidation and the Symbolic Uses

But the hegemonic regime is not merely a resister of demands; it is also a processor and maker of demands. Relying on the ability of a dominant political elite to impose its preferences on society, the hegemonic state, acting in line with its penchant for central direction and encapsulated decisionmaking, deals with situations of intense ethnic and regional conflicts by using five basic strategies of control and their accompanying policy packages.[37] When pursuing a strategy of *subjection*, a dominant ethnic or class coalition uses the power of the state to maintain a structure of inequality; the government employs coercive mechanisms as necessary to ensure the self-determination of the dominant interests (minority or majority) without making significant concessions to the counterpulls of subordinate political interests (South Africa, Burundi, Ethiopia, Amin's Uganda, Arabs in Zanzibar).

Viewing intergroup conflicts as intense and potentially destructive, hegemonic state elites may opt for a strategy of *isolation*, that is, attempting to manage conflict by separating the contending groups into distinct political systems (the 1964 referendum on Bunyoro's "lost counties" in Uganda). More commonly, however, isolation reflects a balance of state and ethnoregional forces on the ground and is manifest in relationships of de facto autonomy (Chad in the early 1980s, UNITA in Angola), de facto partition (Cyprus, Lebanon), attempted secession (Biafra, Katanga), or full separation and the emergence of distinct, sovereign entities (Bangladesh and Pakistan). A dominant political elite pursues a strategy of *cultural assimilation* when it uses the machinery of the state to interpenetrate and absorb politically weaker identity groups into the core culture. The dominant elite may be representative of a numerically preponderant collectivity (Sudan) or a minority (the American-Liberians, 1847–1980), but either way, the state's extension of rules (for example, the system of *shari'a* law

---

of Terror in the USSR," *American Political Science Review*, vol. 81 (December 1987), p. 1089. See also Sammy Smooha, "Control of Minorities in Israel and Northern Ireland," *Comparative Studies in Society and History*, vol. 22 (April 1980), pp. 256–80; and Percy C. Hintzen and Ralph R. Premdas, "Guyana: Coercion and Control in Political Change," *Journal of Interamerican Studies and World Affairs*, vol. 24 (August 1982), p. 352.

37. For a more extended discussion of these conflict-regulating strategies, see Rothchild, "State and Ethnicity in Africa," pp. 38–50.

to southern Sudan) and its suppression of linguistic, religious, and other cultural traits evoke a powerful counterreaction among the peoples affected.

When a dominant political elite pursues a strategy of *avoidance*, it seeks to insulate the state from direct confrontations among social groups. It attempts to elude openly expressed divisiveness by circumscribing and containing conflict. Thus President Siaka Stevens imposed a single-party system in Sierra Leone in 1978 to prevent an "unnecessary" institutionalization of "tribal or ethnic . . . warfare"; and General I. K. Acheampong, seeking in part to restrain interethnic conflict, proposed the establishment of a representative, nonparty system of government for Ghana in 1977.[38] Finally, the hegemonic state elite can pursue a strategy of *displacement*, endeavoring to transform the interethnic encounter by moving an ethnic population permanently from one locale to another. As a state-engineered solution to the ethnic or nationalities "problem," displacement in Africa has taken many forms: the transfer of urban enclaves (South Africa's Group Areas Act); programs to shift rural populations (Tigreans in Ethiopia, 1984–85); local "regroupement" of ethnic peoples (colonial Algeria); assisted emigration (Jews from Ethiopia); and disguised or undisguised deportations or expulsions (Asians from Uganda; blacks from Mauritania in 1989).

In the hegemonic regime, then, state elites tend to perceive ethnic conflict as intense and threatening to the organizing principles of the political system. They therefore use the hierarchically based control at their disposal to resist communal demands or to attempt to structure societal relations in line with their preferences. This elite dominance can be creative, as in the case of President Nimeiri's 1972 decision to seek a political solution to the southern Sudanese call for regional autonomy, or the action taken by various Nigerian governments to restructure the Nigerian federation, splitting it up from its original three to a current twenty-one states, thereby enabling a variety of ethnic minority states to play an increasingly active role in a more fluid and decentralized polity.[39] But the hegemonic regime approach

38. *West Africa*, April 26, 1982, p. 1115; and Donald Rothchild, "Military Regime Performance: An Appraisal of the Ghana Experience, 1972–78," *Comparative Politics*, vol. 12 (July 1980), pp. 462–66.

39. See Edgar O'Ballance, *The Secret War in the Sudan: 1955–1972* (London:

is not without its costs. The suppression of communal demands, if it can be achieved, may result in the appearance of normality; however, it fails to come to grips with grievances still festering beneath the surface. As noted above, deterrence inhibits open expressions of opposition. Yet there are definite limits in Africa to the hegemonic state's coercive powers, and where individuals and groups successfully defy state norms, there is little to stop them from opting for a kind of de facto autonomy (Angola's UNITA, Ethiopia's Tigre or Eritrea). Paradoxically, the lengths to which the more ideologically inclined hegemonic states (such as Ethiopia and Angola) go in coercing compliance only makes their rebellions and internal wars more devastating. Such regimes tend to be poorly informed and to lack the ability to forge coherent interelite linkages through reciprocity and political exchange. Hence they tend toward military solutions to the ethnic and regional challenges, leading to intractable conflicts between determined adversaries. All too often, as the cross-national literature on conflict indicates, hegemonic regimes are reasonably effective in blocking protests and low-intensity conflicts, but are more likely to face rebellions than are the open and more responsive regime types.[40]

By contrast, the hegemonic exchange and polyarchical regimes allow a broader range for legitimate conflict among the elite representatives for ethnic, regional, and other interests. Viewing intergroup relations in more pragmatic terms, their state elites are more prepared to open channels for the articulation of collective demands and to be responsive to these claims as they arise. Yet the hegemonic exchange and polyarchical regimes differ significantly in the ways they have come into being and in their organizing patterns. The hegemonic exchange regime, which emerged for the most part during the decolonization process and reflected the leader's preparedness to co-opt and engage in limited exchange relations with his country's powerful ethnoregional intermediaries, is largely a transitional arrange-

---

Faber and Faber, 1977), p. 116; and Larry Diamond, "Introduction," in Larry Diamond, Juan J. Linz, and Seymour Martin Lipset, eds., *Democracy in Developing Countries: Africa* (Boulder, Colo.: Lynne Rienner, 1988), p. 11.

40. Ekkart Zimmermann, "Macro-Comparative Research on Political Protest," in Ted Robert Gurr, ed., *Handbook of Political Conflict* (Free Press, 1980), p. 210.

ment among elites born of the need to recognize the configurations of societal identity and power during the early years of independence. In some instances, the polyarchical regime also manifested the continuities of the decolonization process; not feeling particularly threatened by the bargain struck with the outgoing imperial authority at the time of independence, leaders in Botswana, Gambia, and Mauritius essentially preserved intact the basic laws and structures inherited from the colonizers. In addition, in two important examples of regime change in Africa, leaders in Senegal and Algeria moved in a deliberate manner from hegemony to polyarchy, partly displaying a shift of preferences and partly a desire for enhanced international legitimacy for their political systems.

Polyarchies, which institutionalize competitive elections and a degree of public accountability, are clearly more effective in regularizing public access to decisionmakers than their hegemonic exchange counterparts. Nevertheless, by the way that the hegemonic exchange regime establishes informal routines on broadly balanced and inclusive coalitions and proportional decision rules on civil service appointments, fiscal allocations, university admissions, and educational scholarships, it is responding, albeit in a less public manner, to the appeals of ethnic, regional, and other intermediaries. More than the hegemonic regime, then, the polyarchic and hegemonic exchange regimes are processors rather than makers of demands. They are more inclined to accept the legitimacy of autonomous social interests, and, in an effort to promote certainty on the part of various political actors, are inclined to work toward national unity by reconciling and negotiating with these powerful social forces. In large part, their pragmatism is born out of a recognition of the "softness" of their state institutions; yet in some cases (Botswana, Senegal), it also demonstrates elite preferences for regulating conflict through more cooperative rituals of encounter. Regardless of the source of this pragmatism, the effect is to channel social conflict along predetermined paths, giving a sense of regularity and predictability to the routines and rules of the political system. The hegemonic exchange and polyarchical regimes' preparedness to accommodate ethnic and regional demands follows logically from their governing elites' perception that claims on the state are generally reasonable and that the intensity of intergroup conflicts is likely to be low or medium.

Their strategies for coping with conflict are indicative of this basic assessment. A willingness to engage in political exchange and reciprocity naturally gives rise to a proclivity to accept *buffering* as a conflict-regulating strategy. Buffering, which takes such forms as good offices, conciliation, mediation, and arbitration, involves initiatives by the state or by internal or external third-party interveners to organize the rules for social interaction. As the costs of intransigent behavior become excessive, the antagonists may come to see a third-party actor as indispensable in facilitating a mutually beneficial agreement. Thus the state has played a critical role in mediating between ethnic, regional, and other interests at the domestic level, organizing the basis of intergroup relations on such thorny issues as recruitment and resource allocation. And at the international level, various nongovernmental and governmental bodies have played a useful role in facilitating regularized patterns of interaction (Sudan in 1972, Zimbabwe, Namibia).

State elites can adopt a strategy of *protection*, granting constitutional and legal guarantees to minorities to reassure them about their status in the new political order (Nigeria, 1979). Moreover, despite the evident constraints of economic scarcity, state elites can, and have, pursued a strategy of *redistribution*. In Kenya, Ghana, Nigeria, and Cameroon, governments have at times given tangible evidence of their concern for the less advantaged peoples and regions by redistributing fiscal resources to the poorer parts of their country, increasing the likelihood that the less advantaged will support and comply with state regulations.[41]

Finally, polyarchies, and to a lesser extent hegemonic exchange regimes, initiate strategies of *sharing*. In situations where demands are moderate and groups share pragmatic perceptions of one another's intentions, a sense of common fate may develop. Collective conflict does not disappear, but rather focuses largely on such negotiable issues as resource allocation and the distribution of political positions and social opportunities. As routines of political exchange become accepted, informal practices of cooperation become evident in executive, legislative, and party affairs. Sharing also gains expression from time to time through formal rules on elections (Mauritius), application

41. See Rothchild, "Middle Africa: Hegemonial Exchange and Resource Allocation," pp. 168–175.

of the principle of Nigeria's "federal character" when making federal appointments, executive power sharing (Nigeria), regional autonomy (Sudan, 1972), and federalism (Nigeria).[42]

The hegemonic exchange and polyarchical states show ample opportunities for learning over time, creating new possibilities for mutual adjustment between the state and its various partially autonomous ethnic and regional interests. Such regimes adapt to their political reality by displaying a greater preparedness to negotiate with the autonomous forces in their society. The result is a greater responsiveness to demands and an increased ability to develop elite linkages. But the legitimacy that prevails in such regimes can involve costs. The larger number of powerful political actors participating in decisionmaking causes leaders to invest more resources in the negotiating process in order to arrive at agreements; moreover, the continuous political interplay that marks these regimes sometimes makes broad-ranging plans difficult to implement and may contribute to indecision, mediocre appointments, and various abuses and corrupt practices.

CONCLUSION

This chapter has attempted to give an insight into conflict management as a system of interactions. It sought to present an overview of state-society relations, linking collective grievances and demands to the structuring of regimes and their strategies and policies. Ethnic and regional demands and state responses are seen as interwoven and reinforcing. Whereas demands for inclusive state coalitions and proportional distributions are accepted as negotiable and legitimate and can be handled within the political order, demands for separation and secession are generally non-negotiable and threatening to the political system, and they have potentially destructive consequences in terms of social coherence and state legitimacy.

Because of the critical feedback effect and a variety of pressures external to the system, the relationships between demands and state responses are by no means fixed in place. The possibility of altering both demands and state responses, and therefore developing new

42. On the politics of sharing, see Peter P. Ekeh and Eghosa E. Osaghae, eds., *Federal Character and Federalism in Nigeria* (Ibadan: Heinemann, 1989).

routines and new regime choices, is quite apparent. For example, with continued rule harmful to the corporate interests of the military, their officers have sought on occasion to disengage from politics and to return to the barracks; thus military-led regimes in Nigeria and Ghana have carefully organized a move to civilian-led polyarchies, only to see these constitutions overthrown and new military-led regimes installed in their place. Zimbabwe's leaders, determined to consolidate their political power over an ethnically and racially divided society, have shifted from a colonially negotiated polyarchy to a hegemonic regime, while Senegalese leaders, for reasons already mentioned, have orchestrated a dramatic change toward greater political liberalization. Similarly in Algeria, leaders of the National Liberation Front decided to introduce a multiparty system; this move toward polyarchy was both a response to domestic pressures and a desire to be in line with the liberalizing trends of the Maghreb and Eastern Europe.[43] No one could have foreseen that the Nimeiri coup in the Sudan would have contributed decisively to the creative negotiations leading up to the Addis Ababa agreement in 1971–72, or that he would soon undercut the very political reality that he had helped to devise. Similarly, the willingness of Angola's governing Popular Movement for the Liberation of Angola to consider negotiating with Jonas Savimbi's National Union for the Total Independence of Angola, a movement built upon a popular following among the Ovimbundu-speaking people in the south-central parts of the country, represents an unexpected shift in 1989 in the preferences of the state elite, and creates new opportunities for a rechanneling of conflict.

One can anticipate that state responsiveness to the demands of the disadvantaged to catch up will have a positive effect, and that state insistence on regional submission or a military solution will provoke defiance. Moreover, the timing of demands and responses is likely to prove critical to the process. Appeals for reform may not endure for long against the claims of extremists. Hence if state elites can look ahead and respond creatively to group demands before they harden and escalate, then the possibilities for developing acceptable rules of relations would seem to be enhanced.

43. Jean de la Gueriviere, "Demands of Democracy," *Manchester Guardian Weekly*, October 15, 1989, p. 15.

In brief, the development of a responsive state appears critical. Not only does such a state encourage ethnic intermediaries to frame their demands in moderate terms, but it facilitates action before reformist possibilities have been eclipsed by the emergence of an intransigent opposition. In addition, the responsive state facilitates conflict management by giving ethnic and regional intermediaries an increased opportunity to pull back from inflexible stances, and without an extraordinary loss of face. Thus state responsiveness lends an indispensable aura of legitimacy to the political system, creating the time and space within which potential adversaries can develop new perceptions about one another and in the process open up new possibilities for cooperative behavior.

PART 4
The Economics of Conflict

Chapter 8

THOMAS OHLSON

Strategic Confrontation versus Economic Survival in Southern Africa

South Africa has, for some fifteen years, been waging an undeclared war against its independent neighbors in defense of the apartheid system. The seven members of the "alliance" of Frontline States (FLS) are the principal victims of this aggression: Angola, Botswana, Mozambique, Namibia, Tanzania, Zambia, and Zimbabwe. This war has seriously affected the socioeconomic development processes in these countries, which are already hampered by colonial heritages, distorted economic structures, natural disasters, and errors in policy implementation. The main aim of this chapter is to analyze the prospects for conflict resolution in southern Africa, taking into account the economic burden of the conflict for the actors involved. It is thus of primary importance to understand the basic conflict issues. What is the conflict about? How polarized are the issues? What is the balance of forces? What is negotiable, what non-negotiable?

The point of departure is as follows. There are two basic and interlinked dimensions to the conflict in southern Africa. First, there is the issue of racist minority rule. Until the recent changes began to indicate a shift, the policy of the South African government has been to preserve it; the neighboring countries, having defined apartheid as the root cause of instability and conflict in the region, want it abolished. Second, there is the issue of regional economic relations. Apartheid South Africa's project is predicated on the need for regional hegemony and the economic subordination of other regional states. The neighbors seek a lessening of economic dependence on South Africa and a more equitable regional economic order allowing for true socioeconomic development. This situation also has global aspects: South Africa sees itself as representing the current world economic order in the region, whereas many of South Africa's neighbors see the economic dimension as linked to the wider struggle for a different international economic order, in which increased South-South co-operation and collective self-reliance will help bring about a redistribution of global production and trade, leading to a more stable, equitable, just, and secure world.

The linkage between the two conflict dimensions emerges in part from the fact that large segments of the ruling white minority in South Africa (as well as many other actors in the region and the world) see the antiapartheid-liberation struggle in South Africa and in the region not only as challenging the political system of apartheid but also as potentially challenging the capitalist economic system in South Africa and elsewhere. The neighboring, independent states—in their declaratory policy, if not necessarily in the practice of each member state—see South Africa as an exploitative economic force in the region, both because of their direct economic dependency on South Africa and because of South Africa's role as a conduit for "neocolonial" ties with the major Western industrialized countries.

It will here be argued that the basic incompatibilities explaining the conflict in southern Africa are intimately linked to the existence of the apartheid system in South Africa and that they are firmly entrenched in the basic objectives and policies of the actors. The conflict is thus characterized by seemingly indivisible values on both sides. This implies that concessions made in a regional conflict resolution process will arise not out of political goodwill based in some form of disarmament-development philosophy, but as a consequence of shrinking space for maneuver caused by various pressures, economic pressures in particular.

I begin by attempting to further the understanding of the basic conflict issues and incompatibilities in the region by describing the strategies and aims of each actor. The next section therefore deals with the objectives and dynamics of South Africa's regional strategy, and the following section describes the regional strategy of the neighboring states. Then comes a short discussion of changes and tendencies in the international system and the current interests of the major powers with respect to southern Africa. The subsequent two sections analyze the economic effect of the regional conflict on South Africa and on the Southern African Development Coordination Conference (SADCC) states, respectively. The final section focuses on conflict resolution in the light of the two conflict dimensions identified and outlines some probable short-term "pre-postapartheid" scenarios.

SOUTH AFRICA'S REGIONAL STRATEGY

The basic aims of South Africa's regional strategy have been the preservation of white minority rule and the maintenance of regional dominance throughout southern Africa. It has centered on crushing domestic opposition and keeping the liberation struggle as far away as possible from South Africa. In the past, the latter aim meant supporting— including with military aid—the colonial regimes in the region. Now, after the liberation of Angola, Mozambique, and Zimbabwe, it takes the form of destabilization in order to maintain apartheid South Africa as a regional power, surrounded by a string of subjugated states that do not fan the flames of revolution in South Africa, but rather serve as markets for South African products and suppliers of labor, raw materials, and, where necessary, transport services.

To achieve the central aims of its regional strategy, Pretoria has thus sought to establish and maintain an economic, political, ideological, and military-strategic hegemony over the other states or territories of southern Africa. While the aims have remained constant, the means and the strategy to achieve them have varied with shifts in the regional and internal balance of forces.[1] There is, however, a clear undercurrent trend toward militarization of the South African state and increasing use of military force.[2]

This militarization process, as well as the inherently violent and

1. For analyses of the evolution of destabilization, see Robert Davies, *South African Strategy towards Mozambique in the Post-Nkomati Period*, Research Report 73 (Uppsala: Scandinavian Institute of African Studies, 1985); Joseph Hanlon, *Beggar Your Neighbours* (London: James Currey, 1986), chaps. 2–7; and Joseph Hanlon, "Political Economies in Conflict: SADCC, South Africa and Sanctions," in David Martin and Phyllis Johnson, eds., *Destructive Engagement: Southern Africa at War* (Harare: Zimbabwe Publishing House, 1986).

2. *Militarization* can best be described as an interactive process of increasing the influence of the military at all levels of society. One can distinguish a military level proper, at which the increase in the means to perform military action (such as fighting wars) can be measured; an economic level, at which the increased costs of the military sector can be measured; an ideological-cultural level, at which an increased importance is attributed to military values or values connected to the military (such as nation, security, honor, law and order) throughout society; and, finally, a political level, at which an increased political influence of the military is felt.

aggressive nature of the apartheid system, is a fundamental point of departure for any discussion on conflict resolution in the region. In our analysis of South Africa's behavior, we must guard against two dangers. One is to ignore the systemic nature of apartheid and imagine that change will come about simply through the goodwill of more enlightened leaders in the Nationalist party (NP), coupled with astute diplomacy. The other is to view the system mechanically as a monolith, completely ignoring the contradictions within it and refusing to undertake initiatives designed to release and encourage forces for change.

Reasons for Militarization

There are three basic, interrelated explanations for the trend toward militarization and violence in South Africa. First, apartheid is essentially a system with colonial characteristics, in its racist minority rule and control of the majority of the population as well as in its economic structure. The specific type of capital accumulation in South Africa thus depends on a high level of coercion and state-enforced control in a system that forces the majority of the population to provide cheap labor while it prevents their social and political mobilization. These ends can be achieved only through the joint build-up of a political-ideological structure to justify this form of exploiting the labor force and a military or police apparatus with the technological and manpower means to exercise control.

Second, and in addition to the indicated lack of support from the majority of the domestic population, South Africa also needs a strong military establishment to try to control the region. Military strength is seen by the apartheid regime as a necessary compensation for South Africa's ideological-normative weakness relative to its neighbors. In the same manner, destabilization and coercive diplomacy are in part seen as long-term instruments for increasing acceptance on the regional level of at least parts of South Africa's policies.

Third, South Africa belongs to a small group of countries often referred to as "pariah states." The common characteristic of pariah states is that they, for a variety of reasons, have an isolated position in the international system. A more politicized definition would underline that pariah states—even though they sometimes tend to pursue policies and strategies that may threaten the wider strategic interests of global powers or international capital—are peripheral states in which the ruling group or class can survive only through some form of alliance with key interests in the center. At the same time, the internal policies or external behavior of pariah states often generates action against them, such as boycotts or embargoes, from at least parts of the international community. As their international ostracism expands in this manner, pariah states tend to feel an increasing need to enhance their overall military capabilities. Similarly, the use of violence increasingly tends to become the sole method of conflict resolution for the pariah state.

These built-in, systemic factors determine and necessitate the existence and growth of a process of militarization in South Africa. To this, and related to the second factor above, should be added what may be called situational factors. The first example of this is found in connection with the new balance of forces in the region that emerged after the liberation of Mozambique and Angola in the mid-1970s. The South African response to this shift manifested itself in the so-called total strategy.

The Total Strategy

The struggles of the liberation movements in Angola and Mozambique and the ensuing rapid collapse of Portuguese fascism and its colonial empire not only meant the loss for South Africa of two vital buffer states, but also gave a moral and material boost to liberation movements in Rhodesia, Namibia, and inside South Africa, which resulted in a major change in the regional balance of forces. The government of Balthazar Johannes Vorster had for some time been enhancing its capacity for external military action, but tried initially to advocate a regional "détente" of sorts. These attempts failed and were followed by the invasions of Angola in 1975–76, the student revolt and the Soweto killings in 1976, and the mandatory U.N. arms embargo in 1977. Pretoria's strategic equilibrium disintegrated, regionally and within South Africa. The Vorster government was subjected to much criticism from military and financial circles in South Africa for its inability to deal properly with the new dimensions of South Africa's external and internal problems. As a result, it was replaced by the technocratic and security-oriented government of Pieter Willem Botha in 1978.[3]

The top military strategists who first formulated the total strategy in the 1977 Defence White Paper saw a need to reorganize fundamentally the apartheid state's capacity to make military interventions in the region. They also argued that the mobilization of all available resources—economic, political, sociopsychological, and military—was essential to defend and advance the interests of the apartheid state, which, it was argued, was threatened by a total onslaught, a Soviet-orchestrated strategy to take over the whole region. When Botha assumed power in 1978, the total strategy was adopted as official state policy. That led to a restructuring of regional policy in at least three important respects with a view to adapting to the changed regional conjuncture.[4]

Modification of strategic objectives. Because of the changed regional situation, Botha relaunched the old and somewhat vague Vorster concept of a "Constellation of Southern African States" (CONSAS), a regional economic and security alliance with South Africa as the dominant power, to counteract the influence of "Marxism" in the area. Through joint economic projects and security pacts, the superiority of capitalism to socialism and Marxism was to be demonstrated. In other words, the total strategy was not only—or even primarily—concerned with the direct use of military power. Economic and security cooperation was assigned a major role in line with the view often voiced by total strategy advocates that the solution to South Africa's problem is 20 percent military and 80 percent political. This main objective failed, in no small part because of the outcome of the liberation struggle in Rhodesia and the coming to power of Robert Mugabe's Zimbabwe African National Union (ZANU) government in Zimbabwe in 1980. Instead, the other countries in the subregion cre-

---

3. For a fuller discussion, see Dan O'Meara, "From 'Muldergate' to Total Strategy: The Politics of Afrikaner Nationalism and the Crisis of the Capitalist State in South Africa," Maputo, 1984; and Deon Geldenhuys, *The Diplomacy of Isolation* (Johannesburg: Macmillan, 1984).

4. Robert Davies and Dan O'Meara, "Total Strategy in Southern Africa: An Analysis of South African Regional Strategy since 1978," *Journal of Southern African Studies*, vol. 11 (April 1985).

ated the Southern African Development Coordination Conference to promote economic cooperation and decrease dependence on South Africa. The establishing of SADCC had two main implications for South Africa. First, co-optation of its neighbors had to be replaced by coercion and destabilization. Second, other, more limited South African objectives became all the more important:

—that regional states both refuse to permit Namibian and South African liberation movements to operate from their territories and take steps to prevent them from operating clandestinely;

—that regional states moderate their antiapartheid stance;

—that regional states do not develop into strong and independent economies with a capacity to defend themselves militarily;

—that regional states do not develop strong ties, especially of a military nature, with socialist countries;

—that regional states maintain and deepen their economic links with, and dependency on, South Africa.

On the basis of these objectives, Angola and Mozambique were defined as the principal adversaries in the region and were singled out as the main targets of destabilization.

Creation of new instruments to achieve the objectives. These instruments constitute a mixture of military and economic tools, some of them in the form of carrots, others in the form of sticks. After 1980 a preference for economic and military sticks over economic carrots can be observed, especially with respect to the Frontline members of SADCC. Most important, the South African Defence Force (SADF) was restructured and turned into a conventional force to be used against neighboring countries, domestic arms production was stepped up, and the police and the military were reinforced to improve the capability to fight a counterinsurgency war. The official military budget (which excludes substantial amounts of security expenditures hidden elsewhere in the budget) tripled in the ten-year period from 1977–78 to 1987–88.

In addition to this general expansion, particular capabilities were also developed for aggression against neighboring states. These include *reconnaissance commandos and other special forces* for hit-and-run operations; *ethnic battalions* stationed near the borders and composed of black soldiers of the same language-cultural group as the people of the neighboring state (these troops are ready for raids into those territories and to support surrogate forces); *surrogate forces*, such as the National Union for the Total Independence of Angola (UNITA), the Mozambique National Resistance (MNR), the Lesotho Liberation Army (LLA), and "super-ZAPU" (Zimbabwe African People's Union), drawing recruits from the country concerned but supplied, trained, and led by the SADF, in particular by the Directorate of Special Tasks within the SADF's Department of Military Intelligence (DMI). The surrogate forces are the most important of the new military instruments, because from Pretoria's view the strategic effect of their actions makes them highly cost-efficient. They also offer "plausible deniability," that is, there is only a low risk of overt exposure of their South African patronage.

There are two basic types of economic tools. In the terminology of South African strategists, economic links were seen to be capable of being used either as carrots (techniques of persuasion or incentive levers) or sticks (techniques of coercion or disincentive levers). The precise mix has largely been determined by the willingness of the country in question to act in a manner conducive to the five objectives listed above.[5]

Restructuring the decisionmaking process. In the last years of the Vorster government, a great deal of bureaucratic infighting developed among various ministries, state bureaucracies, and parts of the military and security apparatus. These disagreements particularly concerned several aspects of regional strategy and policy. The need for more cohesion and the subsequent elaboration of the "total strategy" by the military in 1977 grew out of these conflicts.

The Botha government set out to end the infighting and the ad hoc and incoherent decisionmaking by restructuring the political process. The most notable features of this reorganization have been, first, a decisive centralization of power in the hands of the prime minister and (after 1984) the executive state president and a corresponding diminution of the role of the cabinet and the parliament. Second, a military-dominated, extraparliamentary government structure, the National Security Management System (NSMS) has been created on

5. Deon Geldenhuys, "Some Strategic Implications of Regional Economic Relationships for the Republic of South Africa," *ISSUP Strategic Review* (University of Pretoria), January 1981.

all levels alongside, but superior to, the formal government structure. At the top of this parallel structure has been the State Security Council (SSC), the main decisionmaking body in South Africa, at least until late 1989.[6]

The significance of this action cannot be overestimated: in practice it has meant that no important decision can be taken in South Africa without the consent of the military. Similarly, the military has been independently able to take decisions and implement them (given the consent of the state president) without having to bother with cabinet consent. In sum, the total strategy emanated from the military and signified the ascendancy to power by the military. Therefore, in a number of important respects, South Africa has been regarded as a military-ruled state.[7]

The Cuito Cuanavale Syndrome

Drastic changes in the regional balance of forces occurred in 1974–75 (the liberation of Angola and Mozambique) and in 1980 (the outcome of the independence process in Zimbabwe and the creation of SADCC). From the point of view of the South African government, both events

6. The NSMS is described in Gavin Cawthra, *Brutal Force: The Apartheid War Machine* (London: International Defence and Aid Fund for Southern Africa, 1986), pp. 31–38; *Star*, November 16, 1988; and *South Africa Barometer*, vol. 2 (November 18, 1988). On November 28, 1989, F. W. de Klerk announced that the NSMS would be replaced by a looser system of coordination in which civilian authorities would come into contact with the security forces only "when there was a need for joint action." He said that the "advantage with this new approach is that the government is confirmed as the maximum authority in matters of strategy and coordination." See *Notícias* (Maputo), November 30, 1989, p. 1.

7. Just to give one example, SADF generals expressed their views on the power of the SADF in a 1988 Supreme Court case. The court was hearing an application for the SADF to be restrained from harassing the End Conscription Campaign (ECC). Defense Minister General Magnus Malan said that any actions taken by the SADF fell outside the jurisdiction of the court because South Africa is engaged in war. The ECC advocate alleged that Malan had invoked martial law by affidavit and then tried to keep it secret. The minister's lawyer agreed that martial law did in fact exist in South Africa, but did not require to be proclaimed; see *Southern Africa Report*, vol. 6 (September 9, 1988).

represented deteriorations in its national security environment and generated shifts of emphasis in regional strategy. It seems likely that 1989–90 will mark a third important shift in the regional power equation, primarily through the decolonization of Namibia.

To understand this new stage, it is necessary to address the erroneous and misleading view that the SADF suffered decisive and irreversible defeats on the military battlefield and, broken and humiliated, sneaked out the backdoor to lick its wounds while the politicians were left with the gruesome task of negotiating the terms of surrender with the victorious Angolan and Cuban representatives. The SADF did not suffer a decisive defeat, nor did it all of a sudden become militarily weak in an overall sense. The "triumphalism" implied in the above viewpoint only serves to obscure the real significance as well as the limitations of the military setbacks suffered by the SADF. There are strong indications that the SADF was successful in southern Angola under the circumstances. After all, the SADF never had more than 9,000 troops inside Angola (South African sources claim the number was about 3,000), which is only a fraction of what the SADF could theoretically field; yet by all accounts they performed well and sustained only limited losses against the numerically superior Angolan and Cuban troops. The important thing is that, for the first time since its participation in the Second World War, the SADF was confronted with a proper, full-size, well-equipped, and battle-hardened conventional force. The SADF did not manage to defeat this force despite making full use of the qualitatively most sophisticated weapons and equipment at its disposal. The battle at Cuito Cuanavale was, in essence, a military setback with wide-ranging political ramifications: it revealed the inherent dangers for South Africa in trying to achieve political goals with military means in the present conjuncture, and it also had an effect on the standing of the military within the apartheid state in general.

Two separate sets of vulnerabilities can be distinguished. The first concerns what can be broadly termed *human and personnel factors*. Most important here is the high-loss sensitivity of white troops. By its own account, the SADF lost more than fifty white soldiers in Angola— substantially more, according to Luanda. It seems clear that the idea of an all-out infantry assault on Cuito Cuanavale was rejected by the politicians in Pretoria, mainly because it entailed the risk of losing up to three hundred whites. That this level of casualties was deemed unacceptable is an important indication of just how sensitive South

Africa is to white losses. Other indicators of this sensitivity are the public refusal of 143 white conscripts to accept an SADF call-up order and a South African Institute for International Affairs poll that showed 57 percent of white adults believed Botha should negotiate with SWAPO and 75 percent opposed increased military spending.[8] Experiences from other wars show that public opinion—and, thus, also political decisionmakers—is heavily influenced by casualty figures.

In order to avoid major white losses in future large-scale fighting, South Africa could either attempt to recruit foreign mercenaries on a much larger scale than is currently the case or integrate more blacks into the SADF. The first alternative is very costly and unlikely to produce a sufficient number of recruits. The second alternative has already proved to be, if not counterproductive, at least potentially problematical. The series of mutinous protests among black soldiers in Namibia during late 1987 and the coup attempt in Bophutatswana illustrate the problem of giving blacks the task of defending the apartheid system.[9] The sensitivity to white casualties is thus a major window of vulnerability and, furthermore, one that will prove difficult to close both in the short and in the longer term.

The other set of vulnerabilities has to do with *weapons and equipment*. There are a number of integrated aspects, which add up to the loss of air superiority. First, there is the issue of fighter aircraft. South Africa possesses a fixed number of relatively modern or modernized Mirage fighters. It cannot openly acquire new fighters from abroad, because of the mandatory U.N. arms embargo in force since 1977, nor has it mastered the technology to manufacture modern fighter aircraft. The South African Air Force (SAAF) is therefore extremely loss sensitive when it comes to its most sophisticated jet fighters. Second, South Africa lacks dedicated attack helicopters. Third, SADF air defenses are vulnerable, because access to modern antiaircraft missiles and to associated up-to-date radar systems is limited. Fourth, the SAAF has for years unsuccessfully tried to improve its airborne long-range surveillance capabilities by finding a replacement for its obsolete Shackleton surveillance planes. Fifth, South Africa has limited access to the most modern C3I (command, control, communications, and intelligence) systems, as well as to up-to-date technology

8. *Weekly Mail*, August 5–11, 1988; and *SouthScan*, vol. 2 (August 10, 1988).
9. *Weekly Mail*, November 20–26, 1987.

related to electronic countermeasures, counter-countermeasures, and electronic warfare vital for aircraft protection and for airborne attacks on defensive missile sites and such other radar- and missile-protected targets as armor concentrations, road or rail junctions, power stations, bridges, and so on.

Most of these factors can be explained by the arms embargo. Despite its many significant loopholes, the embargo continues to be effective. The weaknesses described here were of course not unknown to the South African strategists and the upper echelons of the military. But the practical implications were not experienced until the Angolans and the Cubans introduced modern equipment of Soviet origin into the front line of battle. This equipment was basically identical to that supplied to the Syrians by the Soviet Union in the early 1980s. It was the same weaponry that the Israeli air force literally wiped out in the Bekaa Valley in the 1982 Lebanon War. The Israelis succeeded through a combination of maximum use of superior high-technology electronic equipment and advanced weapon systems launched from modern weapon platforms. Six years later, largely as a result of the arms embargo, the SADF failed to copy the Israeli victory.

A number of military setbacks in southern Angola during 1987–88 revealed some key military vulnerabilities in the SADF. The weaknesses related to human and personnel factors will be difficult to alleviate. The insufficiency of their weapons and technology was known, but its significance was brought home by the Cuito Cuanavale experience. Major efforts to rectify these weaknesses have been under way for several years—with considerable outside help, mainly from some Western major powers and from Israel. (The acquisition of foreign military technology in spite of the arms embargo is discussed later.) Two more factors must be underlined: first, with the exit of Cuban forces from Angola, the military balance is again changing in South Africa's favor (though with an independent Namibia); and second, despite the arms embargo, South Africa remains the strongest military power in the region, in both qualitative and quantitative terms. The point is that the setbacks in Angola—combined with the existence of a strained domestic economy and changes in the international climate—changed once again South Africa's strategic situation, resulting in further modifications in the formulation and conduct of regional strategy.

Internal Contradictions and the Safety-Profitability Problem

It was argued above that, in a strategic situation of increasing crisis internally and isolation internationally, the "securocrats" in Pretoria have so far played a leading role, determining both the general lines of internal and external policy and the operational modes to be used for their implementation. Yet, although the National Security Management System has rationalized the formulation and execution of policy, it has not created a monolith nor has it eliminated all contradictions within the white minority. The turn toward escalating aggression and destabilization against the independent states in the region has revealed some contradictions within the ruling group.

First, and most important, there are the recurring contradictions between monopoly capital and the government. In 1984 relations were more than cordial: the Nkomati Accord with Mozambique and the "reformed apartheid" program at home heralded the revitalization and further expansion of South African monopoly capital at home and in the region. These hopes had faded by mid-1986, after the popular rejection of the Black Local Authority (BLA) system and the ensuing popular protests against the apartheid system, Botha's famous "Rubicon speech," the failure of the Commonwealth's Eminent Persons Group to pressure the NP government into initiating a process of real democratization, and the declaration of the state of emergency. The conclusion is that, even if monopoly capital is often critical of some of the government's policies, there is no "break" as such. Rather, the monopolies are vacillating: moving closer to the government position when they feel the government is capable of guaranteeing workable conditions for capital accumulation and a relatively stable economic environment, distancing themselves when they feel it is not. Currently, the monopolies are participating actively in sanctions-busting, and some of them have long been reaping substantial profits from the wars in the region through their involvement in the arms industry.

Second, there are the differences between what is simplistically referred to as the "Foreign Ministry faction" and the "SADF/military intelligence faction," often termed the differences between "doves" and "hawks." These differences are often misinterpreted. It is important to underline that the adherents of the former faction accept and support the basic goals of maintaining white minority rule and South Africa's regional hegemony. They also support the more short-term objectives of the "total strategy." Nor do they reject military action as one of the means to achieve these objectives. The differences concern choice or nuance: they are about the precise mix and timing of military aggression and economic and diplomatic action, and not over whether or not military and economic aggression should be applied.

A similar line of reasoning should be applied to the issue of "reforming" apartheid. The "factions" in this context are often referred to as *verligte* (enlightened; reformist) and *verkrampte* (narrow-minded; ultraconservative). Here, too, it must be underlined that there are no fundamental disagreements within the government. There may be some differences about the pace and level of abolishing some of the expressions of petty apartheid, but until recently they did not extend to questioning the basic objectives of maintaining white minority rule and securing regional hegemony.

Some of the modalities, limitations, and dynamics of the internal contradictions in the context of regional policy can be illustrated by the 1988 negotiations on Namibian independence. The process leading up to the signing of the Brazzaville Protocol on December 13 and its subsequent ratification in New York on December 22 was somewhat paradoxical. Initially, South African politicians ordered an invasion of Angola in order to save UNITA and at the same time strengthen South Africa's position in any future talks. The military tried to achieve a quick defeat of the Cuban and Angolan forces, but failed. This led to a situation where the main concern of the military was to get out of Angola. The politicians, however, found themselves caught in a quagmire of military setbacks and external diplomatic pressures aimed at Namibian independence. Cuito Cuanavale was therefore a setback for the "securocrats" and made the project of the "doves"—diplomacy in order to buy time—more viable.

This affected the balance of forces within the ruling white minority. The business community, both English- and Afrikaner-based, probably tended to favor a "high road" solution that would further peace and stabilize the regional security situation, thus enhancing their possibilities to expand their economic activities in the region.[10] Foreign

10. The "high road–low road" scenarios are described in Clem Sunter, *The World and South Africa in the 1990s* (Cape Town: Human and Rousseau, Tafelberg, 1987).

Affairs officials and many senior military officers, with a good grasp of the global political implications arising from a continued militaristic regional behavior, were probably also in favor of a negotiated settlement, but wary of compromising South Africa's national security. At least parts of the military and security apparatuses saw Namibian independence as a "sell-out" and a marked deterioration of South Africa's security position. Those who made the final decisions in the negotiations thus had to balance the two regional objectives of "apartheid safety" and "apartheid profitability," while also taking into account international financial and political pressures as well as weighing the effect of the alternatives at hand on the unstable internal political scene.

If the positions of these factions are projected onto the wider issue of South Africa's regional strategy as a whole, there emerge two basic "option clusters" for South African regional policy in the short-to-medium term. The first one is based on détente and a restructuring of regional strategy toward a more "benign" South African behavior. The advantages of economic carrots as opposed to military and economic sticks are emphasized. Favored by those who underline the importance of regional economic cooperation and peaceful relations between the various countries in southern Africa, it is based on the view that destabilization has served its purpose and that now is the time to reintroduce the total strategy as it was originally conceptualized together with a brushed-up version of the CONSAS scheme. This course is believed to be the best way of securing the goal common to both factions and of placating the international community so as to ward off the threat of sanctions. The other basic option rests on a mixture of a continued "confrontationist" behavior and Afrikaner nationalist fundamentalism. Its advocates emphasize the rule of force, finding support in the traditional Afrikaner *laager* mentality and in the notion that "apartheid safety" is far more important than "apartheid profitability." There is of course a third option open for the South African government: to *follow both the détente and the confrontationist routes simultaneously*, as seems currently to be the case in the South Africa–Mozambique relationship.[11]

11. A peculiar feature of current South African behavior toward Mozambique is that, while military and economic destabilization continues unabated, South Africa is also offering economic carrots. One interpretation of

It is in the context of these strategic options that the above-mentioned different views on the mix and timing of "carrots and sticks" are relevant for regional conflict resolution. In moments of deep economic, political, or security crisis or when the different factions have important domestic or international forces behind them, such differences can assume major importance.

Assessment

The preceding analysis of the regional objectives of the South African government generates a number of important conclusions with a bearing on conflict resolution:

—The basic aims of South Africa's regional strategy have been to preserve white minority rule and maintain hegemony throughout southern Africa. The tactics to achieve these strategic objectives have varied with shifts in the regional balance of forces.

—The apartheid system has a built-in tendency toward aggression and the use of violence, and it is the root cause of conflict and instability in the region. The prospects for peace and genuine socioeconomic development in the region are therefore limited until apartheid is ended.

—The basic element of regional strategy has been not to allow political stability and economic development in those neighboring countries that are openly critical of the apartheid system or to pursue strategies designed to offer concrete alternatives to one-sided economic dependence on South Africa.

—Contempt for world opinion has so far been accompanied by a search for military "quick-fix" solutions to regional problems, partic-

---

this is that it exemplifies the contradictions within the white minority in South Africa. Those in favor of détente would like to expand cooperation with Mozambique, but the forces in favor of confrontation are acting on their own and outside political control. Another interpretation is that this seemingly erratic behavior is in fact an *intentional strategy*—an analogy to the "good guy–bad guy" interrogation technique in which the objective of both interrogators is to break the will of the prisoner. Support for this interpretation can be found in the earlier description of the total strategy, the specific objectives of South Africa's destabilization of Mozambique and their underlying explanations, and in the role and composition of the State Security Council.

ularly with respect to Angola and Mozambique. It must nevertheless be hoped that the current diplomatic process, made possible by changes in the balance of forces, will yield some positive results.

—Although the apartheid system is condemned by the major Western powers, there are indications of a gradual convergence of the strategies and objectives of the major Western powers and those of important parts of the South African white minority on the southern Africa region. A kind of "Pax Pretoriana" (preferably without apartheid) in the region—rather similar to the original CONSAS idea—is apparently more acceptable to the West now that South Africa has agreed to the implementation of U.N. Resolution 435 on Namibia.

—The South African government, united on regional policy objectives, has two basic options on which policy tools it should use in the future: détente or confrontation. Whether it will revert to the latter, or be allowed to pursue a combination of the two, is largely a function of which types of external pressure are applied.

THE REGIONAL STRATEGY OF THE FLS-SADCC MEMBER STATES

The purpose of this section is to identify the aims, objectives, values, and strategies of South Africa's neighbors. The common goals and the areas of strategic cooperation between the Frontline States and the Southern African Development Coordination Conference (which comprises the Frontline States plus Lesotho, Malawi, and Swaziland) constitute the other part of the regional conflict map. First, I look at the common strategy behind and general basis for regional cooperation against apartheid South Africa, examining both the unifying forces and the limits to such cooperation. I then consider some of the political, diplomatic, economic, and military aspects of strategic cooperation in the region.

Parameters of FLS-SADCC Cooperation

South Africa's objectives on the regional level—political, economic, and military hegemony—are not accepted by most of the other states in the region. They subscribe to a different conceptualization of how peace should be won and how regional relations should be structured.

The apartheid system is seen as the root cause of the conflict in the region. Furthermore, at least in the declaratory policy of most of the FLS-SADCC states, independence is more than political independence—it is also the freedom to formulate and execute a socioeconomic development strategy. Development is more than economic growth—it is also the reduction of inequalities and injustices between and within regional states. Peace is more than the absence of physical violence and war—it is also the absence of structural violence and exploitation within and between regional states. Security, finally, is more than the military capability to fend off external threats to national core values—it also encompasses the broader insight that underdevelopment, resource waste, the polarization of wealth within and between nations, violations of human rights, illiteracy, malnutrition, diseases, and other nonmilitary aspects of security contribute significantly to tensions, conflicts, and insecurity. Thus national security must be seen in the broader context of collective or common security. National security measures that threaten security on such broader levels are seen as illegitimate.

The broad objectives listed provide necessary but not sufficient guarantees of actual cooperation. The main unifying factor—and the one that allowed the operationalization of regional cooperation—is the common antipathy against white minority rule: apartheid is seen as the main regional obstacle against moving closer to the preferred paradigm outlined above. The commitment to true independence for the remaining white-dominated states and territories of southern Africa thus functions as a substitute for a common ideology among South Africa's neighbors. Still, there are a number of important impediments to regional cooperation. One is the subordinated position of the region in the international division of labor and the economic structures and dependencies inherited from colonialism. Another is the dominating economic and military role of South Africa in the region and the obvious hostility of that country toward any attempts at reducing its position in the region. A third is the political and economic heterogeneity of southern Africa's independent states.

Joint formulation and execution of policy among the FLS-SADCC states is located within a complex set of propelling and inhibiting forces. They constitute a group of newly independent, economically weak, and politically diverse states together trying to pursue a difficult strategy against a background of continuous and growing external threats to their political and economic stability.

Modes of Cooperation

Diplomatic and political cooperation within the FLS dates back to early attempts at bringing unity to the struggle for Rhodesian liberation. In 1974 Presidents Kenneth Kaunda of Zambia, Seretse Khama of Botswana, Samore Machel of FRELIMO in Mozambique, and Julius Nyerere of Tanzania initiated informal discussions within the "Four Presidents Group." They took upon themselves the task of trying to unify the various Rhodesian liberation movements. During the first year and a half, this crisis-management function had only the nominal approval of the Organization of African Unity (OAU). De facto delegation of OAU authority to the FLS (as the group was referred to as of early 1976) on the search for a Rhodesian settlement came about in June 1976 at a meeting of the African Liberation Committee (ALC) of the OAU.[12] There were at least three reasons for this disposition: the geographic proximity to the scene of battle and the close contacts between the FLS leaders and the nationalist leaders in Rhodesia; the lack of unity in the OAU over which line to follow; and the need to work out a comprehensive response to the Kissinger peace proposals (which were presented in Lusaka, indicating a tacit U.S. acknowledgment of the central role played by the FLS presidents).

The modus operandi of FLS collaboration established in this early period—ad hoc summitry of a functional nature, rather than the establishment of permanent secretariats and other fixed structures—remains to this day. It is also probably the only workable way of operating, given the inhibiting factors mentioned above. This way, each national leader can pursue the foreign policy of his country, while the summitry format allows for flexibility, pragmatism, and rapid, collective responses to questions of vital importance to the common goals. The approach established when addressing the Rho-

12. Robert Jaster, "A Regional Security Role for Africa's Front-Line States," in Robert Jaster, ed., *Southern Africa: Regional Security Problems and Prospects* (London and New York: International Institute for Strategic Studies and St. Martin's Press, 1985), p. 93.

desia issue continued throughout the Lancaster House negotiations and was carried over to the other three main issues where the FLS has been diplomatically active: Namibia, the wars in Angola and Mozambique, and the issue of sanctions against South Africa.[13]

Military cooperation is another important aspect of regional strategic interaction. Such cooperation goes back to the early 1960s and the initiation of armed liberation struggle in the Portuguese colonies. Tanzania and Zambia provided rear bases and training for the liberation movements. There was also direct cooperation between the liberation movements, for example, the guerrilla training program and logistical support provided to ZANU fighters inside Mozambique as of mid-1970, when FRELIMO still saw ZAPU as its political ally among the Rhodesian liberation movements.[14] Later on, independent Mozambique and other FLS member states offered crucial assistance to the Patriotic Front in the final stages of the war—for example, apart from logistical support, Mozambique had some five hundred troops fighting alongside the PF guerrillas in 1978–79. Since South Africa initiated large-scale destabilization in Mozambique in 1980, military training has been provided to the Mozambican armed forces from Zimbabwe and Tanzania. At the same time, Mozambique and Zimbabwe have agreed to exchange information and intelligence in the areas of defense and security.[15] The presence of Zimbabwean troops in Mozambique was stepped up in mid-1985, and they were joined by Tanzanian troops.

Because of the sensitive nature of the subject, few details are known about the modalities of military cooperation. It appears that such cooperation is more bilateral in nature than most of the diplomatic activity within the FLS framework. This could, however, result from an intentional FLS policy, according to which those most capable and concerned give direct military aid, whereas other FLS states contribute to the best of their abilities with various forms of nonlethal support.

13. On the important role of the FLS in the Lancaster House negotiations, see Jeffrey Davidow, *A Peace in Southern Africa: The Lancaster House Conference on Rhodesia, 1979* (Boulder, Colo.: Westview Press, 1985); Jaster, "Regional Security Role."

14. David Martin and Phyllis Johnson, *The Struggle for Zimbabwe* (New York: Monthly Review Press, 1981), pp. 21–34.

15. BBC, *Summary of World Broadcasts* (SWB), ME/6662/B/3, March 2, 1981.

Economic cooperation is the last but not least important form of strategic cooperation against South Africa's hegemonic aspirations. The CONSAS plan, as noted above, was unacceptable to most of South Africa's neighbors. The experiences from the political cooperation that had developed within the FLS framework indicated the necessity of economic cooperation, both against dependence on South Africa and for national and regional economic development.

Economic cooperation within the FLS evolved around a small secretariat established in Gaborone, Botswana, in early 1979, and the SADCC guidelines were adopted in Arusha in July the same year. The formal founding of SADCC took place on April 1, 1980, in Lusaka, its prospects having been greatly enhanced by the outcome of the Rhodesian liberation struggle and the ZANU election victory. At the Lusaka summit the heads of state of the six FLS countries, Lesotho, Malawi, and Swaziland formulated the following four basic objectives of SADCC: (1) the reduction of economic independence, particularly, but not only, on South Africa; (2) the forging of links to create a genuine and equitable regional integration; (3) the mobilization of resources to promote the implementation of national, interstate, and regional policies; and (4) concerted action to secure international cooperation within the framework of a strategy for economic liberation.[16]

SADCC has identified some five hundred projects at a total approximate value of US$6.5 billion. About 40 percent of this sum has been guaranteed by extraregional donors, in particular, the European Community, individual EC countries, the Nordic countries, Canada, the United States, and the World Bank.[17] Given its importance to SADCC success, it is not surprising that the transport sector has been given top priority by the organization and by external donors. Some two-thirds of externally generated financial resources have benefited SADCC's Maputo-based transport and communications commission. The degree of independence from the South African transport, port, and shipping network is determined by the degree to which the al-

16. SADCC, "Southern Africa: Toward Economic Liberation: A Declaration by the Governments of Independent Africa Made at Lusaka on the 1st April, 1980," Record of the Southern Africa Development Coordination Summit Conference, Lusaka, 1980.

17. Coralie Bryant, *SADCC*, U.S. Information Agency leaflet (Washington, 1988).

ternative regional transport corridors and outlets can be made operational in spite of South Africa's efforts at making them inoperative.

Like the FLS, SADCC seeks to minimize interstate bureaucracies and has instead opted for concrete and decentralized efforts in areas of common economic-strategic significance. Each member state is responsible for a particular part of SADCC's program. No SADCC institution can make decisions that are binding for the individual members or for the region as a whole. Rather, the idea is to maximize cooperation in areas of joint concern, with national interests as the starting point.

Assessment

What leverage can the FLS-SADCC states exert toward the achievement of their goals in a process of conflict resolution? First, in diplomacy and international politics, the FLS has over the past fifteen years acquired considerable weight within larger forums, such as the OAU, the Commonwealth, the Non-Aligned Movement, and the United Nations. It played a key role in the negotiations leading up to Zimbabwe's independence and was equally instrumental in the almost simultaneous process leading up to the adoption of U.N. Security Council Resolution 435 on Namibian independence. The FLS has also had a significant role in influencing public opinion and political decisionmakers in the West on sanctions against South Africa. The credibility of the FLS undoubtedly also helped SADCC to get external financial support in its initial phase. Within the FLS itself, there have been cases of uncoordinated initiatives, lack of follow-up on decisions taken, and serious disagreements in cases where national and collective interests have collided. Examples include Angolan independence, military support to ZANU and ZAPU, the opening of trade routes through Rhodesia by Zambia, and the issues of sanctions and dialogue with South Africa. But such differences have been overcome and the resilience acquired through FLS summitry and joint action is a major asset. FLS political cooperation has led to an entrenched "collective" thinking, which has carried the alliance through difficult moments and which will be important for future cooperation in the region.

Assessing military cooperation is more difficult. It is unquestionable that this particular form of strategic cooperation was instrumental in the struggle for Zimbabwean liberation and that military aid from

Zimbabwe and Tanzania has been central to Mozambique's struggle for its continued territorial sovereignty and national independence. It is doubtful whether it is justified to expect much more in terms of joint or bilateral military action, given the strong linkages between the military and the national (as opposed to supranational) values the military is tasked with protecting. Military collaboration can of course take many other, less visible forms. For example, much might be achieved through an expansion of the exchange of military intelligence and more coordinated arms procurement policies.

The successes and failures of SADCC, finally, cannot be analyzed without considering the balance of economic forces in the region and the region's subordinated position in the global division of labor. Against that background, SADCC's objectives are anything but modest. It is easy to argue that the West and its financial institutions have supported SADCC—and, in particular, projects in the private sector—as a face-saving exercise making up for the refusal to take firmer action against South Africa in the form of comprehensive economic sanctions. In this manner, the West has managed to prop up the capacity to import and consume in the SADCC countries in spite of the devastating economic effects of destabilization. At the same time, the West has further increased its economic and diplomatic leverage over the SADCC states. Some observers have also noted that most SADCC projects are not only foreign-funded and technical in nature but also rather nationalist in character. This might be interpreted as a form of depolitization of SADCC, that is, something that could further bilateral North-South relations rather than regional integration.[18]

On the face of it, dependence on South Africa has not been reduced, not even in the crucial transport sector, where South Africa handled 21 percent of the SADCC states' external trade in 1988, the same percentage as in 1981.[19] Nevertheless, this implies a major effort within SADCC, given the attempts of South Africa during the 1980s to close the alternative SADCC trade routes, especially through Mozambique. Industrial production and intra-SADCC trade are other areas where

18. Samir Amin, Derrick Chitala, and Ibbo Mandaza, eds., *SADCC: Prospects for Disengagement and Development in Southern Africa* (London: Zed Books, 1987), chaps. 1, 9.

19. *Notícias* (Maputo), June 2, 1989.

few advances have been made. But SADCC has been successful in mobilizing strong international support behind its program, it has convinced the world that a regional economy dictated by the needs of apartheid South Africa is unacceptable, and it has to some extent nurtured the kind of collective thinking that grew out of FLS cooperation. Yet the restructuring of economic relations within each of the SADCC member states, the restructuring of relations between them, and between them and the world economy are still distant goals. Advances toward these goals appear increasingly to be seen by the FLS-SADCC countries as being predicated on peace in the region and a gradual withering away of white minority rule in South Africa.

MAJOR POWER INTERESTS AND CHANGES IN THE INTERNATIONAL SYSTEM

Longer-term trends and dynamics in the international system have had an effect in the United States and the Soviet Union on current foreign policy formulation about regional conflicts in the Third World. Here I briefly consider the current policies and interests of the Soviet Union and the major Western powers about southern Africa, including a discussion on the 1977 mandatory embargo on arms sales to South Africa, since the implementation of this embargo illustrates the incoherence and contradictions often visible in the policies of the major Western powers.

Soviet Interests

The basic element in current foreign policy formulation in the Soviet Union rests on a vital reformulation of the concept of security, and especially of how national and international security interact. The current Soviet conceptualization of security takes a systemic approach: security has to be defined together with, and not against, other states. Joint survival, peaceful coexistence, and international cooperation are better ways of enhancing security on all levels in the international system than the threat of mutual destruction.[20]

20. See Mikhail Gorbachev's statement in CC-CPSU, *Political Report of the CPSU Central Committee to the 27th Party Congress* (Moscow: Novosti, 1986), p. 94.

This reformulation can perhaps be summarized in the following points:

—a rejection of the power-based concept of security and the so-called security dilemma, which is seen as causing a spiraling arms race that threatens global stability;

—a notion that interdependence, rather than an anarchic power struggle, should be, and indeed is becoming, the main driving force in international relations;

—an acknowledgment of the importance of nonmilitary aspects of security;

—a reappraisal of the role of the Third World as an arena for the competition between socialism and capitalism.

These positions can in part be taken at face value as representing a genuine, normative view of how international relations should be conducted. But the reasons for this conceptual adaptation—which was initiated before the advent of Mikhail Gorbachev's *perestroika* and *glasnost*—are also to be found in a pragmatic appreciation of the world and the position of the Soviet Union within it.

What does this imply for Soviet policy toward regional conflicts in the Third World? First, it suggests a reduced importance of such conflicts for the USSR, especially those situated outside areas of major strategic importance to it. There is a Soviet preparedness to make concessions if this serves the overall objective of global stability. Second, the Soviet Union is now looking for political settlements—rather than military solutions—to all Third World regional conflicts. Third, it prefers to reach these solutions through active interaction with the United States and other major powers, given the escalatory risks of regional conflicts, the need for world stability, and the interdependent nature of the international system. Fourth, such political solutions should be based on the specific reality of the region in question and should preferably strengthen, or at least not diminish, the political standing of the Soviet Union—and of that party to the regional conflict with which the USSR has friendly ties—in the region and in the international system.

The role of the Soviet Union in the four-party negotiations on Angola and Namibia illustrates these four points. A similar approach is emerging in the situation in Mozambique, that is, a mutually agreed-upon scaling-down of the military presence and an offer to contribute to a political solution, should the Mozambican government so request.

On the liberation struggle in South Africa, the Soviet Union prefers a negotiated solution; whether conditions for such a solution are currently seen to exist is, however, more ambiguous.

The Interests of the Major Western Powers

The conceptualization of security has not as yet undergone similar changes in the major Western countries, where the power-based security paradigm still prevails.[21] In the United States, for example, Third World policy during the Cold War era was formulated on the basis of entrenched assumptions about the ideological and strategic bipolarity of the international system and the role of the United States as leader of one of the two "blocs" in world politics. Translated into general policy objectives, this implied the promotion of U.S. national security interests, the cultivation of a free-market system, and the support of anticommunist values. On a somewhat more selective basis, the United States has also promoted civil liberties and human rights in Third World countries. These objectives have determined the formulation of U.S. policy on southern Africa. The other major Western powers, including the United Kingdom, West Germany, France, and Japan (as well as the European Community) have relatively fewer geostrategic concerns to take into account. Their Third World policies are more exclusively steered by pragmatic trade and investment considerations and other economic and commercial interests. Both their reluctance to apply sanctions on South Africa and their aid programs in the Frontline States illustrate this.

One important question in this context is whether there is a common fundamental guiding principle in the policy formulation of the major Western governments toward southern Africa. In my view there is: the preservation of capitalism. Since such an objective is increasingly becoming regarded as incompatible with apartheid, it is dependent on some form of postapartheid settlement. This complex objective—which also implies a negative attitude toward attempts at socialist transformation in the region—has generated policies that have often come across as contradictory and incoherent.[22] A good

21. According to this view, the concept of security is defined primarily in national and military terms.

22. See John Marcum, Helen Kitchen, and Michael Spicer, "The United States and the World," in Peter Berger and Bobby Godsell, eds., *A Future*

example of such incoherence is the arms embargo of 1977 (discussed below). The other important question is whether objective circumstances are now emerging that might prompt the leading Western powers to modify their policies toward southern Africa and, if they are, how.

The long-term dynamics and shorter-term shifts in the international system listed earlier, as well as the common wish in the West to vitalize the regional economies and attain a deepened access to the potentially important southern African market, may indicate future Western policies less amenable to apartheid South Africa's maneuvers in the region. The view that Mozambique and Angola have been, or are being, successfully "weaned away from communism" points in the same direction. Moreover, there is in the West a growing realization that the only solution to apartheid's permanent crisis is the abolition of that system and the introduction of a system of universal franchise and equal political and economic rights for all South Africans.

What matters is whether the West is prepared to use its considerable economic leverage in the region to put the necessary pressure on the South African government. Of decisive importance here will be the continuing antiapartheid struggle of the mass democratic movement and other democratic forces inside South Africa and how the government responds to it; domestic policy concerns and public opinion pressures in the major Western countries; and the continuation of détente between the United States and the Soviet Union, including agreement on the conflict in southern Africa. In the past, these and other factors have not been convincing enough. As will be seen, the major Western powers have, albeit indirectly, supported apartheid South Africa's domestic and regional ambitions.

COHERENCE OR INCOHERENCE? THE ARMS
EMBARGO EXAMPLE

South Africa is the most embargoed nation in the world. International opposition to South Africa's policy of apartheid and to its policy of regional aggression in southern Africa has since 1963 been expressed

South Africa: Visions, Strategies and Realities (Cape Town: Human and Rousseau, Tafelberg, 1988), pp. 240–41.

in numerous U.N. Security Council resolutions concerning the trade in arms and military technology with South Africa. In spite of that, the arms trade with South Africa has continued. Weaponry, arms production technology, industrial inputs, electronics, semi-fabricates, and spare parts have continued to reach South Africa, most often from the same Western countries that agreed in the United Nations to abide by the embargo restrictions. South Africa has thus been able to build up both its armed forces and a capable military-industrial complex on a scale that will not soon be attainable for all its African neighbors.

The U.N. arms embargoes, of which the 1977 mandatory embargo on sales of arms and related material is the most important, were achieved only after a long history (since 1956) of demands in the United Nations, not only for an arms embargo but for comprehensive economic sanctions against South Africa. Those who were most reluctant—and vetoed all proposals for a mandatory arms embargo up to 1977—were those Western powers with strong financial interests in South Africa. Thus for the block of African and other Third World states, the arms embargoes finally agreed to by the Western powers should actually be regarded as a compromise. They were imposed as an alternative to mandatory and general economic sanctions. Bearing this in mind, what were the specific circumstances and reasons that made the 1977 embargo come about? Four general reasons can be distinguished.

First, the so-called oil crisis in 1973–74 had to a considerable extent raised the political status of some Third World countries in the international system. Many of these states were strongly committed to the antiapartheid cause. For the Western countries—heavily involved in economic interaction with South Africa—the 1977 embargo offered a way in which they could soften nouveaux riches and economically important antiapartheid countries in the Third World, without having to reduce their overall activities in South Africa very much.

Second, the arms market was booming in the mid- and late 1970s. There was little or no danger of underutilization of capacities in the arms industries of the industrialized countries because of the loss of South Africa as a customer. Instead, there was the possibility that antiapartheid governments in Africa and the Middle East—some of which were among the world's leading arms importers at the time—

would blacklist purchases from companies or countries willing to supply South Africa with military equipment.

Third, the invasions of Angola in 1975–76 and the Soweto massacre of 1976 had put measures against apartheid firmly back on the international political agenda.

Fourth, in some of the crucial countries—which either had been important suppliers of arms and military technology to South Africa or could possibly assume that role—political power was at the time with governments taking a more or less firm antiapartheid stand. This was particularly true for the Carter administration in the United States with its U.N. Ambassador Andrew Young, but the British Labour government under James Callaghan and the Social Democratic Government in West Germany to some extent also pursued similar policies. The conservative French government would have come under heavy fire from its main African clients had it chosen to vote against the mandatory embargo. Thus the mandatory arms embargo against South Africa did not result from moral indignation over the system of apartheid, but was to a large extent the result of careful calculations of the national economic and political interests of the leading Western arms-exporting countries.

However, this did not stop the continued flow of weapons and related equipment to South Africa, especially from the major Western powers. The success of the arms embargo has therefore been partial. The basic aims, an end to apartheid and South Africa's regional aggression, have not been attained. One important reason for this partial failure is the vague formulations of the 1977 mandatory arms embargo. They facilitate minimalist interpretations of the embargo and have, in turn, led to a remarkable growth of the South African arms industry.[23] Why is it that South Africa has been allowed such

23. For overviews of the growth of the South African military industry and the multiple links between it and Western interests, see, for example, two SIPRI publications: Signe Landgren, *Embargo Disimplemented: South Africa's Military Industry* (Oxford University Press, 1989); and Michael Brzoska, "South Africa: Evading the Embargo," in Michael Brzoska and Thomas Ohlson, eds., *Arms Production in the Third World* (London: Taylor and Francis, 1986). See also Cawthra, *Brutal Force*, chap. 5; U.N. Economic and Social Council, Commission of Transnational Corporations, *Role of Transnational Corporations in the Military and Nuclear Sectors of South Africa and Namibia—Report of the Secretary-General*, E/C.10/AC.4/1985/4; and Abdul S. Minty, "South Af-

access to military technology despite the universal condemnation of its apartheid policies and its aggressive regional behavior?

There are some general reasons why arms embargoes are difficult to implement in a comprehensive manner. First, there is no U.N. body that can enforce a mandatory arms embargo. The logical measure against a member violating the embargo would instead be to call upon all other member states to embargo that state. To be of any practical value, then, a mandatory U.N. arms embargo has to be translated into national laws and regulations by member countries (if national legislation is not already conforming to the embargo). This gives individual states considerable leeway in interpreting several issues in connection with the embargo.

Second, numerous powerful industrial, economic, military, and political forces and interests run contrary to the basically moral and judicial reasons underlying an arms embargo. Therefore it can be expected that many states will adopt less than maximal interpretations in implementing the embargo. Most of the major arms-exporting countries do not have a comprehensive set of laws and regulations on its arms exports. Arms transfers have a tendency to be approved or disapproved in an ad hoc manner and be based on short-term national economic and political interests.

Third, the abundance of producers and suppliers of military matériel in the world today renders it inconceivable that an international embargo could be fully effective, even in the event of maximalized laws and regulations in the majority of the arms-exporting countries.

Fourth, the international arms market today is largely a buyer's market. There is a general overcapacity in the world's arms industries. Governments increasingly find the economic forces behind the pressures to export arms so strong that they approve arms deals that for political reasons they might rather prevent. This situation reduces the willingness of governments to adopt legislation that further decreases the prospects for its arms industries to gain lucrative export contracts.

Fifth, with the increasing technological complexity of modern weapon systems, the distinction between military and civilian goods, inputs, and semi-fabricates becomes blurred. Dual technology items, that is, items that can be used for both military and civilian purposes, are

---

rica's Military Build-up: The Region at War," in Martin and Johnson, *Destructive Engagement*.

abundant. From the point of view of embargo implementation, this presents a number of difficult problems, ones that increase with the level of scrutiny applied.

Finally, parallel with the overt exchange of goods and services on the international market, there is the shady area known as the international black market, where illegal or semi-illegal transactions take place. If all other methods fail, the embargoed state can always— albeit often at great costs—turn to this last resort for much of its requirements.

Over and above this, the embargo has been weakened for ideological reasons that have come to the fore in the West. Most important, many political leaders (including President Ronald Reagan, Prime Minister Margaret Thatcher, and Chancellor Helmut Kohl) have not been inclined to see it in the economic and security interests of their countries to take firm action on the implementation of the arms embargo. To the contrary, embargo interpretations have been relaxed. The tendency of the Reagan administration and others during much of the 1980s to see all conflicts in the Third World exclusively in an East-West perspective has undoubtedly been of great benefit to the South African arms industry. The apartheid regime has extracted considerable mileage from referring to South Africa's geo-strategic importance, its wealth in strategic minerals, and the risk that all this might end up in the hands of the Soviet Union and its regional proxies. But such mileage may not be extracted as easily in the future, because of the described changes in the international system and in the regional balance of forces. Furthermore, as noted later, it is a mistake to write off the arms embargo as a failure and as evidence to the fact that sanctions do not work.

THE ECONOMIC EFFECT OF CONFLICT: SOUTH AFRICA

It is difficult, if not impossible, to come up with an overall assessment of the total cost, or opportunity cost, to the South African economy of the apartheid system. Far too many unknown variables enter into the equation. This section deals with three specific costs related to the conflict between apartheid and the forces of liberation in the region: the arms embargo, overall security spending, and the effect of sanctions, financial sanctions in particular. It is vital to consider these costs in relation to the advantages provided to those that benefit from the system. Up to the mid-1970s the political system of apartheid and the economic system of capitalism worked well together. The benefits outweighed the costs. Cheap labor guaranteed stable conditions for capital accumulation, and South African capital in all sectors as well as foreign capital reaped huge profits in the country. That began to change with the challenge from the domestic forces of liberation and the changing balance of forces in the region after 1975. The apartheid regime still sees these and other costs incurred in the maintenance of apartheid as necessary to guarantee the twin objectives of white minority rule and regional hegemony.

The 1977 arms embargo has had a detrimental effect on South Africa's military and economy. First, it has to a considerable extent deprived South Africa of major weapon systems available to other arms-importing countries in the world. Second, the 1977 embargo has, in several instances, curtailed South Africa's efforts to obtain the latest military technology. Third, it has also raised the cost to South Africa of acquiring whatever it can in terms of spare parts, components, and technology. Clandestine trade always imposes substantial extra costs for the purchaser.[24]

Moreover, even if (as argued earlier) the arms embargoes have not had an immediate effect on South Africa's actual military capabilities in the regional context, they have put a strain on resources, financially as well as in personnel, including scientists, engineers, and skilled labor. There are no official estimates of these costs, but a recurrent theme in the South African White Papers on Defence and Armaments Supply has been that domestic arms production is very costly. Major advances in arms production are frequently cited in South African media to pacify public opinion and reassure white South Africans. Although the government has an interest in presenting the state-controlled arms-manufacturing umbrella company Armscor as the

24. One estimate is that the excess costs South Africa has to pay for its clandestine acquisitions of arms and military technology are in the range of 20–100 percent; see "UN Arms Ban Proves Costly to South Africans," *Washington Post*, February 24, 1985. This estimate appears conservative, given the fact that Iran, for example, reportedly had to pay between two and ten times the market price for equipment it needed for its war against Iraq.

most successful arms industry in the world, reports of difficulties keep appearing. Questions about the costs of armaments production and about Armscor spending figures have continually been asked by the opposition in parliament, and over the years a number of measures aiming at rationalization and adjustment have been undertaken to improve Armscor's performance. Most recently, a special investigation committee—set up in 1984 and headed by the then chief of the army (now chief of the SADF), J. J. Geldenhuys—tabled a number of proposals on how to rationalize arms production. But the committee's report did not suggest a solution to the problem that the South African market is far too small to make the production of a wide range of armaments economically viable.[25]

The root of the South African arms production dilemma is the drive toward self-sufficiency, or the "siege economy approach." Self-sufficiency is a form of isolation, either self-imposed or brought about from outside. This approach provides jobs and prosperity for some in the short term, but stagnation in the longer term. If a country protects itself and its industries against international competition, it misses out on the prices and bargains on the international market. The cost of this policy is enormous in the long run. For South Africa's arms industry there has not been any choice, given the embargoes and the overall aim to preserve apartheid and regional hegemony. This is precisely where the embargo has had—and continues to have—an effect.

Unlike most other manufacturers, which do not invest in production facilities unless they are sure of profitable sales volumes, Armscor normally has to tool up for uneconomical and short production runs of sophisticated products. Furthermore, these facilities have to be kept in readiness for surge production even when orders have been filled. It is also forced to tie up huge resources in stocks. Armscor often holds up to four years' supply of strategic items not easily available in South Africa. Civilian manufacturers normally hold about three months of material and component stocks. Finally, it has high research and development (R&D) costs and maintains a rigidly enforced security system to protect its industrial secrets, which incurs high costs

25. A summary of the findings and recommendations of the Geldenhuys Committee is given in *White Paper on Defence and Armaments Supply 1986* (Pretoria: Ministry of Defence, 1986), pt. 1, pp. 1–11.

and may also to some extent hamper productivity.[26] Good management, maximum rationalization, and efficient quality control can to some extent alleviate these problems. In the long run, however, the lack of economies of scale proves enormously, perhaps prohibitively, expensive.

In 1982 Armscor launched a big export drive to gain funds for future R&D efforts and counter the trend toward rapidly rising costs. To further its international competitiveness, Armscor partly lifted the veil of secrecy surrounding its products and flooded the world arms market with information about some of its weapons. Advertising campaigns in the international arms press were combined with displays at arms exhibitions in Greece and Chile. Recipients are few, however, especially after the adoption in 1984 of U.N. Security Council Resolution 558 requesting all states to refrain from importing South African arms. Some customers have been mentioned, though, including Israel, Taiwan, Morocco, Chile, Guatemala, Paraguay, and Venezuela. In recent years, massive amounts of 155-mm artillery shells and also large numbers of G-5 howitzers have been sold to Iran and Iraq in exchange for oil. Nevertheless, official claims of exports valued at $927 million to twenty-three countries in 1987 and over $700 million to thirty-nine countries in 1988 seem improbably high, at least in view of the fact that annual sales before deliveries to Iraq and Iran commenced were estimated at $25–35 million.[27]

As regards overall security expenditure in South Africa, it is evident that the enormous growth in South Africa's military expenditure figures during the last thirty years (from 44 million Rand in 1960–61 to 9,937 million Rand in 1989–90) is something that the regime tries to disguise and minimize. It claims that the figures on the average represent some 15 percent of government spending and some 3–4 percent of gross domestic product, figures which are, indeed, not extremely high compared with those of other countries. There are, however, at least three important points to be made in this context.

First, the comparison with state spending and overall GDP is of

26. *Financial Mail*, December 9, 1983, p. 74.

27. For various estimates of South African arms exports, see *Paratus*, November 1982; *Frankfurter Allgemeine Zeitung*, September 13, 1984, Brzoska, "South Africa: Evading the Embargo," p. 208; *Jane's Defence Weekly*, January

TABLE 8-1. *Spending on "Protection Services," 1988–89 and 1989–90*
Millions of Rand

Service	1988–89 budget (A)	1988–89 actual (B)	1989–90 budget (C)	C over A (percent increase)	C over B (percent increase)
Defense	8,196.0	8,742.8	9,937.4	21.2	13.7
Police	1,940.0	2,130.6	2,496.3	28.7	17.2
Justice	277.4	307.5	348.6	25.7	13.4
Prisons	630.4	673.0	751.0	19.1	11.6
Total	11,043.8	11,853.9	13,533.3	22.5	14.2

Sources: *Financial Mail*, March 17, 1989; *Weekly Mail*, March 17, 1989; and *Star Weekly*, March 22, 1989.

limited relevance. The fact that an economy grows does not automatically imply that the country's military needs become any greater. The argument could be turned around: the fact that military spending has grown with—and often outgrown—state spending and GDP is remarkable given the corresponding growth of the South African economy during the period. Second, actual spending is often substantially higher than the budgeted figure. Third, the defense budget represents only a portion of what can be labeled "security expenditure." As a first step toward an approximation of the real level of security spending in South Africa, one may add up the costs of what in South Africa is often referred to as "protection services," that is, the costs for defense, police, justice, and prisons (table 8-1).

The total budget for 1989–90 amounts to R65 billion. The defense budget of R9,937 million thus accounts for 15.3 percent of this total. The inclusion of total "protection services" brings the security spending total to R13.5 billion, or 20.8 percent. But that still leaves substantial security-related spending unaccounted for, including

—large parts of the costs for the South West African Territorial Force (SWATF) and South West African Police (SWAPOL) forces in Namibia (up to independence);

—parts of military intelligence and secret services (Finance);

23, 1988, p. 118; *Daily Telegraph* (U.K.), March 15, 1988; and *Star*, July 26, 1989.

—the "independent homeland" armies (Development Aid);

—construction of military bases, including defense housing and building (Public Works);

—parts of military medical spending and conscript salaries (Health and private sector);

—parts of weapons and other military procurement, research, and development costs (Education, Special Defense Account, and private sector); and

—costs connected with the Joint Management Centres and other parts of the National Security Management System (various departments).

It has been estimated that if all these security-related costs were added up, total defense and security spending would be between R20 billion and R24 billion, or between 31 and 37 percent of total spending. That would probably amount to about 8–9 percent of GDP.[28] Insofar as security spending is one valid indicator of the level of militarization, South Africa is, theoretically speaking, at least twice as militarized as the official defense budget figure suggests.

The recent and substantial increases in security spending (the peace agreement with Angola and Cuba and the bad state of the South African economy notwithstanding) indicate that peace is apparently costlier than war. This is not as paradoxical as it first may seem, given the absolute priority enjoyed by the security apparatuses in apartheid South Africa. A rolling back of South Africa's outermost defense perimeter might lead to increased security spending because of the modernization and growth of conventional arsenals (the need for which was underlined by the Cuito Cuanavale experience) and further emphasis on conventional rather than guerrilla war; a larger need for permanent deployment of soldiers, weapons, and other equipment along the borders; and an increased emphasis on internal security. Economic necessities, however, may force a decrease in the 1990–91 budget.

Military and security expenditures constitute consumption of resources and contribute little to the productive growth potential of an economy. That becomes a problem when the civilian sectors of the economy also fail to generate growth, as has been true of the South African economy since the mid-1980s. The South African manufacturing sector is not a net earner of foreign exchange: the country is dependent

28. *Weekly Mail*, April 7–13, 1989.

on mineral exports and importation of capital goods. The late Gerhard de Kock, former governor of the South African Reserve Bank, estimated that approximately 80 percent of South Africa's imports are capital equipment and intermediate goods without which the economy cannot sustain itself.[29] Foreign exchange to pay for these imports comes mainly from two sources: exports of primary goods, chiefly minerals, and foreign investment (loans, risk capital, or technology transfers).

As of 1985 Western commercial bankers have expressed a profound lack of trust in the prospects of the South African economy. A freeze on new lending was accompanied by a reluctance to renew credits, creating a snowball effect that soon began to be seriously felt in South Africa. With prospects of huge profits drastically diminished, private investors became reluctant to enter the South African market. Many foreign investors began to disinvest. Public creditors followed suit and refused new loans and debt renegotiations. Trade sanctions were introduced by more and more countries. As Alan Hirsch aptly put it, "The ability of the West to take a moral stand in the 1980s was assisted by the illness of the golden goose."[30]

Debt repayment has thus become a serious problem for the South African government. The hostility of the international financial market has led to deficits since 1985 on both the long-term and the short-term capital account. With limited foreign reserves, South Africa has had no option but to finance these deficits with a surplus on the current account, mainly through increased exports of gold and other minerals. The lack of fresh capital from abroad and the mounting debt problem force the economic decisionmakers to put the brakes on demand, thereby limiting both private expenditure and economic growth. The 5 percent annual growth rate claimed necessary to overcome the economic problems, repay debts, sustain the security effort, pay for socioeconomic upgrading in the townships, and so on, is now untenable—it would overheat the economy.[31]

29. Quoted in *South African Barometer*, vol. 1 (March 27, 1987), p. 20.

30. Alan Hirsch, "The Paperback Which Reveals a More Likely Commonwealth Line," *Weekly Mail*, August 18–24, 1989, p. 14.

31. For a thorough discussion of the emergence, extent, and implications of the current economic crisis in South Africa, see "The 1989/90 South African Budget and the Continuing Crisis of the Apartheid Economy," *Southern Africa Dossier* (Centro de Estudos Africanos, Maputo), April 1989.

In the present circumstances, the low growth rates and the debt burden indicate that, to many influential interest groups inside and outside South Africa, the maintenance of the apartheid political superstructure does not stand the test of cost-benefit analysis. It will take much more pressure, however, to also make the Nationalist party government realize that apartheid can be made neither profitable nor secure. Its current attempts at breaking out of its international isolation through "shuttle diplomacy" and domestic "reform" have as one main objective the easing of the pressures from international financial markets.

THE ECONOMIC EFFECT OF CONFLICT: THE SADCC MEMBER STATES

The economic effects of war and destabilization in the states belonging to SADCC are well documented. Here I review some of the statistical data published in recent years in four areas: war-related deaths, refugees and displaced persons, the effect on health and education, and regional GDP losses from South Africa's war of aggression. It should be kept in mind that statistics—demographic and economic—are unreliable, especially in Angola and Mozambique.

The United Nations Children's and Educational Fund (UNICEF) has estimated that at least 1.3 million people were killed either directly or indirectly in Angola and Mozambique during 1980–88. At least 850,000 of these were children below the age of five. The concept "war-related death" includes deaths directly caused by military action, death by starvation caused by the security situation, and deaths resulting from the combined effects of malnutrition, disease, and the breakdown of the rural health services network.[32] The brutal slaughtering and maiming of civilians by the Mozambique National Resistance (MNR) has led high-ranking officials in the U.S. Department of State to compare the MNR with the Cambodian Khmer Rouge and

32. UNICEF, *Children on the Frontline: The Impact of Apartheid, Destabilization and Warfare on Children in Southern and South Africa*, 3d ed. (UNICEF, 1989), pp. 10, 24–25.

describe the situation in Mozambique as "one of the most brutal holocausts against ordinary human beings since World War II."[33]

In addition, in Angola and Mozambique more than 11 million people—roughly half the rural population in both countries—are displaced from their homes and land. Some 9 million of these are displaced inside their own country, while an estimated 1.5–2 million have been forced to flee to neighboring countries, thus imposing a heavy burden on their countries of refuge.[34]

Real and sustained socioeconomic development without a healthy and reasonably well-educated population is impossible. After independence, these sectors were given top priority in most southern African states, and in many cases these public sector programs achieved substantial successes. This was particularly true in Mozambique, where vaccination and literacy schemes were hailed as model undertakings by the global community. Destabilization has changed that. By mid-1989 more than 2,655 primary schools, or about 45 percent of the total, had been destroyed or otherwise forced to close in Mozambique, affecting more than 500,000 children and over 7,000 teachers. Similarly, some 850 rural health posts and 10 out of a total of 27 rural hospitals were destroyed or seriously damaged. In 1981 the equivalent of $5.40 was spent on the health of each Mozambican. By late 1988 this figure was less than $1.[35]

The first comprehensive estimate of regional GDP losses due to war and destabilization was presented by SADCC to the OAU summit in 1984. This estimate covered 1980–84 and totaled just over US$10 billion,[36] which at the time equaled 10 percent of the combined GDP of

33. Deputy Assistant Secretary of State for Africa Roy Stacy, speaking at a donors' conference in Maputo; quoted in James Brooke, "U.S. Assails 'Holocaust' by Mozambican Rebels," *International Herald Tribune*, April 26, 1988. The reference to the Khmer Rouge was made by Assistant Secretary of State Charles Freeman during a visit to Brazil in March 1989; quoted in *Notícias* (Maputo), March 14, 1989.

34. UNICEF, *Children on the Frontline*, p. 20.

35. Partido Frelimo, *Relatório do Comité Central ao V Congresso* (Maputo: CEGRAF, 1989), pp. 212, 238; and David Martin and Phyllis Johnson, *A Candle on Kilimanjaro: The Front Line States vs. Apartheid*, report prepared for the meeting of the Commonwealth Foreign Ministers on Southern Africa, Canberra, August 7–9, 1989, pp. MO28–31.

36. SADCC, "The Costs of Destabilization of Member States of SADCC,"

the nine SADCC member states for the same period. The most recent estimates cover 1980–88 and come from the U.N. Economic Commission for Africa and from UNICEF. Using basically the same methodology as the SADCC study and certain assumptions on exchange rate calculations, they estimated the loss in Angola at US$30 billion, in Mozambique at $13.5 billion, and in other SADCC countries at $17 billion. The total cost of some US$60 billion indicates a total GDP loss more than three times the total foreign debt of all the SADCC member states.[37]

There are other, more political costs, which are interlinked and result primarily from war and destabilization, as well as from the efforts at alleviating the adverse effects of the conflict. One is the strong donor dependency that has resulted, especially in Mozambique. Another is the loss of freedom of economic action. Certain negative consequences also arise from the necessary changes in economic policy. Again, this is currently most visible in Mozambique, where the program for economic rehabilitation, mainly known under its Portuguese acronym PRE, severely curtails the ability of the state to channel resources to the health and education sectors and also drastically reduces the living standard of the urban poor. Furthermore, as a result of destabilization, the economic interaction with and dependence on South Africa has not been reduced, nor has intra-SADCC economic cooperation increased anywhere near as much as would have been possible under more peaceful conditions. As noted, some of these changes in economic policy result from earlier errors in the formulation and implementation of development policies; however, the current lack of economic maneuvering space is mainly explained by South Africa's war of destabilization.

---

reprinted as Annex B, *Overview* (to Harare annual conference) (Gaborone, 1986).

37. See UNICEF, *Children on the Frontline*, annex A, pp. 35–38; U.N. Economic Commission for Africa, "South African Destabilization: The Economic Costs of Frontline Resistance to Apartheid," quoted in *SouthScan*, vol. 4 (October 20, 1989), p. 298; and North-South Roundtable, *Total Response to Total Strategy: Toward Economic Recovery and Development in Southern Africa*, report from a North-South Roundtable Consultation in Juliasdale, Zimbabwe, December 1–3, 1988, p. 14.

PROSPECTS FOR CONFLICT RESOLUTION BASED ON ECONOMIC RATIONALITY

The overall conclusion emerging from this chapter is that firm pressure is one key to conflict resolution in southern Africa. Such pressure—in the form of military and economic destabilization—has been used by South Africa (and, indirectly, by many Western states) to force South Africa's independent neighbors to back down on the economic level of the conflict (and pay an exorbitantly high price in human and socioeconomic terms in the process). The responsibility to influence the outcome of the other level of conflict and eliminate institutionalized racism in the region thus rests heavily with those Western powers that have the instruments to do so.

The conflict in southern Africa is to be understood in the overall context of the current world economic order and the existence of institutionalized racism and white minority rule. South Africa and its neighbors cannot in the long run continue to live side by side with their differences on these two issues. A successful process of conflict resolution must nevertheless be predicated on these two levels of conflict and on their interaction. From this perspective, all of South Africa's strategies and tactical maneuvers—diplomatic, political, economic, and military—since at least the early 1960s have been reactive and defensive undertakings aimed at preventing or postponing the downfall of the apartheid system. South Africa's regional strategy should thus, more correctly, be labeled a *counterstrategy*. This counterstrategy has mainly been offensive rather than defensive, militaristic and aggressive, not peaceful and conciliatory.

With the direct and indirect support of the major Western powers, South Africa has used its economic and military might in the region according to the principle "offense is the best defense." While the maneuvering space for apartheid South Africa has continually diminished through dramatic changes in the regional balance of forces, South Africa's policy of destabilization has had a severe effect on the surrounding newly independent states. The prospects for a restructuring of regional economic relations away from neocolonial features and toward more economic freedom of action has thus been curtailed. In this respect, destabilization has indeed been successful. Mozambique may serve as an illustration. Whereas in the past the goals of socialist transformation, socioeconomic development, an end to apartheid, and peace in the country and in the region were seen as inextricably linked, the policy objectives are now in order of priority: peace, socioeconomic recuperation (without socialist transformation), an end to apartheid, and, in the longer term if at all, socialist transformation. Furthermore, the interdependence of the objectives is no longer considered automatic.

The present climate appears to favor negotiations toward political solutions both to the conflict between apartheid and the forces of liberation inside South Africa and the other conflicts in the region caused by apartheid South Africa. Negotiations are also seen in a more favorable light in Pretoria. That is not, however, to be interpreted as representing profound changes in the subjective views of the decisionmakers. Instead it should be seen in the light of changes in the objective circumstances within which decisions are made. These "new realities" include

—the military setbacks at Cuito Cuanavale, which highlighted the limitations of militaristic aggression as a means of guaranteeing long-term security for apartheid;

—the failure of both "Total Strategy" and its successor WHAM ("Winning Hearts and Minds") to create a new supportive alliance capable of resolving the domestic crisis of apartheid, as well as the gradual withering away of white political cohesion on what the future path of South Africa should be;

—the growing pressures of international isolation, and most particularly the effects of South Africa's exclusion from the "normal facilities" of international financial markets on the South African economy;

—the changing international environment, resulting particularly from the adoption of the policies of *glasnost*, *perestroika*, and "new thinking" in the Soviet Union. This has led to growing cooperation between the Soviet Union and the West in seeking "political solutions to regional conflicts." There is also in the West a growth in antiapartheid sentiment.

Even before F. W. de Klerk became state president in 1989, it had become clear that these new realities had coalesced to produce new objective circumstances that the authorities in Pretoria could not ignore. The military option in Angola had become extremely costly in military, political, and economic terms. Pretoria's known involvement in destabilization elsewhere in the region, most notably in Mozambique, was threatening to become expensive diplomatically and ideologically, since it would lead to an increase in South Africa's international isolation at precisely a moment when economic pressures dictated the necessity for a major effort to reduce this isolation. Meanwhile, the government needed space, time, and a degree of legitimacy to tackle the question of how to proceed with domestic restructuring, given the growing recognition that neither Total Strategy nor WHAM was capable of producing a viable solution to the continuing crisis of apartheid.

These new realities are not necessarily all negative for Pretoria. The South African government has involved its diplomats in various negotiations in order to substitute some endorsement by the region and the international community for its lack of domestic legitimacy. Through maximum utilization of its current international goodwill (after the Namibia Accord and the substitution of de Klerk for Botha), South Africa is currently using diplomatic and economic action to gain tacit support for three of its currently most important regional policy objectives: (1) breaking out of the international isolation through an acceptance of its "constructive" political role as a regional peacemaker; (2) gaining greater access to the regional markets by promoting itself as the regional economic powerhouse through which the region can be economically "restabilized"; and (3) winning regional and international endorsement for the modified "internal reform" program of the NP and thus warding off further sanctions.

There is no single inevitable future for South Africa or for the region. Rather, several possible scenarios exist and are being struggled for by different forces. Which one materializes in practice will depend on the strategies pursued by the various national, regional, and extraregional forces involved in the main conflict—that between apartheid and the forces of liberation inside South Africa. The new realities in South and southern Africa have widened the range of possible near-term scenarios, but apartheid South Africa remains a powerful economic and military force, and whereas the new South African government talks about profound domestic change, it has also firmly rejected the prospect of a system of universal franchise in a unitary state. Nevertheless, the transition to a phase of regional relations involving some element of dialogue between Pretoria and its neighbors has opened up new terrain with certain possibilities for the apartheid regime to buy time and enhance its image with the major Western powers. These factors also have to be taken into account in considering the range of possible scenarios in the region in the immediate future. There are several assumptions about the international, regional, and domestic domains that are likely to influence future scenarios:

—The conflicts in South and southern Africa will not be considered sufficiently important by the superpowers to provoke large-scale military intervention, either directly or indirectly.

—The superpowers and other large powers with interests in the region will continue to favor a nonrevolutionary transition to democracy in South Africa.

—South Africa's external trade and financial linkages, as well as its economic growth, will continue to be hampered by internal political opposition and external action, sanctions in particular.

—South Africa's neighbors will continue to be willing to offer substantial concessions on both their economic links with South Africa and their domestic socioeconomic development projects as long as they can see light at the end of the tunnel.

—The goal of FLS-SADCC diplomacy will continue to be raising the costs to Pretoria of supporting the destabilization of its neighboring states and bringing about a withdrawal from such policies, thus securing national independence and creating conditions for economic recovery. Among the FLS-SADCC member states there is also an interest in exploring whether the new realities are conducive to some form of a negotiated end to apartheid.

—There is widespread dissent within South Africa's white population, a dissent that covers the entire South African political spectrum. This discord will grow as the extreme right, with its socially and geographically limited support base, finds its breathing space further diminished and as the more powerful interests linked to "big business" find the prospects for capital accumulation and economic growth hampered by apartheid and the external reaction against it.

—The ruling Nationalist party strata are also likely to become further divided. Such divisions within the ruling bureaucracy, paired with a split white political constituency as a whole, will make it difficult to formulate a long-term strategy and mobilize the resources required to support it. The capacity of the regime to control events is likely to diminish.

—The leadership of the African National Congress (ANC) and the mass democratic movement will continue to be disposed toward conciliation, at least until all attempts at a negotiated transformation to democracy have proved futile.

On the basis of these assumptions, at least three scenarios can be envisaged: (1) reformed apartheid or power sharing without a transfer of power, (2) power sharing after a transfer of power, and (3) nonracial democracy.[38]

Reformed Apartheid

The domestic scenario currently envisaged by the de Klerk government, reformed apartheid is based on the Five-Year Action Plan of the NP and has been further elaborated upon in various official statements. It falls well short of a postapartheid solution, since its objective is to preserve, not eliminate, the basic pillars of the apartheid system. This scenario could have at least three different effects on the region as a whole, depending on the balance of forces.

The first possible regional "sub-scenario" would emerge if South Africa succeeded in using the current diplomatic and economic openings to reduce significantly its international isolation and obtain a degree of international endorsement for its "reformed apartheid" program. If these objectives were to be realized, a greater convergence between South African and Western policy could be expected around a project seeking to "restabilize" the region under South African hegemony. This concourse could lead to Western participation in joint ventures with South Africa channeling aid and investment into projects that would tend to strengthen rather than lessen ties of dependence. Such a strategy has been elaborated in South Africa and tentatively named a "Marshall Plan" for southern Africa. It implies that the West will close its eyes to the crisis of apartheid inside South Africa and to apartheid's role as the root cause of conflict on the regional level or, alternatively, will believe that the newly elected white minority government and its state president somehow will seriously involve itself in negotiations leading to its elimination from political power.

38. These scenarios, as well as other points made in this section, were developed jointly with my colleague Robert Davies, whose substantial input is gratefully acknowledged.

At the security level, this scenario would initially suggest some withdrawal from certain forms of destabilization. Since the crisis of apartheid would remain essentially unresolved, however, a strong impulse toward seeking to export the crisis of apartheid to the region would remain—especially at moments when the domestic crisis of apartheid was felt most intensely. A complete unilateral abandonment of "war by proxy" by South Africa would be extremely unlikely, although cycles of ups and downs in such support are possible. Any more permanent reduction in the level of destabilization would probably continue to depend on acceptance by a victim state of some form of "Pax Pretoriana" terms. That is, a measure of peace (in the sense of absence of war) could be bought, but only at the cost of significant concessions to South African demands that would place severe constraints on the capacity to assert real independence. For the region, this scenario would also mean that the apartheid regime could acquire the resources to overcome its current military and financial vulnerabilities.

A second possible regional sub-scenario would result from an early collapse of Pretoria's current diplomatic, economic-oriented approach to the region. If that were to occur, and there was not sufficient international pressure to render the costs prohibitive, a rapid return to the cycle of escalating regional aggression could be expected. Yet there could be certain changes in the selection of the major targets of destabilization, with Zimbabwe and an independent Namibia coming in for more attention. For Mozambique, such a scenario would mean not only the continuation of the bandit war but also the possibility that Zimbabwe might find itself so tied down by destabilization at home that it would be obliged to reduce its commitment to Mozambique.

A third sub-scenario would be that the momentum of changes in the international system and new regional realities succeeds in continuing to restrain those in Pretoria favoring militaristic options, while not capitulating to the strategies of South Africa's diplomats or allowing apartheid to break out of its international isolation. Such a scenario would amount to keeping destabilization at bay and simultaneously keeping apartheid weak. Undiminished or increased international pressure is central here. For the independent states of southern Africa as a whole, such a scenario would open up a certain space for the advance of SADCC projects currently blocked by destabilization, and it would be conducive to the role SADCC plays in the strategic planning of the major Western powers. The antiapartheid struggle would be able to derive maximum benefit from the new regional conjuncture, while minimizing the openings created for the apartheid regime to overcome its current economic and military vulnerabilities.

Clearly this third scenario is the one preferred by the FLS and SADCC member states. It is, however, the alternative that requires the most skilled diplomacy and the most active and carefully formulated strategy. This effort will have to be rooted in a recognition that success depends on being able to force South Africa to respond to proposals from the region (or from extraregional interests), rather than the other way around. It implies an element of dialogue with Pretoria that does not spill over into legitimation of Pretoria's policies and objectives. Also required is the formulation of policies on economic interaction that do not simply offer an open door for South African capital, but seek to obtain the best terms possible in relations that remain unavoidable and allow other forms of economic cooperation where this is compatible with national and regional plans and priorities. The central focus of regional economic policy would continue to be firmly located within the SADCC perspective of reducing historical ties of dependence on South Africa. Such strategy formulation should be based on the insight that the present South African government is intransigent on the key issues. The offering of carrots by extraregional forces is therefore as counterproductive now as it was in the past. Further progress depends on increasing external pressure.

The reformed apartheid scenario and its three regional sub-scenarios have one thing in common: they describe a situation still profoundly characterized by the struggle to maintain or end apartheid. The other two possible domestic scenarios refer to situations in which there has been more substantial change in either the political or socioeconomic pillars of apartheid.

Power Sharing after a Transfer of Power

This scenario could, in a somewhat oversimplified manner, be described as the project of South African big business, with the support of foreign financial and monopoly capital interests. The trademark of various proposals along the lines of "power sharing after a transfer of power" is that qualitative changes must take place in the *political* system—with some proposals suggesting the total elimination of racist minority rule—but with simultaneous restrictions built into the constitution and elsewhere to limit the capacity of a new government to bring about changes in the restructuring of the South African *economy*.

While having many characteristics in common, proposals along these lines also display important differences. For example, it is not clear whether this scenario will lead to a "power-sharing, general affairs government" and a system of "own affairs" ethnic bodies or just a single parliament or assembly. An imposed power-sharing arrangement against the wishes of the majority may not bring about an end to destabilization, as can be remembered from the Smith-Muzorewa government in Rhodesia-Zimbabwe. Another important issue is whether such a government will want to assert itself as a regional power. If such a position is sought, then it can be expected that the government will want to maintain existing patterns of subordination and domination in the region. A passive approach on the issue of regional economic transformation will similarly tend to reinforce existing patterns; at the same time it can be expected that international support for SADCC—and perhaps also internal SADCC cohesion—will diminish if apartheid is abolished.

Nonracial Democracy

This projection is the scenario of the various organizations subscribing to the Freedom Charter and more recent perspectives outlined in the ANC constitutional guidelines and the declaration on South Africa endorsed by the OAU and the Non-Aligned Movement. Their goal is to eradicate both the political and socioeconomic pillars of apartheid and transform South Africa into a unitary, nonracial, and democratic state based on justice and equality. Little is known about the regional policy to be pursued by such a government. There is, however, an awareness within the liberation movement that, although South Africa will have to be inward-looking for an extended period of transformation and consolidation, there is an urgent need to direct regional economic relations toward more equitable forms of economic interaction, especially in the areas of migrant labor, transport, and trade.

POSTSCRIPT

Postscripts are nice. They offer the author the opportunity to say: "The analysis made above is essentially correct, but the dynamic of events demands a few additional remarks and modifications." The degree of turbulence currently experienced in southern Africa would justify an entirely new chapter dealing with the prospects for conflict reduction and resolution in the region. The more limited objective here is to highlight some crucial and interlinked developments that have a direct bearing on the central topic of the chapter as defined in its title. More specifically, the emphasis is on the problem of continuing destabilization and its implications.

First, it is necessary to return to what I have designated the basic conflict in the region. It was argued that this conflict is intimately linked to the existence of the apartheid system and that it has two dimensions: a political struggle over institutionalized racism and an economic struggle over development strategies and regional economic relations. This basic conflict is now moving toward a form of resolution. It is tempting to imagine an old FRELIMO or MPLA (Popular Movement for the Liberation of Angola) militant describing this resolution in the following stark way: "Apartheid seems to be losing and imperialism seems to be winning." This particular outcome will lead to new conflict formations within and between regional states just as any other outcome would have done. In addition, previously suppressed conflict issues will resurface once the overriding conflict has receded into the background.

Whatever the final structure of the international system emerging out of the current transition process, it will operate in a framework characterized by political pluralism and market economy rule to a much greater extent than in the past. The same is true for southern Africa, including Angola and Mozambique. Also, the Nationalist party government in South Africa has dramatically changed its position on many of the pillars of apartheid since this essay was written in the fall of 1989. While the government then located itself in the reformed apartheid scenario, it now appears to have *shifted to the scenario called "power sharing after a transfer of power."* In other words, the NP has dropped its long-standing objective of maintaining political and economic power in the hands of the white minority and is now concentrating on safeguarding economic power for its constituency. This approach implies that the creators of apartheid are now willing to get rid of this system in exchange for an end to international isolation and a central role for South Africa in the economic reconstruction of a capitalist southern Africa (the restabilization scenario). If such a scenario is acceptable, even desirable, to the NP, to South African big business, to the major Western powers, to neighbors in the region, and to the international financial institutions, then there would be few, if any, reasons for South Africa to continue to destabilize its neighbors.

Yet the disturbing fact is that military destabilization of Angola, Mozambique, and other regional neighbors continues. Assistance to UNITA and the MNR (or Renamo, its Portuguese acronym) is still coming from South African territory. This continuation of support has not been given much coverage in the international press during 1990–91 for several reasons: first, because the support is much more low key than before; second, because the Angolan and Mozambican governments see it in their best interests not to go public on every instance, given the delicate internal process in South Africa; and, third, because the focus of world attention has been on events in Eastern Europe and the Middle East. But the assistance continues.

In the Mozambican case, this was implicitly admitted by the South African Foreign Minister Roelof Botha when he visited Maputo in November 1990. At a press conference, he told reporters that the Pretoria government was unable to guarantee that logistic support could not reach Renamo from South African soil, even though the government had ordered all such support to cease.[39] More concrete evidence of such aid comes from statements by former Renamo officials, signals intelligence, and eyewitness accounts of equipment deliveries, plane drops, Renamo bands entering Mozambique from South Africa and returning there after attacks, and hit squad activities in Maputo.

This situation raises two crucial questions. First, what is the logic and rationale behind the continuing military destabilization? A tentative answer is that, even if the outcome outlined here is acceptable to the NP and to the big companies, it is far from self-evident that it

39. *MozambiqueFile*, AIM monthly newsletter, no. 173 (December 1990), p. 23.

is acceptable to all sections of the white minority. There are groups that do not want an outcome based on the political elimination of formal apartheid structures in South Africa and the victory of capitalism over socialism in the region. This refusal is rooted in identity issues, that is, individuals' or groups' self-perceived sense of their position in society.

Three important types of individuals or groups that may experience a threat to their identity from the abolition of apartheid structures are (1) segments of the security forces, such as strategic planners in police or military intelligence think tanks, operatives from police or military hit squads, and middle-level officers who for a considerable time have been exposed to the most militarized aspects of apartheid ideology; (2) white farmers in border areas; and (3) the poorest segments of the white population in both urban and rural areas.

For people in those three categories it would be particularly difficult to move away from the apartheid paradigm that is implanted in every South African from birth. Apart from the general cultural and ideological pressures, they feel specific threats to their very existence. The first group may have fears of being tracked down and killed, of being expelled from the defense force or from the country, or even of having a black commanding officer. The second group may fear personal bankruptcy if the ready availability of cheap farm labor disappears through legislative changes. The third group may psychologically fear the disappearance of their legal right to kick downward, since there will be no one left to kick at while they themselves will continue to be subjected to kicking from above in their new and, for them, extremely awkward position at the bottom of the social ladder alongside their nonwhite counterparts.

Thus there is a motive (survival of individual and group identity) as well as an infrastructure (planning and control from within the security forces apparatus, operational assistance from farmers in supplying the instruments of destabilization into the neighboring countries, operational assistance from lower strata of the white minority in instigating and fanning the flames of so-called black-on-black violence inside South Africa). Further infrastructural support comes from such external forces as the religious extreme right, fanatical anticommunists, colonial revanchists, and opportunists in neighboring countries who see potential gains from further weakening the MPLA and FRELIMO governments.

The second crucial question is whether these activities have tacit government sanction or whether they simply illustrate the fact that President de Klerk and his allies in government are not in full control of the security forces. It is difficult to speculate on this, especially when observing events from a distance. Three points can be made. First, it is conceivable that de Klerk tacitly supports the continuation of destabilization. The rationale would be that he judges it helpful in securing the best possible deal out of the current domestic process as well as for achieving the three regional policy objectives mentioned earlier in this chapter. In that case he would no longer be content with "plausible deniability"; he would need "absolute deniability." Second, it is possible that he is against the continuation of destabilization (which is what he publicly claims) and that, when faced with allegations of support, he is left with the argument that no country can fully control what goes on either inside or at its borders. His situation would then be similar to that of Soviet President Gorbachev on the morning after the Vilnius massacre in Lithuania in January 1991, when Gorbachev swore himself free of responsibility because he was asleep at the time of the event. The third and most important point is that any external actor who has the will and the power to influence the situation in South Africa and speed up the process of eliminating apartheid will have to work hard to establish which of the two positions mentioned is the correct one. The reason for that is clear: the mix of carrots and sticks will look different depending on what the position of the South African government really is. This problem would become particularly difficult if the government itself felt ambivalent on the matter.

In sum, considering the effect of global change, the process of political and economic restructuring in Angola and Mozambique, the continuation of destabilization, and the volatile internal situation in South Africa, what are the actions and outcomes that in the present regional conjuncture would seem to best promote peace and security in southern Africa? On the regional level, the actors should begin to lay an institutional basis for concrete discussions on such vital regional matters as security, trade, migrant labor, transport, mining, and energy. There should be a total and unconditional end to all forms of external support for UNITA and Renamo. In addition, all available domestic resources in Angola and Mozambique should be mobilized to facilitate the return to the land and the rehabilitation of the socioeconomic infrastructure in rural areas. That is, a bottom-up type of rural development strategy based on dynamization, local resources, and local initiative needs to be adopted. Also essential is a major effort to reach the poorest, most marginalized, and "semi-banditized" segments of the rural poor in Angola and Mozambique. If that is not done, a perpetuation of violence in rural areas is unavoidable. Substantial amounts of donor funds must be earmarked for support of the efforts described in the last two points. There must be implementation of some form of a distributionist welfare system, particularly aimed at the urban poor. Furthermore, there needs to be a general recognition—in the region and among donors—of the important role of the state, not only as a facilitator for the operation of market forces but as an actor in its own right. It will also be necessary to create political and other institutions, methods, procedures, and norms that can strengthen regional and national values, further the nation-building process, and prevent future conflict issues from triggering overt violence.

Chapter 9

NICOLE BALL

The Effect of Conflict on the Economies of Third World Countries

The period following the Second World War has been one of enormous contradictions for most Third World countries, and those in sub-Saharan Africa are no exception. Decolonization has afforded local populations in Africa, the Caribbean, Asia, the Middle East, and portions of Latin America the opportunity to regain control of the political and economic life of their countries. Governments have had the opportunity to determine priorities based on the needs of local populations and to allocate resources accordingly. Access to education and social services has increased since the end of the colonial period. According to the World Bank, in the low- and middle-income countries a larger, often substantially larger, share of children now receive formal primary and secondary education; life expectancy has risen; and the number of doctors and nurses per thousand individuals has grown.[1] The prices paid for primary commodities have at times been very high, and the industrial sectors of Third World countries have grown and diversified over the last forty years. World Bank statistics show that the share of manufactured goods in total exports has increased, as has the share of industry in total production in the low- and middle-income countries.[2]

At the same time, the anticipated benefits of economic and political

1. World Bank, *World Development Report, 1990* (New York: Oxford University Press, 1990), tables 28 and 29, pp. 232–35, for health and nutrition and education indicators; and World Bank, *World Development Report, 1986* (New York: Oxford University Press, 1986), table 27, pp. 232–33, for life expectancy indicators.

2. World Bank, *World Development Report, 1990*, table A–5, p. 162, for the structure of production, and table 16, pp. 208–09, for the structure of merchandise exports.

independence have frequently not materialized or have been squan-
dered. Wealth has been concentrated in the hands of a relatively
few individuals. Economic planners have focused on urban areas
and the industrial sector at the expense of rural areas and the agricultural sector. Management capacity and entrepreneurship have
been weak in many parts of the Third World with the result that
multinational corporations have frequently held a substantial amount
of power within particular economies. Rates of unemployment and
underemployment have been high. Despite the growth of the industrial sector, the Third World continues to be heavily reliant on
the more industrialized countries for manufactured goods, and there
is still considerable reliance on exports of traditional raw materials
to earn foreign exchange. Indebtedness has reached crisis proportions in many Third World countries.

Third World political systems have tended to be characterized by
political and administrative centralization, bureaucratization, corruption, and the absence of participatory government. Conflicts among
groups with different ethnic or religious backgrounds have proved
difficult, if not impossible, to resolve. Far from having created independent governments capable of allocating scarce national resources in an equitable manner among all societal groups, decolonization
has produced a situation in which economic systems function to the
benefit of a relatively small group of individuals and control over the
political system is seen as the means of guaranteeing continued elite
dominance. The ordinary citizen frequently has little or no opportunity to influence the policymaking process or to participate fully in
the economic system.

Sub-Saharan Africa is in a particularly precarious situation. In a
1986 analysis of development in sub-Saharan Africa, the World Bank
reported that

> even after this year's projected increase, per capita income will
> have fallen by about 12 percent since the start of the decade. In
> countries such as Chad, Niger, Tanzania, and Togo, the drop
> since 1980 will be roughly 30 percent—similar to that in the United
> States during the Great Depression of the 1930s. The decline in
> Africa's per capita output during the 1980s, together with the
> decline in the 1970s, will wipe out all its rise in per capita output
> since 1960. As a result, low-income Africa is poorer today than

in 1960. Improvements over those years in health, education, and infrastructure are increasingly at risk. For the first time since World War II, a whole region has suffered retrogression over a generation.[3]

The situation in the region's middle-income countries is not much brighter.

By all measurements, sub-Saharan African economies lag behind other Third World economies. Food production per capita declined between the beginning of the 1970s and the early 1980s throughout much of the region and stagnated during the remainder of the 1980s. Gross national product (GNP) per capita declined between 1973 and 1988 in sub-Saharan Africa (excluding South Africa). Gross domestic savings either declined or stagnated throughout the region during the same period. Manufacturing accounted for a slightly larger share of gross product in 1987 than it had in 1965 but actually declined or stagnated throughout much of the period. Unfortunately, what did increase was the rate of population growth and indebtedness. Indeed, measured as a share of GNP, low- and middle-income countries in sub-Saharan Africa had by far the most burdensome external public debt of all Third World regions by 1987.[4]

Sub-Saharan Africa has also seen numerous conflicts, which have ranged from relatively low-level, if protracted, border disputes that are a legacy of the colonial period or ethnic rivalries predating colonial conquest to full-blown wars of secession or national liberation that have consumed far greater human and financial resources. In addition, governments in many African countries have relied heavily on their security forces to come to power and remain there. In some

3. World Bank, *Financing Adjustment with Growth in Sub-Saharan Africa, 1986–90* (Washington, 1986), p. 9. Data on per capita gross national income for 1980–88 for individual countries in the region are found in World Bank, *Trends in Developing Economies, 1990* (Washington, *1990*).

4. World Bank, *World Development Report,* 1990, table A.2, p. 160, for GNP per capita; table A.11, p. 167, for savings rates; table 3, pp. 182–83, for the structure of production; table 4, pp. 184–85, for food production indicators; tables 23 and 24, pp. 222–25, for external debt and external public debt, respectively; and table 26, pp. 228–29, for population growth indicators; and World Bank, *Financing Adjustment,* table 21, p. 87, for food production indicators. See also World Bank, *Trends in Developing Economies.*

cases, the security forces are *the* dominant political force in society. As a result, military expenditure has often absorbed a significant share of state and government resources (table 9–1). In examining the economic performance of African countries, it is therefore important to consider the effect of the security sector. This chapter will be devoted to an examination of four types of effects that conflicts and expenditure in the security sector can be expected to have on African economies: (1) effects generated by direct expenditure on the security forces; (2) indirect effects of expenditure in the security sector; (3) short- and long-term disruption of the economy from conflicts; and (4) effects of a politically active security force.

DIRECT EXPENDITURE ON THE SECURITY FORCES

All security expenditure has an opportunity cost. Once resources are allocated to the security forces, they cannot be used for any other purpose. It is not clear, however, that the developmental effects of spending in the security sector are always negative. Some forms of security expenditure may promote economic growth by, for example, increasing demand for domestically produced goods and services. Other forms of security expenditure may increase the value of factors of production by, for example, providing training that can be transferred to the civilian sector when soldiers leave the armed forces. To evaluate whether such positive effects are in operation, it is necessary to be able to answer two questions: *how much* is being spent in the security sector, and *on what* is it being spent?

How Much Is Spent?

There are serious questions of accuracy surrounding Third World economic and social indicators. At the beginning of the 1980s, a World Bank official admitted to this author that international agencies use each other's statistics without really knowing how accurate they are, and the situation cannot be said to have improved substantially over the last decade. Security expenditure data are particularly problem-

TABLE 9-1. *Military Expenditure of Twenty Sub-Saharan Countries with Per Capita Income below $350 in 1987*[a]

Country	1970		1977		1987	
	Percent GNP	Percent CGE[b]	Percent GNP	Percent CGE[b]	Percent GNP	Percent CGE[b]
Ethiopia	2.3	12.4	5.7	29.2	8.5	24.0
Chad	2.9	12.4	3.3	28.7	3.5	40.1
Zaire	5.4	14.5	1.9	10.8	3.0[c]	18.2[c]
Malawi	0.5	1.5	1.9	8.0	1.4	5.1
Mozambique	n.a.	n.a.	3.7	15.6	8.4	34.6
Tanzania	1.4	6.0	3.2	12.2	3.3[d]	14.3[d]
Burkina Faso	1.3	11.3	3.0	20.8	3.1	17.6
Madagascar	1.4	8.1	2.7	12.8	2.1[c]	7.2[c]
Mali	2.3	17.8	2.6	18.5	2.5[d]	7.2[d]
Burundi	1.3	12.7	2.7	12.4	3.1	12.7
Zambia	1.9	5.6	13.8	33.0[c]	6.6[e]	19.6[e]
Niger	0.8	6.5	0.6	4.6	0.7[c]	5.7[c]
Uganda	1.8	10.8	1.8	21.0	1.4[d]	15.6[d]
Somalia	3.5	25.3	3.1	16.2	3.2[c]	30.0[c]
Togo	1.2	8.5	6.2	13.3	3.3	13.3
Rwanda	2.0	23.5	2.1	15.8	2.0	12.0
Sierra Leone	0.8	5.4	1.0	4.1	0.8[d]	5.0[d]
Benin	n.a.	n.a.	1.4	5.3	2.1[c]	15.5[c]
Central African Republic	2.9	12.4	1.9	10.3	n.a.	n.a.
Kenya	1.0	4.9	2.4	11.1	2.4	8.0

Source: U.S. Arms Control and Disarmament Agency, *World Military Expenditures and Arms Transfers, 1988* (Washington, 1989), table 1; and U.S. Arms Control and Disarmament Agency, *World Military Expenditures and Arms Transfers, 1970–1979* (Washington, March 1982), table 1.

n.a. Data not available.

a. The order of the countries reflects their level of per capita income, with the poorest country at the top.

b. Central government expenditure.

c. Data from 1986.

d. Data from 1985.

e. Data from 1984, and very uncertain.

atic.[5] All security expenditure is not conveniently listed in government budgets and accounts under "Defense" or "Armed Forces," making it necessary to comb through a number of categories to compile a (reasonably) accurate figure. What is more, different countries include different types of expenditure under headings of the same name and, from time to time, move expenditure from one category to another.[6] Expenditure recorded in budgets can be for amounts requested, amounts appropriated, or amounts actually disbursed. A more problematic practice involves the concealment of security-related expenditure. Easiest to conceal are those involving foreign exchange that can be funded off-budget or through special accounts, a frequent occurrence in Latin America.[7] Thomas Ohlson's exposition of the official defense budget of the South African government highlights several of these issues quite clearly. First, and most important, large portions of what can be properly identified as security expenditure are found outside the defense budget. Not only must all or part of the expenditure on police, justice, and prisons be included in the total, but outlays on military intelligence and the secret services are found in the budget for the finance ministry, "homeland" armies are funded through de-

5. For a detailed examination of the issues surrounding the measurement of security expenditure, see Nicole Ball, *Security and Economy in the Third World* (Princeton University Press, 1988), pp. 84–122; and Nicole Ball, *Third World Security Expenditure: A Statistical Compendium* (Stockholm: National Defense Research Institute, May 1984).

6. For example, the paramilitary Garde Républicaine in the Central African Republic has at times been listed under the Ministry of Defense and at other times under the Ministry of the Interior. See Ball, *Security and Economy*, p. 86; Ball, *Third World Security Expenditure*, pp. 114–15.

7. The example of the Indonesian armed forces, which has consistently financed as much as 50 percent and perhaps more of its security expenditure off-budget, indicates that concealment can include more than those expenditures requiring outlays of foreign exchange. See Ball, *Security and Economy*, pp. 112–14; Harold Crouch, "Generals and Business in Indonesia," *Pacific Affairs*, vol. 48 (Winter 1975–76), pp. 519–40; David Jenkins, "The Military's Secret Cache," *Far Eastern Economic Review*, vol. 107 (February 8, 1980), p. 70; David Jenkins, "The Military in Business," *Far Eastern Economic Review*, vol. 99 (January 13, 1978), p. 24; and David Jenkins, "The Defence Budget Gives Little Away," *Far Eastern Economic Review*, vol. 121 (September 15, 1983), p. 46.

velopment aid, and expenditures on military procurement (domestic and imports) are spread throughout several accounts.[8] Second, table 8–1 demonstrates that actual expenditure is frequently higher than that initially requested or approved. It is important to obtain actual expenditure figures when computing the cost of security expenditure to an economy.

The Composition of Security Expenditure

Although an accurate total of security expenditure is an important first step in assessing the economic effect of the security sector, it is far from all that is needed. "What the armed forces are buying with their money" can be divided into salaries, purchases of operating material, weapons procurement, construction, and research and development (R&D) costs. Each of these categories of expenditure can affect a country's economy in different ways. Paying salaries can increase the demand for locally produced goods or, because of training received in the armed forces, can expand the available pool of skilled workers or competent managers available to the civilian sector, both of which could promote growth. But if a large proportion of military personnel choose to spend their salaries on imported goods, then the benefits to the domestic economy are correspondingly reduced. Similarly, if military personnel are trained at the expense of civilians or if the training they receive is not transferable to the civilian sector, economic growth might be hindered.

It is frequently argued that the domestic procurement of weapons and other materials required by the security forces can increase investment and expand the industrial capacity of the economy as a whole. Military-related investment can also occur at the expense of more productive civil-sector investment and may encourage an emphasis on "inappropriate" technologies, ultimately reducing the growth potential of an economy. Procurement of military-related material from abroad can impose an intolerable burden on an economy short of foreign exchange, but it may be an acceptable burden for an economy not faced with such shortages. Because sub-Saharan Africa's per capita external public debt is the heaviest in the Third World, any addition to it must be considered very carefully. It was suggested

8. See Thomas Ohlson's essay in this volume (chapter 8).

during the course of this conference that the most heavily indebted African countries are those whose military-related debt as a share of total debt is the largest.

It is therefore extremely important to have as detailed as possible an understanding of the sectors in which security expenditure occurs and the sectors from which expenditure might be diverted. While the latter exercise may, of necessity, be somewhat speculative, it needs to be undertaken if a complete picture is to be obtained of the direct economic effects of security expenditure on an economy.

SOME INDIRECT EFFECTS OF EXPENDITURE IN THE SECURITY SECTOR

Like any other form of public spending, security expenditure can both increase and decrease the resources available for investment in productive undertakings. The intensity and manner in which security spending affects economies vary from country to country and over time depending on a number of economic, political, and social variables. Disentangling the effects of outlays on security from general economic trends (both domestic and international) can be difficult or even impossible. At the same time, there are several indirect effects that security expenditure has on Third World economies. Whereas the direct effects pertain to how much is spent and where in the economy it is spent, indirect effects relate to the efficiency with which resources are employed and derive from the degree to which resources are misallocated or misused.

Industrial Resources

Development strategies implemented throughout the period after the Second World War have tended to emphasize industrialization as the most efficient means of promoting economic growth and modernization in the Third World, which has frequently resulted in relative neglect of the agricultural sector on the part of development planners. This imbalance has occurred despite the fact that a good argument can be made for the simultaneous development of industry and agriculture.[9] In Nigeria during the 1970s and 1980s, for example, the government (which was controlled by the armed forces up to 1979) gave priority to heavy industry, construction, transportation, and defense and security, with the latter receiving nearly half again as large an allocation under the Third Plan as agriculture, irrigation, livestock, forestry, and fisheries combined. Investment that occurred in the agricultural sector was directed toward export crops and primarily benefited the larger farmers and transnational corporations. The reliance on imported food grew rapidly during the 1970s, and the collapse of oil prices in the early 1980s meant that these food imports were increasingly difficult to finance while the domestic agricultural sector labored under severe constraints.[10]

By according preference to the urban-industrial sector, the government of Nigeria, and those of many other Third World countries, has worsened the situation of smallholders and landless peasants. By failing to eradicate rural poverty, it has weakened the long-term prospects of attaining self-sustaining growth by reducing domestic demand. The security sector frequently affects the assignment of investment priorities. Third World armed forces generally favor industrialization because they believe it enhances economic independence and lays the basis for the domestic production of weapons. When they hold power, as they have in many Third World countries, their ability to influence investment priorities naturally increases.

By building up a defense-industrial sector, not only is any bias in favor of the urban-industrial sector increased, but capital-intensive processes will be favored over labor-intensive ones, and large investments will be made in industries that may well produce goods and industrial inputs that are too specialized for the civilian market. The abundance of labor, much of it unskilled, and the shortage of

9. See, for example, A. F. Ewing, "Some Recent Contributions to the Literature on Economic Development," *Journal of Modern African Studies*, vol. 4, no. 3 (1966), pp. 342–43, where it is argued that a lack of growth and development in the agricultural sector limits demand for industrial products and exacerbates problems of unemployment and underemployment.

10. These constraints are enumerated in Toyin Falola and Julius Ihonvbere, *The Rise and Fall of Nigeria's Second Republic, 1979–84* (London: Zed Press, 1985), p. 141. See also the discussion there on pages 122–45, as well as Otto Sano, *The Political Economy of Food in Nigeria 1960–1982*, Research Report 65 (Uppsala: Scandinavian Institute of African Studies, 1983), esp. pt. 1.

capital that characterize many Third World economies argue in favor of investing scarce capital in production processes that are as labor-intensive as possible. An initial emphasis on labor-intensive processes by no means excludes all capital-intensive methods of production. Nor does it contradict the goal shared by many Third World development planners to create producer-goods industries. It is, however, the appropriate place in which to begin the industrialization process.[11] Many Third World leaders and planners have taken the position that the industrialization process can be "forced" by inaugurating domestic production of weapons. Not only does this approach distort industrial development where it succeeds, but the chances of failure are enormous, resulting in the loss of substantial amounts of investment capital.[12]

In the African context, the issue of domestic production of weapons is, of course, primarily one for South Africa. Most African "arms producers," such as Burkina Faso, Cameroon, Congo, Sudan, and Ghana, produce no more than small amounts of ammunition or carry out assembly of naval craft, as do Gabon and Senegal. Only Nigeria has attempted more substantial domestic production, but without much success, largely because of insufficient capital. It is worth pointing out, however, that a frequently mentioned reason for pursuing the creation of a Nigerian arms industry is to promote industrialization.[13]

The South African government has been "forced" by its previous

11. Carl Dahlman and Larry Westphal, "Technological Effort in Industrial Development: An Interpretative Survey of Recent Research," in Frances Stewart and Jeffrey James, eds., *The Economics of New Technology in Developing Countries* (London and Boulder, Colo.: Frances Pinter and Westview Press, 1982), p. 110, for example, argue that "where the scope for choice is quite broad . . . relatively labour-intensive techniques, rather than the current 'best practice' techniques of the industrial economies, tend typically to be more appropriate for developing-country economies."

12. M. Brzoska and T. Ohlson, "Conclusions," in Michael Brzoska and Thomas Ohlson, eds., *Arms Production in the Third World* (Philadelphia: Taylor and Francis, 1986), pp. 279–90, point out that arms production of any magnitude will not succeed in the absence of a strong, diversified civilian economy.

13. M. Brzoska, "Other Countries: The Smaller Arms Producers," in Brzoska and Ohlson, *Arms Production*, pp. 258–60, 271–74.

unwillingness to share power with the majority of the country's population to create and sustain an arms industry that is larger and more technologically sophisticated than the government can economically support over the long term. This is particularly true given the embargo on the transfer of military technology, which has not stemmed the flow of production technology and components to South Africa but which has raised the cost of these items considerably. It is clear that the success of the South African arms industry has depended very much on the fact that the country already had a substantial industrial base when arms production began to be emphasized in the early 1970s. This base enabled the South African arms industry to modify existing technology to suit the requirements of the South African Defence Forces. There can be no doubt, however, that heavy investment in the defense-industrial sector has helped determine the direction of industry in South Africa in general.[14]

Manpower Resources

Another area in which resources may be misallocated when they are allotted to the military sector is manpower. Military service removes (with a few exceptions) young men from the civilian economy when they are in their most productive years. During wars or periods of protracted conflicts, the manpower needs of the armed forces rise and a larger proportion of the economically active population is removed from the civilian economy. Countries such as Ethiopia and South Africa, which have for many years pursued military solutions to conflicts that require negotiated political solutions, have experienced a constant drain on manpower resources.[15]

14. See chapter 8 in this volume; M. Brzoska, "South Africa: Evading the Embargo," in Brzoska and Ohlson, Arms Production, pp. 193–214; Signe Landgren, Embargo Disimplemented: South Africa's Military Industry (Oxford: Oxford University Press, 1989); and Ewan W. Anderson, "South Africa," in James Everett Katz, ed., Arms Production in Developing Countries (Lexington, Mass.: Heath, 1984), pp. 321–38.

15. It should be pointed out that sub-Saharan Africa, with its very large populations, tends to have a smaller proportion of its economically active population involved in the armed forces than do other Third World regions. Nonetheless, it has been estimated that just over 6 percent of Ethiopia's 15–44-year-old males were enlisted in the security forces in 1980. (If one adds

It is frequently argued that training received in the military out-
weighs the negative consequences of manpower diversion, but this
is true only to the extent that the training received in the military has
applications in the civilian sector and that trained military personnel
return to civilian life. Spinoff from military training can be anticipated
in two areas: administrative skills and technical skills. Different types
of technical skills can be learned in the course of military training:
basic ones such as driving vehicles, plumbing, reading, and writing,
and more advanced ones such as operating and repairing sophisticated weapon systems, and electrical, chemical, and mechanical en-
gineering. To evaluate the effect this training has on the civilian
economy, it is necessary to consider several issues. Are the skills
learned in the normal course of training? What skills are actually
taught? Are the skills transferable to the civilian sector? Do the armed
forces train more individuals than they can employ, or are they in
competition with the civilian sector for skilled manpower? It is only
once these questions have been answered that the full effect of military
technical training can be known. In terms of administrative skills, it
has been claimed that military officers possess organizational skills,
a rational and efficient approach to problems, and a familiarity with
hierarchical structure that enables them to cut through the uncertainties that are said to hinder development led by civilian politicians.

Since many sub-Saharan African armed forces are volunteer forces,
the number of men released into the civilian economy each year is
limited.[16] The fact that conscript forces discharge more men is not
necessarily helpful, because conscripts form the group most likely to
receive the most military-specific, least transferable training. Many

women in that age group to the pool of economically active individuals, then
that figure drops to about 3 percent.) Other sub-Saharan African countries
with a significant percentage of their 15–44-year-old male population engaged
in military-related activities in 1980 are Guinea-Bissau (9.3), Somalia (8.6),
Congo (4.3), Gabon (3.9), Cape Verde (3.8), and Mauritania (3.4). Information
for South Africa was not available. See Ball, *Security and Economy*, app. 4, pp.
410–11.

16. Twenty-eight of thirty-seven sub-Saharan African armed forces sur-
veyed in the mid-1980s were volunteer forces. The conscript forces include
Benin (where men and women are subject to conscription), Burkina Faso,
Ethiopia, Guinea, Madagascar, Malawi, Niger, Senegal, and Zimbabwe. See
Ball, *Security and Economy*, p. 308.

skills taught in the course of normal training are military- or weapon-specific, and even in countries that have purchased large amounts of sophisticated military equipment, only a small proportion of the armed forces can be defined as technically skilled. A further problem is that even skills that can be transferred to the civilian sector may not transfer automatically and further training may be necessary.

Military officers have been involved in governing and administering many Third World countries, but they have not in general proved to be more competent than their civilian counterparts. Indeed, as a group they have certain shortcomings that have reduced their effectiveness. Military officers frequently lack the bargaining skills necessary to reach compromises essential for governing complex bureaucracies and pluralistic societies, and those involved in administering civilian organizations sometimes cannot accept suggestions from their own advisers, expecting instead that these advisers will uncritically support government policies. The militaries that have been most successful at governing have been those in which officers have given civilians an important role in initiating, formulating, and executing economic policies, as is the case in Nigeria, Mauritania, Liberia, and Mali.

The armed forces can release skilled manpower into the civilian economy, but it can also experience shortages of trained manpower. Particularly in countries where unemployment is high or where training opportunities are limited and the pool of skilled labor inside and outside the armed forces is limited, skilled technicians may be encouraged to remain in the military for a large part of their working lives.[17]

Corruption

While external economic conditions over which Third World governments have little, if any, control frequently handicap development efforts, the failure on the part of these governments to manage their available resources effectively has contributed to maldevelopment. In the mid-1980s, it became increasingly common to read that economic difficulties in the Third World are "due, among other factors, to a

---

17. See, for example, Bruce Arlinghaus, *Military Development in Africa: The Political and Economic Risks of Arms Transfers* (Boulder, Colo.: Westview Press, 1984), p. 75.

serious 'misallocation of resources' and to corruption." In 1985, the Organization of African Unity (OAU) announced that many African countries were on the verge of "economic collapse" because of a combination of "an unjust and inequitable economic system," natural disasters, and "domestic policy shortcomings."[18] A survey of twenty-nine coups that occurred in sub-Saharan African countries between 1958 and 1980 reported that corruption was cited as a justification for the coup in 40 percent of the cases.[19]

During the 1950s and 1960s, a school of political theory emerged which argued that because of their "public-service tradition," the armed forces in the newly decolonized areas of the world were able to put the concerns of society as a whole before such particularistic interests as family, class, ethnic group, religion, or region. It was thought that this ability made the armed forces especially well suited to lead the battle against corruption in their countries.

When these ideas were first propounded, few Third World countries outside Latin America had been independent for any length of time. The experience of Latin America suggested very strongly that rule by the armed forces or individual military men (known as *cau-*

18. The first citation is from Roy Stevens, "Momoh Takes Over in a Time of Trouble," *Africa Now*, October 1985, p. 61. The second citation is from Edward Gargan, "Rise in Africa Debt," *New York Times*, August 26, 1985. Writing about sub-Saharan Africa in the mid-1980s, Richard Sandbrook commented that many governments "lack the capacity to establish the crucial conditions for capital accumulation and, additionally, act in economically irrational ways. This nondevelopmental or even antidevelopmental thrust is manifest in the mismanagement, inefficiency, and pervasive corruption of the public sector as well as political instability and inability to prevent widespread evasion of laws and regulations." "The State and Economic Stagnation in Tropical Africa," *World Development*, vol. 14, no. 3 (1986), p. 321. See also Africa Leadership Forum, Secretariat of the Organization of Africa Unity and Secretariat of the United Nations Economic Commission for Africa, "Report on a Brainstorming Meeting for a Conference on Security, Stability, Development and Cooperation in Africa," held on November 17–18, 1990, in Addis Ababa, Ethiopia (New York, 1991).

19. Staffan Wiking, *Military Coups in Sub-Saharan Africa: How to Justify Illegal Assumptions of Power* (Uppsala: Scandinavian Institute of African Studies, 1983), p. 99. The most frequently cited justification, "economic failures," appeared in just over 50 percent of the cases.

dillos) almost certainly guaranteed corrupt, inefficient government, but that experience was rejected by the theorists precisely because the militaries there were organized along traditional lines and projected an image of "administrative incompetence, inaction, and authoritarian, if not reactionary values." The armed forces in other Third World regions were believed to possess a "dynamic and self-sacrificing military leadership committed to progress and the task of modernizing traditional societies that have been subverted by the 'corrupt practices' of the politicians."[20] Unfortunately, the events of the last thirty years have amply demonstrated that the Latin American experience was indeed relevant. Corrupt behavior appears to respect no ideological or occupational boundaries, and the failure of civilians has in no way guaranteed the success of the military.

A comparison of the problems confronting Ghana at the time of Kwame Nkrumah's overthrow in 1966 and the record of his military successors is instructive in this regard. By the mid-1960s, Ghana's economy was in shambles. Real economic growth had been negligible since the beginning of the decade. The country had a large foreign debt and was also running a substantial balance-of-payments deficit. Real earnings were lower in 1965 than they had been in 1955, and unemployment was rising. Inefficiency and corruption characterized the government, leading to "a high level of cynicism toward anything and everything governmental."[21]

Citing economic mismanagement and a deterioration of law and order (but, interestingly, making no references to ethical issues), the armed forces, led by Lieutenant General Joseph Ankrah, overthrew the Nkrumah government on February 24, 1966.[22] Far from offering

---

20. Lucien Pye, "Armies in the Process of Modernization," in John J. Johnson, ed., *The Role of the Military in Underdeveloped Countries* (Princeton University Press, 1962), p. 69.

21. Robert M. Price, "Military Officers and Political Leadership: The Ghanaian Case," *Comparative Politics*, vol. 3 (April 1981), pp. 361–62. See also Robert M. Price, "Neo-Colonialism and Ghana's Economic Decline: A Critical Assessment," *Canadian Journal of African Studies*, vol. 18, no. 1 (1984), pp. 163–93.

22. Wiking, *Military Coups*, p. 86. It is important to understand that before the coup, Nkrumah had placed the regular army on an austerity budget, had created the President's Own Guard Regiment, raising concerns within the regular army that its position of authority was in danger of being eroded,

an alternative to chaotic, corrupt, and inefficient civilian rule, however, this first period of military rule in Ghana, which lasted until 1969, served only to deepen the political and economic crisis. The armed forces allied themselves with the police, which had strongly advocated and implemented repressive legislation under Nkrumah and which had an apparently well-deserved reputation for corruption.

In the economic sphere, the armed forces failed to set a good example for financial austerity. While public expenditures on industries and agriculture were sharply cut back, outlays on the armed forces increased substantially. Particularly noteworthy was the large allocation of foreign exchange to the armed forces, which exceeded that available to all other government ministries, departments, and agencies. Aware of the extensive governmental and administrative corruption that had plagued the country, Ghanaian military officers were nonetheless just as capable as their civilian predecessors of taking part in what was described by Major-General A. K. Ocran as "the plunder of the public treasury." Robert Price has commented: "The impact of this first period of military rule on efficiency, honesty and austerity in Ghanaian public life is perhaps best summed up by a popular record released in Ghana during 1968, the title of which is, 'The Cars Are the Same, Only the Drivers Have Changed.' Not surprisingly, the record was banned soon after its release."[23]

The Ghanaian example is not an isolated case, either in Africa or in many other parts of the world. Corruption results in a substantial, if unrecorded, amount of forgone revenue for many developing countries and conditions the form that development takes by determining which sectors and individual firms obtain funding. During periods of conflict, the opportunities for corruption may increase, but it poses

---

and had proposed to begin training military officers in the Soviet Union, rather than in Great Britain. The coup was, in essence, a turf battle, with the armed forces making it very clear that they intended to maintain their professional autonomy and prerogatives.

23. The first citation is from A. K. Ocran, *A Myth Is Broken* (London: Longmans, 1968), p. 2. The second citation is from Price, "Military Officers," p. 372. The cars referred to in the title of the song were the imported vehicles, often Mercedes-Benz, favored by Ghanaian officials, both civilian and military. On these points, see also Bjorn Hettne, "Soldiers and Politics: The Case of Ghana," *Journal of Peace Research*, vol. 17, no. 2 (1980), pp. 173–93; and Price, "Neo-Colonialism."

a substantial obstacle to development even in times of peace. The problem is not that military officers are more corrupt than civilians; it is, given their importance within the political system of so many Third World countries, that they are not less so. All too often they have no compunction about ensuring that they, their families, and close associates obtain the greatest financial benefits from the position of power they enjoy within society.[24]

DISRUPTION OF THE ECONOMY BY CONFLICT

A number of short- and long-term economic disruptions resulting from the conflict in southern Africa are described in detail in chapter 8, by Thomas Ohlson. They can be divided into three main groupings. First and perhaps most pernicious is the inability to plan rationally, particularly in a situation of prolonged conflict. This difficulty arises because of a dependency on external sources of funding that may be slow in arriving, funds that may be offered for a purpose other than what the government would like to fund; because of difficulties in obtaining financial resources from the local population, whose ability to earn their livelihood has been severely disrupted; and because of war-related destruction of infrastructure. Second are manpower-related problems. The personal toll of conflict, manifested in refugees, displaced persons, and deaths, results in reductions of output, particularly in the agricultural sector. Third, there are the reductions in gross domestic product (GDP) that derive from direct war damage, loss of income from exports, tourism, aid, and the like, as well as higher costs in such sectors as transportation and energy.

It was pointed out in the course of this conference that official GDP figures do not show a decline for countries such as Mozambique or Angola that are involved in long-term conflicts. What this finding probably demonstrates is the serious problems involved in measuring GDP and other economic activity in the poorest countries. Otherwise,

24. See, for example, David J. Gould, *Bureaucratic Corruption and Underdevelopment in the Third World: The Case of Zaire* (New York: Pergamon Press, 1980); James C. Scott, *Comparative Political Corruption* (Englewood Cliffs, N.J.: Prentice-Hall, 1972); and Nicole Ball, "The Military in Politics: Who Benefits and How," *World Development*, vol. 9, no. 6 (1981), pp. 575–77.

it is simply not possible to understand how a country in which a large proportion of the population has been forced to become internal or external refugees does not suffer from a decline in gross domestic product. We must look behind the gross figures in order to accurately represent the ways in which conflict disrupts the economic activities of African peoples.

In chapter 8, Ohlson explains how the conflict in southern Africa has disrupted Mozambique's economy. All that is necessary here, therefore, is to underline that this issue is clearly an important one for Africa as a whole, given the fragile state of regional economies and the involvement of many countries in more or less protracted conflicts during the last thirty to thirty-five years.

THE POLITICAL ROLE OF THE ARMED FORCES

An examination of the political role of the armed forces brings together the three strands of inquiry that the Brookings Africa program has expressed an interest in exploring: conflict and conflict resolution, economic development, and political development.

A frequent outcome of wars and long-term conflicts is the increased involvement of the security forces in the political systems of the states party to the conflict. Few countries in sub-Saharan Africa have not experienced some degree of military rule. Some countries, Nigeria, for example, have been under direct military rule for more than half the time since becoming independent. Others, such as South Africa, where civilians have ruled without interruption, have nonetheless accorded the security forces an important role in determining government policy.[25]

In many parts of the world, including Africa, political systems are dominated by a relatively small number of elite groups (distinguished by such characteristics as class, race, ethnicity, religion, and occupation). These groups also dominate the economy, and they seek to restrict access to power in both spheres. Thus the general public has little or no opportunity to participate in the policymaking process or in the formal economic system. These domestic inequalities, along

25. See the discussion on the South African National Security Management System and the State Security Council in chapter 8.

with an international economic system not designed to operate in the interests of Third World countries, are at the root of underdevelopment. For political development that meets the needs of all social groups to take place, there must be, among other things, a relatively equitable distribution of resources and a political system that both allows all groups to articulate their demands and is capable of producing workable compromises between competing interests.

The inability or unwillingness of many governments to attack seriously the domestic inequalities at the root of underdevelopment has led many of them to arm themselves against their own people as well as against potential external enemies. Security expenditure in Third World countries is heavily weighted toward paying, feeding, housing, and clothing the troops and purchasing basic operating materials for the armed forces.[26] This pattern of expenditure suggests that in most Third World countries the primary use of the security forces is a domestic, political one. By relying on the armed forces to remain in power or by producing political and economic conditions that provide the military with the justification for intervention, many civilian governments have facilitated the entry of the armed forces into the political arena.

Regrettably, the involvement of the security forces in politics only makes the process of creating political systems capable of mediating among the interests of different societal groups more difficult. Most Third World security forces have not supported the growth of participatory forms of government or the implementation of development strategies designed to promote the well-being of the poorer segments of the population. On the contrary, they have increasingly assumed the positions of mediator among competing elite groups and of guarantor of elite-dominated political and economic systems. Indeed, the armed forces have themselves become one of the elite groups. By helping to maintain a system in which the state is seen as a source

26. See the discussion in Ball, *Security and Economy*, pp. 106–11, on the composition of security expenditure. Even though many Third World governments underreport the amount of money they spend on weapons, weapon procurement accounts for a surprisingly small share of most Third World security budgets. See also Ball, *Third World Security Expenditure*, pp. 107–70, and Ball, *Security and Economy*, pp. 398–99, for disaggregated security-expenditure figures for African countries.

of wealth to be tapped by a privileged minority of the population, the security forces seriously complicate the task of implementing the structural changes necessary for the attainment of self-sustaining growth and the improvement of the lives of the poorest groups in society. Rather, they contribute to maldevelopment.

It is clear that one of the main requirements of development, and one of the main challenges for the 1990s, is the creation and nurturing of participatory political and economic systems. The changes that began in the Soviet Union and Eastern Europe in 1989 provide clear opportunities and lessons for Third World governments. Opportunities arise out of the reduction in tensions between East and West and the encouragement of peaceful resolution of conflicts, which should have a direct effect on local and regional security. This should, in turn, make it harder for the armed forces to justify an active domestic political role for themselves. Lessons are to be learned from the link between domestic political reforms and successful economic development. Security forces that have posed a serious obstacle to political development in the Third World by preserving elite-dominated political systems have also frequently complicated the resolution of domestic and international conflicts by seeking military solutions to problems that are inherently political and economic and by *creating* conflict through their refusal to countenance economic and political pluralism.

To the extent possible, it is incumbent on the governments of the major industrialized powers, particularly the United States and the Soviet Union, to encourage the peaceful resolution of conflicts and to support the implementation of economic and political reforms that will give all segments of society in the Third World the opportunity to contribute to the decisionmaking process and to benefit from economic development. Ultimately, however, it is the people and governments of the Third World that must seize the opportunities presented by the changes occurring in East-West relations and create a more equitable future for themselves. A first step in this process for many countries in Africa and other parts of the Third World is to remove the military from politics. As a contribution to this process, the Brookings Africa program should seriously consider examining the relationship among the political role of the security forces, economic development, and political development.

Chapter 10

ATIENO ODHIAMBO

The Economics of Conflict among Marginalized Peoples of Eastern Africa

I am a historian interested in the histories of those nomadic communities that inhabit the borderlands that Kenya shares with Uganda, Sudan, Ethiopia, and Somalia: in order, the Turkana, Pokot, and Karimojong; the Toposa, Dongiro, and Dasenetch (Shangilla); the Gabbra, Oromo, Orma, and Burji; and the Somaali clan-families of Darod, Hawiye, Degodia, Rahanwein, and Ogaden. These groups occupy the margins of the state systems that rule over them. Their viewpoints, if any, hardly penetrate to the capitals of the hegemonic states that have continually coerced their allegiances; Nairobi, Kampala, Addis Ababa, and Mogadishu are faraway places in "foreign" lands, centers from which emanate discourses about control and subjection. These marginal peoples have therefore not heard of *glasnost* and *perestroika*, nor are their own discourses audible to the superpowers. So although these communities are talked *over* as part of the geopolitical configuration that constitutes "the Horn" of Africa, it is a glaring omission that they are neither talked *about* nor constituted as "peoples" with "identities" in any colonial or postcolonial discourse.

Yet they have their own historical discourses, ones grounded in the *long memory* that these peoples have retained, over their last long "century," which runs from about the middle of the European seventeenth century to the present. This long century has had, as its signifiers and markers, etymological and ecological disasters. Destruction of society through warfare and decimation of people and animals by drought have been the trademarks of the region. It is a fragile ecological environment whose occupants have had more than their share of disaster: drought, diseases, and famines; cataclysmic scourges of rinderpest at the beginning of this century and now AIDS at its trailer- and tanker-dominated end. In the last one hundred calendar years, the peoples have undergone military conquests by the British,

Italian, and Amharic imperial conquerors, who sustained their domination through the violence of punitive expeditions, collective punishments, and closed districts ordinances. In the postcolonial era, the states have treated the homelands of these nomadic groups as "security" areas, that is, as terrains over which the state may wage its own internal wars against its citizens. The rhetoric on the etiologies of these state-versus-people wars is likewise monopolized by the state.

Yet these are peoples with voices, which they have used to address their own agenda, an agenda of survival, of coping with disasters. This coping has taken place at three levels. The first level is the household. Families have had to face up to the natural and man-made disasters, coping with contradictions through the constitution and reconstitution of themselves, pursuing such strategies as migration, pawning, suborning, and ritually separating younger from elder, male from female. The hardest-hit segment of these household populations has been and continues to be the women and the children. This sad fact suggests a number of appropriate research topics, including Gender and Disaster, Children and Conflict, and the challenges of reconstituting family and household in the anticipated era of postconflict resolution.

The second level of articulation has been the community, wherein these groups have had to reconstitute themselves over time in terms of identity: Orma today, Wardai tomorrow, "Galla" the day after, and Oromo on the market day is an accessible enough construct. This process of relocation has led communities to acquire new neighbors, kinship networks, and overarching networks of survival within the operational areas of disaster. These communities-in-flux attest to the genius for endurance of these peoples, who have had to build up and sustain their cultural components of survival. In colonialist discourses, these cultural activities were variously labeled murder, raiding, and warfare, but in the postcolonial discourses, they are ominously referred to as "warlike activities" with the consequential state juridical charges of high treason. The more characteristic response, however, has been the permanent military occupation of these people's homelands by the state armies, which are often undisciplined and murderous. The nomads are frequently forced by these alien presences to recall their recent history. Through their prisms they see the state primarily as a cattle-rustling apparatus intent on impoverishing the communities. Clearly, a research and policy agenda aimed at conflict resolution should include discussions about the demilitarization of state boundaries, the reconstruction of new state–civil society relations along these marches, and new directions in conflict management between the communities outside the state's parameters.

The third level of concern is the intervention of the states into the conflict arenas within these regions, in particular, the management of access to favorable ecological niches by the nomads. These have been communities on the march: their repeated migration, dispersal, and resettlement have primarily been quests for favorable pastures and water holes. The modern state has sought to arrest the nomadic practices by appropriating peoples and livestock, and by limiting their movements within state boundaries. What is more, the state system has partitioned these Africans; the Somaali and the Maasai are the most glaring examples. Irredentism, the flipside of partition, thus becomes our other urgent research topic.

The converse of this scenario is also problematic. In eastern Africa, the state comes in many forms: "overdeveloped," "brokenbacked," "soft," "mashed potato," "gentle," and "absent." It is the "absent" state that is the most hazardous for the nomads. In situations in which they belong to the absent or weak state, segments of the neighboring state, if relatively strong, can raid with impunity the unprotected citizens and appropriate their resources. The absent state has also manifested itself in those situations in which bandits temporarily overrun a state institution, such as a police station or a district headquarters, before retreating into the fastnesses, only to have the so-called real state later turn up and inflict dire punishment on the local civilians. This particular issue raises the wider question of the state's accountability to the local populations.

I hasten to add that in eastern Africa there is also what might be referred to as the "imaginary" state. This situation obtains in such places as the Elemi Triangle between Kenya, Uganda, and Sudan, where for ninety years there has been no state. But current rumor flies that there is some oil or some new cache of ivory and all of a sudden the state appears. Sudan and Kenya were recently (1989) revising their boundaries using military maps drawn by European conquerors from 1898, and vigorous discourse carries on. These two countries are under threat of war because there is presumed to be some oil around the Elemi Triangle. There are several fundamental

questions. Who is engaged in warlike activities in these neighborhoods? Who is involved in problem solving? Who is involved in conflict resolution?

To speak more directly to the agenda of the economics of the conflict: seeing that the neighborhoods are disturbed at the levels of
households, community–civil society, and state systems, the logical
conclusion is that conflict is endemic and enduring. Therefore, the
call to arms has likewise been a permanently appropriate response,
which in turn is backed by a permanent state of armed preparedness.
Where these arms have come from is further commentary on the
region's history. Arms have been accumulated from the era of Menelik
II of Ethiopia and Lord Lugard in East Africa, through the First and
Second World Wars, to the Mau Mau era in Kenya, as well as from
the postcolonial armories through mutinies and perennial civil wars
in Sudan, Uganda, Somalia, and Ethiopia. In addition, there are privileged auxiliaries plying arms in the region: poachers, playboys (such
as Adnan Khashoggi and H. Haryanto, alleged by the Kenya state to
be privy to its overthrow in 1982–83), and the private security systems
such as Wells Fargo and Securicor. There are enough arms in the area
to sustain regional conflicts for a long time after superpower rivalries
have SALT-ed their way into peace. And there is an inordinate supply
of military know-how in the countryside: dismissed soldiers, policemen, and prison guards; disbanded armies; and disgruntled guerrillas—all eyeing the national armories. Compounding this situation are
the institutional arms in the hands of the overdeveloped security
systems: the Special Branch, the General Service Unit, and Director-
ates of Intelligence and Military Intelligence, all of which have been
deployed in regional conflicts. Independent sources that supply arms
to such groups as bank robbers also contribute to the turmoil.

In sum, there is a plethora of arms at the centers of state power.
But how do they get to the marginalized peoples I study? The role
of the African educated elites in the procurement and distribution of
arms to marginalized peoples raises for me the question of the *moral
responsibilities of the African intelligentsia* for the fueling and fanning of
regional conflict. That calls for policy thinking.

On the wider canvas of state-to-state relations, it is first important
to reiterate that bilateral relations between, say, France and its African
neocolonies, or Great Britain and its African military clients, have yet

to be affected by the spirit of *perestroika* and *glasnost*. Second, the superpowers are talking to each other, but those African countries that host military bases and facilities of the Soviet Union and the United States have not yet been directly engaged by the superpowers in the discussions leading to the de-escalation of conflict in the Horn. It is a fair measure of the compromise to their sovereignty that the African leaders are currently absent at the rendezvous with history.

PART 5
Conflict Management and Resolution

Chapter 11

I. WILLIAM ZARTMAN

Conflict Reduction: Prevention, Management, and Resolution

Conflict is an inevitable aspect of human interaction, an unavoidable concomitant of choices and decisions. Although conflict is inherent in decisions even when there is only one person, social conflict—as discussed here—is necessarily brought on by the presence of several actors and compounded by several choices. It cannot be avoided. The problem, then, is not to court the frustrations of seeking to remove an inevitability but rather of trying to keep conflict in bounds. Conflict can be prevented on some occasions and managed on others, but resolved only if the term is taken to mean the satisfaction of apparent demands rather than the total eradication of underlying sentiments, memories, and interests. Only time really resolves conflicts, and even the wounds it heals leave their scars for future reference. But short of such ultimate healing, much can be done to reduce conflict and thereby release needed energies for more productive tasks.

Before turning to the methods of conflict reduction, one needs to understand better the importance of conflict itself. Although protracted conflict is dysfunctional, some conflict is not only inevitable but functionally necessary and useful. Since conflict comes from an incompatibility of goals or actions,[1] it is above all necessary as a test of costs and commitments. Sometimes these are already evident beyond all doubt, but even when they are logically determinable, they often need testing in reality. Beyond logic, the other alternative to conflict as a means of establishing costs and commitments is through precedent, on the basis of past performance, experience, and similar situations. This alternative is particularly weak in the Third World. Thus in new nations, where past performance is scarce, experience rare, and the similarity of situations hard to establish, direct involve-

1. See Lewis Coser, *The Functions of Social Conflict* (Free Press, 1956), p. 8.

299

ment in conflict is often the only way to ascertain the necessary information required for a decision. There is no way of knowing how committed Burkina Faso or Morocco is to its borders, or how costly a demand for Tamil autonomy or Eritrean independence will be without testing it. Similarly, on the other side, there is no way for the Tamils or Eritreans to show their commitment or for the Burkinabe or Moroccans to force their challengers to calculate their costs without the use of conflict. Since sociopolitical stakes are frequently not frivolous, the establishment of costs and commitments is a crucial exercise whose frustration or curtailment would reduce the necessary information for conducting international relations. As a result, conflict reduction runs up against not only the habits, inertia, and even enjoyment of conflict by the parties but also its usefulness to the basic purposes and existence of its practitioners and their associates. The bounds within which conflict is properly to be kept are not always obvious.

The proper bounds of conflict and conflict reduction are not its only ambiguity. The term itself is used in two ways. It has been referred to explicitly as an incompatibility, a condition inherent in multi-issue and multiparty situations, but it has also been used implicitly to mean the violent stage or expression of that incompatibility. The two overlap. Conflict reduction means both reducing incompatibilities, where possible, and returning the pursuit of those incompatibilities to nonviolent or political means. The ends and means are inextricably linked, a commonplace that is often forgotten in conflict management. Politics is the process of handling demands, and demands unhandled can escalate from politics to violence; conflict management that does not deal with basic causes is likely to be short-lived. Thus in addition to the usual consideration of conflict resolution, or the satisfaction of demands after violence, and of conflict management, or the reduction of the means for the pursuit of conflict, the following discussion will also include conflict prevention, or the preemptive satisfaction of demands before they become the basis of violence.

This chapter reviews the methods of conflict reduction using the analytical artifice of the number of parties involved: unilateral methods or conflict prevention, bilateral methods of negotiating the management and solution of violent conflicts, trilateral methods of mediation, and multilateral methods of institutionalized conflict reduction. Examples from African conflicts are used to illustrate the discussion to help identify the appropriate conditions and practices for each method, as well as the reasons for their underutilization in current African practice.

UNILATERAL PREVENTION

There is no substitute for dealing with grievances and demands early in their history; such is the normal business of politics and governance. Examples of "normal politics" are infinite, since they include all the cases in which violent conflict did not occur because it was handled preemptively. Yet normal politics—and its foreign policy equivalent, normal diplomacy—is not always a natural occurrence. Governments are reluctant to take on demands that challenge their programs, their authority, or their resources, often in the hope that the problem will go away. Sometimes it does, making it contradictory but no less important to emphasize that those problems which do not would better have been handled early. The advantage of early attention to problems is that demands can be met at a lower level, since unattended grievances usually undergo an escalation of ends as well as means. (The purported disadvantage is that demands may escalate nonetheless, as giving a hand may lead to taking an arm. But such fears are usually exaggerated, since change usually requires absorption and a pause before new changes are demanded.) Satisfaction of demands does not mean giving in to them; it means responsive and respectful attention to them in the search for mutually satisfactory solutions. It means above all the recognition of the legitimacy of the other party's concerns. Salient among such problems are ethnic protests in internal politics and incidents of neighborly relations in international politics, both of which are difficult to treat successfully by ignoring them. Examples can be chosen for each to show both policies of successful treatment and instructive failures.

Ethnic, subnational, or regional grievances are a frequent challenge to the nation-building policies of a new state, to programs for allocating its scarce resources, and ultimately to its own authority and legitimacy. Dealing with ethnic grievances is not simply a matter of handling demands that arise incidentally, since they are often a reaction to legitimate nation-building concerns and they often have long histories with no clear beginnings. Yet conflict prevention means implementing policies that reduce perceptions of ascriptive blockage on the part of the ethnic group, subnation, or region, foreclosing its search for escalated means to attract government attention to its problems or escalated ends to ensure a satisfying response.[2] As important as any specific policy is a tactical skill and familiarity with the rules and practices of protest on the part of both government and citizens— the single most important problem that turned recent internal conflicts in the Baltic states (1988-91), Tiananmen square (1989),[3] and the Kabylia in Algeria (1980) into violence. The latter case serves as a good example of both temporary successes and failures in internal conflict prevention.

Algeria's Berber minority was the spearhead of the nationalist struggle against French rule as well as the largest and poorest subnational group in the country, two characteristics that were closely interrelated. After Algerian independence, segments of Berber society in the Kabylia region continued their protest by the only method they know, the use of armed rebellion to draw government attention to their socioeconomic needs and to their political demands for greater representation.[4] In 1963 and again in 1964, the government of Ahmed ben Bella combined military and political measures to defeat the rebellion and reintegrate the rebels, using first the external challenge of a Moroccan war and then the promise of a political alliance as the basis for reintegration. It took more positive measures from the successor government of Houari Boumedienne to meet the substance of Kabyle grievances through regional development efforts and greater political representation, coupled with a clear no-nonsense attitude on regional separatism.[5] The combination of measures that raised sat-

2. See Joseph Rudolph and Robert Thompson, "Ethno-Territorial Movements and the Policy Process," *Comparative Politics*, vol. 17, no. 3 (1985), pp. 291–311; and Joseph Montville, ed., *Conflict and Peacemaking in Multiethnic Societies* (Lexington, Mass.: Heath, 1989).

3. See Scott Simmie and Bob Nixon, *Tiananmen Square* (University of Washington Press, 1990).

4. See William B. Quandt, *Revolution and Political Leadership* (MIT Press, 1969), pp. 220, 270; and David Ottaway and Marina Ottaway, *The Politics of a Socialist Revolution* (University of California Press, 1970), pp. 92–105.

5. See Jean Leca and Jean-Claude Vatin, *L'Algérie politique* (CNRS, 1975), p. 302; Charles Micaud and Ernest Gellner, eds., *Arabs and Berbers* (Lexington,

isfactions and those that lowered expectations was an effective way of preventing further internal conflict.

The death of Boumedienne at the end of 1978 and the selection of his successor, Chadli Benjedid, on the basis of a new program of consumerism and liberalization upset the expectations that had underlain internal peace in the Kabylia region. Ben Jedid's early measure for greater political liberties, which raised Berber hopes without indicating any new limits on pluralism, expression, and subnational identity, set the stage for tests of the new political atmosphere. A minor bureaucratic decision forbidding poetry readings in the Berber language in 1980 led to a situation wherein neither the protesters nor the authorities had any experience in conducting or in handling protest. Although momentary riots were brought under control, an uneasy and uncertain truce characterized the following decade into 1990. When the official version of national history was rewritten in 1984 in the "enriched" National Charter, the Berber element was upgraded. But when the establishment of an Algerian human rights league became conceivable, the first such organization was a Berber interest group, and it took a four-year process at the end of the decade to dilute its ethnic protest nature. When Algeria opened the possibility of multiple political parties in 1989, a new Berber party (the Rally for Culture and Development) was among the first to register and an old one (the Social Forces Front) soon followed, leaving a third group of politically conscious Berbers rejecting any political party as the proper vehicle for their cultural concerns. Ethnic particularism remains an issue in Algeria, and on occasion it triggered the use of police powers in the 1980s. Yet, although Berber cultural expression has not received the full freedom demanded, there is no discrimination against Berbers themselves, and the search for an appropriate response to Berber demands can be seen as part of normal politics in the general search for stable policies within the liberalization and pluralization of the Algerian polity.

The normal frictions of neighborly coexistence also provide many sources of conflict in international relations, which can often be dealt with through normal diplomatic practices of problem solving and

Mass.: Heath, 1973); and Ottaway and Ottaway, *Politics of a Socialist Revolution*, p. 254.

conflict prevention. The most basic of these problems come from the line that divides neighbors, one that is exceptionally sensitive and exceptionally uncertain in the case of new states. There are two types of border problems: territorial disputes over the location of the border itself, and relational problems about the conditions of existence near the border. Territorial problems sometimes concern the conditions of existence around the border, and sometimes they involve actual demands and contests over the appropriate location of the boundary line. Difficulties can also arise over the interpretation of a treaty, the location of the line on the ground, or the appropriateness of an outmoded determination even when the territorial division itself is not under dispute. New states are often reluctant to arrive at a definitive settlement on boundaries, suspecting some hidden advantages that they might not yet know of, at the very moment when greater certainty is what is needed. Similarly, new states are often suspicious about transborder incidents, interpreting them as evidence of official designs on their territory from their neighbors, just when greater sangfroid is needed to handle incidents that are most often private and natural but that can easily escalate to interstate conflict.

Boundaries in Africa have often been described as a Pandora's box, a source of both real and potential conflict that threatens the emerging interstate order of the continent.[6] The description has proved apt on many occasions when African states have pursued their conflicts over boundaries defined and undefined, but it has also led to many measures—both collective and individual—of conflict prevention. The most significant collective effort was the 1964 resolution by the Organization of African Unity (OAU) reinforcing the provisions of the OAU Charter on the sanctity of inherited boundaries, the doctrine of *uti possidetis*. But other measures of normal diplomacy are also useful for supporting the norm with specific measures of implementation.

African states have taken unilateral actions to prevent boundary conflicts in specific cases by initiating policies to remove the uncertainties from their borders through demarcation and to remove the

6. See Carl Widstrand, ed., *African Boundary Problems* (Uppsala: Scandinavian Institute of African Studies, 1969); I. William Zartman, *International Relations in the New Africa* (Englewood Cliffs, N.J.: Prentice-Hall, 1966; rpt. University Press of America, 1987); and Saadia Touval, *Boundary Politics of Independent Africa* (Harvard University Press, 1972).

artificiality from their borders through rectifications that bring geo-graphic lines into closer harmony with human realities. Algeria is one country that has made border demarcation a prime condition of nor-mal relations with its neighbors. Throughout the 1980s, borders de-limited by treaty were demarcated on the ground on Algerian insistence by joint commissions with Tunisia, Niger, Mali, and Mauritania, and plans were finally reaffirmed as part of the rapprochement with Mo-rocco after 1988 to demarcate Algeria's western frontier. In other, select cases, African states have initiated border negotiations with their neighbors to readjust geometric lines to take transhuman mi-grations into account, so that migratory groups need not cross inter-national frontiers in search of traditional watering holes and seasonal pastures. Thus in 1962, Mauritania sought a resolution of its trans-border problems with Mali and the next year finally arrived at a settlement based on a more manageable border, buying good relations and an uncontested border with the cession of small pieces of territory to its neighbor. At the other end of the continent, Egypt, under the colonial protection of Great Britain, readjusted its administrative bor-der with Sudan so as to coincide with traditional grazing habits on either side of the frontier in 1902; a politically motivated flare-up in 1958 between the two now-independent neighbors brought them to the verge of open conflict, but since then, under the impetus of solving additional border problems raised by the creation of Lake Nasir behind the Aswan High Dam, Egypt has come to regard the administrative line as the international boundary. Conflict is often useful as a way of making artificial boundaries African, since "nations have fought and died" in the defense of borders formerly regarded as only colo-nially imposed. But independent diplomacy is an equally sovereign but less costly way of accomplishing the same result. Since uncertainty and artificiality are two major sources of conflict,[7] unilateral measures to reduce such attributes reduce conflict.

Why then are such measures not used more often? It is worth noting, for the sake of perspective, that the picture is not as bleak as the question would imply. In a continent as fraught with the potential for ethnic and boundary conflict as Africa, the number of actual cases is statistically small. Indeed, it would be worth studying some cases

7. See Martin Patchen, *Resolving Disputes between Nations* (Duke University Press, 1988), chap. 11.

in which conflict has been handled preemptively alongside others in which it has not in order to learn from positive as well as negative examples. But negative cases remain and need to be explained. The best general explanation probably lies in the fact that conflicts are not prevented because their issues run counter to other predominant (although not necessarily justified) issues connected with the establishment of the new states and nations themselves. Thus ethnic protests conflict with nation-building endeavors (a legitimate concern) and with the efforts of some ethnic groups to prevail in the postcolonial power struggle over others (a less legitimate even if explicable concern). Border conflicts arise from the suspicion of state leaders over the aims of their neighbors and over their own uncertainty about where and how well their writ runs in the far reaches of their territory. Such causes bring conflict and the need for conflict prevention at the same time. They also bring the need for conflict management and resolution measures when conflict prevails over prevention.

BILATERAL MANAGEMENT AND RESOLUTION

Contrary to popular images of American games, conflicts do not simply end in a scorable win, lose, or draw, although that notion provides a good starting point for analysis. More like a cricket match (at least in American eyes), conflict life is dominated by a fourth outcome, that of going on and on, as each side awaits the moment when a decisive escalation is possible and propitious. This is the southeast square of the Prisoners' and Chicken Dilemma Games (and their variations), where the strategy is to move the outcome into (and out of) the other squares only when such moves are possible and propitious. The necessary condition for such movement, then, is not merely a stalemate, as found in the Prisoners' Dilemma, where the parties can continue their conflict indecisively, but a mutually hurting stalemate, as in the Chicken Dilemma, where the game's going on and on is the worst possible outcome.[8]

The second ingredient of the mutually hurting stalemate is the

8. See I. William Zartman, *Ripe for Resolution* (Oxford University Press, 1985); and Steven J. Brams, *Rational Politics: Decisions, Games, and Strategy* (Washington: CQ Press, 1985).

impossibility of a decisive escalation to victory on the part of either side; the northeast and southwest squares are (perceived to be) closed. Since this condition, like the first, is a matter of perception rather than of incontrovertible reality, it involves testing as well as testifying, probing as well as persuading. Frequently, a peculiarly delicate type of escalation is required, an "escalation to call" as opposed to an "escalation to raise." Through this device, parties show that they are willing and able to raise the means of conflict to the point of blocking the other side, making the opponent's search for victory impossible, but not to the point of prevailing over the other side, thus showing that the escalating side cannot achieve victory either. Often, this delicate operation is accompanied by intimations that further escalation—"to raise"—might be conceivable, painful though that would be, if the responding side does not agree to join in the search for a draw as an outcome.[9]

The final ingredient of the mutually hurting stalemate is a way out, involving both the perception that a mutually agreeable formula for a solution is available (even if all its details are not worked out as yet) and a mutual sense of requirement or a feeling that both sides will respond to concessions by the other with concessions of their own. Parties painted into a corner are no closer to a solution if they do not see a way out. But parties locked in a mutually hurting stalemate, hardened by conflict, and navigating the tricky shoals of partial escalations may find it very difficult to engage in the mental about-face required to come up with an agreeable formula and convey a sense of requital.[10]

It is this shift from unilateral efforts to try to impose a solution to bilateral efforts to try to find a solution, or from a winning to a reconciling mindset, that creates the biggest problems for conflicting parties. Typically, they do not simply make a decision to shift mindsets and abandon their previous conflict; rather, they bring a new track on line and check out its potentialities and implications, pursuing conflict and conciliation at the same time. Inevitably this produces attitudinal schizophrenia, policy disputes, and conflicting actions

9. See I. William Zartman, "Strategies of Deescalation," in Paul Kriesberg, ed., *Timing and Deescalation* (Syracuse University Press, 1991).

10. See I. William Zartman and Maureen Berman, *The Practical Negotiator* (Yale University Press, 1982).

and signals, all of which complicate the domestic decision to pursue bilateral conflict management and resolution as well as the smooth conduct of the bilateral process.

Many different types of mutually hurting stalemates have been produced in Africa, leading to different kinds of conflict management and resolution. First is a simple stalemate, resulting from the pursuit of an initial round of escalation that depletes military stocks and resources and leaves the parties exhausted, looking for a way out. They have tested the conflict for the possibility of a quick and decisive victory, and have found themselves blocked. A good example is the Moroccan-Algerian war of October 1963, when a Moroccan encirclement of Tindouf, followed by an Algeria encirclement of Figuig, at the western and eastern ends of the border, respectively, created a deadlock out of which the parties could not emerge militarily. Negotiations ensued to terminate hostilities, to determine their origins, and to resolve the border issue—in other words, to manage the conflict preparatory to its resolution. Resolution ultimately occurred in bilateral negotiations a decade later with the friendship treaty of Ifrane of 1969, the framework agreement of Tlemcen of 1970, and the Rabat border convention of 1972, ratified in 1973 by Algeria and, because of intervening conflicts, only in 1989 by Morocco.[11]

Second is a compound stalemate, in which the parties replenish their stocks while pursuing the armed conflict through several more rounds of escalation until they reach the limits of escalation and stalemate. This is similar to what occurred in the Biafran War, 1966–70, and the Ogaden War, 1977–78, although the result in both cases was not stalemate but victory. Bilateral negotiations completed the resolution of the conflict in Nigeria, but it took nearly a decade to produce some timid conflict management measures and no resolution between Ethiopia and Somalia. Multiple escalations produce increasing pressures for victory rather than stalemate, by the process variously referred to as entrapment, investment, or overcommitment.[12] Bilateral negotiation becomes correspondingly difficult.

Repeated stalemates, arising from escalated crises, constitute a third

11. See Zartman, *Ripe for Resolution*, ch. 2.

12. See Dean Pruitt and Jeffrey Rubin, *Social Conflict* (Random House, 1986), pp. 121–25; and Zartman, *Ripe for Resolution*, pp. 270–71.

category that falls between the first two. Repeated stalemates are usually obtained by parties that are not capable of real escalation, but that return periodically to try to break out of the effects of a simple stalemate after the passage of some time. The decennial wars between Mali and Burkina Faso (Upper Volta) in 1964, 1976–77, and 1985–86 produced multiple occasions for bilateral conflict resolution that became more and more difficult because of the repeated nature of the crises.[13]

Finally, there is the grinding stalemate, produced by the conflict that drags on and on, characterized by gradual intensifications and occasional escalations. Such a situation can produce a number of opportunities for bilateral management and resolution along the way, but it also creates a counterpressure on the parties to look for ways out through escalation and then for ways to close potential escalatory loopholes. Grinding crises tend also to be characteristic of conflicts involving the standing or legitimacy of the parties themselves as an issue. Examples are the sixteen-year conflict over the western Sahara or the twelve-year conflict resolution efforts over Namibia and associated issues.

Each of these ways in which a conflict can drag on provides its own types of opportunities for productive stalemate and negotiation. Yet in reality there are so few instances of bilateral conflict turning to bilateral conflict management and resolution that examples in Africa are rare. Left to their own devices, parties to a conflict find it hard to make the conversion to a bilateral track of conflict resolution. Two partial examples are illustrative. In 1986, an exhausted and beleaguered Somalia proposed to a similarly exhausted and beleaguered Ethiopia a formula for the management of their territorial dispute; it took two more years before an affirmative response was forthcoming from Ethiopia and an agreement to bury the means of conflict and begin discussing its substance could be signed. The demarche was limited to conflict management, and although the interaction was bilateral, it took place at meetings of the Inter-Government Authority on Drought and Development under pressures from member and other interested states; it was thus "augmented bilateralism."

13. See David Crum, "Mali and the UMOA," *Journal of Modern African Studies*, vol. 22 (September 1984), pp. 469–86.

Another example was the long-awaited summit between King Hassan II and President Benjedid in 1983 as a result of five years of bilateral expectations and initiatives. Within six months after the summit, any understanding between the parties had collapsed in a downward spiral of misread commitments and perceived duplicity. Only when a return engagement was scheduled in the presence of a third party four years later did it produce more effective results.[14]

Why has it been so difficult to move from unilaterally pursued conflict to bilateral conflict resolution? Much of the answer is in the question. Even under the most mutually painful of stalemates, the shift of mindsets and strategies is difficult to accomplish. This has already been seen in the different types of stalemates, which become more difficult to turn to management and resolution as they become more prolonged. Indeed, the very painfulness of the stalemate gives the parties additional reason to resent each other. As the Moroccan-Algerian case clearly shows, any degree of trust becomes very difficult to achieve. These procedural impediments make it difficult for the parties to come up with formulas susceptible of attracting the agreement of the other side. As the examples also suggest, the best that is usually possible in such situations is an agreement on conflict management, reducing the pressures and preoccupations of hostility that block creative measures on resolution itself. Conflict management gives the parties time to refocus on ways out of their dispute.

Yet conflict management contains a trap and a contradiction. Conflict management measures give the parties time to refocus on ways out of their painful stalemate; yet the measures remove the painful aspects of the stalemate, and hence remove the pressures to turn stalemates to resolution. On the one hand, management measures may serve merely to make the conflict bearable, enabling the parties to carry on the conflict on a more affordable level. On the other hand, management contains the promise of resolution, so that extended periods of conflict management without the follow-up phase that resolves the issues themselves can create even greater frustration and renewed conflict at a higher level. Conflict management without a reasonably rapid follow-up with efforts at conflict resolution leads to greater conflict. Yet experience has shown that parties have difficulty in consummating either phase on a bilateral basis.

14. See Zartman, *Ripe for Resolution*, pp. 122–25, 60–73.

TRILATERAL MANAGEMENT AND RESOLUTION

It is not clear which conflicts need mediation and which do not; rather, the general characteristics presented seem to suggest that most conflicts contain enough inherent obstacles to resolution by the conflicting parties alone to be able to benefit from a little help from their friends. However, it is clear that some types of conflicts are less susceptible to mediation than others, and, relatedly, some types of mediators are more acceptable than others. Superpower conflicts are rarely open to mediation, suggesting that mediators should come from the same or higher general "level" of power as the parties. Mediators tend to function best when they come from the parties' region, although regional identity is open to definition by the parties themselves. Internal conflicts are difficult to mediate since mediation itself suggests that the government is unable to handle its own business and therefore implies interference in internal affairs. Thus nonstate actors— private individuals and organizations—are more easily acceptable as mediators in internal disputes than are other states. It is also increasingly clear that, while mediators need to be dedicated to the search for a jointly acceptable solution, they need not be free of ties to either of the parties; "biased" mediators may often be what is needed, since their ties provide them with a basis for leverage over the parties. But the concomitant assumption is that they will be able to deliver the agreement of the party to which they are closest.[15]

Mediation is a trilateral exercise of a delicate type. Although mediators cannot be parties in the dispute, they can be expected to have interests involved in the management and resolution of the dispute. Although they probably will not and should not have an interest in a particular solution, they can be expected to have an interest in obtaining a solution of whatever kind is agreeable to the parties. Mediators will at least have an interest in their reputation as media-

15. See Kenneth Kressel and others, *Mediation Research* (San Francisco, 1989); Saadia Touval and I. William Zartman, eds., *International Mediation in Theory and Practice* (Boulder, Colo.: Westview Press, 1985); Jacob Bercovitch, *Social Conflicts and Third Parties* (Boulder, Colo.: Westview Press, 1984); Jacob Bercovitch and Jeffrey Rubin, eds., *Mediation in International Relations* (SPSSI, 1990); and Christopher Mitchell and Keith Webb, eds., *New Approaches to International Mediation* (Greenwood Press, 1988).

tors, and they will probably have interests in maintaining or improving their own relations with the parties involved in the conflict. Yet despite all these interests, mediators are only a catalyst to the dyad of conflict. They dare never allow themselves to become fully absorbed in that dyad, either by joining one side or by abandoning their good offices, or else they lose their function as mediators.

Yet it is that very danger which provides mediators with one of their rare sources of power or leverage. Mediators can threaten either to withdraw from the conflict reduction process if the parties do not cooperate ("a pox on both your houses") or they can threaten to join one of the sides or otherwise support its cause if the other side does not cooperate ("a pox on one of your houses"). Thus former President Jimmy Carter, in launching his 1989 "observer" role in the Ethiopian-Eritrean talks, indicated to both sides that if the talks broke down and the mediation effort were rejected, he would feel obliged to draw up a public balance of the process and indicate who was responsible for the collapse.

Mediators have only two other sources of leverage. The most important is simply the ability to formulate an outcome that is attractive to both sides, or, more precisely, to deliver to each party the other party's agreement to an outcome that is attractive to the first party. The second wording is a more accurate portrayal of both the difficulties and the process of mediation, and clearly indicates the extent to which the leverage of the mediator is at the mercy of each of the parties. As the last source of leverage, the mediator can make side-payments to the parties, providing incentives to come to an agreement that are not available as benefits from the agreement itself. Yet the latitude for purchasing agreement when its terms are otherwise unattractive to the parties is slim, in addition to being dependent on the availability of resources.

These sources of leverage correspond to the three levels of the mediation function. Mediators can act as communicators, as formulators, or as manipulators, depending on the depth of involvement in the management and resolution process. As communicators, mediators remain a pure catalyst, performing the communications functions that conflict prevents the parties from accomplishing alone. Mediators become holders of trust for the two parties and allow them to exchange messages and proposals that they could not otherwise do without losing face or appearing weak. As formulators, mediators also overcome the inabilities of the parties, but in this case by providing new ideas of their own about ways out of the conflict. Rather than serving as a merely procedural pipeline, formulators add some substance of their own. As manipulators, mediators deal with incentives and outcomes as well as proposals and communications between the parties. They may provide side-payments when the parties' own resources are too limited to make conflict reduction attractive, or they may act to reinforce the stalemate or even block the escalation attempts that press the parties to find an agreement.

Despite the precariousness of mediation, trilateral management and resolution of conflicts has a much better record in Africa than does bilateral management.[16] The basic conditions for the two are similar. Both require a mutually hurting stalemate and a way out, although part of the job of the mediator is to enhance the parties' perception of the opportunity in time and outcome as present and possible. In Africa as elsewhere, that exercise is the source of the mediator's leverage; African mediators have very limited resources for side-payments and relatively little clout in their threats to take sides or drop the mediation. African mediators act mainly as communicators and formulators and rarely as manipulators. As in many other cases, African mediation efforts are essentially an ad hoc exercise; even when a particular attempt is mandated by the OAU, the mandate is merely a hunting license, not a formalization of the process. Finally, African mediations may be individual or collective, as in the case of a carefully balanced ad hoc commission selected by the OAU, but they tend to involve many would-be mediators. When these are commission members, their efforts are more or less coordinated; when they are individuals, they may often get in each other's way. Multiple efforts are a desirable feature of mediation, but so is coordination. Uncoordinated, many mediators present the parties with continual occasions to try to improve the latest offer, by turning to another mediator, and thus they destroy the mediator's basis for leverage.

Little is known about the internal dynamics of African—or any

16. I. William Zartman, "African Mediation," in John Harbeson and Donald Rothchild, eds., *African International Relations* (Boulder, Colo.: Westview Press, 1991).

other—mediation; there are few records of "who said what to whom with what effect."[17] The basic dynamics are simple: by persuasion, mediators must help parties see that there is a common present condition that is more painful than possible futures and a common potential outcome that is preferable to the real present or to other attainable futures. Another function of mediators relates to risks and trust. The mediator must be the repository of a trust that is absent between the two parties, and must persuade them to use and then dispose of the mediation services as a crutch. Similarly, the mediator must help the parties to evaluate and handle the risks involved in the leap from a conflicting to a conciliating mindset and from conflict to agreement. In all these ways, the mediator helps the parties conceive and evaluate a different future.

The cases already cited provide some limited examples of the African practice of trilateral conflict reduction. Third-party venue and pressure were instrumental in staging the Somali-Ethiopian summits of 1986 and 1988, enabling the two heads of state to engage in bilateral conflict management. An OAU commission established after the 1963 war enabled Morocco and Algeria to engage in a cooling-off period and an exchange of briefs until they were able to resolve their border conflict bilaterally. In the Moroccan-Algerian summits of the 1980s, the mediator's role was more important. Its absence was felt in 1983 through the nonperformance of crucial functions that only a mediator could handle. Four years later, a mediator, King Fahd of Saudi Arabia, called another summit and persuaded the parties to come, then brought them to a minimal agreement on conflict management measures and served as witness to the initiation of a process of conflict management. As that process began to take on a life of its own, because of the comprehensive nature of the mutually hurting stalemate and the possibility of a way out, the mediator quietly withdrew. In the recurring Burkinabe-Malian border conflicts, a number of neighboring states served as mediators to get the bilateral management and resolution process moving, as also happened in the equally protracted conflict between Libya and Chad over northern Chad.

Many other cases involve even more active mediations. Layers of mediators—starting with the World Council of Churches and All-

---

17. See Touval, *Boundary Politics*; and William B. Quandt, *Camp David* (Brookings, 1986).

Africa Council of Churches, backed up by the Assistant Secretary General of the OAU, Mohammed Sahnoun, with Emperor Haile Selassie as the mediator of last resort—were responsible for the Addis Ababa Agreement between the Sudanese government and the southern Sudanese in 1972. It was based on a stalemate that, though mildly painful, was well perceived by both sides, on a mutually satisfactory formula for resolution, and on effective persuasion, threats, and trust by the mediators.[18] At the other end of the spectrum lie the innumerable examples of personal mediations in smaller disputes between African states and ultimately African heads of state. The conflicts can be internal, as in the 1989 mediations by Mobutu Sese Seko in the Angolan civil war or by Kenneth Kaunda and Daniel Arap Moi in the Mozambican civil war, or international, as in the mediation attempts by a number of heads of states in the 1989 conflict between Mauritania and Senegal. None of these recent examples have seen an outcome as yet.

Mediation works, yet conflicts continue. Are there identifiable problems in the African conduct of trilateral conflict reduction that can be addressed? Problems that do *not* exist include the supply of available mediators and the legitimacy of the operation. Probably the biggest problem lies outside the exercise and inside the conflict itself. Mediation, like conflict prevention, works best early, right after the first flare of the conflict and as a simple stalemate sets in. As the conflict continues, the parties become used to it and even begin to find it useful: many unrelated decisions and postponements can be justified by an ongoing conflict. Also, the problem of entrapment or sunk costs arises, making resolution a more and more expensive affair. As seen, compound, repeated, and grinding stalemates are more difficult to turn into opportunities for resolution, since the parties have learned from their first experience that an apparent stalemate can be lived with or broken by escalation. This is not to say that mediators are at the total mercy of the perfect stalemate, for that would be to forget that the mediator's job is to bring about a perception of mutual hurting stalemate among the parties. But the mediator must have a minimum

18. See Dunstan Wai, *African-Arab Conflict in the Sudan* (London: Holmes and Meier, 1981); Hizkias Assefa, *Mediation of Civil Wars* (Boulder, Colo.: Westview Press, 1987); Mitchell and Webb, *New Approaches to International Mediation*; and Montville, *Conflict and Peacemaking*.

of reality on which to build, and continuing conflicts make the job more difficult. The real problems of African conflict reduction are the long and deep conflicts—Ogaden, Eritrea, Aozou, Sahara, southern Sudan, Angola, Mozambique, and so on.

There are also narrower, tactical reasons why mediation in these cases has failed or has not yet succeeded, all of them relating to a lack of focus in the process. Some involve the mediation itself: many mediators working uncoordinatedly allow the parties to slip away in search of better alternatives. A similar problem involves other external supporters: outside powers offer support to factions to continue the conflict and undermine the perception of a stalemate. Furthermore, impoverished Africa has few resources to make mediated futures attractive.

MULTILATERAL MANAGEMENT AND RESOLUTION

Conflict reduction can also be a collective, institutionalized exercise in certain types of cases. As seen, parties feel most comfortable when they are in control of their own management and resolution process in interaction with the opposing party, although they usually have difficulty in pursuing conflict and conciliation at the same time. Mediated management and reduction is only augmented bilateralism, with the third party helping the others to do what they could not accomplish alone. But negotiation under the pressure and scrutiny of a large number of peers is uncomfortable and not conducive to success. This fact is obvious, yet it is generally overlooked in the frustrated calls for a greater OAU role in African conflict resolution. There are many things the OAU cannot do, and it does well not to do them.

The first of two functions a multilateral institution can perform in regard to conflict has to do with the principles of the conflict. All positions find their justification in principles and all conflicts are grounded in conflicting principles (or conflicting applications of principle). Sometimes such principles are fixed; in other cases, conflicts take place within the context of evolving or changing principles. The first involve regime testing; the second, regime change.[19] International institutions, as the site for the collective exercise of "parliamentary diplomacy," are an important element in both the affirmation and the evolution of regimes, contributing powerful support to the norms of international interaction. As such they also function as the battle-ground for the testing and defense of these norms, declaring which norms apply to which cases. Such declarations, however, do not resolve conflicts; they merely reinforce the claims of certain norms over others, leaving the ultimate resolution to an agreement among the parties, justified in terms of some of the norms.

Whether by affirming or by changing principles or norms, multi-lateral institutions help limit conflict. The OAU declaration on inher-ited boundaries, cited earlier, has affected conflict in two different ways. In many, often unheard of, cases, it has prevented conflict, by signaling to potentially revisionist states that their case would be difficult, costly, and unsure. In a few other cases, notably those two —Somalia and Morocco—that signaled their exception to the reso-lution in 1964, it has limited action, even if it has not eliminated the possibilities of conflict. The norm has not by any means eliminated the problem and the conflict over the Ogaden (indeed, the conflict is between the legal norm and a socioeconomic fact), but it has rein-forced one side and has generally indicated that any conclusive, re-solving formula will be one that deals with the fact of nomadism and Somali social structure within the framework of existing boundaries. Nor has the norm resolved the problem of the Western Sahara, but it has been the basis of a gradual recognition that only a referendum on self-determination will produce a final resolution of the conflict. Similarly, in the Namibian or Biafran conflicts, the OAU's role was to reaffirm governing principles—state integrity and decolonization, respectively—and not to mediate the conflict between its own and others' principles.[20]

The other role for multilateral conflict reduction is in legitimizing

19. See Stephen Krasner, ed., *International Regimes* (Cornell University Press, 1983); Gilbert Winham, ed., *New Issues in International Crisis Management* (Boul-der, Colo.: Westview Press, 1988); and Victor Kremenyuk and others, *Inter-national Negotiation* (Jossey-Bass for ILASA, 1990).

20. See Yassin El-Ayouty and I. William Zartman, eds., *The OAU after Twenty Years* (Praeger, 1984).

the choice of mediators, and even on occasion of parties. Internal disputes with grinding stalemates, as seen, are often characterized by a struggle of one party to gain recognition and legitimacy before it can undertake conflict-resolving negotiations. The OAU alone cannot give that legitimacy, but it can contribute. More frequently, OAU designation of mediators not only gives them standing but also imposes a certain degree of coordination. It has been proposed that the OAU create a Committee of Elders, modeled on the Interaction Council of former heads of state and government, to provide a pool of former leaders who might be available for mediation of disputes.[21] Any such mechanisms reinforce the position of the potential mediators, who need all the help they can get in their delicate role.

FURTHER DIRECTIONS IN CONFLICT REDUCTION

Conflict reduction is well developed in Africa, but so is conflict. Both leave us much to learn. One immediate challenge concerns the trends in both processes. Conflict is associated with change, as accepted patterns and expectations are upset. Development is major change, and particularly the important aspects of political development associated with establishment of new states and nations are powerful generators of conflict. One can expect to find conflicts over boundaries and over ethnic subnationalisms as a concomitant of state- and nation-building. But for how long? Can these initial problems in settling in be expected to disappear a generation or so after independence? Or can they be expected to increase as states and nations only then come to closer grips with the reality of their boundaries and neighbors, or of their internal structures? Or, in the terms of the previous section, how long does it take for the new regime of Third World independence to become established, and for regional security regimes to become operative, and what trends can be expected in testing as well as in changing these regimes?

A better understanding is needed as well of the mechanisms and process of conflict management and resolution as outlined above. It has already been pointed out that little is known about the dynamics

21. See Sam Amoo, "Conflict Resolution in the OAU," Ph.D. dissertation, Johns Hopkins University, 1989.

of mediation, a subject obviously difficult to research. There is some work on stalemate and escalation, but these processes are still not fully explored. Unfortunately, much of the conceptual work available is difficult to translate into reality.

There are many studies about the nature of current conflicts, in Africa and elsewhere, but they tend to be either historical or polemical. The first give a thorough analysis of the causes and evolution of the conflict, the second of the rightness of one side. But there is little study of the conflicts as a problem, requiring imaginative ideas and propitious conditions for a solution. Solutions are at best added as an afterthought to studies, and are not considered academic since they are unfootnotable. Yet more serious attention to possible outcomes, including discussion of their conditions and implications within the context of both historical and theoretical knowledge, is a challenging exercise that would be helpful as well, and it would alter the current attitudes that consider conflicts as deviant and disruptive behavior rather than an indication of a problem to be solved.

Finally, a better understanding is needed of the processes of successful conflict prevention, so that they may be replicated. Like psychology and journalism, political science is caught up with the abnormal or disturbing event, rather than with studying the real life of the politician—making decisions that deal with day-to-day problems as well as with flashy crises. Conflicts can be played back comparatively: how did another country handle a similar situation to avoid a similar problem? Conflict reduction should more commonly be expanded to include prevention as well.

Chapter 12

CRAWFORD YOUNG

Self-Determination, Territorial Integrity, and the African State System

The United Nations General Assembly, after many months of preparatory labors and hard bargaining, adopted by consensus in 1960 a landmark declaration asserting a comprehensive set of international norms regarding the right to independence of territories subjected to colonial rule. Self-determination, as sacred right and juridical entitlement of colonized peoples, acquired new standing in this convenant. And yet, equally affirmed were crucial limitations on its orbit of application, eloquently illustrated in the contrast between articles 2 and 6:

> Article 2: All peoples have the right to self-determination; by virtue of that right they freely determine their political status and freely pursue their economic, social and cultural development.

> Article 6: Any attempt aimed at the partial or whole disruption of the national unity and the territorial integrity of a country is incompatible with the purposes and principles of the Charter of the United Nations.[1]

In this fundamental declaration, the United Nations General Assembly Declaration on the Granting of Independence to Colonial Countries and Peoples solemnly enunciated the profound contradictions in the concept of self-determination. It was asserted as bedrock principle of the contemporary law of nations, and inscribed in article 1 of the U.N. Charter. Yet its very articulation at once called forth territorial integrity doctrines circumscribing its application, if not emptying the notion of its substance.

1. U.N. Resolution 1514(XV), December 1960.

SELF-DETERMINATION: THE CONTRADICTIONS

From its first reception as international norm, self-determination has been chained uneasily to the state-protective ideas of national unity and territorial integrity. At the close of the First World War, two great statesmen, Vladimir I. Lenin and Woodrow Wilson, in different ways gave decisive impetus to the idea. For Lenin, self-determination was an arm of combat against the dying Czarist state. Once Bolshevik revolution triumphed, ingenious gloss was required to ensure that this explosive principle did not dismember the fledgling socialist polity. As his then-lieutenant, Joseph Stalin squared the circle in 1923: "There are occasions when the right of self-determination conflicts with . . . the higher right of a working class that has assumed power to consolidate its power. In such cases—this must be said bluntly— the right of self-determination cannot and must not serve as an obstacle to the exercise by the working class of its right to dictatorship."[2]

Wilson believed he had discovered an ethical principle for the democratic disposition of the European domains of the multinational empires of Austria-Hungary, Ottoman Turkey, and Czarist Russia. Unlike that of Lenin, the Wilsonian vision of self-determination as popular sovereignty in action never extended beyond Europe. Wilson was shocked at the parade of would-be nationalities he beckoned from obscurity by his words, many hitherto unknown to him. In subsequent testimony to the Senate Committee on Foreign Relations, he confessed: "When I gave utterance to those words [that all nations had a right to self-determination], I said them without the knowledge that nationalities existed, which are coming to us day after day. . . . You do not know and cannot appreciate the anxieties that I have experienced as a result of many millions of people having their hopes raised by what I have said."[3]

Ambiguity thus permeated the doctrine of self-determination from its birth as commanding norm in international politics to its subsequent equivocal assimilation into the corpus of international law. In the aftermath of the First World War, it was partially applied in the

---

2. Joseph Stalin, *Marxism and the National and Colonial Question* (Moscow: Foreign Language Publishing House, 1940), p. 148.

3. Quoted in Alfred Cobban, *The Nation State and National Self-Determination* (Crowell, 1970), pp. 64–65.

dismantling of Austria-Hungary, the Balkan domains of the Ottoman Empire, and those European segments of Russia that the successor socialist state was unable to reincorporate (Finland, Poland, the Baltic states). And subsequently, it was assimilated as a powerful doctrine of liberation by subjugated peoples of Asia and Africa.

The dilemmas of self-determination are numerous. What is the "self" that may legitimately invoke this claim? Is it defined by territoriality, ethnocultural commonality, subjective collective self-assertion, or some combination of these? Is self-determination to be exercised only once, at the moment of the covenant, or is it subject to continuous review? Must it be solemnized by some participative act of the human collectivity in question, or may a political movement purporting to speak contractually for a "people" exercise this right? Is there some "critical date" at which the people entitled to exercise self-determination are fully constituted, with those arriving after excluded from the choice? Does self-determination comport with an unassailable right of separation? Is it circumscribed by some criterion of "viability" of a sovereign unit? This roster of interrogations, suggestive rather than exhaustive, suffices to illustrate the contradictions embedded in an apparently self-evident postulate.[4]

The object of this chapter is to revisit the concept of self-determination in Africa, to examine its interaction with the cognate principles of territorial integrity and boundary inviolability during the three decades of African independence. The intertwined crises in the Horn, in recent years the most critical zone of conflict between these principles, require special attention in the concluding section. African states, in their effort to secure their liberation and sovereignty, have struggled with the need to at once use and limit self-determination; in so doing, an African concert of nations has emerged, part of a global community of states yet constructing its own regional customary international law. In the process, one may observe—as else-

<hr>

4. Among the many works treating the subject that are particularly relevant to the African dilemma are Rupert Emerson, *From Empire to Nation* (Harvard University Press, 1960); Lee C. Buchheit, *Secession: The Legitimacy of Self-Determination* (Yale University Press, 1978); Benjamin Neuberger, *National Self-Determination in Postcolonial Africa* (Boulder, Colo.: Lynne Rienner Publishers, 1986); and I. M. Lewis, ed., *Nationalism and Self-Determination in the Horn of Africa* (London: Ithaca Press, 1983).

where—the interaction of political vectors, evolving international norms, and the brute facts of force. All three dimensions must enter the calculus; each is affected by the other two, and none alone can supply an authoritative formula.

The difficulties of domesticating self-determination as an interstate norm in Africa become manifest in two spheres. First, territorial integrity necessarily poses issues of boundary determination between sovereign polities. Second, the question arises whether any "people," however defined, may claim separate sovereignty outside the framework of decolonization—whether such demands must be stigmatized as secessionism, or may be exalted as liberation. I begin with a review of the evolution of self-determination doctrines as an international norm.

SELF-DETERMINATION AS AN INTERNATIONAL NORM

The Versailles Conference in 1919 witnessed frequent invocation of self-determination and gave the appearance of partial incorporation of the concept as a new value in the law of nations, though in reality its application was riddled with inconsistencies. Alfred Cobban later mused on the ironies of Versailles, asking how it was that, upon close examination, a European settlement "was not founded on self-determination," yet "was believed to be so founded, perhaps even by many of those who drew it up."[5] The doubtful standing of self-determination as an international norm was made clear by the International Commission of Jurists, which asked in 1920 for an opinion on the status of the Swedish-populated Aaland Islands in the Baltic Sea, under Finnish sovereignty:

[I]n the absence of express provisions in international treaties, the right of disposing of national territory is essentially an attribute of the sovereignty of every State. Positive International Law does not recognize the right of national groups, as such, to separate themselves from the State of which they form part by

5. Cobban, *Nation State*, p. 75.

the simple expression of a wish, any more than it recognizes the right of other States to claim such a separation.[6]

However, the postwar era brought radical changes. The United Nations system emerged as an important arena of norm creation, coexisting uneasily with the older Westphalia state-as-subject model, with international law the exclusive product of sovereign transactions by independent polities.[7] Self-determination found its way into article 1 of the U.N. Charter, and article 73 concerning non-self-governing territories suggested its application to colonized peoples. Territorial integrity, however, was equally sanctified in the Charter, and while acquisition of territory by force—fully legitimate before 1914, and in a penumbra of uncertainty between the wars—was proscribed,[8] the inherent right of a state to self-defense was acknowledged.

The growing force of Third World nationalism, and the swelling ranks of U.N. membership drawn from these regions, led to a series of solemn General Assembly resolutions seeking clarification of self-determination, adopted by overwhelming majorities; these included most notably the 1960 Declaration on the Granting of Independence to Colonial Countries and Peoples and the 1970 Declaration on Friendly Relations and Cooperation among States. In this unfolding debate, the dialectic between self-determination and territorial integrity produced a normative drift toward restriction of self-determination to circumstances in which colonial, alien, or racist rule prevailed.[9] U.N. Secretary-General U Thant lent the authority of his office to a highly restrictive interpretation, arguing that "self-determination of the peoples does not imply self-determination of a section of a particular Member-State." To hammer home his circumscribed concept of the U.N. Declaration self-determination statement, he added that "when a State applies to be a member of the United Nations, and when the United Nations accepts that Member, then the implication is that the

6. Buchheit, *Secession*, p. 71.

7. The complex interaction of Westphalia and U.N. models of international law is given elegant exposition by Antonio Cassese, *International Law in a Divided World* (Oxford: Clarendon Press, 1986).

8. R. Y. Jennings, *The Acquisition of Territory in International Law* (Manchester University Press, 1963).

9. Cassese, *International Law*, pp. 134–36.

rest of the membership of the United Nations recognizes the territorial integrity, independence and sovereignty of this particular Member-State."[10]

Tensions and contradictions persisted, as stubborn empirical facts in given instances eluded the normative web intended to enclose them. Powerful moral imperatives of solidarity with oppressed communities in unique settings (Palestine/Israel, South Africa) generated a quest for universalizing norms deduced from these circumstances, which might then serve as liberating weapons; generalizing from the particular always risks introducing inconvenient implications into the normative order. In the nooks and crannies of self-determination doctrine in international law lie unresolved conundrums: for example, the legitimacy of forcible annexation of formerly colonized territories (Goa, East Timor); the status of enclaves whose population rejects incorporation into the surrounding country (Gibraltar). There is, in short, no universal consensus in international law about the balance of norms applicable in all instances in which self-determination and territorial integrity conflict; indeed, a number of authoritative treatises deny that self-determination is more than a widely recognized political principle. R. Y. Jennings, for one, takes such a view, arguing, "It is not capable of sufficiently exact definition in relation to particular situations to amount to a legal doctrine; and it is therefore inexact to speak of a 'right' to self-determination if by that is meant a legal right."[11]

In short, no degree of assertion can remove all ambiguity or eliminate the conflation of the political and the juridical in debates about self-determination. In the interstices of ambiguity flow the determinants of force and *faits accomplis*. Lee Buchheit, in a masterful analysis, gives succinct statement to a core contradiction that continues to plague the quest for universal norm construction:

> International law is thus asked to perceive a distinction between the historical subjugation of an alien population living in a different part of the globe and the historical subjugation of an alien population living on a piece of land abutting that of its oppres-

10. Buchheit, *Secession*, p. 88.
11. Jennings, *Acquisition of Territory*, p. 78.

sors. The former can apparently never be legitimated by the mere passage of time, whereas the latter is eventually transformed into a protected status quo.[12]

AFRICAN RECEPTION OF THE SELF-DETERMINATION DOCTRINE

I turn now to the application of self-determination and territorial integrity norms in the African environment. Here one at once encounters a paradox: nowhere in the sweep of the world between the Caribbean and Oceania where at least formal colonialism has been liquidated in the postwar world was the potential tension between self-determination and territorial integrity more acute. Yet a surprisingly sturdy regional customary international law has been erected, building on the global doctrines of the U.N. system yet using a specific African architecture. To a degree few would have dared hope in the 1950s, interstate comity has been preserved within the new African international order, with most difficult boundary issues resolved or neutralized and ethnic self-determination marginalized. But a few deadly disputes have persisted, which seem unlikely to yield to the existing African normative code; these are above all located in the Horn of Africa.

The first articulation of African norms expressed the voice of nationalist movements rather than states. At this juncture, the territoriality of the African state system was not fully clear, and the pan-African vision was a powerful value. Thus self-determination was ascendant; territorial integrity lurked far in the background. The 1945 Manchester Pan-African Congress excoriated "the artificial divisions and territorial boundaries created by the Imperialist Powers" as "deliberate steps to obstruct the political unity of the West African peoples," and, for the Horn, declared that "in the interest of justice as well as of economic geography this Congress supports most heartily the claims of the Somalis and Eritreans to be returned to their (Ethi-

12. Buchheit, *Secession*, p. 18.

opian) Motherland instead of being parcelled out to foreign powers."[13] The 1958 Accra All-African Peoples' Conference adopted a resolution denouncing "artificial frontiers drawn by the imperialist Powers to divide the peoples of Africa, particularly those which cut across ethnic groups and divide people of the same stock," and calling for "the abolition or adjustment of such frontiers at an early date." As states supplanted political movements as normative sources, such explosive sentiments were soon supplanted by more prudent doctrines of guaranteed perpetuation of existing territorial arrangements. Indeed, the consensus of the first African assembly of states, also convened at Accra in 1958, was summarized in a closing speech by the host, Kwame Nkrumah, in words clearly embodying territorial integrity: "Our conference came to the conclusion that in the interests of that Peace which is so essential, we should respect the independence, sovereignty and territorial integrity of one another."[14]

With the 1963 creation of the Organization of African Unity (OAU), the commitment to territorial integrity was firmly implanted; the OAU Charter refers to "territorial integrity" no fewer than three times. At the 1964 Cairo OAU Summit, the fundamental commitment to territorial integrity became far more explicit; all member states "pledge themselves to respect the borders existing on their achievement of national independence," a resolution voted by acclamation (although Somalia and Morocco demurred). As O. S. Kamanu cogently observed, the OAU went well beyond the United Nations Charter (which imposes a merely passive obligation on signatories to refrain from violating the territorial integrity of any state) to assert an affirmative obligation on OAU member states to defend the sovereignty and territorial integrity of all African states.[15] OAU resolutions do not have the full force of law; however, as the authoritative commentator on

13. Saadia Touval, *The Boundary Politics of Independent Africa* (Harvard University Press, 1972), pp. 21, 23.

14. Touval, *Boundary Politics*, pp. 54, 56–57.

15. Onyeonoro S. Kamanu, "Secession and the Right of Self-Determination: An O.A.U. Dilemma," *Journal of Modern African Studies*, vol. 12, no. 3 (1974), pp. 371–73. For a useful review of the OAU record on this issue, see the special issue of *Africa Today*, edited by Amare Tekle, "The OAU at 25: The Quest for Unity, Self-Determination and Human Rights," vol. 35, no. 3–4 (1988).

the jurisprudence of African boundaries, Ian Brownlie, observed, "the resolution, the conduct of governments based upon it, provides the basis for a rule of regional customary international law binding those states which have unilaterally declared their acceptance of the principle of the *status quo* as at the time of independence."[16] In juridical terms, this position was assimilated to the legal doctrine of *uti possidetis*, a concept that asserts the territorial continuity of African units in spite of the transfer of sovereignty and irrespective of the international legal merits of their original demarcation. Prescriptive dignity is claimed for *uti possidetis* not only because of its origins in Roman law but because of a belief among specialists in African international law that the doctrine has had a commendable career in preserving territorial integrity and state system stability in Latin America. A close inspection of Latin American history provides little support for this conviction, but the important juridical fact is that *uti possidetis* has acquired robust authority in Africa.

The reception of *uti possidetis* in an emerging system of African international law has beyond a doubt facilitated norms of interstate boundary harmony in Africa. The OAU doctrines have certainly inhibited the potential disposition of external actors to seek global strategic advantage through support of forces seeking territorial alterations, although such hesitations may be overridden when temptations become too strong.[17] Within Africa as well it has rarely been disputed in principle although, as discussed later, it has on occasion been breached in practice.[18]

"Self-determination" as an enunciated principle did not thereby

16. Ian Brownlie, *African Boundaries: A Legal and Diplomatic Encyclopedia* (University of California Press, 1979), p. 11.

17. For example, in the French support for the Biafran secession, or in the Belgian and to a lesser extent French and British aid to the Katanga regime of Moise Tshombe in 1960–63. John Ravenhill argues that external respect for the OAU territorial integrity doctrine is significantly weakening; "Redrawing the Map of Africa?" in Donald Rothchild and Naomi Chazan, eds., *The Precarious Balance: State and Society in Africa* (Boulder, Colo.: Westview Press, 1988), pp. 282–306.

18. For an exception, see the passionate attack by a Moroccan jurist, Abdelhamid El Ouali, " 'L'uti possidetis' ou le non-sens du 'principe de base' de l'OUA pour le réglement des différends territoriaux," *Mois en Afrique*, nos. 217–18 (February–March 1984), pp. 3–30.

disappear. It was indeed affirmed in ringing terms in the 1981 African Charter on Human and Peoples' Rights, drafted under OAU auspices. "All peoples" were said to enjoy this right, although no definition of "people" was supplied. Actual state behavior leaves no doubt that territorial integrity takes primacy. Self-determination in practice appears to refer to the right of civil society or segments of it to shape their own destiny within the framework of an established nation-state.[19]

At the moment of African norm creation, there was solid reason for apprehension concerning the stability of the African state system. Although there is an element of artificiality in many—perhaps most—boundaries, African frontiers seemed singularly fragile. With a handful of exceptions, states lacked historical pedigree; innumerable instances exist where cultural communities are divided by the colonial partition. The anxieties as well as the hopes awakened by the surge to independence, and often turbulent political mobilization that attended it, gave rise to a large number of ethnic self-determination claims. Between the 1963 and 1964 OAU summits, the brief but potentially serious border wars between Ethiopia and Somalia, and Algeria and Morocco, portended a dangerous future. As well, the form assumed by the OAU as interstate cartel sounded the death knell of the grandiose project of a pan-African unification that might have rendered moot lesser boundary conflicts and self-determination demands. The fervor with which *uti possidetis* was adopted reflected the elemental imperatives of survival.

TERRITORIAL INTEGRITY: THE BOUNDARY DIMENSION

I turn first to the frontier issue. Disputes of this nature have three primary sources. First, the boundaries and territorial personality of administrative units within the zone of occupation of a single colonial power were frequently ambiguous and historically fluctuating. Sec-

19. See the useful discussion by a Sudanese international law specialist, Abdullahi Ahmed An-na'im, "The Right to Self-Determination in the Horn of Africa: Perils and Promises," *ACAS Bulletin*, vol. 27 (Spring 1989), pp. 20–27

ond, conflicts germinated from the disposition of former German and Italian possessions after the First and Second World Wars, respectively. Third, for states with a historical personality, claims rooted in a logic other than the colonial partition competed with the territorial grid imposed by imperialism.[20]

On the first issue, frontiers separating zones occupied by different colonial powers had been the object of formal international treaties and were generally clear if not rational. Administrative subdivisions within a sphere ruled by a single colonizer were a different matter altogether. In the administrative federations of Afrique Occidentale Française (AOF) and Afrique Equatoriale Française (AEF), especially the former, the territorial units that ultimately acquired sovereignty were subjected to repeated reconfigurations;[21] thus, for example, Upper Volta (Burkina Faso), created only in 1919, was eliminated in 1932, only to be resurrected in 1947. In the southern reaches of the Maghreb territories, demarcation between areas of French occupation was incomplete, especially between Morocco and Algeria; indeed, in this instance there was extended jostling between competing colonial bureaucracies (Foreign Ministry and Interior Ministry). In the Comoros, the four islands had somewhat separate colonial administrative personalities, which served as the basis for the hotly disputed decision to count independence referendum results separately in 1974, leaving Mayotte under French sovereignty. Cabinda (until 1955) and Fer-

20. For major useful studies on African boundary issues, see Touval, *Boundary Politics*; Carl Widstrand, ed., *African Boundary Problems* (Uppsala: Scandinavian Institute of African Studies, 1969); P. Bouvier, "Un problème de sociologie politique: Les frontières des Etats africains," *Revue de l'Institut de Sociologie* (Brussels), vol. 4 (1972), pp. 685–720; A. I. Asiwaju, *Partitioned Africans: Ethnic Relations across Africa's International Boundaries 1884–1984* (London: C. Hurst 1984); Jon Woronoff, "Différends frontaliers en Afrique," *Revue Française d'Etudes Politiques Africaines*, vol. 80 (August 1972), pp. 56–78; and Yves Person, "L'Afrique Noire et ses frontières," *Revue Française d'Etudes Politiques Africaines*, vol. 80 (August 1972), pp. 18–42. The African boundary doctrine received international support from the 1969 Vienna Convention on the Law of Treaties, article 11 of which stipulates that succession of state does not affect a boundary established by a treaty. For a definitive treatment of the legal details of particular African frontiers, see the massive juridical text by Brownlie, *African Boundaries*.

21. For examples, see Person, "L'Afrique Noire."

nando Poo (until 1963) were separate administrative units from An-gola and Equatorial Guinea, respectively, some of whose residents disputed using the final colonial entity as the territorial basis for de-colonization.[22] Overall, a large fraction of interstate boundary litiga-tion has involved areas formerly under French domination, especially in the vast zone of compact colonial sovereignty stretching from Al-giers to Brazzaville.

A second type of dispute arose owing to the partition of the German territories of Togo, Cameroon, and Tanganyika as mandate territories after the First World War, and to years of uncertainty concerning Italian colonies, occupied militarily by Allied forces early in the Second World War. In Togo and Cameroon, self-determination through a referendum was applied in the British-occupied zones, although with a crucial difference in the rules: tally as a single unit in the Togo case, separate counting in the two territorial segments of British Cam-eroon (and thus contrasting outcomes). Tanganyikan nationalists, un-like their Togolese and Cameroonian counterparts, never laid claim to Ruanda-Urundi, but the insistence of the latter two territories on independence as separate units was opposed by the African voices in the Trusteeship Council. As for the former Italian colonies, the confused international politics of their postwar disposition sowed the seeds of the Horn crisis today, and for that matter of the Libya-Chad boundary conflict.

The third category of conflicts affected six states with a historical personality that was not simply a product of the colonial partition. Liberia believed itself to be the victim of French and British encroachment in the early colonial years, in territories to which the Americo-Liberian fledgling state had laid precarious claim. Egypt had not only lost the Sudanese territories conquered in the 1820s by Khedive Mohammed Ali, which till the eve of Sudanese independence it hoped to recover, but also nursed grievances about the southern frontier imposed by the

22. Neuberger, *National Self-Determination*, pp. 18–60. When independence brought the capricious tyranny of Francisco Macias Nguema and the destruc-tion of the once-prosperous Fernando Poo economy, the dominant Bubi pop-ulation had cause to regret its attachment to mainland Rio Muni. However, separation has not resurfaced as an issue. Ibrahim K. Sundiata, "The Roots of African Despotism: The Question of Political Culture," *African Studies Re-view*, vol. 31 (April 1988), p. 16.

British. Especially troublesome were the territorial ambitions of Morocco, which drew inspiration from maximal images of its *blad-as-siba* (zone of dissidence), the fluctuating regions of sporadic royal suzerainty. Ethiopia, especially during the Second World War, nurtured hopes of unifying under its flag the entire Horn, and was swift to advance its claims as natural successor power to Italy in Eritrea and Somalia when a British-Ethiopian force liberated the country in 1941.[23] Somalia, alone of African states, asserted a historical personality based on cultural unity rather than precolonial statehood, claiming thereby portions of Kenya and Ethiopia as well as Djibouti.[24] Lesotho and Swaziland have claims on some areas of the Orange Free State and Natal, respectively, which are not actively pursued at present.

Thus the emergent African state system confronted a serious challenge. In the face of its magnitude, the peaceful resolution of most boundary litigation is remarkable, all the more if one recollects the three major wars in Latin America fought over frontier issues, the three wars between India and Pakistan, the 1962 Sino-Indian war, and the extraordinary carnage of the 1980–88 Iran-Iraq war, which originated over disputed territory. The powerful consensus on territorial inviolability, grounded in *uti possidetis*, supplied both norm and incentive for peaceful settlement. Around this African international law grew diplomatic machinery, often under OAU auspices, which facilitated negotiation. A large number of disputes have been resolved or are quiescent. Outside the Horn, the only major border conflicts concern the Aozou strip, claimed by Chad and Libya, and the looming struggle between Namibia and South Africa over Walvis Bay.[25]

23. To recapture the Ethiopian dreams of the time, see the study by two adoptive Ethiopian patriots, E. Sylvia Pankhurst and Richard K. P. Pankhurst, *Ethiopia and Eritrea* (Woodford Green, Essex: Lalibela House, 1953).

24. A paradox in Somali claims requires note. Although the cultural and linguistic unity of all Somalis as a historically constituted people was the justification for pan-Somali claims, in practice the entire administrative units of the Northern Frontier District of Kenya and Djibouti were demanded; these territories, demarcated by colonial rather than cultural logic, both included areas not populated by Somalis.

25. For one listing of the disputes settled, see Touval, *Boundary Politics*, pp. 279–90. See also Habib Gherari, "Démarcation et bornage des frontières algériennes," *Mois en Afrique*, nos. 225–26 (1984), pp. 15–30.

ETHNICITY AND SELF-DETERMINATION

The second main category of challenges to the African state system derives from the cultural heterogeneity of nearly all states and the ambiguities in the doctrine of self-determination as applied to African circumstance. In the history of a nation-state, the advent of independence is invariably a moment of the covenant, a "critical date" when fundamental questions of community and commitment arise; the compact of citizenship is presumptively perpetual. In the years of decolonization or new independence, whispers (or sometimes shouts) of secession were heard by ethnic or regional groups in Zambia, Zaire, Angola, Kenya, Uganda, Sudan, Chad, Central African Republic, Nigeria, Benin, Togo, Ghana, Ivory Coast, Senegal, Equatorial Guinea, Libya, and Mauritania. Informed by the sense of state fragility that even the mere listing of separatist sentiments suffices to illuminate, the alacrity with which the framers of African international law embraced territorial integrity and frontier inviolability finds further explanation. Indeed, in one important sense the difficulty was more profound than most African leaders appreciated in 1960; at that time, the cleavages of cultural pluralism—ethnic, linguistic, regional, religious, or racial—were widely believed to be transitional tensions, to be effaced by the progressive tides of national integration. However, subsequent events and analysis conclusively demonstrate that, while there is an element of indeterminacy in trends concerning cultural identities, many forces commonly associated with "modernization" tend to broaden and deepen cultural identities, even though "nation" as a component of state doctrine may simultaneously strengthen.[26]

In retrospect, the speed with which ethnic self-determination— which has proved so powerful and resilient a force in Asia, Europe, and now the Soviet Union—was rendered illicit in Africa is extraordinary if one recollects the surge of ethnic restiveness at the moment of power transfer. The territorial integrity doctrine swiftly achieved overpowering normative force, not only at the level of state elites but also among the African intelligentsia more generally. One may sug-

26. For evidence, see Donald L. Horowitz, *Ethnic Groups in Conflict* (University of California Press, 1985); and Crawford Young, *The Politics of Cultural Pluralism* (University of Wisconsin Press, 1976).

gest several reasons for ideological assimilation of territorial integrity as a moral code. Such a list must begin with the transcendent force of anticolonial nationalism at that time, with its strong territorial focus and unitarian impulses. At this juncture, the political leadership and the intelligentsia were in most instances united, which denied to potential ethnic self-determination movements the skills of organization and discourse indispensable to their structuration as articulated political forces. Claims for ethnic sovereignty were at this crucial historical point irredeemably contaminated as retrograde vehicles for undermining African independence. Further discrediting the notion of ethnicity as a basis for self-determination claims was the implementation, simultaneous with the surge to African independence, of the South African scheme of "grand apartheid," by which the African population was to be deprived of all civic rights by herding it into ten "homelands" according to state-defined ethnic criteria. Thus stood epitomized a vision of ethnicity as the manipulation of the oppressed by the master race.

Ethnic self-determination could arise in two forms: demands for separate sovereignty expressed by a cultural community within an existing territorial entity, and claims for reunification by a group partitioned among two or more states. Both forms have been surprisingly rare and mainly confined to the first years of independence, except in the Somali case. If one sets aside from the earlier listing of ethnic secession units those that were limited to the immediate conjuncture of independence and that lacked sustained support or purpose, one finds but a few instances, none of which were continuous forces. Buganda proclaimed its separation from Uganda both on the eve of independence, in 1960, and in 1966; in both instances, the kingdom lacked the means to execute its threat, which was not pursued against the coercive supremacy of the territorial state. Also in western Uganda, a regionalist revolt broke out in 1962 among the Konjo and Amba groups in the Ruwenzori mountains. The movement had declined in intensity by 1969, and in 1982 it was ended by a formal agreement with the Ugandan government.[27]

27. See Martin Doornbos, "Kumenyana and Rwenzururu: Two Responses to Ethnic Inequality," in Robert I. Rotberg and Ali A. Mazrui, eds., *Protest and Power in Black Africa* (New York: Oxford University Press, 1970), pp. 1088–

Even more remarkable than the near-absence of ethnic separatist movements has been the low incidence of claims for ethnic regrouping of partitioned peoples. The number of identifiable communities separated by existing frontiers is vast; yet only in the Somali instance has the demand been a permanent political fact.[28] The Ewe, divided between Togo and Ghana, who appear at first glance to offer an example of an ethnic irredenta, on closer inspection demonstrate the intimate interpenetration of ethnic regrouping aspirations, interstate politics, and internal dynamics within the two polities in which they dwell.[29] The crucial point of reference is the former German colonial territory of Togoland; no claim has ever been made for a separate Ewe state. The demand for regrouping within a single state has waxed and waned; the political unit of preference has fluctuated over time, contingent on the relative advantages. In the terminal colonial period, British rule was less oppressive, and the Gold Coast was far more prosperous, making it a more attractive framework for Ewe unification. The use of the referendum mechanism to determine the future of the British Togo mandate fostered intense mobilization on this issue; by the time it occurred most Ewe had come to prefer Togo, where they expected to play a more dominant economic and political role. Although such a role has been denied them in the more than two decades of Gnassingbe Eyadema's rule, the far superior economic conditions in Togo by the late 1960s intensified preferences for reconsideration of the Ghana links, leading to the emergence of the National Liberation Movement of Western Togoland. This agitation

---

1136. Nelson Kasfir holds rich documentation on this movement; I am indebted to him for clarification of its history.

28. Even in this instance, the ideal of the Somali irredenta has diminished with time. With respect to Kenya and Djibouti, the matter is wholly dormant and no longer attracts support from Somali speakers in these states. In the Ogaden, a Somali-Ethiopian accord at least suspending this dispute was signed in 1988, made necessary by the decomposition of both states. Edmond J. Keller, "The O.A.U. and the Ogaden Dispute," paper presented to the International Conference on the Horn of Africa, Alcala, Spain, September 1989.

29. For fascinating detail, see David Brown, "Borderline Politics in Ghana: The National Liberation Movement of Western Togoland," *Journal of Modern African Studies*, vol. 18, no. 4 (1981), pp. 575–609.

in turn diminished in the 1980s, with some economic recovery in Ghana, and the advent of the Jerry Rawlings regime, in which the Ewe played a salient role.

A more transient ethnic regroupment movement, proposing the unification of the Kongo in Angola, Zaire, and Congo-Brazzaville, briefly appeared at the moment of independence. The notion of a resurrection of the storied Kongo kingdom was swiftly eclipsed and never had as much backing as its opponents feared. In reality, "Kongo" is a problematic ethnonym despite a significant shared historical consciousness. The more striking fact is that, although the Kongo are relatively marginalized in the regional coalitions in all three states, the "tous ceux qui se ressemblent, se rassemblent" dictum attributed to Congo-Brazzaville President Foulbert Youlou at the time of independence has never resurfaced.[30]

The most spectacular cases of armed insurrection by groups demanding independence have revolved not around cultural segments but around administrative regions; the four major instances were Katanga, Biafra, southern Sudan, and Eritrea. The superior legitimacy of territorial divisions originating in colonial administrative boundaries was central to the separation effort. Even though in all four examples ethnic factors were present, they did not figure in the official text of legitimation.

In the case of Katanga, a colonial province whose European milieux had long nurtured a culture of particularity profited from the sudden power deflation at the center produced by the mutiny of the national army in July 1960 to claim independence. The secessionist region claimed the right of self-determination at a provincial level, to which the national state responded by invoking the sacred vocation of national unity at another. This debate proved unequal; not a single state could be found to recognize Katangan sovereignty, although France, Great Britain, and especially Belgium provided more or less covert assistance. Denied the gift of external juridical life as a "subject" of

30. Separatist sentiments were widely attributed to the Alliance des Bakongo (ABAKO) at the time of Zairian independence. Although such ideas were nurtured in some quarters, they were never held by the leadership, in particular President Joseph Kasavubu. For evidence, see Loka ne Kongo, "La pensée politique de Kasa-Vubu," Mémoire de licence, Université Nationale du Zaire, Lubumbashi, 1974.

international law by the refusal of the community of states to lay on its hands, Katanga was ultimately vulnerable to international force; U.N. troops liquidated the secession after thirty months.[31] The Katanga case well illustrated the capacity of the African state system— even before the OAU gave it collective expression—to constrain the formation of breakaway states. As Charles de Visscher expressed the matter, even if an entity shows "the characteristics generally attributed to the State," and enjoys momentary autonomy, only international recognition "invests it with a personality in the law of nations."[32]

In the Biafra case, the invocation of a colonial administrative boundary rather than the claim of ethnic self-determination is even more striking, because the crux of the Nigerian crisis of 1965–67 became the Ibo situation. The former Eastern Region of Nigeria, proclaimed as the sovereign state of Biafra in 1967, was over 60 percent Ibo in population, but some Ibo also inhabited the neighboring Midwest Region as well as urban centers throughout the federation. The impetus to separation came from the progressive isolation of the Ibo in political and administrative instances outside the Eastern Region, the fraud and violence associated with the 1964 and 1965 elections that made this trend seem permanent, the decimation of Ibo military leaders in the July 1966 coup, and the calamitous anti-Ibo pogroms in northern cities that year, which drove more than a million refugees back to the ethnic cradleland. Some other southern ethnic communities shared in some of these misfortunes; indeed, initially Biafran leaders hoped to spark a reunification of all southern Nigeria, to undo the 1914 Lugardian amalgamation of the previously separate northern and southern colonies. But the secession had the reverse effect, of supplying a powerful surge of Nigerian national sentiment in support of reconquest.

31. The definitive study of the Katanga secession is Jules-Gerard Libois, *Katanga Secession* (University of Wisconsin Press, 1966). See also Crawford Young, "Comparative Claims to Political Sovereignty: Biafra, Katanga, Eritrea," in Donald Rothchild and Victor A. Olorunsola, eds., *State versus Ethnic Claims: African Policy Dilemmas* (Boulder, Colo.: Westview Press, 1983), pp. 199–232; and René Lemarchand, "The Limits of Self-Determination: Katanga," *American Political Science Review*, vol. 56 (June 1962), pp. 404–16.

32. Charles de Visscher, *Theory and Reality in Public International Law* (Princeton University Press, 1968), p. 175.

The Biafran case was a critical test for OAU doctrines of territorial integrity. At the 1967, 1968, and 1969 OAU summits, Nigerian diplomats had some difficult moments ensuring final African backing for its positions, and Nigeria had to cope with a series of conciliation missions while pursuing its own military response; no fewer than four African states actually accorded recognition to Biafra (Tanzania, Zambia, Ivory Coast, and Gabon, as well as Haiti), and several others contemplated such a move. Julius K. Nyerere suggested *uti possidetis* had to give way to higher moral imperatives; he explained, "It seemed to us that by refusing the existence of Biafra we were tacitly supporting a war against the people of Eastern Nigeria. . . . We could not continue doing this any longer."[33]

In the end, the Biafra secession was defeated not by jurisprudence but by the Nigerian army; from this military fact came a potent reinforcement of African commitment to the concept of territorial integrity. The Nigerian triumph, and magnanimous reincorporation of defeated populations, vindicated *uti possidetis*. However, for a number of months, the military outcome hung in the balance. Had Biafran forces been able to sustain themselves over an extended period, international law would have accommodated itself, over time, to an alternative set of political facts.

TERRITORIAL INTEGRITY CHALLENGED: SUDAN AND ETHIOPIA

The southern Sudan case is far more complex.[34] In contrast to Katanga and Biafra, where regimes in control of provincial institutions declared separation and formed regular armies, in southern Sudan armed re-

---

33. John J. Stremlau, *The International Politics of the Nigerian Civil War 1967–1970* (Princeton University Press, 1977), pp. 129–41.

34. For scholarly monographs reflecting the southern Sudanese perspective, see Dunstan M. Wai, *The African-Arab Conflict in the Sudan* (New York: Africana Publishing House, 1978); and Mohamed Omar Beshir, *The Southern Sudan: Background to Conflict* (London: Blackwood and Sons, 1968). For the northern perspective, see Bona Malwal, "The Challenge of the South to Sudanese National Politics," paper presented to the International Conference on the Conflict in the Horn of Africa, Alcala, Spain, September 1989.

sistance movements emerged in response to regional grievances of the southern provinces. As Dunstan Wai cogently argues, the southern Sudanese were not involved in the independence movement, for the most part had little attachment to the idea of a union of the north and south, and were essentially excluded from the discussions that defined the constitutional framework for power transfer.[35] The south was highly apprehensive at the moment of independence; measures taken by the northern-dominated government to secure its hold on the south intensified these fears, which by 1963 had given rise to armed guerrilla bands. Southern resistance, though feeding on a common set of grievances, never produced a fully unified movement, nor were its goals explicitly enunciated. Nor did it ever enjoy the unanimous backing of all ethnic communities in the south; Khartoum always had some room for maneuver by playing on local rivalries. Although neighboring states at times exhibited some informal sympathy and even offered sanctuary and tolerated arms flow, at an official level African states remained resolutely aligned on the OAU Charter doctrines of territorial integrity. Despite their divisions and isolation, the southern insurgents were ultimately a more formidable foe than the would-be regular armies constituted by Katanga and Biafra; the armies disintegrated after military defeat, whereas guerrilla forces could avoid or absorb losses in given skirmishes. With neither side able to prevail, and southern movements not irrevocably committed to sovereignty, conditions were ripe for creative diplomacy. By conceding a special status for the southern provinces, and other generous provisions of incorporation, President Jaafar Nimeiri was able to achieve settlement in 1972; African international law through its territorial integrity commitments doubtless played a part, as did the mediation of Emperor Haile Selassie of Ethiopia.

Subsequently, Nimeiri, in the twilight of his rule, unraveled what had been so painfully stitched together through promulgation of the September 1983 laws imposing a harsh version of *shari'a* on the country. Renewed insurrection in the south followed at once; significantly, however, the leading insurgent movement, the Sudan People's Liberation Army (SPLA), insisted that its combat was to achieve a reconstructed basis for Sudanese unity, grounded in secular toleration.

35. Dunstan Wai, "Sources of Communal Conflict and Secessionist Policies in Africa," *Ethnic and Racial Studies*, vol. 1 (July 1978).

The choice of the idiom of Sudanese unity as justification for regional resistance can only reflect the pervasive influence of African state doctrine.

The Eritrean case originates in the exceptional circumstances of decolonization of the former Italian colonies, entirely situated in the realm of international negotiation.[36] The 1952 award of Eritrea to Ethiopia with a constitutionally recognized distinct personality and significant autonomy was above all the product of international system dynamics, in which Ethiopian diplomacy played a significant role, but from which Eritrean participation was largely excluded. Although Eritrean political movements with varying degrees of reluctance participated in the new institutions, the full exercise of anticolonial self-determination normally available to distinct colonial territorial units was in effect denied. The U.N. role in sponsoring and legitimating this formula had enduring consequences. Although Ethiopia began at once to dismantle the federal arrangements and autonomy provisions, then abrogated them altogether in 1962, the United Nations covered by its silence this contravention. Abetted by agile Ethiopian diplomacy, this in turn made possible the acceptance by the OAU at its birth of Eritrean annexation as a *fait accompli*.[37]

36. On the Eritrean issue, see Lewis, *Nationalism and Self-Determination*; Richard Sherman, *Eritrea: The Unfinished Revolution* (Praeger, 1980); Berhane Cahsai, "Une étude politique et juridique de la question erythréene," *Mois en Afrique*, nos. 217–18 (February–March 1984), pp. 3–30; John Markakis, "The Nationalist Revolution in Eritrea," *Journal of Modern African Studies*, vol. 26, no. 4 (1987), pp. 643–68; Getachew Haile, "The Unity and Territorial Integrity of Ethiopia," *Journal of Modern African Studies*, vol. 24, no. 3 (1986), pp. 465–88; Okbazghi Yohannes, "The Eritrean Question: A Colonial Case?" *Journal of Modern African Studies*, vol. 25, no. 4 (1987), pp. 51–70; Bereket H. Selassie, *Conflict and Intervention in the Horn* (Monthly Review Press, 1980), and *Eritrea and the United Nations and Other Essays* (Trenton, N.J.: Red Sea Press, 1989); and Gegre Hiwet Tesfagiorgis, "Self-Determination: Its Evolution and Practice by the United Nations and Its Application to the Case of Eritrea," *Wisconsin International Law Journal*, vol. 6, no. 1 (1987), pp. 75–127.

37. The OAU thus perceives a distinction between Western Sahara, accorded recognition as a member state, and Eritrea, which is denied a hearing. The principal difference seems to lie in the evolution of international norms concerning self-determination of colonized peoples, the "critical date" at which these issues were debated in the international arena, and power politics.

Thus the Eritrean liberation movements have never been able to secure a hearing from the OAU and suffer from stigmatization as "secessionists." In recent years, Eritrean juridical arguments focused on the notion that Ethiopia is a colonial state, under which circumstances self-determination takes precedence over territorial integrity. Whatever the empirical merits of this reasoning, its prospects of success in the African and international arena seem slender.

I return to the challenges posed to the African international normative order in the closing section; the key conclusion to retain at this juncture is the effective exclusion of ethnic commonality as grounds for self-determination. To fully measure the significance of this social fact, one needs to juxtapose the African pattern to those of other regions. In the Baltic republics in the Soviet Union, in Tibet in China, in Tamil areas of Sri Lanka, in Kurdish regions of Iraq, Iran, and Turkey, in Scotland, in Quebec province of Canada, ethnolinguistic identity is asserted as prescriptive entitlement to self-determination. Among the major regions where ethnicity is territorially rooted, Africa alone has rendered virtually taboo its articulation as grounds for sovereignty claims. This unique outcome is not because Africa has proscribed ethnic self-determination; in the modern world, nation-state ideology everywhere asserts that an irrevocable covenant binds existing territory and population to the sovereign polity. What makes the African outcome exceptional is the effectiveness of this doctrine at precluding the demands of ethnic sovereignty. One may recollect that the doctrine of self-determination arose in indissociable bonds with the idea of nationality, which originally sacralized communities defined by language and culture.[38]

My analysis thus far would suggest that the consolidation of the African state system is an accomplished fact, and that the OAU Charter prescriptions of territorial integrity and inviolable frontiers are remarkably robust. The crucial challenges to the OAU normative system lie in the Horn, although unresolved issues of territory and sover-

---

38. Among the immense literature on this point, see especially John Breuilly, *Nationalism and the State* (Manchester University Press, 1982); Hans Kohn, *The Idea of Nationalism* (Macmillan, 1943); Anthony D. Smith, *Theories of Nationalism* (Harper and Row, 1971); and Crawford Young, "Nationalizing the Third World State: Categorical Imperative or Mission Impossible?" *Polity*, vol. 15 (Winter 1982), pp. 161–81.

eignty remain in the Western Sahara, the Libya-Chad border, and Walvis Bay. In the first case, by admitting Western Sahara as a member state in the face of Moroccan military enforcement of its annexation claims, the OAU affirmed the superior standing of colonial partition as generative of self-determination rights, when asserted by a liberation movement.[39] In the Chad-Libya case, Libyan occupation of the Aozou strip since 1973, without ever articulating a claim cast in the discourse of international law, has created an impasse that the OAU machinery has yet to overcome. *Uti possidetis* confronts a boundary of unusually dubious parentage, with French border claims originating in treaties signed with Great Britain, whose juridical standing to allocate Ottoman territory is obscure. Although an August 1989 Libya-Chad accord seemed to point to a settlement, early resolution is far from certain.[40] In Walvis Bay, self-determination would provide a safer basis for the Namibian claim that common sense commands than *uti possidetis*; when the German South West Africa colony was created, the enclave was a British (Cape) possession.[41]

39. The best recapitulation of the background to the Western Sahara dispute is Tony Hodges, *Western Sahara: Roots of a Desert War* (Chicago Review Press, 1984). See also John Damis, *Conflict in Northwest Africa: The Western Sahara Dispute* (Stanford: Hoover Institution Press, 1983).

40. The most valuable source for exploring the background to this imbroglio is Bernard Lanne, *Tchad-Libye: la querelle des frontiéres* (Paris: Editions Karthala, 1982). Also useful are Virginia Thompson and Richard Adloff, *Conflict in Chad* (Berkeley: Institute of International Studies, 1981); Robert Buijtenhuis, *Le FROLINAT et les révoltes populaires du Tchad, 1965–1976* (The Hague: Mouton, 1978); and Adrian Pelt, *Libyan Independence and the United Nations: A Case of Planned Decolonization* (Yale University Press, 1970). The Ottoman state sought to reinforce its claims against French encroachment in the southern reaches of its Libyan domain just before Italian conquest. In 1906–11 Turkish garrisons were established in the Tibesti region, thus creating a modicum of "effective occupation." John Wright, *Libya: A Modern History* (Johns Hopkins University Press, 1982), p. 19.

41. The Dutch first established on outpost at this harbor in 1793, and the British seized it in 1795. It was administered as part of Cape Colony and remained separate from the German South West Africa territory created in the 1880s. South Africa attached it to its mandate for administrative convenience, but reattached it to the Cape in 1974 when some form of independence

But none of these issues pose a general challenge to African state stability. The OAU, whatever weaknesses one may detect in its machinery, has created an African international public law with both normative and empirical force. In turn, the broader world order has assimilated African norms, especially through the U.N. machinery. Despite the weakness and vulnerability of many African states, in the classical calculus of power and force, overall African boundaries have acquired international protective security by the end of the third decade of independence. Indeed, Robert Jackson and Carl Rosberg go so far as to claim African sovereignty is above all an international juridical fact.

> The independence and survival of African states is not in jeopardy, however, because their sovereignty is not contingent on their credibility as authoritative and capable political structures. Instead, it is guaranteed by the world community of states, especially as embodied in the United Nations, whose egalitarian international norms are universally accepted. . . . Legal recognition has been far more important than material aid in their emergence and survival to date. Therefore, rather than claiming sovereignty by a demonstration of inescapable reality, most Tropical African states exist primarily by means of international legitimacy.[42]

The institutionalized legitimacy of these norms assures that the boundary disputes that have bedeviled Latin America will not occur in Africa outside the Horn. Nor at least in a near future will ethnic self-determination movements arise to assault the extant state system, again excepting the Horn; only Ethiopia is currently at risk from such movements. If one views the African case comparatively and historically, these are extraordinary accomplishments for the existing African state system.

---

for Namibia was first seriously contemplated. Namibia will need to vindicate its claims on grounds other than standard *uti possidetis* doctrine.

42. Robert H. Jackson and Carl G. Rosberg, "Sovereignty and Underdevelopment: Juridical Statehood in the African Case," *Journal of Modern African Studies*, vol. 24, no. 1 (1986), p. 2.

SELF-DETERMINATION RECONSIDERED: CONCLUDING REFLECTIONS

Yet analysis cannot stop here. The multiple crises in the Horn of Africa raise fundamental issues for the African state system. The human devastation in Sudan and Ethiopia is so great, and the decay of the central states so far-reaching, that some discovery of a path beyond the current entangled impasses is urgent. The appalling tyranny of death and destruction in the Horn cannot indefinitely persist. There must be some alternative to permanent insurgent warfare.

One may doubt whether such a resolution is possible within the framework of the Horn state system as presently constituted. At least the possibility of its revision seems indispensable, through acceptance of self-determination as well as territorial integrity as applicable principles. Not only international legal norms but political history and balances, and the distribution of force, must enter the equation.

But the military and political balances are of fundamental importance. A durable accommodation was probably possible in the 1950s, and again in the middle 1970s; these historic occasions were lost. The intensity of the suffering endured by the Eritrean population during the succession of brutal offensives since 1978 has altered the basic parameters of the situation. So also has the emergence of the Eritrean People's Liberation Front (EPLF) as sole voice, and the thorough social structuration of EPLF zones. There is no prospect that the 1978–88 level of military supply can be sustained by the Ethiopians, nor that diplomacy can seal off all sources of provisions for the Eritrean resistance. The Ethiopian army transparently lacks enthusiasm for further offensives, with their huge cost in casualties for the lower ranks and the severe punishments for commanders as reward for failure. History records many cases in which a state conducts a war without mercy against a segment of its population—for example, the Civil War in America and the crushing of the Basmachi uprising in Soviet Central Asia in the 1920s. When force prevails, a tacit acceptance of the state's authority may over time occur. When it fails, a negotiated restoration of its hegemony seems difficult to imagine. Whether this conflict is "ripe for resolution" is another matter.[43] For Ethiopia, the

43. The phrase is contributed by I. William Zartman in his perceptive review of diplomatic successes in addressing seemingly intractable conflicts;

repercussions in other dissident zones would be serious. For the Eritreans, the issue of communities whose role in the liberation struggle has been peripheral or even hostile (Kunama, Afar) inevitably arises; if Ethiopian "territorial integrity" is open for negotiation, can that of Eritrea remain inviolable should a segment of its population through self-determination express a preference for Ethiopian sovereignty?

In Sudan, the failure to grasp the opportunity now available for settlement means a prolongation of the catastrophic human devastation in the south and continued decay at the center. The integral Islamic state desired by some in the north is beyond reach. Whatever its ethical virtues, such a political formula can never be imposed on the south, either by military force or by a now-shattered state apparatus. The alternative to splitting the Sudanese state is a political settlement acceptable to the south. The SPLA leadership's commitment to unity is not shared by many of its cadres and the rank and file. It cannot persist indefinitely if the dominant Islamic-oriented forces in the northern political equation continue to insist on that which they lack the means to enforce and can never achieve by persuasion.

Given the magnitude of the catastrophe and the impossibility of overcoming human suffering within existing political frameworks, both Ethiopia and Sudan cry out for creative imagination and careful study. The steel grid of the nation-state and its excessively unitarian ideology must somehow yield to more flexible formulations. Whether these may come through some loose-knit, broader Horn umbrella entity, confederal arrangements within existing state units, their reconfiguration by some design that can win the acceptance of all regional and ideological forces, or the acceptance of additional sovereign entities into the African family of states, can be decided only by the protagonists within the region, and a resolution will not come soon. Systematic inquiry into the implications and requisites for the choices that lie ahead, wherever conducted, can be of service only to the parties involved.

In the final analysis, and in the long run, international law accommodates itself to force. This Hobbesian reality is implicitly acknowledged in the *uti possidetis* shield African international law has erected

---

Ripe for Resolution: Conflict and Intervention in Africa (New York: Oxford University Press, 1985).

to protect existing frontiers, which argues inviolable borders irrespective of the legal foundations of their colonial origins. As R. J. Vincent has cogently argued, *faits accomplis* are "creative of values regardless of previous conceptions of rights."[44]

I believe at this juncture that the elements of stability in the African state system are sufficiently institutionalized for the OAU normative code to withstand a handful of derogations without the entire edifice crumbling. As the classic international law text on territorial status concludes, "A law which, within narrow limits, seems to sanction only the maintenance of the *status quo*, is not likely to survive without serious modification in a still rapidly developing society of States."[45] An independent Eritrea, for example, need not shake the foundations of the African international legal order, as Biafran separation might well have done two decades ago. This is not to say that such a settlement will not produce intense strains within Ethiopia, with more assertive articulation of regional claims by Oromo, Tigre, Somali, and perhaps other groups. But Ethiopia will continue to enjoy the inestimable advantage of legal and normative support from the African state system. The instances in which solutions derogating from extant OAU boundary doctrine may be unavoidable are limiting cases of exception, rather than precursors of a flood of frontier litigation and state fragmentation.

44. R. J. Vincent, "Western Conceptions of a Universal Moral Order," *British Journal of International Studies*, vol. 4 (1978), p. 27.

45. Jennings, *Acquisition of Territory*, p. 70.

Chapter 13

WILLIAM J. FOLTZ

The Organization of African Unity and the Resolution of Africa's Conflicts

The Organization of African Unity (OAU) has come under increasing attack in recent years from Africans and from usually sympathetic outsiders. There is nothing new about attacks on the OAU; since its founding in 1963, the organization has been criticized for its failure to promote pan-African political unity, a continent-wide socialist order, higher commodity prices, regional economic integration, and an end to apartheid and neocolonial intervention—most of these wildly beyond the capabilities of any conceivable international organization, or even of a unified and powerful national state.[1] In recent years, complaints have come to focus on the organization's failure to prevent or to resolve the violent conflicts that have caused vast human misery in several parts of the continent and opened the door to penetration by non-African powers. In reviewing the July 1989 OAU assembly of heads of government, *Africa Confidential* confided to its readers that if the OAU's new leadership cannot make dramatic strides in resolving these conflicts, "it is hard to see an effective future for the OAU."[2] The challenge thus posed would be a formidable one for any collective organization. For one as beset by problems, as materially under-nourished as the OAU, and with so little prospect of a new influx of resources, it might seem impossible.

The OAU, however, has not survived for more than a quarter of a century because it has lacked problems or enjoyed material prosperity.

1. A sampling of such literature would include Zdenek Cervenka, *The Unfinished Quest for Unity: Africa and the OAU* (London: Julian Friedmann, 1977); Elenga M'buyinga, *Pan Africanism or Neo-Colonialism? The Bankruptcy of the O.A.U.* (London: Zed Press, 1982); and Sekou Traore, *Questions Africaines* (Paris: Harmattan, 1989).

2. *Africa Confidential*, vol. 30 (August 11, 1989), p. 4.

If nothing else, it is resilient and adaptable to circumstance. This chapter takes a broad look at the way the OAU has functioned up to now, on the presumption that its modus operandi has reflected useful and realistic adaptations to powerfully coercive domestic circumstances and international structures, and that radical changes in the way the organization functions will require changes in these circumstances and structures. Any more effective OAU role in conflict resolution would thus be more likely to involve an adaptation of previous practice than a set of bold new departures.

UNDERSTANDING THE OAU

Any realistic appreciation of the OAU's current weaknesses and capabilities must begin with the organization's origins. Like the United Nations at its founding a generation earlier, the Organization of African Unity was very much a product of its time. The immediate needs and fears of the founding members marked the organization's structure and agenda in ways that have endured. In Africa, the early 1960s saw a triumph of classic Third World nationalist coalitions, movements led by schoolteachers and clerks, which for the most part had come to power without widespread use of violence within the frameworks of the former colonial states. The boundaries of the newly independent states were those that had delimited the largest unit of effective colonial administration, and thus the largest unit of effective nationalist political organization. These boundaries usually had more juridical and administrative reality than social or economic content, but they sufficed to permit political coalitions to be formed and for the leaders of those coalitions to take advantage of the times to negotiate a transfer of sovereignty. Preservation of the political coalition and its authority in the capital put a premium on preservation of the new state's administrative boundary against threats of secession led by entrepreneurial regional and ethnic elites. Also, it led to the rejection of the larger federal and common administrative units that had been constructed for the convenience of the metropolitan powers, but that had not provided a basis for effective nationalist organization and had thus escaped a single movement's control.

Almost without exception, the nationalist coalitions were led by individuals who, through whatever combination of power, brilliance, craft, compromise, and blind luck, came out on top at the time independence was granted. Like most of those around them, these men possessed *political* skills and experience, not economic. If they sought first the political kingdom, it was in part because that was the kingdom they were equipped to rule.

Although domestic politics was the primary arena for the new leaders, international relations heavily affected the local scene. Independence itself was an international event. The national economies were heavily oriented toward the external world, particularly the former metropole. Establishing the tenor of the new state's relations with the former colonial power was the most fateful decision a new regime faced, for from that many of its other decisions, domestic as well as international, followed logically. But African neighbors could not be neglected either: the modal state on the African continent has five neighbors on its highly porous borders. Perhaps most important, independence for the new state came about not so much because of its leaders' own efforts as because of a broad historical movement involving all the rest of the continent, and indeed Asia as well, which led the way toward the dismantling of old colonial empires. A single country's experience was inseparable from—and contributed to—this general movement toward independence. Although generous aspirations toward "pan-Africanism" also played a role, they influenced the organization of Africa's international affairs much less than these immediate realities. African independence from the beginning was a mutual affair.

The OAU Charter that emerged at Addis Ababa in 1963, with principles and procedures refined in the first two years of meetings, provided for an organization of sovereign and juridically equal states whose most authentic voices were to be those of their individual national leaders. On the internal affairs of its member states, the Charter is a most conservative document; six of the seven "principles" enumerated in article III are designed to serve in part or in whole to protect the autonomy of member states from interference or coercion by other members or by the organization as a whole. (The exception is principle 6, pledging "absolute dedication to the total emancipation of the African territories which are still dependent," which in effect calls for change in the internal affairs of territorial entities that are not, or not yet, members of the organization.) The special significance given to supreme national authorities by making the Assembly of Chiefs of State and Government the decisive organ serves further to reinforce the individual leader's authority over his own state bureaucracy and other political elites.

The Charter is conservative also in its concern to protect the organization as a whole from being manipulated by a determined and organized faction. The requirement of two-thirds for a quorum, for the calling of special meetings, and for all decisions in the summit meetings demonstrates a protective preference for inaction and delay over decisive movement, in the absence of general support. Likewise, the few explicit powers given the secretary-general and the secretariat, as well as the refusal to empanel the proposed Commission of Mediation, Conciliation and Arbitration, and the quick hamstringing of the Liberation Committee when it tried to take autonomous decisions, make it clear that executive action is reserved for the chiefs of state and government, and then only for those subjects on which they can achieve broad consensus. Lest even that threaten a state's sovereign prerogatives, further protection is guaranteed by the absence of any formal sanction, such as suspension or termination of membership, that could be applied against a recalcitrant state. (The exception is suspension for nonpayment of dues, a sanction that has not been invoked despite numerous opportunities.)

The OAU is thus not a command organization, nor is it equipped with independent executive instruments capable of enforcing decisions against either members or nonmembers. Yet I. William Zartman is only partially right when he declares, "There is no OAU; there are only members, and their interests come first."[3] Rather than see the OAU in concrete organizational terms, or set up a standard of executive action against which to measure the OAU, it is more helpful to step back and see it first and foremost as a complex pattern of ordered interactions among states. From such a perspective, the OAU provides an institutionalized forum that facilitates the mutual adjustment of member states' policies and actions within an evolving framework

3. I. William Zartman, "The OAU in the African State System," in Yassin El-Ayouty and I. William Zartman, eds., The OAU after Twenty Years (Praeger, 1984), p. 41.

of general norms and operating practices. The norms are consensual expressions of common, or at least widely shared, goals, which may be attained through a variety of agencies, only a few of which will be those directly under the central command of the organization itself.

Seen thus, the OAU will be familiar to students of international relations as a *regime*, a broad category of international arrangements that includes such disparate cases as the General Agreement on Tariffs and Trade (GATT), the Bretton Woods monetary system, the Law of the Sea Treaty, and, in the security realm, the Concert of Europe in the nineteenth century. In a widely accepted formulation, "regimes can be defined as sets of implicit or explicit principles, norms, rules, and decision making procedures around which actors' expectations converge in a given area of international relations."[4] Whereas some regimes may set up elaborate bureaucratic machinery, it is the reciprocal and mutual adjustment of policies, and of expectations of others' policies, by individual states acting in the pursuit of long-range collective interest that distinguishes an international regime, rather than the presence of authoritative executive structures. The marker of regimes is the elaboration of norms of behavior, whether these are set forth in formal agreements or, more commonly, develop continually as well-understood but unwritten common law.

The Organization of African Unity is unusual among regimes in that it contains no great power, or hegemon, able and willing to pay the setup and running costs and to bribe or bully others into complying with the normative order. At its creation, the OAU was a regime of the weak and thus of the equal. "Sovereign equality" of members is a legal fiction common to most international organizations, but this fiction was a functional reality in the OAU's early years. In this club of weak and fragile states, none possessed the military resources capable of coercing its fellows into compliance, or the economic resources to bankroll an enticing new order. Leadership was a matter of political rhetoric and reputation—in effect, the ability to establish and sustain norms. Although over the years a few states have acquired sufficient resources to become clearly more equal than others and have used those resources to coerce their fellows, the

4. Stephen D. Krasner, "Structural Causes and Regime Consequences: Regimes and Intervening Variables," in S. D. Krasner, ed., *International Regimes* (Cornell University Press, 1983), p. 2.

fundamental norms of the African system "have in no instance been clearly and decisively reversed."[5]

OAU NORMS

Three fundamental norms underpin OAU responses to conflict situations: *noninterference* in the internal affairs of other African states, *territorial integrity* and inviolability of the boundaries within which independence is attained, and *African solutions to African problems*. (A fourth, commitment to liberation of territories under white rule, is not directly relevant to this discussion.)[6] The first of these is a standard feature of virtually all international organizations, though the intensity with which the norm is enunciated—and the difficulty with which it is enforced—may reflect the weakness of the new African states and their inability to control their boundaries and much of their internal public space. The other norms are peculiarly African, and so merit particular attention.

The principle of *territorial integrity*, which enshrines the legitimacy of the borders inherited from the colonial period, no matter how arbitrary they may be about geographic feature or human population, is a favorite target of attack by OAU critics. No less a personage than Edem Kodjo, a former OAU secretary-general, calls it "a 'perverse' principle with negative effects."[7] Nonetheless, the stability of African boundaries has been little short of remarkable, suggesting that however "perverse" the principle may be in theory, it responds to some deep needs within the African situation and will not easily be replaced by an alternative norm. The standard explanation for the norm's per-

5. Zartman, "OAU in the African System," p. 29.

6. See William J. Foltz and Jennifer Widner, "The OAU and Southern African Liberation," in El-Ayouty and Zartman, *OAU after Twenty Years*, pp. 249–72.

7. Edem Kodjo, *Et Demain l'Afrique* (Paris: Stock, 1985), p. 272. The respect for borders existing at the time of independence is not mentioned in the charter itself. Rather, this principle was "adopted by the Assembly of Heads of State and Government in Cairo in 1964 [and] has since been considered as being part and parcel of the Charter." Organization of African Unity Charter Review Committee, *Draft Rapporteur's Report*, CAB/LEG/97/DRFT./Rapt.Rpt.(III) Rev. 2, Addis Ababa, May 10–24, 1982, p. 7.

sistence is the Pandora's box analogy: once one border had been changed, clamors would arise for changes everywhere, which would put all states at risk. While the logic is impeccable, it overlooks the broader complex of factors that support the norm. The first of these is internal: the need for ruling elites to control their boundaries and, to the degree possible, regulate the transfers across them. The frailty of their control leads them to reinforce the norm for their own protection.[8] The second anchors the norm in the workings of the international state system since the end of the Second World War, which has found it convenient to support—indeed virtually guarantee—"juridical statehood" of otherwise weak units that in previous eras would have been gobbled up or dismembered by rapacious neighbors or more distant imperialists.[9] This argument draws added support from the paucity of significant boundary changes in Third World areas outside Africa since decolonization. To these, Jeffrey Herbst has added the reminder that something very much like the inviolability of arbitrary boundaries as a principle extends back more than a century to the provisions of the Berlin Conference of 1884–85. The principal colonizing powers sought to reduce their mutual rivalry and the danger of armed confrontation, and so required that only minimal levels of effective administration be established on the ground in order to qualify for international recognition. The contemporary equivalent is the operative OAU norm (discussed below) that equates control of the capital with juridical control of the country within the established borders—whatever they may be.[10]

Whatever emphasis one may place on the various causal factors, the territorial integrity principle would seem solidly entrenched, indeed overdetermined. This may bode well for logical tidiness, no small

8. William J. Foltz, "Political Boundaries and Political Competition in Tropical Africa," in S. N. Eisenstadt and Stein Rokkan, eds., *Building States and Nations: Analyses by Region*, vol. 2 (Beverly Hills, Calif.: Sage Publications, 1973), pp. 357–83.

9. Robert H. Jackson and Carl G. Rosberg, "Why Africa's Weak States Persist: The Empirical and Juridical in Statehood," *World Politics*, vol. 35 (1982); and R. H. Jackson, "Quasi-States, Dual Regimes, and Neoclassical Theory: International Jurisprudence and the Third World," *International Organization*, vol. 41 (1987).

10. Jeffrey Herbst, "The Creation and Maintenance of National Boundaries in Africa," *International Organization*, vol. 43, no. 4 (1989), pp. 673–92.

virtue when it comes to finding a clear decision rule for the policies of fifty-one states, and one that can be clearly communicated to the rest of the world. Like other OAU norms, it serves to reduce confusion and contention among member states. However, by giving absolute priority to the maintenance of existing borders over the otherwise compelling norm of self-determination of peoples—a norm in practice reserved for "peoples under colonial domination"[11]—the territorial integrity principle prohibits the organization and inhibits its members from intervening to resolve regional, ethnic, or other conflicts within African states. Internal conflict resolution is clearly subordinated in OAU practice to the larger goal of maintaining a reasonable level of harmony among the majority of member states.

Even here, however, OAU operating procedures provide more flexibility than is at first apparent. Mergers of existing political units are not only permissible but also may be hailed as steps toward greater pan-African unity. Tanganyika's absorption of Zanzibar after the 1964 revolution raised barely a peep of protest. The key is that the merger appear voluntary, that it produce order, not disorder that would divide neighbors and the organization itself, and that no major neighboring state object vigorously. In the case of the Western Sahara, it was the inability of Mauritania and Morocco to impose order on the ground and Algeria's willingness to invest heavily in the Sahrawi cause for its own foreign policy purposes that frustrated the agreement with Spain to divide the colony between its neighbors. Now that Morocco has succeeded in imposing comparative order behind the defensive berm and that Algeria's foreign policy has changed to emphasize economic cooperation with its North African neighbors, a complex diplomatic dance is likely to ensue within the OAU that will seek to bring its membership more closely into alignment with the reality on the ground.

African solutions to African problems is a well-established norm that in matters of interstate conflict proceeds from the injunction "Try OAU first" (before going to the U.N. Security Council).[12] The legal basis for OAU priority is article 52(2) of the United Nations Charter,

11. OAU Charter Review Committee, CAB/ LEG/97/DRFT./Rapt.Rpt.(III) Rev. 2, p. 8.

12. Berhanykun Andemicael, *The OAU and the UN: Relations between the Organization of African Unity and the United Nations* (New York: Africana, 1976).

which adjures states that are also member states of a regional organization to make every effort to settle local disputes peacefully through that organization before referring them to the Security Council. The measure of the OAU's assiduity in following out article 52(2) is the fact that the first dispute wholly between independent members of the OAU to be brought by one of the disputants to the Security Council was Chad's complaint against Libya in April 1983, at a time when the OAU itself was paralyzed. The complaint was made against the advice of many of Chad's friends, who then worked to be sure the Security Council buried the issue without definitive action. Africa is of course no stranger to the Security Council, but the African issues brought before it have all dealt with liberation or with outside intervention on the continent. Even when issues have had elements of inter-African disputes, as in the Security Council debates after the 1964 Stanleyville rescue mission, the African states have tried to confine the council's debates to the extra-African aspects.

Two reasons are commonly advanced for trying to exclude non-Africans from a role in settling African disutes: that exclusively African action will be substantively more effective in resolving disputes and designing stable solutions, and that the intrinsic quality of the resolution is less important than the fact that Africans do it themselves. The latter would seem to be the dominant principle, known commonly as "air the dirty linen at home." Although the OAU plenary sessions provide the largest laundry, the principle governs African behavior in other international settings as well.

Five concerns underlie the principle of African exclusivity. First is the fear of outside intervention, however well intentioned. Individual African states may welcome great power support, but African *collective* judgment invariably emphasizes the negative externalities of intervention. "We cannot afford to bring bulls into our china shop," as an OAU official assigned to the United Nations once put it. The last two hundred years of African history provide ample support for the concern.

Second is the concern to avoid the public setting of precedent. Once Africa officially and collectively invites outsiders in, ambitious great powers will find it that much easier to return when their intervention may be less welcome.

Third, African states fear that the formal involvement of external powers and external organizational actors will introduce rigidities into the negotiating process that will make it harder for the parties to a particular dispute to reach agreement and that it will establish case law that might be applied inappropriately to other African disputes. Fourth is the concern that external participation will deepen divisions between African states, thus damaging their ability to cooperate in the future and making impossible the public facade of unity required for issues such as liberation.

These are all eminently pragmatic and rational concerns. To them one might add an element common to all weak and embattled groups: a deep concern with their own disunity, which on occasion may lead to dysfunctional attempts to paper over differences. This structural predisposition is common to most groups that must deal with a hostile world from a position of comparative weakness, and is not necessarily some cultural element peculiar to African societies.[13]

It is important to emphasize that the principles just listed are collective norms, which in any specific case may be at variance with the judgment and preferences of the individual African states directly involved. Although defections may occur, most OAU members will not be directly affected by a dispute and thus will have every incentive to uphold the collective norm.

These collective concerns dictate the way African states prefer to address difficult African issues, whether at the OAU or elsewhere. The uncodified rules of procedure are as follows:

—Prefer informal to formal mechanisms of dispute settlement. Ad hoc committees are less disruptive and also less expensive than formal inquiries. They can proceed flexibly and discreetly to work out arrangements specifically tailored to the situation at hand, and since they have no continuous existence, they avoid setting precedents, which might later be applied to any of the fifty-one member states. It is no wonder that the OAU Charter's elaborate juridical structure for dispute settlement, the Commission of Mediation, Conciliation and Arbitration, has never been used.

—Prefer closed over open discussion. Public discussion invites outside commentary and participation and makes it difficult for parties

13. Compare the classic insights of Georg Simmel, for example, in the essay on "Conflict" in *Conflict & the Web of Group-Affiliations* (Free Press, 1955), esp. pp. 98–108; and Lewis A. Coser, *The Functions of Social Conflict* (Free Press, 1956), pp. 87–110.

to the dispute to eschew rhetorical posturing and to cut themselves loose from external obligations and ties, which may be necessary for an agreement to take place. Secrecy within the OAU as a whole has increased over the last fifteen years, to the point where neither votes nor records of debates are now made public.

—Operate at the highest governmental level possible, ideally that of chiefs of state or government. The men at the top have greater flexibility in reaching decisions and cutting deals than do their juniors, as well as the prestige to make decisions stick. This procedural principle has consequences for the way the OAU goes about trying to resolve disputes, for it virtually requires that negotiations be conducted under the auspices of someone who is formally on an equal footing with the spokesmen for the two sides, which is to say that he too is a chief of state. The most obvious such person to conduct the negotiations is the annual chairman of the OAU, but he is likely to be limited by his time, his length of tenure, and perhaps even his budget for foreign travel. He, or his country, may have a history of relations with one of the disputants that would make his intervention inappropriate. This possibility makes decentralization of negotiations imperative, so that other chiefs of state, operating under the general umbrella of OAU norms, can step in to try to bring the parties to agreement. It is more important that a dispute be resolved *within* the framework of the organization than that it be formally resolved *by* the organization.[14]

—No matter where and at what level negotiations are conducted, when agreement is at hand, try to involve all OAU member states in its ratification so as to implicate everyone in the decision. This cooperation will increase pressure on the original disputants to stick to the agreement and diminish the likelihood that anyone will seek extra-African intervention to upset the decision. The other side of this norm is that it invites boycott from those states not wanting to be implicated.

—Proceed by consensus, not by vote, so as to build momentum for agreement, avoid putting individual participants on the spot, and present a united front to the world. It is often claimed that consensus is a highly prized and universal African value; in fact it is the way

14. The distinction is made by B. David Meyers in "Intraregional Conflict Management by the Organization of African Unity," *International Organization*, vol. 28, no. 3 (1974), pp. 345–74.

most collegial bodies, be they university departments or the U.N. Security Council, try to take most of their decisions.

—Make decisions on African matters in Africa. When that is impossible, use the OAU to hammer out differences before meetings convened elsewhere. Africans should control African agendas outside Africa. Hence the importance of the African caucus at the United Nations and regular insistence of African participants at summit meetings of the Non-Aligned Movement on rewriting totally the African sections of the resolutions to bring them into line with official OAU positions.

—Formalistic and unanimous agreement, which permits the reduction of tensions within the group of member states, is to be preferred over decisive and divisive outcomes, even though the latter might have a better chance of resolving the initial cause of the dispute. Consensual agreement followed by hypocritical efforts at implementation is better than no agreement or an arrangement that might lead one side to have recourse to external intervention.

There is nothing mysterious about the African concerns and norms of procedure enumerated above. They all realistically reflect the situation in which the OAU and its member states find themselves and are geared to prevent the worst outcome: the general breakdown of order in the relations among African states. They are not adapted to stopping disputes in their tracks through authoritative action, and certainly not to imposing solutions on disputes within member states. These norms are supplemented by unofficial rules of behavior to be followed when things go wrong. They may be summed up as follows.

—The organization as a whole is bound by the noninterference principle to stay out of civil wars, and it has done so in cases such as the attempted secessions of Biafra, Eritrea, and southern Sudan. The OAU formally deals only with the central government and thereby upholds the norm of territorial integrity. When, as in all three of these cases, the rebels attract the support of certain African states, the OAU has no effective sanctions to bring against the offenders, though they can expect to be denounced in plenary meetings by the aggrieved central government and may face retaliation in the form of support for dissident groups within their borders. The most the OAU can do as an institution is to persuade others to stay out of the quarrel and to offer its ad hoc good offices to smooth out bilateral relations among the member governments.

—The dilemma is more difficult when the issue is not secession, but a fight for control of a member state's government. In this case the operative norm is for the organization and its members to prefer a bad central government over no central government or over divided authority. Therefore, whatever faction controls the capital, as symbol of the juridical state, should be recognized so long as it continues to control the capital. This norm was decisive in the Congo crises of the early 1960s, in the Angolan civil war of 1975–76, and in Chad in 1980–83. The principle is a thoroughly conservative one, which very much reflects the fact that the indisputable point in common among those who attend OAU summits is that they, too, control capital cities.

—Ideally, a central government should deal with its internal problems itself, but if it cannot, it has the sovereign right to bring in outside help. This help can be ranked by gradations of acceptability.

The preferred form is one-to-one support from another African state. The first such occasion was the dispatch of Nigerian troops to Tanzania in the aftermath of the 1964 mutiny. Since then, such supportive armed interventions have become almost commonplace. Guinea has several times sent troops to Liberia and Sierra Leone; Morocco has specialized in providing presidential security guards for Chad (under Ngarta Thombalbaye), Gabon, and Equatorial Guinea, among others; Libya has responded to calls for help from Idi Amin in Uganda and Goukoni Ouedeyye in Chad; Senegal has saved Dawdra Jawara in Gambia; and Tanzania has sent troops to Seychelles and Mozambique. The biggest such rescue operation is the current Zimbabwean military presence in the Beira corridor of Mozambique, an intervention necessitated as much by Zimbabwe's own economic and strategic imperatives as by its sense of obligation to a helpful neighbor. This form of intervention appears most acceptable not only because its source is within the OAU fold but because the provider appears weak enough not to threaten neighboring states. Nonetheless, the ability to provide military support for a government in trouble is a potent resource; it is rapidly becoming a new currency of influence in African affairs.

Less preferred, but still generally acceptable, is bilateral recourse to help from a power outside Africa. The French have frequently provided military support to francophone states in trouble: Mauritania, Ivory Coast, Chad, and Gabon, among others. Great Britain put down the mutinies in Tanganyika, Uganda, and Kenya in 1964 and has played a discreet continuing role in Kenya; the Cubans saved the Congo-Brazzaville government from an angry mob in 1966 and have since played a major role in Angola and Ethiopia. The list could be continued. African states are as united in regretting the necessity of such external intervention as they are in defending every chief of state's sovereign right to invite such help. The prime OAU concern is to contain the damage, to ensure that the intervention is confined to a specific domestic context and does not spread over to affect the balance within neighboring states.

Intervention that combines African troops and great power support raises much more controversy. It evokes Trojan horse metaphors from Africans, who are prone to see this as a particularly insidious form of external intervention using African clients as cover. The American manipulation of African troops in the Congo in the early 1960s left bad memories, which were revived by the Western response to the 1977 and 1978 Shaba invasions. French attempts in the 1970s to build a permanent pan-African force of troops from states friendly to the West were decisively rebuffed, even by most francophone states, as representing "armed neocolonialism." The widespread disillusionment among Africans over the performance of the OAU peacekeeping force in Chad has led that effort to be viewed as yet another case of outside powers, France and the United States, supporting African forces to ensure an outcome favorable to their own interests.

Finally, it is obvious now (although it was not to some American decisionmakers in 1975) that the use of South African forces and Western mercenaries is not only illegitimate but discredits any cause that employs them in the eyes of most OAU members.

This hierarchy of preferences increasingly poses some difficult dilemmas for the OAU and its members. The most acceptable form of invited intervention, contribution of troops by one African state to solve another's problems, inevitably gives the provider influence over the recipient—at least so long as the troops are in place. This worry would perhaps not be significant for the African system as a whole when the differences in effective military power among African states were insignificant. Now that a few states are beginning to acquire more substantial military capabilities, however, the possibility arises that the continent's interstate relations may become clustered around those few powers able and enthusiastically willing to provide military aid.

The solution to this dilemma would be the creation and deployment of a multilateral, wholly African force, independent of any outside involvement and under the command of the OAU. A favorite solution put forward by African academics, by Nigerians in particular,[15] is the creation of a pan-African military force. This was discussed at some length at the 1989 OAU presummit meeting of the Council of Ministers, where it was finally pigeonholed. The practical, and above all financial, costs of maintaining any such arrangement would seem well beyond the organization's capacity. As Kenya's President Daniel Arap Moi is reported to have said about the 1989 proposal, "This is all fantasy. It is not realistic, so let us do what is practical."[16] What might come closer to realism would be standing provisions for the OAU president to deputize one or more willing national military units to respond to calls for assistance as explicit agents of the organization. Even then, as C. O. C. Amate notes, an OAU peacekeeping force would have a much greater chance of success if it avoided situations of internal strife, like that confronted so frustratingly in Chad, and rather was used "to help an OAU member-state under attack from a non-African state or to separate and help maintain a truce between two or more OAU member-states at war with one another."[17] Action on such a basis would absolve the organization from acting contrary to the noninterference and the territorial integrity norms, and presumably would be at the invitation of the African states directly concerned.

THE PROBLEM OF CONFLICT

It is clear from the subject of this volume that the OAU normative order falls far short of being able to prevent or impose solutions on

15. See, for example, Amadu Sesay, Olusola Ojo, and Orobola Fasehun, *The OAU after Twenty Years* (Boulder, Colo.: Westview Press, 1984), p. 99; and T. A. Imobigbe, "An African High Command: The Search for a Feasible Strategy of Continental Defence," *African Affairs*, vol. 79 (1965), p. 315.

16. Quoted in J. Coleman Kitchen, "OAU Assembly XXV," *CSIS Africa Notes*, vol. 101 (August 30, 1989), p. 4.

17. C. O. C. Amate, *Inside the OAU: Pan-Africanism in Practice* (St. Martin's Press, 1986), p. 189.

serious conflicts in Africa and that the seriousness of these conflicts has grown in recent years. Three interrelated systemic factors have in particular made the OAU's task more difficult: the greatly increased level of armaments on the African continent, the growing inequality among members, and the increased tendency of member states to divide into stable factions based on international alignment.

The buildup of armaments and the development of force projection capacity has for some time reached the point where many African armies are able to do serious damage to their neighbors as well as to their own civilian populations, and a few can even threaten governments that are not their own. Even two of the world's most impoverished states, Mali and Burkina Faso, were in 1985 able to do serious harm, mostly to one another's civilian populations. A decade earlier, when a similar border dispute broke out, only isolated units were able to reach the locus of conflict, and the battle was decided by a single salvo from a Malian rocket launcher.

Economic inequalities have risen to a significant degree, thanks largely to the unequal distribution of petroleum deposits and of economic management skills. These differences have in turn exacerbated military inequalities and given some states effective coercive abilities over the policies of others.

From the point of view of keeping the peace in Africa's various subregions, African states may be unequal just the wrong amount. As table 13–1 suggests, no subregion contains a hegemonic power with such a preponderance of resources that it could impose an unchallenged and stable order in the neighborhood. South Africa comes closest statistically, but its neighborhood effects have been anything but peaceful.

The principal cleavage along which member states of the OAU have divided has nothing intrinsically African about it. Rather, it is East-West alignment of the Cold War. African states have divided on this axis since even before the founding of the OAU.[18] Yet the intensified confrontation between the Soviet Union and the United States in Africa beginning in 1975 sharpened the cleavage—a division made dramatically clear in one of the rare public "votes" of OAU members, the decision to attend or to boycott the two Tripoli summits in 1982.

18. Thomas Hovet, Jr., *Africa in the United Nations* (Northwestern University Press, 1963), pp. 144–88.

TABLE 13-1. *Elements of Power in Potential Subregional Hegemons, 1987*

Country	Military expenditures (millions of dollars)	Armed forces (thousands)	GNP (millions of dollars)	Population (millions)	GNP per capita (dollars)
Algeria	1,930	170	65,200	23.5	2,779
Egypt	6,527	450	71,170	51.9	1,370
Libya	3,063	91	27,560	3.8	7,188
Morocco	1,114	200	15,640	24.4	642
Ethiopia	442	300	5,217	46.7	112
Kenya	182	21	7,618	22.4	340
Sudan	231	59	8,691	23.5	369
Cameroon	246	15	12,880	10.3	1,256
Ivory Coast	178	8	9,440	10.8	877
Nigeria	180[a]	138	23,270[a]	108.6	214[a]
Angola[b]	666	74	9,165	8.0	1,145
Zaire[b]	155	53	5,140	31.4	169
Zimbabwe	283	45	5,714	9.4	610
South Africa	3,400	102	77,130	34.3	2,248

Source: U.S. Arms Control and Disarmament Agency, *World Military Expenditures and Arms Transfers, 1988* (Washington, 1989), pp. 32–68.

a. Devaluation of the naira caused the U.S. dollar value of 1987 Nigerian production and expenditure to fall by more than two-thirds from 1985 figures.

b. 1986 data.

If one uses as a measure of alignment a preponderance of votes that year in the U.N. General Assembly that on ten "important" issues accord with the votes of the Soviet Union (Eastern states) or the United States (Western states), with allowance for those whose votes are equally balanced (neutral states), attendance at the summits sorts out as in table 13–2.[19]

The result is even more striking when one realizes that four of the

19. The judgment of which issues are "important" is made here, in Cold War terms, by the United States Mission to the United Nations. The figures cited are derived from those presented to Congress by Jeanne Kirkpatrick in *Foreign Assistance and Related Programs Appropriations, Fiscal Year 1984*, Part I, Hearings before the Senate Committee on Appropriations, 98 Cong. 1 sess. (Government Printing Office, 1983), pp. 519–25.

TABLE 13-2. *Attendance at Two Tripoli Summits, 1982*

State alignment[a]	Both	One	Neither
Western	5	5	11
Neutral	2	0	2
Eastern	23	1	1

a. Alignment is based on the 1982 voting pattern in the U.N. General Assembly on ten important issues relative to the votes cast by the United States (Western) and the Soviet Union (Eastern).

five "Western" states that attended both summits are members of the Southern African Development Coordination Conference, which had made a pact beforehand to attend en bloc so as to try to focus the summits' attention on southern African issues.

The relevance of alignment to the OAU's ability to reduce conflict is that it calls forth automatic support for states on what appears at the time to be ideological grounds, whatever the merits of their international behavior may be, and thus diminishes the gently coercive workings of a normative order. In this way it reinforces alliance patterns based on patronage links between wealthier and poorer African states. Such rigidification is the antithesis of the way the OAU norms are supposed to work.

WHAT NEXT?

Nothing is about to happen that will suddenly transform the OAU into a dynamic force for peace within the African continent. There are no bases on which forceful executive agencies are likely to be constructed. And yet, there are signs that changes in Africa and the world may create a more propitious environment for the OAU system to be effective in restraining and resolving serious conflicts. Of help may be Africa's economic situation, both the serious economic plight of some of the wealthier oil-exporting states and the turn to greater governmental concern with regional economic relations. The former has led to a significant drop in the absolute level of arms expenditure throughout the 1980s, and the drop is concentrated in purchases by the big spenders. The latter, particularly evident in North Africa, provides a serious impulsion to cooperative behavior rather than to conflict through surrogates. By 1989 the surprisingly rapid progression of détente in superpower relations had already facilitated African peace initiatives in southern Africa. It is inconceivable that in that year either the Gbadolite national reconciliation meetings on Angola or the Nairobi meeting on Mozambique would have gone forward with such strong African support without the implied joint blessing of the United States and the Soviet Union. Significantly, both initiatives deal with matters internal to a member state, of course with the acquiescence of the national governments involved. Since each party to these conflicts claims to be fighting for control of the central government, and not for secession, the territorial integrity norm is not involved. Here also the flexibility of the OAU system works well: the initiative has the endorsement of many neighboring chiefs of state, and yet there is no requirement for the continental organization as such taking a formal position on internal matters. Should something approximating agreement be reached, one can expect the OAU as a plenary organization to embrace the settlement, congratulate itself for its efforts, and welcome the concordant parties back into the fold.

Optimism on these cases is certainly premature, and would be even more so in dealing with the vexed situations in the Horn of Africa. Here, too, superpower détente may help, at least by discouraging the superpowers from adding new fuel to the fires. Both the Soviets and Americans show diminishing enthusiasm for continued arms supplies to their regional clients, Ethiopia and Somalia, and any illusions either side may have entertained about the ideological fervor or consistency of their clients must be close to the vanishing point. Neither superpower has a stake in any particular faction emerging on top in Sudan, or in continued strife in the area.

From the OAU's perspective, these conflicts have two components: the core conflicts between each of the three central governments and its domestic opposition or separatist groups, and the support given by each of the three governments (and by other African and non-African states) to these opposition groups. The first of these is difficult for the OAU to address directly, since each government can claim protection by both the noninterference and the inviolability norms. The second, however, gives the OAU more scope for action. The opportunity is there for a concerted diplomatic effort to achieve mutual noninterference by the three governments and on this basis to mount an international campaign to "hold the ring" around each of these conflicts—to persuade outsiders to cease arms supplies and indirect operational support to all parties to the conflicts. The goal would be to create a "ripe moment" at which time some of the flexible conflict-resolution skills within the OAU system could be deployed to help end these tragic conflicts.[20] Should this occur, one may be certain that the process would be protracted, complex, and multi-leveled, and that it would defy neat organizational categories. But that is the way the OAU works at its best, and the world has reason to be grateful for its actions.

20. See I. William Zartman, *Ripe for Resolution: Conflict and Intervention in Africa* (New York: Oxford University Press, 1989).

Chapter 14

STEPHEN JOHN STEDMAN

Conflict and Conflict Resolution in Africa: A Conceptual Framework

Albert Hirschman recently remarked that, given that the enormous revolutionary changes in the world in 1989 swept away decades of expert gospel, it is somewhat bizarre to see so many experts dogmatically professing what the implications of those changes will be. After all, he states, if these pundits were blindsided by the changes, how likely are they to foresee the implications of those changes?[1]

This cautionary note applies equally to those who attempt to fathom conflict and conflict resolution in Africa. Major triumphs of conflict resolution have occurred in Africa in the last twelve years: the negotiated settlement to the civil war in Zimbabwe, the end to the war of independence in Namibia, present developments in South Africa and Angola—all of them mostly unanticipated by students of and participants in the conflicts.

This is not to imply that these conflicts have gone away—far from it. Changes in South Africa have only begun to resolve the myriad conflicts in that country. Nor should one assume that such changes are irreversible. And although the conflict between the races in Zimbabwe has been resolved, new cracks have developed in the political surface there, symbolizing the appearance of other conflictual fault lines. These cases suggest, however, that even seemingly intractable problems can be solved, that fundamental change is the most difficult of processes to predict, and that one must approach the subject of conflict resolution in Africa with an eye toward the unexpected.

Conflict in Africa arises from problems basic to all populations: the tugs and pulls of different identities, the differential distribution of resources and access to power, and competing definitions of what is

1. Albert O. Hirschman, "Good News Is Not Bad News," *New York Review of Books*, vol. 37 (October 11, 1990), p. 20.

right, fair, and just. When individuals and groups turn to violence to solve such problems, conflict takes on a second dimension: security and survival. Conflict resolution becomes as multifaceted as conflict itself: solutions must look to satisfy the hunger of individuals for justice but must also allay the fears of the participants. Conflict becomes prolonged because the antagonists come to fear the consequences of settlement, in which parties choose mutual security arrangements over the individual pursuit of security more than the consequences of continued violence.

A dual legacy of colonialism—patchwork borders and markets designed to benefit the few at the expense of the many—ensures that conflict in Africa is not easily compartmentalized. Struggles over distribution of resources and the demands of subnational groups often spill across borders. Conflict within nations ripples across economically interdependent regions. The ability of some nations in Africa to build institutions that moderate conflict depends on regional and international cooperation for economic and human development. The multilevel nature of much of African conflict means that solutions reached at one level may be necessary but not sufficient for resolving conflict at other levels.[2]

This book has presented the state of the literature on conflict and conflict resolution in Africa and serves as a springboard for future volumes on the subregions of Africa that will examine in contextual detail many of the issues raised here. To follow this volume, the Brookings Africa program has commissioned three regional case studies of conflict and conflict resolution in Africa—on southern Africa, West Africa, and the Horn of Africa. In this concluding chapter, I set out a conceptual framework for the study of conflict in Africa, which I hope will serve to order the many insights within the essays compiled here and generate questions for the regional case studies that will follow.

The conceptual framework offered here includes definitions of key words, a typology of conflict issues and how these issues vary by level of analysis, and, finally, questions about the process of conflict

2. For an argument about negotiations at different levels of analysis and their interrelated nature in South Africa, see I. William Zartman, "Negotiation and the South African Conflict," *SAIS Review*, vol. 11 (Winter–Spring 1991), pp. 113–32.

resolution. In the course of preparing this chapter, I have drawn from the other authors of this volume. When I have found points of consensus among them, I have pointed them out. When, upon reflecting on some of those agreements, I have found internal contradictions, I outline them here. Where scholarly dissensus about sources of conflict and conflict resolution exists, I have simply described competing interpretations.

DEFINITIONS

The normative goal of the Brookings Africa program is to understand various probable scenarios of conflict within the regions of Africa and to elucidate what institutions can be devised that will produce enduring peace in Africa. For many in unjust social and political situations, peace connotes the advocacy of a nonviolent status quo over the attainment of justice. Peace, however, is more than the absence of violence. First, the lack of direct violence in a relationship may mask a profound sense of latent conflict that may be awaiting an opportunity to come to the surface. The lack of direct violence between peoples need not imply the absence of deep-felt animosity among them. Finally, a lack of direct violence may be the result of powerlessness on the part of some of the actors: that is, whatever stability that exists may be a product of domination and coercion. For these reasons, we who are involved in the Africa project see peace in a positive sense—as the presence of political security and stability in the region, equitable economic relations within and throughout the region, new prospects for development, and the fulfillment of basic human needs, including the need for dignity in human relations, for the peoples of the region.

This definition of peace contains a number of words that provoke much disagreement about meaning: conflict, security, and development. One alternative, given their range of outstanding definitions and inherently political nature, would be to dismiss all these terms as essentially meaningless. Yet certainly these words do mean something, and something very important.

Conflict, as I. William Zartman observes, is "an inevitable aspect of human interaction, an unavoidable concomitant of choices and decisions." Conflict stems from the basic fact of human interdependency: for individuals to meet even their basic needs (let alone grand desires), they depend on the active participation of other individuals. As North and Choucri point out, "seeking to satisfy their needs, wants, and desires, people make demands upon themselves, upon the physical environment, upon other people, and upon whatever organizations and institutions appear to be in a position to help them."[3] Conflict arises from the interaction of individuals who have partly incompatible ends, "in which the ability of one actor to gain his ends depends to an important degree on the choices or decisions another actor will take."[4] Although conflict may turn violent, violence is not an inherent aspect of conflict, but rather a potential form that conflict may take.

Development has been defined traditionally in terms of an increase in per capita wealth. In a world where great disparities of wealth and income exist within nations, however, increases in a nation's aggregate wealth need not portend positive change for the population writ large. As Rysard Kapuscinski observes, " 'development' is no indifferent, abstract concept. It always applies to someone, in the name of something. Development can make a society richer and life better, freer, more just—but it can also do exactly the opposite. So it is in autocratic societies . . . [that] development, aiming at strengthening the state and its apparatus of repression, reinforces dictatorship, subjugation, barrenness, vagueness, and the emptiness of existence."[5] Following the United Nations Development Program, development, as used here, means the improvement in the quality of life of people as measured by longevity of life, nutrition, literacy, and access to health care and education.[6]

Security has two senses, both equally important for individuals: free-

3. Robert North and Nazli Choucri, "Economic and Political Factors in International Conflict and Integration," *International Studies Quarterly*, vol. 27 (1983), p. 445.

4. Thomas Schelling, quoted in North and Choucri, "Economic and Political Factors," p. 446.

5. Rysard Kapuscinski, *Shah of Shahs* (Harcourt Brace, 1985), p. 67.

6. The appropriate measures of development become the human development index, based on life expectancy at birth, adult literacy rate, and purchasing power, in lieu of the gross national product. See *United Nations Development Programme: Human Development Report* (Oxford: Oxford University Press, 1990).

dom from danger (protection, defense), and freedom from fear and anxiety (a feeling of being secure). Traditionally, international politics, relying on the so-called realist paradigm, has focused on the first sense of security and ignored the second. In a world with no overarching authority, the realists assert, security can be achieved only through self-help: security must be achieved through unilateral, military actions (the development of armed forces and the acquisition of arms).

Such a limited view, however, is unsatisfactory. First, although the unilateral pursuit of security through military means may reduce some of the dangers from external threats, it can just as easily prompt unanticipated dangers. For example, resources spent in acquiring the capabilities of freeing one from danger can prove economically damaging to the survival of a state. Second, the acquisition of military means brings the possibilities of those means posing a danger to one's own society. Third, the individual pursuit of security through military actions can lead to the classical "security dilemma": the actions that one takes to free oneself from outside danger may increase the danger felt by others, who then increase their own military means and pose a renewed danger.[7]

While the above criticisms are not new, they are not trivial. More fundamentally, however, the pursuit of security as freedom from danger lacks any relationship to security as freedom from fear and anxiety. Indeed, the unilateral attempt to will oneself secure (freedom from danger) can lead to a profound awareness of one's insecurity (fear and anxiety). In this sense the individual pursuit of security can prove to be irrational: the very act of trying to will oneself secure provokes an awareness of insecurity.[8] This paradox can be seen most dramatically in a passage from Thomas Hobbes:

7. For a critique of relying only on military means for achieving security as "freedom from danger," see *North-South, The Report of the Independent Commission on International Development of Issues under the Chairmanship of Willy Brandt* (MIT Press, 1980), pp. 124–25. For a recent discussion of the need to include environmental concerns in the conception of security, see Jessica Tuchman Matthews, "Redefining Security," *Foreign Affairs*, vol. 68 (Spring 1989), pp. 162–77. A large quantity of literature exists on the classic "security dilemma." For a particularly insightful examination, see Barry Buzan, *People, States, and Fear* (Brighton: Wheatshaft Books, 1983).

8. *Irrationality* is a word best used exactingly and sparingly. Here I simply take Elster's meaning of attempting to will the unwillable, for example, the

Whatever therefore is consequent to a time of war, where every man is enemy to every man; the same is consequent to the time, wherein men live without other security, than what their own strength, and their own invention shall furnish them withal. . . .

Let him therefore consider with himself, when taking a journey, he arms himself, and seeks to go well-accompanied; when going to sleep, he locks his doors; when even in his house he locks his chests; and this when he knows there be laws, and public officers armed, to revenge all injuries shall be done him; what opinion he has of his fellow-subjects, when he rides armed; of his fellow citizens, when he locks his doors; and of his children, and servants, when he locks his chests.[9]

When security depends on individual strength alone, fear and anxiety do not disappear, but follow naturally.

It should be clear then that security must connote both the achievement of protection (freedom from physical danger arising from military, economic, or environmental threat) and the attainment of a sense of safety (freedom from fear). Security defined thus cannot be achieved unilaterally, but only through mutual cooperation.

There is a danger in defining the goals of peace so broadly. Is peace always indivisible? At times leaders and people may be faced with concrete choices about components of peace. For example, some have criticized the Lancaster House agreement on Zimbabwe for focusing solely on the conflict between whites and blacks and ignoring other sources of conflict that came to the fore in Zimbabwe after independence. A key question that arises is whether a settlement could have been reached in December 1979 that addressed all major lines of conflict in the country. Or would the search for an all-encompassing settlement have sacrificed a moment ripe for ending the war between the African nationalists and the white-settler state? At best one can say there was a possibility that by attempting to resolve all lines of conflict in Zimbabwe, no settlement at all would have been reached.

---

attempt to make yourself forget something by telling yourself to forget something. The mere act causes the consequences one wants to avoid. See Jon Elster, *Ulysses and the Sirens: Studies in Rationality and Irrationality* (Cambridge: Cambridge University Press, 1978), p. 157.

9. Thomas Hobbes, *Leviathan*, ed. Michael Oakeshott (Oxford: Basil Blackwell, 1957), pp. 82–83.

And even if the settlement reached there was partial, one should not ignore the real achievement of ending a bloody war that killed between 20,000 and 30,000 people.

From a practical point of view, peace as a goal should be seen as indivisible, but peace as a process may be piecemeal, incomplete, and subject to reversal. Per Wastberg once wrote that positive peace is unattainable, but that one must continue striving for it: "None of the great tasks have an end—that is the starting point. Making justice conceivable, sharing power, lessening hunger and stopping illiteracy and spiritual impoverishment—all that would be superhuman if one did not see the actual striving as meaningful and the result as lonely long-term improvements never possible to complete."[10] Thus we see conflict resolution as both outcome and process. It is our hope that within Africa new political and economic institutions will be established to resolve the current political conflicts there. But it is equally important that those institutions be able to cope with new conflicts, so that citizens of the region will have recourse to institutions that are seen to have legitimacy, include citizen participation, protect subnational identities, and foster equitable distribution of resources, rather than resort to violence to achieve their aims.

CONFLICT: THE SUBNATIONAL AND NATIONAL LEVELS

The essays in this volume agree on one point: conflict in Africa today stems primarily from crises of national governance. Beginning with General Obasanjo's preface on the interplay between domestic peace and human rights, the authors gathered here place much weight on the failure of governmental institutions in African countries to mediate conflict. Thus Peter Anyang' Nyong'o speaks of the necessity of "politically enabling environments," based on democraticization, to allow governments in the Nile Valley to initiate bold policies to resolve conflict. Some of the authors go further and see present governments in Africa as provoking conflict. Ibrahim Msabaha, for example, suggests that the biggest single lesson from Eastern Europe for conflict

10. Per Wastberg, *Assignments in Africa: Reflections, Descriptions, Guesses* (Farrar, Straus, and Giroux, 1986), p. 25.

resolution in Africa "is the necessity for democratic reforms that reorient state-society relationships so that the political accountability of the rulers to the governed is the hub of political life." Nicole Ball points to the tendencies of elites to restrict political participation and unequally distribute economic resources as main sources of African conflict. Both Ted Gurr and Donald Rothchild place regime responsiveness to society at the forefront of their explanations of conflict resolution.

The essays in this book illustrate the varied sources of crises of governance in Africa, from ethnic, religious, and regional rivalries in the Upper Nile Valley to race and class conflict in southern Africa. In all these settings, however, conflict can be seen to center on four related, yet conceptually distinct, issue arenas: identity, participation, distribution, and legitimacy. These arenas form the backdrop to Harold Lasswell's famous definition of politics as the struggle over "who gets what, when and how."[11]

I have drawn these conflict arenas from the work of Leonard Binder and others, who posited that political development entails overcoming five crises: identity, legitimacy, participation, distribution, and penetration.[12] Instead of viewing these subjects as historical crises— that, once overcome, signal the attainment of "development"—I view them simply as ongoing conflict arenas within polities. Moreover, I have decided to treat one of their political conflicts—penetration—as different from the others. Penetration seems to me coterminous with state-building: the process of a state extending its boundaries to exert rule over a population and extracting resources of the population through taxation and military drafts. Penetration puts all other conflicts of governance into motion; by its nature state-building generates conflict by making demands on a population.

States seek compliance through coercion, exchange, or normative appeals. In turn the population must react to state demands. It can comply or it can choose to resist and test the ability of the state to extract its resources. It can obey without complying; that is, combine outward acceptance of state authority with hidden sabotage. A pop-

11. Harold Lasswell, *Politics: Who Gets What, When, How* (McGraw-Hill, 1936).

12. Leonard Binder and others, *Crises and Sequences in Political Development* (Princeton University Press, 1971).

ulation can also choose voice and demand that any extraction of resources be done in exchange for services, that extraction be coupled
with political participation in the allocation of resources, and that
obligations are coupled with rights. Finally, a population can choose
exit and attempt to escape the state's reach.

The mere attempt of a state to exert its reach into a population
brings to the fore the issue of identity. *Identity* involves the individual's self-definition and conception of membership in and allegiance
to symbolic social, political, and territorial units. In the words of one
political theorist, identity refers to the question: "In what context do
'I' properly use the word 'we'?"[13] Identity provides a social context
for the individual's calculations of interests, needs, and behavior—
the social counterpart to the economists' emphasis on rational utility
maximization—which can be illustrated by the use of possessive pro-
nouns: "What is mine I appropriate; what is ours we share. What is
mine is not yours; 'we' exclude 'them' from what 'we' share."[14] Identity places boundaries on behavior and sets expectations about morality, altruism, neighborliness, and the like. Since group membership
bestows psychological benefits, it establishes the parameters of sacrifice each individual is willing to make. The rhetoric of leaders focuses
on common identity whenever there are sacrifices that need to be
shared, or gains that exist to be won.

States exist as self-identified and internationally recognized organizations that counterpose themselves to other organizations, such
as lineage, kinship, tribe, village, and market, and they often seek to
replace those organizations as a locus of resource extraction, protection, and service provision. Traditionally, states have appealed to the
national identity to make the establishment of territorial boundaries
and extraction of resources easier. To the extent that a state can establish a national identity, it weakens such powerful organizational
contenders as ethnic groups, regions, political parties, and classes.[15]

13. W. J. M. Mackenzie, *Political Identity* (St. Martin's Press, 1978), p. 12.

14. Mackenzie, *Political Identity*, p. 115.

15. Thus, according to Ernst Haas, "Legitimate authority under conditions
of mass politics is tied up with successful nationalism; when the national
identity is in doubt, one prop supporting legitimacy is knocked away." "What
Is Nationalism and Why Should We Study It?" *International Organization*, vol.
40 (Summer 1986), p. 709.

States also exist as machinery, consisting of bureaucracies, means of revenue gathering, and means of coercion. If ethnic groups or classes or political parties can capture the machinery of state, they can use the identity of the state to justify their domination and exploitation of the population. By justifying their power and advantage with reference to pursuing the state interest, elites in power obfuscate the relationship between regime and state so as to give the pursuit of private interest a public gloss. That is often the case in highly fragmented ethnic polities where political parties are based on ethnic identity and represent a smaller community at the expense of other communities.

When communities claim separate identities, one can either attempt to insist on shared values at the expense of what makes individuals and groups different or one can acknowledge group differences and attempt to build institutions that protect such differences. Often groups conflict because they differ on these two strategies, resulting in the attempts of one group to impose through coercion their solution to identity differences. One can argue that the presence of groups claiming separate identities should not per se endanger peace within larger territorially constituted groups. Rather, what generates conflict in such situations is the tendency for claims of identity to be made in reference to other social groups in ways that make fundamental value judgments about those groups. That is, conflict erupts not from difference but from judgments of cultural superiority and inferiority that accompany claims to difference.

But are such judgments inherent in group claims to identity? Yes, argues Donald Horowitz: individual self-esteem depends on group worth, which is established through comparison. As he states, "groups aim at distinguishing themselves from others, on some positively valued dimension."[16] Such comparisons enormously complicate conflict resolution. Whereas material benefit may lead to outcomes between groups in which both may be better off, prestige is treated as a zero-sum commodity for which relative advantage is all-important.

Participation concerns access to political and economic decision-making and the promotion of human efficacy in determining the world surrounding the individual. To limit the scope of the definition,

16. Donald Horowitz, *Ethnic Groups in Conflict* (University of California Press, 1985), p. 146.

participation refers to voluntary actions and choices that are open to the individual and group for making demands of government and expressing support or lack of support for government policies. Conflict arises when groups or individuals attempt to monopolize meaningful political participation and exclude others from it.

Distribution refers to who benefits and who loses from access to and spread of resources (money, rights, political influence, educational opportunities) in a society and goes to the heart of feelings of justice and fairness. Governments determine distribution through decisions on investment, taxation, and subsidization. By establishing certain property rights and economic priorities, governments can disproportionately benefit different sectors of a population.

Legitimacy refers to the individual's belief in the rightness of the rules governing political competition within a society, and it entails judgments concerning the three dimensions of conflict mentioned above. Legitimacy concerns the rightness of the whole political system, both in terms of process and outcome. It is also a judgment on the rightness of participants. Is opposition deemed legitimate? Are self-identified groups deemed legitimate participants? Is the regime legitimate?

These arenas of conflict can overlap and reinforce one another. Restrictions on political participation may lead to economic advantage for existing elites, which may prompt the dispossessed to feel the system lacks legitimacy. Often identity conflicts coincide with limitations on political participation and skewed distribution of resources. The insistence by one group that another must lose its separate identity can render the political system illegitimate.

CONFLICT AND CONFLICT RESOLUTION: THE REGIONAL LEVEL

Many authors in this book note that if conflict is to be limited in Africa in the future, then regional cooperation and development will have to take place. Peter Anyang' Nyong'o, for instance, observes that the conflicts of the Upper Nile Valley spill over national boundaries. Thomas Ohlson argues that development in southern Africa will depend on South Africa taking on a new role in the region once it achieves majority rule. Msabaha contends that changes in the international environment make regional economic cooperation necessary for development. Zartman points to the need of regional security regimes to ensure stability throughout Africa.

The central focus of regional conflict and cooperation is the trade-off between national interests, priorities, and sovereignty and regional regimes, gains, and cooperation. Political accountability within the world tends to end at national borders. Because political survival depends on appeasing interests and providing services within borders, political elites naturally put national priorities over extraterritorial interests.

Regional cooperation should be seen as a continuum. At one end would be an openly conflictual relationship with nations at war with one another or at high stages of mobilization for war. At the other end would lie a cooperative, integrative relationship in which joint decisions concerning security and development are institutionalized. In between, but closer to the conflictual end, would lie what Barry Buzan calls "immature anarchies," where the parties pursue their own security without common assumptions or expectations about strength.[17] A different point on the continuum exists when actors pursue their security unilaterally, but do so with common reference points about power. The spectrum would range from violence to unilateral security that tended toward open violence, to unilateral security based on common expectations about strength, to mutual security based on explicit regimes, and finally to mutual security based on integrative military, political, and economic institutions.

The development of regional cooperation generates its own issues of identity, participation, distribution, and legitimacy. For instance, in a telling passage about the Horn of Africa, Terrence Lyons writes, "For the Horn of Africa to evolve into a less violent, more cooperative system, agreement must be reached on the definition and identity of the constituent parts. The legitimacy of actors and recognized borders must be established. Such agreement will require the development of solutions to internal political conflicts and the institutionalization of systems of government that encourage participation and inclusion, rather than resistance and alienation."[18]

17. Buzan, *People, States, and Fear*, p. 96.
18. Terrence Lyons, "The Horn of Africa Regional System: Conflict and Continuity," in Howard Wriggins, ed., *Dynamics of Third World Politics* (Columbia University Press, forthcoming).

Identity and Regional Cooperation

A central dimension of regional relationships is to what degree the members believe themselves to be part of a community. The greater the extent to which regional members share common values, the more likely that such members will sacrifice national gain for gains to the region as a whole. Just as individuals' calculation of interests is affected by their sense of group membership, so national calculation of interests in a region is affected by such a sense. Competing identities can conflict with the achievement of regional community, as in the case of southern Africa, where the racist identity of the South African political elite has been the primary cause of conflict in the region and, ironically, the most important stimulus of a community identity among the nations bordering South Africa. Regional identity when fully formed can result in the free flow of persons across borders, a sense of regional citizenship.

Identity conflict at the regional level manifests itself in several ways. The most obvious conflict occurs between the nation state and its sovereign identity and the region and its emphasis on community. A second conflict exists between types of nation states. For instance, Terrence Lyons argues that conflict in the Horn of Africa arises in part because of what he calls different "organizing principles of states."[19] Ethiopia views itself as a multinational empire, whereas Somalia sees itself as a national state. The problem lies in the fact that part of Somalia's nation lies inside Ethiopia's empire. The issue of national identity can also be affected by pan-nationalist commitments or threats. As Lyons also points out, Ethiopia's identity has been forged by its view of itself as a Christian enclave surrounded by Arabic countries. A final conflict of identity between states in a region involves metaphors symbolically linked to deep conflicts within the larger world of international politics: socialist, capitalist, "free world," revolutionary, and nonaligned.

Participation and Regional Cooperation

Regional political decisions can be reached in different ways, ranging from domination by powerful members, to ad hoc national de-

19. Lyons, "Horn of Africa Regional System," pp. 37–38.

cisions, to explicit forums at which all nations within a region can express themselves and reach decisions binding on all involved. Modes of participation can vary from uncoordinated national policies, to the establishment of regimes that provide information to enable coordinated decisions, to the establishment of joint decisionmaking bodies that allow integrated regional decisions.

Distribution and Regional Cooperation

Regional economic development can be pursued in various ways. Economic growth has differential effects on countries within a region, depending on their role as resources supplier, center of manufacture, port of duty, and so on. Decisions on tariffs, customs, and national development projects all have effects on neighboring countries. Such decisions can be taken solely with national growth in mind, or they can be taken with regional development in mind. Regions develop on a continuum from exploitation to equity among members. Modes of distribution can vary from laissez-faire capitalist development across borders, to explicit national development policies, to the establishment of regimes to enable coordinated economic policies, to economic unions based on customs, trade, and finance, to explicit regional development planning bodies that allow integrated regional decisions.

Legitimacy and Regional Cooperation

In regional politics, legitimacy has two aspects. First, it is a judgment about the priority given to regional goals over national goals. Most often the legitimacy of regional cooperation is challenged when regional priorities disadvantage nationally based groups. For example, if a regional decision places industry in one nation at the expense of already organized workers in a different nation, such displaced workers may protest against giving priority to people in another country. To bring in an example from the United States, American auto workers have questioned the legitimacy of a free trade agreement with Mexico, because it will result in loss of jobs of American auto workers to Mexican auto workers, who work for less pay. The American auto workers appealed to the national government for restrictions against a regionally based development, arguing that the interests of

American workers should take precedence over those of Mexican workers. Second, legitimacy in regional politics concerns judgments about the identity of participants. Regional cooperation presupposes a body of members who acknowledge one another as the sovereign representatives of their territories. Yet in both southern Africa and the Horn, states contest the very legitimacy of their neighboring governments and actually undermine one another by supporting insurgent movements.

The interrelationship between conflict at the national and regional levels raises the question of sequence and conflict resolution. Does regional conflict resolution presuppose conflict resolution at the national level? Can conflict resolution be pursued simultaneously across levels? Do some solutions to conflict at the national level interfere with conflict resolution at the regional level? These are empirical questions to which case studies can provide insight.

CONFLICT AND CONFLICT RESOLUTION: THE INTERNATIONAL LEVEL

Recent international changes cast a large shadow over the essays in this volume. Winrich Kühne argues that the end of the Cold War between the United States and Soviet Union may have contradictory effects on conflict and its resolution in Africa. On the one hand, the rapprochement between the superpowers has already led to a mediated settlement to the war between South Africa and Angola, which resulted in the independence of Namibia. On the other hand, the departure of Eastern Europe from Soviet domination will have profound implications for the economies of Africa, as that continent enters "into direct competition" with Central and Eastern Europe for Western economic aid and investment. Kühne predicts that "Western private enterprise will continue to reduce its investments in Africa," at a time when economic development must underpin any transitions to peace there.

Msabaha stresses that events in Eastern Europe provide normative political lessons for the countries of Africa, including the need for multiparty political systems, economic reform, and regional cooperation. New competition from Eastern Europe, combined with Western European economic and political integration, will place a premium on the ability of African states to transform themselves. Moreover, he implies that economic stagnation in Eastern Europe has discredited socialism as a development model for Africa. Msabaha's analysis suggests a deep ambivalence about African engagement with the West: if Western Europe loses interest in Africa, then Africa will be marginalized internationally; if Western Europe stays involved in Africa and presses for political change, such pressure connotes intimidation.

Many of the authors suggest that changes in the international environment may affect security conflicts in Africa. In the introduction Francis Deng and William Zartman query whether the supply of arms and weapons to Africa will decrease in the future. Raymond Copson raises the possibilities for a renewed role for the United Nations in peacekeeping in Africa. Tom Lodge observes that the decline of communism as a political force decreased the security concerns of white South Africans. Clearly, the myriad changes at the international level affect the potentials for conflict and conflict resolution in Africa. What is needed is a way of thinking systematically about those possible effects. As a first cut, I would like to suggest that changes at the international level influence conflict and its resolution at the national and regional levels by affecting actors' resources, opportunities for development, and perceptions of identity and legitimacy.

Regional and national identity can be affected by alliance structures and ideological struggles in the international system. The resolution of the Cold War peels away a layer of conflict-producing rhetoric, obfuscation of motives, and superpower priorities. By eliminating aspects of conflict imposed upon the local participants, conflicts become more amenable to resolution. The participants come to understand the local causes and issues at stake, and they can begin to determine the real needs of their opponents. International change also affects models of identity. Although commentators have argued that socialism's failure eliminates it as a model for national identity, the resurgence of nationalism throughout the world may bring a resurgence in that model of identity.

Participation can be affected by outside military and economic assistance given to political contenders within a nation, or to a nation within a region. With the lessening of conflict between the Soviet Union and the United States, the question arises whether new sources of military aid will flow into the conflicts in Africa. Outside assistance can affect participation by conditionalities placed on aid and loans to national regimes. Distribution can be affected by economic and technological aid from international donors and by external investment. Distribution can also be affected by targets chosen by aid donors— subnational, national, regional—and by the availability of outside markets. Finally, legitimacy can be affected inasmuch as development and security are seen as being imposed from the outside rather than resulting from local and regional initiatives.

PROCESSES OF CONFLICT RESOLUTION

A study of conflict and conflict resolution in Africa must differentiate between two interrelated processes: the resolution of specific, manifest conflicts and the institutionalization of long-term stable ways of bounding conflict. We are then interested in what factors can account for resolving specific conflicts (for example, the civil wars in Mozambique, Sudan, Ethiopia) and what factors are needed to prevent other conflicts in Africa from becoming violent.

The essays collected here contain implicit (sometimes explicit) ideas about conflict resolution, which correspond to various existing theories in the literature on peace and conflict resolution. Four themes run through the book: the relationship between force and conflict resolution, justice and conflict resolution, community and conflict resolution, and understanding and conflict resolution.

Force and Conflict Resolution

In his study of South Africa, Tom Lodge argues that a negotiated change of regime "would require that the popular forces opposing the South African government accept the impossibility of a unilateral victory. At the same time, it would need to be obvious to the rulers and their supporters that the costs of holding on to power were becoming intolerable." The implications of this statement are straightforward: a negotiated resolution of the conflict in South Africa depends, in the first analysis, not on appeals to justice or right but rather on the fact that the cost of unilateral alternatives are unacceptable. Ohlson's study of southern Africa likewise argues that the resolution of the Namibian war of independence was possible because of the costs incurred by South Africa in its conflict with SWAPO and the MPLA. Finally, Crawford Young ultimately concludes that power, as understood by the ability to prevail in military contests, has been the key to understanding the stability of Africa's norm of territorial integrity.

An emphasis on force and power can be seen in the concept of ripeness as developed by Zartman. He argues that specific conflicts can be resolved when the parties reach "a mutually hurting stalemate." The sense of stalemate is heightened by the perception that the actors stand on a precipice where the costs of conflict are likely to escalate dramatically. Settlement becomes possible because the actors fear the consequences of continued conflict where both sides stand to lose. Crucial to achieving this situation is the attainment of some kind of symmetry in power between the parties.

The realist tradition in political science is believed to be the only exponent of power and coercion as a basis for conflict resolution. Yet sole proprietorship of asserting the importance of power does not belong to the realist. Adam Curle, a long-time peace activist, asserts that the achievement of conflict resolution in situations of gross asymmetry is impossible: only through a "revolutionary transformation" can some conflicts be resolved.[20]

Disagreements arise, however, on the efficacy of power alone to settle conflicts. For example, Zartman stresses that a mutually hurting stalemate makes possible only the achievement of some kind of settlement. The parties must still reach an agreement that meets their minimal needs, a process that involves intensive problem solving. Within the realist tradition itself, some argue for the inadequacy of power alone in resolving conflict and establishing order. Henry Kissinger, for example, argues for the necessity of the actors to view a system as legitimate and to agree on basic rules of competition.[21] Hans Morgenthau, in a passage from *Politics among Nations*, contends that for a balance of power to exist, there must be a prior moral consensus among the actors in conflict.[22]

Justice and Conflict Resolution

A number of essays here stress the importance of justice for the resolution or bounding of conflict. Kühne, for instance, argues that

20. Adam Curle, *Making Peace* (London: Tavistock, 1970), p. 24.
21. Henry Kissinger, *A World Restored* (Houghton Mifflin, 1957), pp. 1–2.
22. Hans Morgenthau, *Politics among Nations*, 5th ed. (Knopf, 1978), pp. 221–28.

"it is equally mistaken to ignore or underestimate the existence of exploitation and the social danger resulting from it. The extremely uneven distribution of income and wealth in developing countries, poverty, famines, and exploitation, as well as the horrendous gap between rich and poor on the North-South axis, are without doubt explosive factors." Nicole Ball contends that economic and political inequality form the root of much conflict in Africa, and until disparities between peoples are reduced, conflict will continue. Obasanjo sees justice, peace, and stability as indivisible and places the achievement of justice at the forefront of conflict resolution in Africa. Finally, Lodge contends that without economic redistribution—the basis for achieving substantive justice in a highly inequitable society—conflict in South Africa will be redefined but not eliminated.

This line of argument has a long tradition in conflict and peace research and can be summarized by a line from Martin Luther King, Jr.: "True peace is not merely the absence of tension, but it is the presence of justice."[23] We best understand this quotation as a judgment on the prerequisites of an enduring, stable peaceful relationship. It is a causal statement: for peace to endure the parties previously in conflict must perceive that solutions are based on the satisfaction of needs, a sense of fairness, and an acknowledgment of an intrinsic right to participate in decisions about one's fate. Solutions to conflict must be based on more than the actors' ability to punish each other. Finally, it holds that unjust relationships between peoples, not marked by open violence and repression, will eventually be transformed into open violent confrontation.

Community and Conflict Resolution

Some of the authors argue that community, by which I mean shared values, norms, and institutions, is crucial for conflict resolution. Representative of this line of thought are those who argue for the necessity of democratic transformation for placing conflict within bounds. Msabaha, for instance, discusses the importance of civil society, "the development of norms and practices of democratic citizenship," and

23. Martin Luther King, Jr., *A Testament of Hope: The Essential Writings of Martin Luther King, Jr.*, ed. James Melvin Washington (Harper and Row, 1986), pp. 50–51.

the triumphing of African "glasnost." Donald Rothchild asserts that the development of a bargaining culture has been crucial for moderating conflict within African states. A sense of shared fate prevents ethnic differences from becoming completely debilitating. In the international arena, both Young and William Foltz point to the role of norms of noninterference in internal politics as a means of minimizing interstate conflict in Africa. (Yet it must be pointed out that Young's analysis sees norms as secondary to power.)

An emphasis on community forms a central tenet of many solutions to conflict. Early advocates of international organization, such as William Penn and L'Abbé de Saint-Pierre, believed that the people of Europe had a shared interest in peace that was blocked by their apparent interest in absolute independence for each state. Saint-Pierre's solution was forthright: the need to create an "all-powerful and immortal society" that would embrace all of Europe and obliterate separate sovereignties.[24] With its emphasis on commonality and sharing, community asserts that conflict comes from perceptions of difference, and therefore that solutions to conflict must work to create a common identity among peoples. Norms create pressures to act in accordance to shared community standards of right and wrong; values create a sense of shared priorities; and institutions create a sense of shared expectations.

The realist critique of community as a solution to conflict is so well known as to need little recounting here. Frederick the Great's response to Saint-Pierre forms the basis of the realist critique: "The thing is most practicable; for its success all that is lacking is the consent of Europe and a few similar trifles."[25] Of course, we live in a day when we are witnessing the flourishing of the European Community and its economic and political institutionalization. What should be apparent from witnessing this change, however, is that the development of a sense of shared community is both a long-term process and a process little understood. Although one can point to the usefulness of shared community for moderating conflict, it is not clear how one goes about making it happen.[26]

24. See the discussion of Saint-Pierre and Penn in F. H. Hinsley, *Power and the Pursuit of Peace* (Cambridge: Cambridge University Press, 1962), pp. 33–45.

25. Hinsley, *Power and the Pursuit of Peace*, p. 45.

26. For analyses of the formation of a European community, see Ernst

This predicament leads to a final thought on community and conflict resolution. The attempt to create or impose a sense of community can exacerbate conflict instead of lessening it. In the words of John Burton, "The relevant questions to pose when considering unsolved social problems are not whether shared values, coercion, or both create an integrated society; but under what conditions and by what processes can there be a harmonious and cooperative society despite the absence both of shared values and of coercion."[27]

Understanding and Conflict Resolution

Rothchild and Zartman agree that mutual understanding, here meant to imply the analytic aspects of problem solving, is essential for conflict resolution. Zartman posits that parties in conflict must find formulas that satisfy their basic needs, and Rothchild emphasizes that parties much reach common understandings about the routines of political bargaining. Such understanding centers on the ability of parties in conflict to identify and acknowledge the needs of their antagonists and to see how unilateral actions affect the other.

Conflict resolution is inherently a problem of bargaining and problem solving, involving the distribution and achievement of shared values. Burton argues that participants in conflict must redefine their conflict in such a way as to minimize the adversarial aspects of bargaining, especially the assumption that what one side gains, the other must give up. "There is an implied assumption that the analysis of a particular conflict, within this analytical framework, itself leads to the resolution of the conflict. There is a hypothesis that once relationships have been analyzed satisfactorily, once each side is accurately informed of the perceptions of the other, of the alternative values and goals, of the alternative means and costs of achieving them, the possible outcomes acceptable to the parties are revealed."[28]

Haas, *The Uniting of Europe* (Stanford University Press, 1958); and Karl Deutsch and others, *Political Community and the North Atlantic Area* (Princeton University Press, 1957).

27. John Burton, *Deviance, Terrorism and War: The Process of Solving Unresolved Social and Political Problems* (St. Martin's Press, 1979), p. 54.

28. John Burton, *Dear Survivors* (Boulder, Colo.: Westview Press, 1982), p. 122.

CONFLICT RESOLUTION: PROBLEMS AND PARADOXES

To summarize to this point, the authors in this volume treat conflict resolution in two senses: the actual resolving of specific violent conflicts that are raging now, and the bounding of conflict in general. Those who deal with the former address the conditions for settlement in such ongoing conflicts as in Sudan, Angola, South Africa, and elsewhere. Those who address the latter see conflict as an inchoate result of the crisis of governance in Africa. To resolve conflict in Africa, the authors suggest solutions variously based on force, justice, community, and understanding.

In this section I point out various problems and paradoxes involved in conflict resolution. These problems center around the compatibility of solutions to conflict, whether "all good things go together," and transitions to institutionalized bounded conflict.[29]

Compatibility of Solutions

The authors who acknowledge a role for power and force in resolving conflict in Africa (Zartman, Lodge, Ohlson, Young) tend to examine specific conflicts in their contextual complexities. The conflicts they mention—South Africa, Angola, Nigeria-Biafra—have all entailed overt violence between the antagonists. Actors have chosen violence as a way of maintaining or combating domination in the attempt to inflict harsh costs on their opponents, so as to achieve a unilateral resolution of the conflict.

Conflict emerges from tangible interests, but as soon as the conflict turns overtly violent, concerns about security and survival coexist with the issues that caused the conflict. Resolution of conflict necessarily becomes more difficult, since problem solving must work on two distinct levels: the issues that prompted the conflict in the first place, and the ending of the violent expression of the conflict. The

---

29. "All good things go together," comes from Samuel Huntington's *Political Order in Changing Societies* (Yale University Press, 1968), and Robert Packenham's seminal examination of the ideology of American development doctrines of the 1950s and 1960s, *Liberal America and the Third World* (Princeton University Press, 1973).

latter often takes on a significance and priority larger than the issues that began the conflict. Overcoming fear and conquering distrust become as important as attaining justice.

Violence causes key changes in conflict. Actors begin to form what Rothchild calls "essentialist" perceptions of their adversaries: to see opponents as possessing a character that precludes compromise and to believe that such a character is engrained and unchanging. The opponents come to see the very essence of the opponent as a threat to their survival. Survival stakes then drive the actors to believe that any settlement will be tactical on their opponent's part, a lull in which the enemy still plans their elimination. Actors in intense, violent conflict face a stark dilemma: what to fear more, settlement—and the incumbent risks of treachery and deceit that come from disarmament—or continued conflict and the costs of violence and vigilance?[30]

Donald Horowitz observes that many participants in ethnic conflicts come to believe that their physical survival is at stake.[31] Recent research in South Africa illustrates the relationship between fear and conflict. Pierre Hugo distinguishes two kinds of fear among white South Africans: fears of a nonviolent nature—concerning possible decline in standards of living, political status, and privilege—and fears of a violent nature, associated with racist stereotypes of black-against-white atrocities. Hugo argues that the latter are more important for understanding white resistance to majority rule than the former. He presents two kinds of evidence: first, how South African media accounts of majority rule in other countries in Africa have often sensationalized violence and presented it as a part of African nature, and second, survey data of Afrikaners considering their fears of majority rule. He concludes, "In South Africa the interests of whites have been so distorted by racial demonology that they will have to come to see not only that rejecting majority rule embodies the potential of serious hurt to themselves, but that such hurt is fairly imminent."[32]

30. For a discussion of this dilemma in civil war negotiations, see Stephen John Stedman, *Peacemaking in Civil War: International Mediation in Zimbabwe, 1974–1980* (Boulder, Colo.: Lynne Rienner, 1991), pp. *11–20*.

31. Horowitz, *Ethnic Groups in Conflict*, pp. 175–81.

32. Pierre Hugo, "Towards Darkness and Death: Racial Demonology in South Africa," *Journal of Modern African Studies*, vol. 26, no. 4 (1988), p. 589.

Hugo's conclusion implies that there are two possible alternatives for achieving a settlement in violent conflict: increase the costs associated with no settlement or decrease the costs associated with settlement. When conflict involves unequal parties, any status quo continues to benefit the more dominant party. The use of violence by the underdog attempts to make a status quo untenable by raising the costs of no settlement.

Examples from Africa, such as Zimbabwe and Angola, point to the partial efficacy of force in reaching political settlements. In the case of Zimbabwe, the white minority government did not seriously undertake negotiations until it faced military elimination at the hands of the Patriotic Front. In Angola, the Cuban military helped to force a settlement on Namibia, by raising the costs of South African intervention in Angola.[33]

The problem of force and conflict resolution lies in its paradoxical relationship to the other necessary aspects of peacemaking. A balance of power brought about through the use or threat of force may make possible the reaching of just settlements. Just settlements, however, depend on the parties understanding the needs of the other. Yet the use or threat of force provokes fear and insecurity, which make the task of understanding difficult. This can be seen in the South African case. Lodge argues that the conflict there is about political and economic interests and not about misperception. But that is only a half-truth: power and wealth and their distribution are at stake in South Africa, and some will win more than others. At least one side, however, the ANC, has made it clear that its goal is not to substitute black domination over whites for white domination over blacks. As long as the white community wrongly perceives black domination and retribution as goals of the ANC, settlement will be difficult to attain.

33. On the relationship between the military situation in Zimbabwe and the settlement of that civil war, see Stedman, *Peacemaking in Civil War*. On the Namibia settlement, see Michael McFaul, "Rethinking the 'Reagan Doctrine' in Angola," *International Security*, vol. 14 (Winter 1989–90); Donald Rothchild and Caroline Hartzell, "The Road to Gbadolite: Great Power and African Mediations in Angola," paper presented at the 1990 American Political Science Association Convention, San Francisco, California; and I. William Zartman, *Ripe for Resolution*, 2d ed. (New York: Oxford University Press, 1989).

Do "All Good Things Go Together"?

A number of essays in the volume assume that measures taken to increase participation—that is, democraticization—are necessarily compatible with measures to increase economic growth. For instance, Msabaha concludes that the lesson for Africa "is that democratization of civil society is necessary, because the single-party state predominant throughout the continent coincides with economic stagnation and decay." Indeed his reading of the developments of Eastern Europe suggests that gradual improvement in economic conditions naturally follows political reform. Ball cites as a lesson from Eastern Europe, "the link between domestic political reforms and successful economic development." She argues that political reform is necessary "for implementing the structural changes necessary for the attainment of self-sustaining growth and the improvement of the lives of the poorest groups in society." Anyang' Nyong'o states that democraticization must precede steps toward economic change in the countries of the Upper Nile Valley.

An obvious point to be made concerns the misreading of the Eastern European example. First, there is no evidence that the economic liberalization that has been taken will be successful in bringing about development in those countries; in some countries, the short-run costs of economic liberalization could be devastating. Nor is there any evidence that the policies under consideration will lead to equitable development and an improvement of living standards for the poorest in those countries. Second, when the prices of economic reforms are high in the short term, it is not clear that political democratization lends itself to supporting such reforms.[34] Third, as Lodge points out in his discussion of South Africa, there will be a trade-off between negotiated democracy in South Africa and redistribution of wealth.

34. On the Soviet Union, see Ed Hewett, "The New Soviet Plan," *Foreign Affairs*, vol. 69 (Winter 1990–91), pp. 146–67. On Eastern Europe, see Charles Gati, "East-Central Europe: The Morning After," *Foreign Affairs*, vol. 69 (Winter 1990–91), pp. 129–45. Two recent unpublished papers by Thomas Biersteker explore the compatibility of economic and political reform: "The 'New' Conditionality: Linking External Assistance to Political Reforms in Developing Countries," and "The Relationship between Economic and Political Reforms: Structural Adjustment and the Political Transition in Nigeria."

Such a trade-off might imply long-lasting political instability: if many Africans feel that majority rule has not benefited them materially, then their allegiance to constitutional settlements may be nonexistent.[35]

A different juxtaposition of good things concerns the goals of regional and international cooperation and the goals of national self-determination. Msabaha quotes a recent statement by Julius Nyerere, which lays out his views on African development in the future. Nyerere argues that five elements are crucial for economic growth, of which I will mention three. The first states that a prerequisite to development is a "policy of national self-reliance. Without national self-reliance, the reality of national independence is compromised. True independence is possible only on the basis of equal self-reliance." Another prerequisite is "the collective self-reliance of the South: bilateral, subregional, and regional cooperation as a base for inter-regional and global South-South cooperation." Finally, Nyerere asserts the importance of "South-South solidarity in all international negotiations." My objection can be stated simply: national self-reliance is necessarily at odds with regional cooperation and international solidarity in international negotiations. Regional cooperation demands that criteria for development be expanded to take into account regional priorities that conflict with national priorities.

Good Governance: The Problem of Transition

An emphasis on good governance, either in its limited interpretation as improved administration or in its more sweeping interpretation as democratization, begs the question of how to achieve such a goal. That is, we may all agree that good government is necessary for

---

35. Within the course of a month I heard two optimistic presentations about the future of negotiations in South Africa. At the first presentation, a commentator from the far left in South Africa raised the issue that much of the political violence today stems from unemployed youth who show no allegiance to market economies or negotiated solutions. He argued that this was a good thing because these youths would wreck any compromise between whites and the ANC leadership. At the second presentation, an American commentator from the far right made the same point, but suggested that since any negotiated settlement would be undermined, support for negotiated power-sharing may be a bad idea.

limiting conflict in Africa, but unless we spell out how to achieve that goal our analysis remains incomplete. A yawning gap lies between the normative theory of how governments in Africa should act and the explanatory theory of how governments in Africa do act. Mentioned throughout the book is the tendency of leaders in Africa to enrich themselves at the expense of the masses and exclude many from participation in government. How then is this to change? In short, we need to know how latent conflict between powerholders and governed can be transformed into power-sharing and how political competition can be bounded and institutionalized.

Two issues must be confronted immediately. The first concerns the value of the principle of self-determination. As mentioned in the Young and Foltz chapters, the principle of self-determination, which is so engrained in African international norms, has been useful for moderating conflict between states in Africa, yet has not contributed to resolving conflict internal to African states. By stressing the need for governmental change to eliminate conflict, we abandon the self-determination principle. Second, if we find that conflict-producing governments in Africa will not change through moral exhortation, then the goal of reducing internal conflict in African states must confront the principle of noninterference in African politics. Indeed, Ball goes so far as to urge Western governments to pressure African countries for internal reforms, including removing the military from political power. While Msabaha agrees that internal changes in government are needed, he is reticent about external pressure playing a role in producing that change. Thus he argues quite vociferously that the internal failings of African governments are responsible for economic and political conflict within their nations, and he demands far-reaching political reforms (of more than just the administrative variety). But he also describes the actions of Western aid agencies that tie aid to political reform as exploitation. I point out these problems to show that principles we may hold in the abstract are not necessarily complementary. If we believe that internal governance is at the root of conflict in Africa, we will have to choose among competing "goods": self-determination (meaning state sovereignty), nonintervention, or conflict resolution.

If we believe that a crisis of governance lies at the heart of conflict in Africa, and we believe that new institutions that will increase participation, legitimacy, and redistribution are necessary to bound conflict in the future, then we must analyze how to build and sustain those institutions—in short, we need a theory of transition. The assertion that bad governance lies at the heart of conflict in Africa implies that a latent conflict exists between those in power and those who are ruled. As Ball states, "In many parts of the world, including Africa, political systems are dominated by a relatively small number of elite groups [that] dominate the economy and . . . seek to restrict access to power in both spheres. Thus the general public has little or no opportunity to participate in the policymaking process or in the formal economic systems."

How, then, does one get such elite groups to share power? In Donald Rothchild's terms, how does one get hegemonial regimes to become hegemonial-exchange regimes, and how does one get hegemonial-exchange regimes to become polyarchical?

The literature on negotiation, strategic interaction, and regime transition provides some possible answers. The first thing is to examine the alternatives of the participants. Here I would distinguish between the ruling elite that benefits from having power, individual members of the ruling elite who compete among themselves for power, and the state, meaning those in the government and military who have been socialized into being concerned about "the national interest," which may not coincide at all with the interests of the political elite in power. The calculations about the benefits and costs of domination versus power-sharing may differ for ruling parties and the state. Those calculations may differ for individuals within the ruling elite who have personal ambitions for power.

From the perspective of a ruling elite that dominates an economy and polity, one would want to know why it would choose to share power. What does the ruling elite stand to gain from power-sharing? What does it stand to lose from continued domination? Variables that would affect such calculations include the degree of social mobilization of the excluded, the dependency of the ruling elite on external aid, and the coherency of the ruling elite itself. From the perspective of the state such calculations would include the ability of the state to penetrate society, demand revenues, and gain compliance from the population. Thus the state may have an interest in power-sharing because of fiscal crisis and the possible gains in legitimacy that may result from broader participation. Finally, individuals within the ruling elite may have an interest in power-sharing as a way of achieving their personal ambitions within their party. When the interests of a political elite in power, individual interests of those within the political elite, and interests of the state diverge, the possibility arises for a transition. This observation is in keeping with results of the Schmitter and O'Donnell study of transitions to democracy, which found that splits in the ruling elite were crucial for initiating transitions away from authoritarianism.[36]

Political elites compete for gain, power, and advantage. Those same elites can place limits on their competition or not. Agreements on power-sharing provide protection against competition run amok: such cooperative agreements are attempts to assure the participants that competition will not eliminate any actor and that political power will continue to be contested in the future. In polyarchies, political parties compete for power with the understanding that the rules of vying for power involve protection for the losers: the losers will not be eliminated and will have the opportunity to continue to contest the game of power in the future. Thus Dahl observes that polyarchy depends on a "system of mutual security."[37]

Therefore one should focus on the attempt of actors to ensure that competition will continue in the future. Such attempts involve an awareness of the costs of unfettered competition, an acknowledgment that such competition could lead to possible ruin or elimination of all involved, and the willingness to forgo attempting to eliminate contenders for power, even though a possible short-run benefit may accrue from doing so. Domestic political cooperation can collapse if one of the actors comes to believe that competition is finite, that a monopoly of power can be attained. When this happens, a game of ruin for the participants results—civil war—with no guarantee that a winner will emerge. The principal problem then is how parties come to expect that competition will stretch into the infinite future. How do players come to believe that their opponents will not use judicial political advantage to eliminate them, take advantage of them eco-

36. Guillermo O'Donnell and Phillipe Schmitter, *Transitions from Authoritarian Rule: Tentative Conclusions about Uncertain Democracies* (Johns Hopkins University Press, 1986).

37. Robert Dahl, *Polyarchy* (Yale University Press, 1971), p. 16.

nomically, or exclude them politically? Schmitter and O'Donnell argue that informal "pacts" are crucial for dealing with the uncertainties of transition.[38]

A problem arises when one party, though juridically able to contest for power, is unable to attain power. That is, for structural reasons a party becomes de facto excluded from the power-sharing arena and demands a change in the rules of political competition. This problem often occurs when parties are based on ethnic membership, where there is little uncertainty about parties' electoral support. To paraphrase Donald Horowitz, elections based on ethnic affiliations are censuses, not elections.[39]

A different problem occurs when one party actively uses its short-term position to constrict the participation of the loser and takes actions to restrict the loser from the state's distribution of resources. A crucial question is whether the prospect of competing for power again in the future is enough to ensure that an opposition will remain "loyal." The stability of polyarchy is aided if the winner, when doling out the spoils of victory, leaves some nourishment at the loser's table.

A final problem occurs when arrangements that were designed at one point to offer participation and distribution of rewards to parties become frozen and no longer reflect the changes in the power positions of the actors. Institutions governing political competition must be responsive to changes in the larger society. For example, constitutions as political institutions are static devices while societies are organic entities. A major problem of relying on a constitution as an institution that bounds competition is that constitutions are written to take into account the demographic, economic, and political relationships existing at a particular time. Such relationships shift as populations, technologies, and resources change, and so can render institutions outmoded. The incurring gap between an institution designed for society at time 1, attempting to meet the changes in society

---

38. O'Donnell and Schmitter, *Transitions from Authoritarian Rule*, pp. 37–47. On a comparative note, Richard Hofstadter estimated that it took over forty years for the United States to develop stable norms governing party competition. Hofstadter, *The Idea of a Party System: The Rise of Legitimate Opposition in the United States, 1780–1840* (University of California Press, 1969).

39. "Majority rule in perpetuity is not what we mean by 'majority rule.' " Horowitz, *Ethnic Groups in Conflict*, p. 86.

at time 2, 3, or 4, will prompt new bases of conflict and competition that can veer out of bounds.[40] In this formulation, legitimacy can be seen as a kind of slack in the system that allows institutions time to change in accordance with changes in society.

QUESTIONS FOR FUTURE RESEARCH

I began this chapter with a number of ideas about conflict and conflict resolution and found that they were useful for summarizing a wealth of material presented in this volume. I also found that these ideas suggest a number of questions for future in-depth research.

At the subnational and national levels, studies of conflict should address who the actors are and how they define their needs and goals. Do those needs and goals conflict with those of other actors? Is there the potential for cross-cutting identities among the population, or do cleavages seem to run in the same direction? Going beyond the question of identity, the case studies should examine patterns of participation and distribution. What opportunities exist for political participation in the specific country? How do restrictions on participation affect current politics? What changes will have to be made in the future to ensure access and participation to all who desire it? How are resources distributed in the country? What can be done to make for more equitable distribution in the country? Finally, we need to know how the participants view the results and the process of political and economic decisionmaking. What claims to legitimacy are made by the regime? Does the population feel that in terms of process and outcome the regime is legitimate? Does the regime view political opposition as legitimate? Are various self-identified groups seen as legitimate participants in the nation?

40. If one substitutes domestic for international, and parties for countries in the following quote by George Kennan, the same point is made: "International political life is something organic, not something mechanical. Its essence is change; and the only systems for the regulation of international life which can be effective over long periods of time are ones sufficiently subtle, sufficiently pliable, to adjust themselves to constant change in the interests and power of the various countries involved." *Memoirs, 1925–1950* (Little, Brown, 1967), p. 229.

The interwoven pattern of national and regional conflict in Africa demands that we consider national conflict in its regional context. What opportunities exist for regional cooperation in political, economic, and security issues? Is there a regional identity that could facilitate such cooperation? How can such an identity be promoted? Are there competing identities—national, ideological, subnational—within the region? Do existing national and subnational conflicts spill over national boundaries? And what of regional mechanisms for decisionmaking? Are there existing regimes or integrated decisionmaking bodies to foster regional political participation? How are regional economic decisions reached? Who gains and who loses within the region? Are there gains to be realized from regional economic cooperation? What institutions are available for regional development? How does one ensure a fair distribution of resources throughout a region? Finally, do the participants throughout the area see regional cooperation as fair?

Given the enormous changes that have occurred in the international environment in the past few years, we want to know what effects these changes will have on conflict and its resolution in Africa. How does international engagement or disengagement affect the four issue areas of conflict at the domestic and regional levels? How does international engagement or disengagement affect the resources, perceptions, and possibilities for settlement of specific, violent conflicts already manifest in Africa?

The framework here suggests a number of questions concerning specific violent conflicts under way in Africa. What are the resources of the participants in conflict? Do they each have the ability to impose severe costs on the other? What are the demands of the participants? Is there a range of solutions that will meet the demands of the participants? Do the participants share important values? How do the participants perceive each other's goals? Is there a mutual understanding of the conflict and its sources?

Finally, in cases where latent conflict has yet to become manifest, and can be limited by the bounding of conflict, we need to know about possible transitions to good governance. Are state institutions in given countries captured by class or ethnic interests? Do the institutions tend to provoke conflict, or do they have the capacity for managing conflicts? Are the institutions responsive to demands from the larger society? What possibilities exist for the reform of captured institutions to manage conflict? Are the ruling elites unified? Does there exist a state identity that sees its interests apart from those of the ruling elite? Are social groups able to mount sustained mobilization to press for change? How coherent are the groups? What resources are at their disposal? What is the potential for intergroup coalition formation and bargaining? Finally, what are the expectations of the participants about their opponent's future behavior?

A CONCLUDING NOTE

In its aspiration to be scientific, the study of conflict often loses sight of the purpose of our endeavor. Recalling Albert Hirschman's article on paradigms as a hindrance to understanding, we should not lose sight that the payoff of a work is not the framework or the theory; the payoff is whether a work has helped us to understand a problem.[41] And when we are grappling with a specific problem in its context, a context that must be taken seriously if we intend to resolve real conflicts, we should not be surprised if the limits to our frameworks are great. And we should not be so committed to them that the framework is more important than solving the conflict.

41. Albert O. Hirschman, "The Search for Paradigms as a Hindrance to Understanding," *World Politics*, vol. 23 (April 1970), pp. 329–43.

Contributors

Nicole Ball
National Security Archive

Raymond W. Copson
U.S. Library of Congress

Francis M. Deng
Brookings Institution

William J. Foltz
Yale University

Ted Robert Gurr
University of Maryland

Winrich Kühne
Stiftung Wissenschaft und Politik

Tom Lodge
Social Science Research Council

Ibrahim S.R. Msabaha
University of Dar es Salaam

Peter Anyang' Nyong'o
African Academy of Sciences

General Olusegun Obasanjo
African Leadership Forum

Atieno Odhiambo
Rice Univeristy

Thomas Ohlson
Centro de Estudos Africanos

Donald Rothchild
University of California, Davis

Stephen John Stedman
Johns Hopkins University

Crawford Young
University of Wisconsin, Madison

I. William Zartman
Johns Hopkins University

Index of Names

General Index

Addis Ababa agreement of *1972*, 26
African Charter on Human and Peoples' Rights, 329
African National Congress: belief in insurrectionary accession, 126–28; Congress of South African Trade Unions relationship, 138–39; diplomacy, 128; effect of white minority factions, 128–29; guerrilla armed force, 133–34; ideological traditions, 125–26; military assistance, 117; negotiation, 125–30; negotiation guidelines, 130–32; outside South Africa, 133; as social movement, 132–36; South African Congress of Trade Unions, 135; Soviet Union, 129–30; structure, 132–33; suspension of guerrilla armed force hostilities, 147
African norms, self-determination, 326–29
Afro-Socialist regimes, future of socialism, 52–55
Agrarian social structure theory, revolution, 178
All-African Peoples' Conference of *1958*, 327
Angola: covert assistance, 29; military destabilization, 268; National Union for the Total Independence of Angola, 19; political compromise with National Union for the Total Independence of Angola, 33;

Popular Movement for the Liberation of Angola, 19; poverty, 25–26; refugees, 257; war casualties *1980s*, 23
Apartheid: economic effects, 249–56; Frontline States, 219, 236; South Africa, 36; threat to identity from abolition, 269
Armed forces. *See* Military
Arms control, *perestroika*, 80–81
Arms embargo, South Africa, 230, 245–49
Arms supply, 36–38; eastern Africa, 295; Israel, 29; Organization of African Unity efficacy, 362; Soviet Union, 28; Uganda, 112
Avoidance strategy, state-ethnic relations, 209

Berber population, conflict prevention, 302–03
Biafra, self-determination insurrection, 337–38
Black community, South Africa, 124–38
Black Local Authority system, South Africa, 231
Boundary disputes: colonial partition, 330–32; self-determination, 329–32; territorial integrity, 329–32
British colonialism, Nile Valley, 95
Buffering strategy, state-ethnic relations, 209
Burundi, Hutu uprising, 24

82; defined, 70–71; group
interaction, 78, 89–90;
implications of changes in, 68–
91; post–*1990*, 82–90; Third
World poverty, 75
Iraq, Kuwait invasion by, 84
Isolation strategy, state-ethnic
relations, 208
Israel, arms supply, 29

Japan, economic assistance, 31
Justice, conflict resolution
relationship, 384–85

Katanga, self-determination
insurrection, 336–37
Kenya, 102–03; Eastern Europe
parallel, 62; economic trends,
102–03; nomadic peoples, 292–
96; Preferential Trade Area, 103
Khatmiyya, Sudan, 105
Kuwait, Iraqi invasion of, 84

League of Nations, influence of,
73
Legal norm, international
relations, 78–79, 89–90
Legitimacy: and conflict, 377; and
regional cooperation, 380–81
Lesotho Liberation Army, South
African surrogate force, 226
Libya: neighbor interference, 35;
Uganda connection, 112–13
Literacy level and coups, 172
Lusaka Summit of *1970*, Third
World poverty, 75

Mahdist movement, Sudan, 105
Malawi, *1964–67* revolt, 175
Manchester Pan-African Congress
of *1945*, self-determination, 326–
27
Manpower, military, 282–84
Marginalized peoples. *See*
Nomadic peoples

Market economy: Eastern Europe,
42; sociopolitical discussion, 58–
61
Marxist-Leninist dissolution, 42–67
Mediation: conflict resolution,
311–16; function, 312–13;
Organization of African Unity,
313–16; problems, 315–16;
willingness, 35
Mediator: institutional standing,
318; leverage, 312; stalemate
requirement, 313
Militarization, South Africa, 222–
23
Military: corruption, 284–88;
manpower, 282–84
Military assistance, 36–38, 47, 359–
60, 382–83: African National
Congress, 117; Ethiopia, 100–01;
Soviet Union, 28–29. *See also*
Arms supply.
Military cooperation, Frontline
States, 238
Military destabilization: Angola,
268; Mozambique, 268
Military expenditure: composition,
278–79; debt, 278–79; direct
effects, 275–79; indirect effects,
279–88; industrial resources,
279–82; South Africa, 252–54;
sub-Saharan Africa, 275–79
Mixed economy, practical
implications, 59–60
Mozambique: Front for the
Liberation of Mozambique, 26–
27; military destabilization, 268;
poverty, 25–26; refugees, 257
Mozambique National Resistance
(Renamo), 256; neighbor
interference, 27; South Africa
surrogate force, 226

Namibia: one-party system, 61;
Security Council, 69; United
Nations Transition Assistance